ELLEN G. WHITE:
THE AUSTRALIAN YEARS

Ellen G. White in 1888

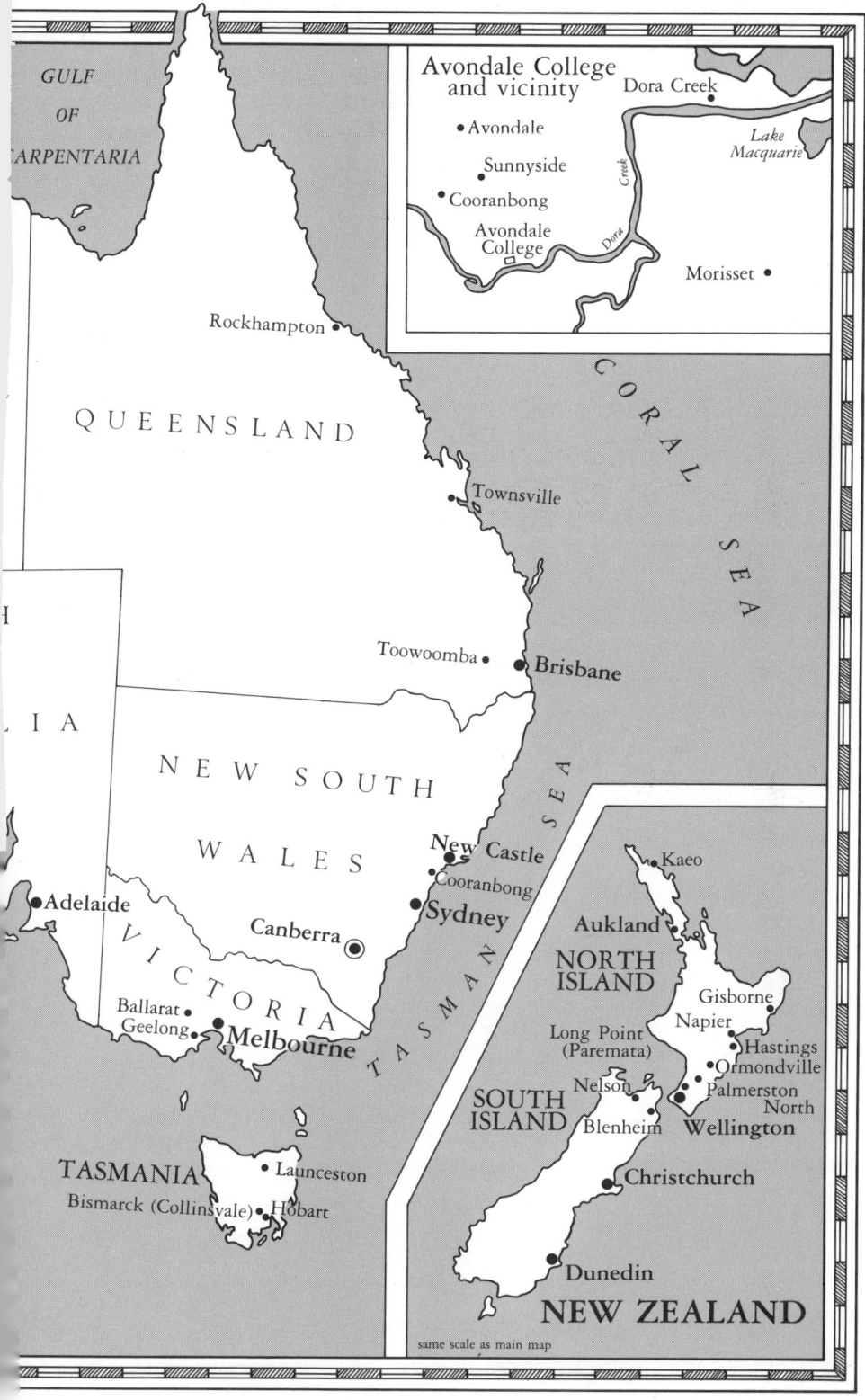

ELLEN G. WHITE:

Volume 4

THE AUSTRALIAN YEARS

1891-1900

Arthur L. White

Review and Herald Publishing Association
Washington, DC 20039-0555
Hagerstown, MD 21740

Copyright © 1983 by Review and Herald Publishing Association
Editor: Raymond H. Woolsey
Book design: Alan Forquer
Printed in U.S.A.

Library of Congress Cataloging in Publication Data
(Revised for volume 4)
White, Arthur L., 1907-
  Ellen G. White.

  Bibliography: v. 4, p.   ; v. 5, p.
  Includes index.
  Contents: — v. 4. The Australian years, 1891-1900 — v. 5. The early Elmshaven years, 1900-1905.
  1. White, Ellen Gould Harmon, 1827-1915.
2. Seventh-day Adventists—United States—Biography.
BX6193.W5W44   1981   286.7'3 [B]   81-15847

ISBN 0-8280-0122-7 {V.4}

Contents

Foreword	8
1. The Call to Australia	11
2. Ellen White Begins Work in Melbourne	22
3. Ministry in Great Pain and Suffering	31
4. The Australasian Bible School	42
5. The Servant of the Lord Could Rejoice	48
6. Influence at Administrative Convocations	58
7. On to New Zealand	69
8. The New Zealand Camp Meeting	77
9. The Winter in New Zealand	89
10. Evangelism—The Struggle for a Foothold	99
11. The Evangelistic Thrust in Australia	113
12. The American Mails—Almost Overwhelmed	125
13. The Move to New South Wales	138
14. A Place for the School	146
15. The Ashfield Camp Meeting in New South Wales	162
16. "Is There Not a God in Israel?"	176
17. Tasmania—The Convention and the Wedding	188
18. The Beginning at Cooranbong	215
19. Travels in the Last Few Weeks of 1895	228

20.	Fannie Bolton and Her Witness—True and False	237
21.	Bearing Testimony by Voice and Pen	251
22.	1896—A Year of Good News and Bad News	260
23.	Meeting Doctrinal Error and Apostasies	272
24.	The Avondale School—Working Toward the Target Date	287
25.	Avondale—A New Start in Christian Education	304
26.	The New Church Building at Avondale	315
27.	Sunnyside and Beyond—1897	323
28.	The Stanmore Camp Meeting and the Health-Food Business	334
29.	The First Half of 1898	342
30.	Divine Guidance in Important Moves	352
31.	The High Point in Australian Camp Meetings	363
32.	Writing on the Life of Christ—*The Desire of Ages*	375
33.	The American Mails and Agonizing Situations	394
34.	Wrestling With Distressing Financial Problems	408
35.	The Work in Australia Comes of Age	420
36.	Finishing Touches of Ellen White's Ministry in Australia	434
37.	Ellen White's Last Year in Australia	448
	Bibliography	461
	Index	463

Abbreviations

AH	*The Adventist Home*
BE	*Bible Echo*
CDF	*Counsels on Diet and Foods*
CH	*Counsels on Health*
CM	*Colporteur Ministry*
CT	*Counsels to Parents and Teachers*
DF	Ellen G. White Estate Document File
Ed	*Education*
EGW	Ellen G. White
Ev	*Evangelism*
GCB	*General Conference Bulletin*
HS	*Historical Sketches*
Letter	Ellen G. White letter
LS	*Life Sketches of Ellen G. White*
MS	Ellen G. White manuscript
RH	*Review and Herald*
SHM	*Story of Our Health Message*
1SM	*Selected Messages,* book 1 (2SM, etc., for books 2, 3)
SW	*The Southern Work* (1966 reprint)
TM	*Testimonies to Ministers*
UCR	Australasian *Union Conference Record*
WCW	William C. White
1 WCW	William C. White letter file, volume 1 (2 WCW for volume 2, etc.)

FOREWORD

An Explanation the Author Would Like to Have You Read

THE nine years Ellen White spent in Australia introduced her to new and different living and working conditions. It also placed upon her responsibilities in some areas she had not previously borne. Nearing her sixty-fourth birthday, she was reluctant to interrupt her work of writing and leave America for a distant field of labor, but near the close of her sojourn she could write, "God sent me to Australia."—Letter 175, 1899.

The resources from which this volume was developed have been full and exceptionally rich. Ellen White, anticipating a published account of her work overseas, reported, "I have kept up my diary, as far as possible, of our labors in Australia and in Europe."—Letter 36, 1910. Her experience in producing biographical sketches of her life in 1860, 1876, and 1885 led her to see the value of such records. The manuscript "Australian Experiences"; her diaries; her reports of activities in the *Review and Herald;* and her correspondence, especially letters to her sons Edson and William and two or three close associates in America, have provided the prime sources.

Ellen White performed a dual ministry in Australia. She virtually pioneered the work in that new field; at the same time she nurtured and counseled, through her letters, the church in America, presenting what God set before her in vision. She wrote carefully and with sympathy and understanding, but at times there were firm messages pointing the way God would have His work managed, or correcting a course of action on the part of individuals that if unchanged would be detrimental to them and to the cause of God, and perhaps even lead to their own ruin. Through foreshortening in this volume, they may seem abrupt and at times harsh, but the reader must remember that in their original form they came to the recipient in an appropriate setting, in a sympathetic mood and aimed at winning confidence.

Sums of money are mentioned from time to time, sometimes in British pounds and at other times American dollars. The reader will be spared some confusion if he keeps in mind that through the decade Ellen White was in Australia, the currency exchange was steady, the pound being equivalent to five American dollars.

This volume, *Ellen G. White: the Australian Years*, is a central volume in a series of six. It is not a history of the church in Australia, although it is in the setting of historical development. It is not a slavish chronicle, but a biography, aimed at guiding the reader through nine years of challenging pioneer work. The author has kept in mind the following aims and objectives:

1. To write for the average reader, but in such detail and with such documentation as will meet the expectations of the scholar.

2. To leave the reader with the feeling that he or she is acquainted with Ellen White as a very human person.

3. To portray accurately the life and work of Ellen White as the Lord's messenger in the Seventh-day Adventist Church, not by a recounting of her active ministry day by day, but by a selection of events and happenings that illustrate her lifework and make a contribution to the cause.

4. As far as possible, to keep these events in a year-by-year development, picturing her home life, her travels, her weaknesses and strengths, her burden of heart, and her earnest devotional life.

5. To select and present, in detail, significant events, two or three in a given year, that best illustrate her prophetic mission, depicting the interplay between the prophet and church leaders, institutions, and individuals, and recounting the sending of testimonies and the response to these messages.

6. To provide a knowledge of the principal points of the history of the church in a unique way as it is seen especially through the eyes of, or in relation to, the messenger of the Lord.

7. To make the work not only an interesting narrative but a selection of illustrative experiences with which the reader may at times vicariously associate himself.

FOREWORD

8. To keep constantly before the reader the major role the visions played in almost every phase of the experiences comprising the narrative.

9. Where convenient to the purposes of the manuscript, to let Ellen White speak in her own words, rather than providing a paraphrase. This ensures an accurate conveyance of the unique and fine points of the messages in the very expressions of the prophetic messenger herself. Thus, many important statements are provided in a form that will be of value to all readers.

10. To provide a documented running account of the literary work done by both Ellen White and her literary assistants in the production of her articles and books.

11. And in all of this, to present in the narrative, in a natural way, confidence-confirming features.

This biography has been prepared in response to the earnest request of the trustees of the Ellen G. White Estate. The work was done in the offices of the Estate at the headquarters of the General Conference of Seventh-day Adventists, in Washington, D.C.

A task of such proportion as this could not have been accomplished singlehandedly within a decade. Even before the responsibility of writing fell on my shoulders, there was the painstaking effort of Miss Bessie Mount, who, in anticipation on the part of the White Estate of such a work, was assigned the task of assembling biographical materials and preparing a card index to biographical data. This initial contribution to the biography has been most useful. I am deeply grateful to other members of the White Estate staff who have served tirelessly in research, and copying and recopying chapters in preparation.

The critical reading of the manuscript by well-qualified persons in Australia and America has been much appreciated by the author, and their suggestions have contributed to its accuracy.

If Ellen White becomes better known as an individual—as a wife and mother, a neighbor and a friend—as well as the messenger of the Lord, laboring tirelessly in the pulpit and on the public platform in declaring God's messages and in counseling often and writing incessantly, with an influence felt around the world, the objectives of the author will have been largely met.

Arthur L. White

CHAPTER 1
(1891)

The Call to Australia

TO ELLEN WHITE the year 1891 gave promise of being a good year for writing and book production. The crisis at the General Conference session of 1888 at Minneapolis and the resistance on the part of some church leaders to the wholehearted acceptance of the message of righteousness by faith had, upon the confessions of certain key men, largely subsided. In her oral ministry and writing Ellen White had for much of two years helped to stem the tide of negative reaction, and the Bible-based doctrine of justification by faith was by 1891 quite generally accepted.

During the preceding five or six years she had made good progress, with the aid of her literary assistants, in enlarging and preparing for colporteur sale volumes one and four of *The Spirit of Prophecy*. *The Great Controversy* bore the publication date of 1888, and *Patriarchs and Prophets* came from the press in 1890. Both were substantial, well-illustrated books, appropriate for sale both to the world and to the church. It was now Ellen White's ambition to take up the life of Christ, bringing out a book that would stand between the *Patriarchs* and *Controversy*, replacing *The Spirit of Prophecy* volumes two and three. She felt that if she could just have a good year without too many interruptions, she could get this done and have the book in the field fulfilling its mission.

The manuscript for *Steps to Christ* was in the hands of a religious publisher in Chicago. The little volume had been prepared at the suggestion of evangelists that some of the choice materials from Ellen White on conversion and the Christian life could have a wide sale and most fruitful mission. It was suggested also that if the book were put out by a religious book publisher in Chicago or New York, its circulation and acceptance would be enhanced. Fleming H. Revell was pleased to receive the manuscript for publication.

The work of the church was expanding overseas. A decade and a half earlier, in 1874, John N. Andrews had been sent to Europe to lead out in the work there. Indeed, it was on April 1 of that year that Ellen White, residing in California, had been given a vision that the time had come to break away from limited ideas of the work and take broader views. The "young man" she had "frequently seen" in her visions declared:

> Your light must not be put under a bushel or under a bed, but on a candlestick, that it may give light to all that are in the house. Your house is the world. . . . The message will go in power to all parts of the world, to Oregon, to Europe, to Australia, to the islands of the sea, to all nations, tongues, and peoples.—LS, p. 209.

Eight months later, at the dedication of Battle Creek College, Ellen White described a vision given the day before in which she saw printing presses in different countries, publishing the message. When James, her husband, pressed her to name the countries, she said she could not recall the names. "Oh, yes," she said, "I remember one—the angel said 'Australia.' "—DF 105j, WCW, "A Comprehensive Vision." S. N. Haskell was present, and he made up his mind he would proclaim the message in Australia. But it was ten years before the church reached the point in growth that it felt it could support him in carrying the message to that faraway land in the South Pacific.

At its 1884 session the General Conference took an action to send Haskell to lead out in opening up the work of Seventh-day Adventists in Australia. Being a practical man, he chose four families to help him start the work in the southern continent: J. O. Corliss, evangelist and editor; M. C. Israel, pastor and evangelist; William Arnold, a colporteur; and Henry Scott, a printer. The five families traveled to Australia in 1885, arriving in June, the winter season in Australia. They threw themselves wholeheartedly into the work; through two evangelistic efforts, supplemented by book

THE CALL TO AUSTRALIA

distribution, there soon was a church of ninety members in Melbourne and a fledgling monthly magazine, *The Bible Echo and Signs of the Times.*

Six years later, 1891, the combined membership in Australia and New Zealand had reached seven hundred; among these were a number of young people eager to enter the work of spreading the church's message in the South Pacific. As Haskell, who had returned to the States, revisited the field, he saw clearly the need for a training school, and voiced his convictions in a letter to O. A. Olsen, president of the General Conference.

THE GENERAL CONFERENCE TAKES ACTION

The twenty-ninth session of the General Conference was held in Battle Creek, Michigan, commencing Thursday morning, March 5, 1891. It was a meeting marked with a broadening vision, particularly in lines of education. On Friday morning Haskell, having recently completed a tour among missions in Africa, India, and other countries, spoke on the importance of training workers in their native countries rather than sending them overseas where they often lost touch with their home situations. Sunday morning W. W. Prescott, General Conference educational secretary, gave his report, in which he mentioned a number of calls for schools. He stated that "a request also comes in for the opening of a school in Australia."—GCB 1891, p. 39. On Monday morning, the Committee on Education brought in the following recommendation:

We recommend, 1. That as soon as practicable, an English Bible school be opened in Australia, to continue from twelve to sixteen weeks.

2. That at least two teachers be sent from this country to have charge of this school.

3. That the expense of maintaining this school be met by the brethren in Australia in such a manner as may seem best to them.

4. That the establishment of this school be regarded as the first step toward a permanent school for children of all ages, in case the brethren in Australia so desire.—*Ibid.,* p. 48.

Haskell was convinced that if Ellen G. White were to visit the field she could bring strength and inspiration, and promote the school idea as a training center. Others were inclined to side with him in this. So the idea of a visit by Ellen White to Australia began to develop.

Ellen White hoped that there would be no invitation for her to leave America. "I long for rest, for quietude, and to get out the 'Life of Christ,'" she wrote.—MS 29, 1891. In fact, in anticipation of a concerted program of writing, she had purchased a lot in Petoskey, in a resort area on Lake Michigan, and was having a home built where she and her staff could work without the interruptions they would have to contend with in Battle Creek.

It was just at this point that word of the invitation of the Foreign Mission Board reached her, asking her to go to Australia. The action read:

> *Whereas,* In our judgment it would be a great blessing to the cause in Australia and adjacent colonies for Sister White to visit that field; Therefore,
>
> *Resolved,* That we hereby invite her to do so, as soon as the coming autumn, if her own judgment, and the light she may have in the matter, shall be in accordance with this request; it being understood that W. C. White shall accompany her on this visit.—GCB 1891, p. 256.

The meeting in Battle Creek at which this action was taken was chaired by O. A. Olsen, president of the General Conference; the secretary was W. C. White, her own son. Looking back on what her two-year visit to Europe had meant to the cause, church leaders anticipated that the Australian sojourn would occupy about the same period of time.

On June 2, 1891, the *Review and Herald* carried an article written by Olsen entitled "Our Duty to Advance," in which he informed the church at large:

> Since the conference, the Foreign Mission Board has recommended that Sister White go to Australia, if it be in harmony with her sense of duty; also that Elder W. C. White accompany her. There has been a long and urgent call from Australia for Sister White to come there, but the way has not been open; and even now it seems like an unreasonable undertaking for her, at her age and in her worn condition, to

THE CALL TO AUSTRALIA

attempt such a journey; but she is of good courage, and has responded favorably, and it is quite probable that she and Elder White will sail for Australia next November.

TO GO OR NOT TO GO

The action of the Foreign Mission Board calling for Ellen White to go to Australia carried a clause that left the final decision with her. As the summer wore on, she sought the Lord for light, but she received none.

On August 5, 1891, she wrote in her diary:*

> This morning my mind is anxious and troubled in regard to my duty. Can it be the will of God that I go to Australia? This involves a great deal with me. I have not special light to leave America for this *far-off country*. Nevertheless, if I knew it was the voice of God, I would go. But I cannot understand this matter.
>
> Some who are bearing responsibilities in America seem to be very persistent that my special work should be to go to Europe and to Australia. I finally did go to Europe and worked there in that new field with all the power and influence God had given me. My home and my goods in America became scattered, and I sustained much loss in this line. I offered my home for sale, and Dr. Kellogg purchased it. The price I received I needed, and it was a small price. I did wish it could have been double, for I had, with W. C. White, to open new fields, and I invested this means in school homes, in meetinghouses, and in opening new fields.—MS 44, 1891.

Time was running out. Soon a decision had to be made. On August 20 she wrote:

> There is much talk in regard to our journey to Australia, but I cannot see my way clear to go. Brethren say that Sister White will have no such burdens to bear, as she has here in America, that she can write her books so much more readily without carrying

---

* Ellen White kept a journal, sometimes with just brief entries as to her activities and other times serving as a place in which she might write at some length on subjects to which the Lord led her mind. These blank books in which she thus wrote she called her diary. These materials have been copied and introduced into the manuscript file, bearing appropriate numbers that appear here as source credits.—Author.

so many responsibilities, but I know it is no use to tell them that all their flattering anticipations on my behalf does not lessen my ideas that going to Australia means work, responsibility to bear a message to the people who are not what the Lord would have them to be. If it were not thus, I would feel authorized to remain in America. As it is, I dare not mention the state of things in the office [of publication in Australia] presented to me, for I am then sure they would firmly conclude I must go.

There is work to be done there, and although those who have been there all testify that they will gladly receive any message that the Lord will give me to bear to them, I am not so sanguine in regard to this as my brethren in Australia. They know nothing of me and my work personally, only through my writings. Reproof is unpleasant to the natural heart, and the reproof coming to the people as I know it will come to them with opposition. Already envy and evil surmisings and jealousies are at work, lest someone shall have a higher place in the work than themselves. There is want of spiritual knowledge, spiritual eyesight to discern the work that needs to be done as the Lord shall open the way.—MS 29, 1891.

Nonetheless, she decided to go. As she later wrote of it, she had adopted the practice of responding to the requests of the General Conference unless she had special light to the contrary (Letter 18a, 1892). The brethren had asked her to go; in vision she had been shown conditions in Australia, which to her seemed to be an indication that she should go; and since the Lord gave her no direct word as to the course she should follow, she would go, even though she wished she might be released from going.

In mid-August the Foreign Mission Board and the General Conference Committee took action appointing G. B. Starr and his wife to accompany Ellen White and her party to Australia (RH, Oct. 13, 1891).

The September 15, 1891, *Review and Herald* carried the word:

> Sister White left Battle Creek [Wednesday] September 9, in company with Brother W. C. White, and others, on her Western journey. She will attend the camp meetings in Colorado and California, and then sail for Australia.

THE CALL TO AUSTRALIA

THE THREAT OF THE WALLING LAWSUIT

While at the Colorado camp meeting in Colorado Springs, Ellen White met with a unique experience. Her diary entry for September 12, penned on Saturday night, declares:

> Today, a lawyer came into my tent and presented me with papers made out in behalf of W. B. Walling, suing me for $25,000 damages. He charges that I have alienated from him the affections of his daughters, Addie and May.—MS 34, 1891.

The two girls were the daughters of Ellen White's niece, who in 1873 resided with her husband, Will Walling, in Colorado. When trouble developed in the family, Walling asked James and Ellen White to take and care for the children for a few months. Once relieved of their care, however, he took no steps to terminate the temporary arrangement. James and Ellen White—and Ellen alone after her husband's death—reared and educated the two girls as if they were their own. Now, some eighteen years later, when the girls were young women, the father, who was living alone, sought their return to make a home for him. They refused, choosing to stay with their Aunt Ellen, and Walling brought suit against Ellen White, claiming that she had alienated the affection of his daughters.

Litigation continued over a period of four years until finally Ellen White, through Harmon Lindsay, an officer of the General Conference to whom she had entrusted her business affairs while in Australia, arranged for a settlement out of court. Ellen White made a cash payment to remove the nuisance lawsuit and to render unnecessary the girls' having to appear in court to testify against their father.

STILL IN UNCERTAINTY CONCERNING AUSTRALIA

In the South Pacific, anticipation of Ellen White's visit heightened. James Harris, of New Zealand, wrote:

> Our Sabbathkeepers, and indeed outsiders also, are on the tiptoe of expectation in the contemplated visit of Sister White. We believe her sojourn among us will disarm much of the prejudice at present existing in the minds of those opposed to our principles and teaching.—RH, Oct. 13, 1891.

THE AUSTRALIAN YEARS

At the last minute Sara McEnterfer was stricken rather seriously with illness. As it was clear she could not accompany Ellen White across the Pacific, Miss Fannie Bolton was chosen to go in her stead. She had been one of Ellen White's literary assistants, and it was thought she could render a dual service (*ibid.*, Sept. 15, 1891). But Ellen White still questioned the matter of going. To O. A. Olsen she wrote on October 12:

> I am considering, Can it be my duty to go to Australia? Shall I not meet the same objections in the sanctuary line in Australia that I met in Switzerland? What can I do? I am presenting the case before the Lord and I believe He will guide me.—Letter 57, 1891.

Why, as one who was so close to the Lord, and one to whom He had so often communicated in positive ways that could leave no question, was she left without some special light from God? Was it that she, like others who serve in God's cause, after carefully and prayerfully examining all the factors involved, must make a decision? Was this an experience that would prepare her for the difficult days ahead? The question was one to which she would have occasion to come back again and again. But the die was cast. She would go.

OFF TO AUSTRALIA

About twenty-five friends of Ellen White, W. C. White,* and the three assistants who traveled with them, were at the wharf in San Francisco Thursday afternoon, November 12, 1891, to bid them farewell as they embarked on the *S.S. Alameda* for Australia. The three assistants were May Walling, Fannie Bolton, and Emily Campbell. Ellen White readily chose Emily to be her cabin mate. She was energetic, outgoing, even-tempered, a schoolteacher with whom she became acquainted in Michigan. Mrs. White felt she would make a valuable member of her staff, even though she had to learn to type on shipboard.

George B. Starr and his wife, Nellie, who in the initial planning were to be a part of the group, had gone on to Honolulu a few weeks

---

* W. C. White was a widower, his wife, Mary, having died in 1890. Anticipating that the stay in Australia would be limited to two years and that much of this would be in travel, he left his two motherless daughters, Ella and Mabel, in Battle Creek, living in his home in the care of Miss Mary Mortensen.

THE CALL TO AUSTRALIA

before, when it was seen that Ellen White would be somewhat delayed.

In the baggage were trunks holding copies of the E. G. White manuscripts and letters, letter books, E. G. White books, reference books, and other working materials that would be needed in setting up an office in Australia. The letter-size manuscript documents were folded in half and placed in oilcloth bags made for the purpose. Ellen White, of course, had writing materials readily at hand so that she could work as she traveled.

After one day of rough weather the sailing was pleasant, the captain remarking that he could hardly remember having so pleasant a voyage. Ellen White describes the ship and the journey:

> Our vessel, though comparatively small, and not so elegant as many of the Atlantic boats, was thoroughly comfortable, convenient, and safe. The officers were kind and gentlemanly. We had about eighty cabin passengers, and forty in the steerage. Among the former were about eight ministers, several of whom were returning home from the great Methodist Conference in Washington. Religious services were held in the social hall twice each Sunday, and occasionally on deck for the steerage passengers.—RH, Feb. 9, 1892.

She also reported that she had an excellent stateroom, and that "no one could have better attention than we have had."—Letter 32a, 1891. The women placed their chairs on the deck in front of her room. Her hip troubled her some, but with soft mattresses in her deck chair she was quite comfortable.

THE DAY IN HONOLULU

It took seven days to sail from San Francisco to the Hawaiian Islands. Of their arrival Ellen White wrote:

> We were glad indeed to reach Honolulu. Elder Starr and wife, who had preceded us five weeks in order to bring help to our people and others on this island, met us together with other friends. As soon as we walked the gangplank and stepped on the wharf, men, women, and children greeted us so heartily that we could not feel otherwise than at home. With the exception of May and Fannie, we all assembled at Brother Clinch's house to

consult in what manner we could best spend the twelve hours allotted us till the boat sailed.

They were so anxious that I should speak that I consented to do so. Oh, how pleased they were, for it was more than they expected. Brother Burges and Elder Starr went at once to see that the people were notified of the appointment. The large hall of the Young Men's Christian Association building was secured in which to hold the meeting.—*Ibid.*

The day was spent in sightseeing; a picnic lunch at the "pali," a natural attraction in the mountains near Honolulu; a visit to the Kerr home; and then the meeting in the YMCA hall.

THE VOYAGE TO SAMOA AND AUSTRALIA

As they left Honolulu, Elder and Mrs. Starr joined the traveling group. During the seven days to Samoa they crossed the equator. Somewhat to Ellen White's surprise, she found the weather not uncomfortably hot. On Thursday, Thanksgiving Day, she celebrated her sixty-fourth birthday. The sea was calm, and in her comfortable rocking chair on deck she had opportunity to contemplate. Thoughts of God's preserving care and lovingkindness filled her mind, and she wrote:

At times I have been afflicted in body and depressed in spirits, but the Lord has been my Redeemer, my Restorer. Many have been the rich blessings imparted to me. In the time of my greatest need, I have been enabled to hold fast my confidence in my heavenly Father. The bright beams of the righteousness of Christ have been shining into my heart and mind, the powers of darkness are restrained; for Jesus our Advocate lives to make intercession for us.—RH, Feb. 16, 1892.

Reaching Samoa Friday morning, the ship cast anchor offshore from Apia, its principal city. Samoans hastened out to the side of the vessel in their boats and canoes, laden with articles for sale. There was an abundance of fruit—pineapples, bananas, oranges, mangoes, limes, coconuts, and some fruits Ellen White had never heard of. They also had shells and coral, mats, baskets, and fans woven from native grasses. Ellen White chose to remain on the ship while her traveling companions went ashore for the brief stay.

THE CALL TO AUSTRALIA

Traveling west and south to New Zealand, they crossed the international date line. For the first time in her life Ellen White experienced a six-day week, for Tuesday, December 1, was dropped from the reckoning. They reached Auckland, New Zealand, on Thursday morning, December 3. Edward Hare and others took them to his home for lunch. After sightseeing in the afternoon, they met with a sizable congregation in the Seventh-day Adventist house of worship, one of the very few in the South Pacific.

Approaching Australia on Monday, the seventh, she brought her shipboard writing to a close. She noted that she had come short of meeting the goal she had set for herself in writing:

> I have not been able to do much writing on this voyage. I have written about one hundred and fifty pages, but I expected to write as much as three hundred pages. I simply had to keep still, and be content not to do much of anything. I have not been able to walk on deck without an assistant, but my limbs* are now growing stronger. I was almost completely exhausted in mind and body when I came on board the vessel.—Letter 32a, 1891.

ARRIVAL AT SYDNEY, AUSTRALIA

At seven o'clock Tuesday morning the steamer entered Sydney harbor. The sea had rolled heavily in the night, and the passengers had kept close to their berths. But with the morning the whole party was on deck to see this harbor, reputed to be one of the most beautiful in the world. As they pulled near the wharf they could see a group of friends waiting to welcome them. Ellen White recognized A. G. Daniells and his wife, Mary, although it had been some years since they were together in Texas. With the others she was unacquainted. Before the ship touched the wharf, they were shouting back and forth, and when the gangplank was down, they were soon shaking hands.

They took breakfast at the Daniells home, and while they were eating, others came in. Soon there was a season of worship, with praise to God for the safe passage across the broad Pacific.

---

* Note: Both ankles, broken in an accident on a camping trip in the Rocky Mountains, were improperly set, leaving her with a permanent weakness.

CHAPTER 2
(1891-1892)

Ellen White Begins Work in Melbourne

ON FRIDAY evening, and again on Sabbath morning, Ellen White spoke in a hall in Sydney. In describing the experience, she reported that the people said:

> They had never before heard words that gave them such hope and courage in regard to justification by faith and the righteousness of Christ. They said that they felt that the treasure house of truth had been opened before them, and the words had taken hold upon their souls, filling them with joy and peace and the love of God. . . .
>
> The presence of Jesus is with us. The Lord has put upon me the spirit of intercession, and I have great freedom and assurance in prayer. . . . I am not sorry that I am here.—Letter 21, 1891.

Taking the train for the overnight trip to Melbourne, they arrived Wednesday morning, December 16. Here were located the publishing house and conference headquarters. A large group was assembled in Federal Hall, the meeting room on the second floor of the Echo Publishing Company, to extend a hearty welcome to Australia. G. B. Starr, W. C. White, and Ellen White each addressed the group. Thanks was given to God for bringing the visitors safely to Australia (MS 47, 1891).

RECOGNIZED THE PRINTING PRESSES

The newcomers were taken to the printing office below the hall. As they entered the pressroom Ellen White recognized the presses

ELLEN WHITE BEGINS WORK IN MELBOURNE

as those shown to her in the vision of January 3, 1875. She declared, "I have seen these presses before," and continued, "I have seen this place before. I have seen these persons, and I know the conditions existing among the workers in this department. There is a lack of unity here, a lack of harmony."—DF 105j, WCW, "A Comprehensive Vision." She had a message for the foreman working there. But she would have more of that to say and write later.

G. C. Tenney, president of the conference, writing for the *Review and Herald* in anticipation of Ellen White's visit to Australia, had declared:

> I need hardly say that this event is anticipated by us all with great interest. I believe it is most opportune. The position that Sister White and her work occupy in connection with our cause renders it imperative that our people should become personally acquainted with her, so far as possible.
>
> The evidences, from a Bible standpoint, of the authenticity of the work of the Spirit of Prophecy in connection with the last church are all-sufficient, but a closer acquaintance with the work of Sister White seems to be demanded, in order to satisfy the honest inquirer that it fills the requirements of God's Word.—RH, Nov. 17, 1891.

Now it was taking place. Ellen White was with them, worshiping and ministering in their midst.

On the next Thursday evening, December 24, the fourth annual session of the Australian Seventh-day Adventist Conference opened in Federal Hall. About one hundred people were present, representing the several churches in Australia. Since the next day was Christmas, Mrs. White delivered an appropriate message on "the birth and mission of Christ, illustrating the love of God and showing the propriety of making gifts of gratitude, as did those who brought their gifts to Jesus, rather than to waste means in useless gratification" (BE, Jan. 1, 1892).

Federal Hall was too small for the Sabbath-morning service, so Ellen White spoke in a larger hall. She was led to comment, "When they understand I am to speak, they have large numbers present."—MS 45, 1891. For the Sunday-night meeting, the nearby Fitzroy Town Hall was secured; there she spoke on the plan of salvation and the love of God for fallen man to an audience that sat attentively for an hour and a half.

In her diary she wrote:

> I was not well December 26 and December 27 [Sabbath and Sunday]. I had strong symptoms of malaria. I could eat but little through the day and had quite a fever, but the Lord strengthened me when [I was] before the people.—*Ibid.*

She little realized the ominous nature of the situation, for this was the onset of a prolonged and painful illness that was to affect her ministry in Australia materially.

THE BUSINESS SESSION OF THE CONFERENCE

On Monday morning, December 28, as forty delegates took up the business of the session, two new churches were admitted, committees were appointed, and resolutions were brought before the delegates for consideration. These were not numerous, but they were important. The first read:

> 1. *Resolved,* That immediate attention be given to the Bible-reading work [Bible studies in private homes], and that suitable persons be selected and thoroughly trained for this kind of labor. —BE, Jan. 15, 1892.

The next item had to do with the literature ministry and called for a faithful follow-up work where books were sold. This was followed by a resolution of gratitude to the General Conference for sending the newly arrived workers to "visit, counsel, and assist" at this present juncture of their experience.

THE CALL FOR A SCHOOL

The delegates were quite conscious of the action taken by the General Conference in its March session toward starting a school. That matter was presented at the Melbourne session, with Tenney and W. C. White making appropriate remarks. Ellen White read important matter in regard to the church's schools and the work that should be done in them. She reported:

> Suddenly and unexpectedly to me the Spirit of the Lord came upon me, and I was moved to give a decided testimony

ELLEN WHITE BEGINS WORK IN MELBOURNE

concerning the spiritual condition of many who had taken their position upon the truth in the colonies. After addressing the people I returned to my temporary home and tried to write.—MS 45, 1891.

At the session, work continued, and resolutions on the matter of establishing a school were brought forward and acted upon. These read:

> *Whereas,* There is an increasing demand for educated laborers in Australasia and adjoining fields, and in view of the fact that many young men and women now stand ready, and are waiting to enter a school where they may receive education and training for the work; and—
>
> *Whereas,* The distance and traveling expenses to America are so great as to make it impracticable for any large number to attend our colleges; therefore—
>
> 4. *Resolved,* That it is our duty to take immediate steps toward the establishment of a school in Australasia.
>
> 5. *Resolved,* That six persons be chosen by this conference, to act with two to be chosen by the conference in New Zealand to represent that field, and one chosen by our missionaries in Polynesia to represent that field, to act as a committee on location.
>
> 6. *Resolved,* That a committee of seven on organization and plans be elected by this conference.
>
> 7. *Resolved,* That in the interval preceding the location of this school, the erection of buildings and opening, the executive committee be authorized to arrange for and conduct such terms of a workers' training school as they deem advisable.—BE, Jan. 15, 1892.

THE UNUSUAL MONDAY-EVENING MEETING

Before Ellen White had left America the situation in Australia, and particularly Melbourne, had been opened to her in vision. This was one of the reasons she dreaded going to Australia. Now on that Monday evening she was impressed by the Spirit of God to call the ministers together for a special meeting in one of the publishing-house offices. While G. B. Starr preached to the congregation in the meeting room above, she bore her testimony. Of this she wrote in her diary:

> In the evening I attended a meeting for the ministers held in the Echo office. I talked for half an hour plainly and decidedly, calling them by name and telling them the Lord had shown me their dangers. This was a precious season.
>
> Brother Curtis made a heartbroken confession. He humbled himself as a little child. He wept aloud and confessed that he had not had the Spirit of the Lord with him in his preaching. He was discouraged and did not feel that he should receive credentials. Brother Hare also confessed that he could see no success attending his labors and that he had been envious and jealous of Brother Daniells. Brother Steed and Brother Tenney made humble confessions and then we bowed before the Lord and had a precious season of prayer, and the Lord blessed us.
>
> The brethren confessed to one another and fell on one another's necks, weeping and asking forgiveness. We were together for about three hours, while Brother Starr was speaking to the congregation in the room above. The Lord is at work, and we praise His holy name.—MS 45, 1891.

The next morning Ellen White addressed the conference, as she did each morning, and then gave her time to writing.

TESTIMONY CONCERNING THE ECHO PUBLISHING HOUSE

That Tuesday morning she picked up her pen and began to write concerning the publishing house and its problems. The eight-page testimony opened:

> In connection with our publishing work in Australia, there has been a combination of circumstances that have not resulted favorably to the interests of the work.—MS 13, 1891.

Later she wrote more, elaborating on the problems as she saw them in the publishing house.

> I attended two committee meetings, and presented the true condition of things in the Echo office. This institution had been gathering up branches of work which it was not able to carry, and this was hampering, entangling, and impeding its forces.

ELLEN WHITE BEGINS WORK IN MELBOURNE

Too many lines of work were carried on, which were merely dead weights. Seemingly a labored effort was being made to keep up appearances for the sake of appearances.

The publication of the Echo was being made at continual loss. Jobs were secured at altogether too low a price, and loss was the result. Funds were being sunk in nearly all lines that were being carried forward. There was not sufficient business ability in the office or wise generalship to bind up the work in a way that would save expense.

I was shown that this was not the way to do business. It is not the will of our heavenly Father that His work should be so conducted as to be a continual embarrassment. The office should not be eaten up by its own expenses. Work that could not be done without this cost should be abandoned.—DF 28a, "Experiences in Australia," pp. 26, 27.

In this latter statement, as well as in the eight-page testimony, Ellen White specified a major factor that contributed to difficulties among the workers: their failure to exchange among themselves knowledge in the carrying through of certain processes in the plant. She wrote:

Some of the workers were not willing to help and instruct their fellow workmen. Those who were inexperienced did not wish their ignorance to be known. They made many mistakes at a cost of much time and material, because they were too proud or too self-willed to seek instruction. This ignorance could have been avoided if those at the work had shown kindness and love toward each other. The workers in the Echo office had very little insight into the right methods of obtaining success. They were working at cross purposes with each other. The office was sick, throughout all its departments.—*Ibid.*

In the heart of the testimony she read to the committee meeting, she revealed the source of the information and counsel she was passing on to them:

Brethren and sisters connected with the work of the Echo office, these words I have written were spoken to you by my guide.—MS 13, 1891.

THE AUSTRALIAN YEARS
A. G. DANIELLS ELECTED PRESIDENT

The nominating committee brought in the name of A. G. Daniells for president of the Australian Conference, and he was elected. The choice was not an easy one. Writing of the experience to O. A. Olsen six months later, Ellen White explained their dilemma found in the extremely short supply of leadership material available. The delegates were divided in their preferences. She told the nominating committee that not one of the men from which they must choose "was competent for the situation; but we must have a president; and I presented before them the objectionable features of each case. I told them that Elder Daniells was certainly standing in the best condition spiritually of any of them, and would be better fitted for the work than any other man in Australia."

"Well," she said, "they selected Elder Daniells, and this we are sure was the best thing they could do, for decided changes for the better have been made."—Letter 40, 1892. Earlier, in her letter to Olsen, she declared: "Few thought that Elder Daniells could be the one for the place of president; but with W.C. White as his counselor, he has done well."

In later years Daniells told in rather general terms of this experience:

> I was elected to the presidency of the newly organized Australian Conference, and continued in that office during the nine years of Mrs. White's residence in that field. This official responsibility kept me in unbroken association with her. Our mission field was vast. Our problems were heavy, and some of them very perplexing. . . .
>
> Our membership increased encouragingly, and it became necessary to establish a training school for Christian workers, also church schools for the children of our believers. Then followed the erection of a sanitarium for the treatment of the sick, and the establishment of a factory for the manufacture of health foods.
>
> I was young, and utterly inexperienced in most of these undertakings. As president, I was held more or less responsible for progress in all these endeavors. I needed counsel. This I sought at every important step from Mrs. White, and I was not

ELLEN WHITE BEGINS WORK IN MELBOURNE

disappointed. I was also closely associated in committee and administrative work with her son, W. C. White. His counsel was very helpful to me; it was based on a longer experience than my own, and also upon his intimate knowledge of the many messages of counsel that had been given through his mother during past years, in meeting conditions similar to those we were facing.—A. G. Daniells, *The Abiding Gift of Prophecy,* pp. 364, 365.

The conference session was profitable and instructive to the relatively new believers, few of whom had been in the message for more than six years. On Sunday, January 3, it closed, but the program continued for another full week in "An Institute for Instruction in Christian Work" and devotional meetings. Two of the popular classes were in cooking and in nursing the sick; Mrs. Starr and Mrs. Gates taught the cooking, and Miss May Walling gave practical instruction in the care of the sick. She had just recently completed the nurses' course at the Battle Creek Sanitarium. The people attending felt they had gained a good deal of practical instruction and were highly satisfied.

Mrs. White devoted this week to house hunting. She and her office family needed to have a place to live and work. The overall plan was that she would make Melbourne her headquarters for six months, and write on the life of Christ. From there she would visit the principal churches and even spend two months in New Zealand in connection with their conference session.

On Sunday morning, January 3, Stephen Belden drove Ellen White in his carriage five miles north to a suburb known as Preston. She was pleased with the country atmosphere and with the area generally, but the cottage they went to see was not large enough for the group that had to work together. Tuesday morning they were back in Preston, this time with better success. She noted in her diary:

> We found a nice brick house with nine rooms which, with a little squeezing, would accommodate Elder Starr and his wife and our workers. There is a beautiful garden, but it has been neglected and is grown up to weeds.—MS 28, 1892.

Wednesday they were there again, this time to make arrangements to rent the unfurnished house for six months. The next two days were spent in buying furniture, dishes, and other household necessities. Sunday morning she was up early packing and getting ready to move into their new home. By noon they were in their new quarters, and quite content with the prospects: a large lot; pure, invigorating air; a yard full of flowers "of fine rich quality"; and good soil.

Because the new "home" was five miles from the city and the publishing house, Ellen White purchased a horse and carriage, a double-seated phaeton in which she could ride with comfort. They secured a good healthy cow to provide their milk supply, and a stable was built to accommodate the horse and cow (Letter 90, 1892). A girl, Annie, was employed to assist with the housework. May Walling did the cooking. Because their plans called for only a six-month stay, they bought secondhand furniture, improvising somewhat with packing boxes. Some of the old carpeting used in packing the goods shipped from America served as floor covering. Economy was the watchword.

The women helpers took the yard work under their care, and the garden responded well. Wrote Ellen White:

> The girls went to work in the garden, pulling weeds, making flower beds, sowing seeds for vegetables. It was very dry, so we bought a hose, and Marian [Davis] was chief in the flower garden. With water, the flowers sprang up. Dahlias, the richest beauties, are in full bloom, and fuchias flourish. I never saw them blossom as they do here; the geraniums, Lady Washingtons, in immense bunches of the richest colors to delight the eye.
> —MS 4, 1892.

But for Ellen White, who began to feel ill during the conference session, there was an acceleration in her suffering. From week to week she seemed to be in more and more pain and was becoming more helpless. Nevertheless, she did not turn from her writing. On January 23, near the onset of her illness, she stated in a letter to S. N. Haskell:

> I am now writing on the life of Christ, and I have had great comfort and blessing in my writing. It may be I am a cripple in order to do this work so long neglected.—Letter 90, 1892.

CHAPTER 3
(1892)

Ministry in Great Pain and Suffering

TO ELLEN WHITE, the illness that began almost as soon as she reached Australia was one of the most mysterious experiences in her life. This is how she herself depicted it:

> When the work, newly started in Australia, was in need of help, our brethren in America desired me to visit this field. They urged that as one whom the Lord was especially teaching I could help the work here as others could not. I felt no inclination to go, and had no light that it was my duty. The journey was a dread to me. I desired to remain at home and complete my work on the life of Christ and other writings.
>
> But as the matter was introduced, and the responsible men of the conference expressed their conviction that I in company with others should visit this field, I decided to act in accordance with their light. I feared that my own unwillingness to go was the reason why I had no more evidence on the point.
>
> I made the long journey and attended the conference held in Melbourne. I bore a decided testimony. The Lord gave me tongue and utterance to reprove, to entreat, and to present principles of the greatest importance to the people and to the work. The burden was heavy upon me, and just before the conference closed I was stricken with a severe illness. For eleven months I suffered from malarial fever and inflammatory rheumatism.
>
> During this period I experienced the most terrible suffering of my whole life. I was unable to lift my feet from the floor without

THE AUSTRALIAN YEARS

suffering great pain. My right arm, from the elbow down, was the only part of my body that was free from pain. My hips and my spine were in constant pain. I could not lie on my cot for more than two hours at a time, though I had rubber cushions under me. I would drag myself to a similar bed to change my position. Thus the nights passed.

But in all this there was a cheerful side. My Saviour seemed to be close beside me. I felt His sacred presence in my heart, and I was thankful. These months of suffering were the happiest months of my life, because of the companionship of my Saviour. He was my hope and crown of rejoicing. I am so thankful that I had this experience, because I am better acquainted with my precious Lord and Saviour. His love filled my heart. All through my sickness His love, His tender compassion, was my comfort, my continual consolation.

Physicians said I would never be able to walk again, and I had fears that my life was to be a perpetual conflict with suffering. But I would not give up, and the constant effort that I made, because of my faith that I could still be the Lord's messenger to the people, accomplished a great change in my health. Some of the meetings that I attended at this time were from four to twelve miles from home. On some of these occasions I was enabled to speak for a full hour at a time. The fact that I could speak in public in spite of my crippled condition was an encouragement to my brethren and sisters.

CONTINUED TO WRITE

During those eleven months of suffering I continued my work of writing. My right arm from the elbow down was whole, so that I could use my pen, and I wrote twenty-five hundred pages of letter paper for publication during this period.

When I was first convinced that I must give up my cherished plan to visit the churches in Australia and New Zealand, I questioned seriously whether it was ever my duty to leave America, and come to this far-off country. Many sleepless hours of the night I spent in going over our experience since we left America for Australia. It was a time of continual anxiety, suffering, and burden bearing.

MINISTRY IN GREAT PAIN AND SUFFERING

I felt at first that I could not bear this inactivity. I think I fretted in spirit over it, and at times darkness gathered about me. This unreconciliation was at the beginning of my suffering and helplessness, but it was not long before I saw that the affliction was a part of God's plan. I carefully reviewed the history of the past few years, and the work the Lord had given me to do. Not once had He failed me. Often He had manifested Himself in a marked manner, and I saw nothing in the past of which to complain. I realized that like threads of gold, precious things had run through all this severe experience.

Then I prayed earnestly and realized continually sweet comfort in the promises of God: "Draw nigh to God, and he will draw nigh to you." "When the enemy shall come in like a flood, the Spirit of the Lord shall lift up a standard against him."

These promises were fulfilled to me. I knew Jesus came sacredly near, and I found His grace all-sufficient. My soul stayed upon God. I could say from a full heart, "I know in whom I have believed." "God is faithful, who will not suffer you to be tempted above that ye are able; but will with the temptation make a way of escape, that ye may be able to bear it."—MS 75, 1893.

Thus Ellen White, while making a recovery, could write setting forth her philosophy of the experience of prolonged suffering and could dare to hope that she had some good years ahead. Following are some highlights in this agonizing experience.

STRICKEN! "WHAT SHALL I DO?"

At first, while in the uncertainty as to her future, she had some decisions to make. She had come to Australia as the Lord's messenger to minister to the people. To what extent could she do this while her activities were curtailed by physical suffering? She could not travel, and her oral ministry must be within easy driving distance. She could write, for miraculously her right hand was free from pain, but this writing had to be done under certain conditions.

It was mid-February, 1892—late summer in the Southern Hemisphere. After being confined to her home in Preston for a full month and experiencing no improvement in health, she determined to speak to the congregation in Melbourne. Sabbath morning,

THE AUSTRALIAN YEARS

February 13, she was taken in her carriage to Federal Hall at the publishing house. Her son Willie and J. H. Stockton carried her up the long flight of stone steps to the chapel. There she stood and spoke for nearly an hour. Of the experience she wrote: "The Lord refreshed me while speaking to our people, and I received no harm."—MS 40, 1892.

As her physical condition worsened she could not stand to speak, but she would not give up; she spoke while sitting in a chair on the platform. By this time, work was begun in remodeling the physical plant of the Echo Publishing House, in the process of which the meeting room became a part of the factory. Nearby Albert Hall was rented for Sabbath meetings.

Of her experience she wrote on Sunday, March 27, to her son Willie, who was in New Zealand attending the meetings she had expected to attend:

> Last night I slept little. I had one hour's nap in the first trial after going to bed, then slept no more until midnight, then one hour's sleep, then two hours' wakefulness. I cannot handle myself any better than I have done for weeks.
>
> Sabbath it rained some—was very cloudy. I had told them I would speak to them, but I was unusually weak and the weather threatened every moment to be rainy. I finally decided to go and the clouds dispersed. There was a large congregation and they listened with interest. It rained and was cold when we started homeward, Marian, Annie, May, and I. We had meeting in Albert's Hall. I was glad I went; do not think it hurt me.—Letter 64, 1892.

She referred again to the Sabbath meeting:

> I am glad I spoke last Sabbath. Sister Daniells said that she was surprised, knowing my feebleness, that I spoke with such clearness and power. If the Lord will give me strength to do a little here, I know that little is needed. I will not give up my courage. I will hope in God, although I cannot rise up or sit down or move without pain. . . .
>
> The Lord has . . . care for me. He will not leave me to suffering and despair. I shall speak Sabbaths, for the thought I can do that much refreshes me.—Letter 65, 1892.

MINISTRY IN GREAT PAIN AND SUFFERING

As she wrote to Elder and Mrs. Haskell a week later, she reported:

> I manage to speak Sabbaths. Stephen Belden and Byron or some other brother is at hand when my carriage drives up to the hall, and one on each side helps me to the hall and up the steps onto the platform, to my chair.
>
> I have spoken seven times in this fashion; it is quite a humiliation to me, but the Lord does give me words for the people. I am blessed myself and the congregation is blessed. I spoke last Sunday afternoon to our sisters on dress reform. We had a good attendance and I hope the words spoken will enlighten some befogged minds.—Letter 10, 1892.

Thus she continued for a few more weeks, until her physical condition worsened to the point that she could no longer meet speaking appointments. However, conference and publishing-house officials frequently visited her at her residence for counsel.

WRITING UNDER GREAT DIFFICULTIES

Writing she could do, but not without suffering. In almost desperation she wrote on April 6:

> I am unable to move hands or limbs without pain. My arms are so painful, the writing I have done for the last few months has been in constant suffering. For the last two weeks my arms have been more helpless, and I may be compelled to lay down my pen until the Lord in His mercy sees fit to restore me. I am worn out for want of sleep, and nature refuses to be cheated longer; I fall asleep in my chair, fall asleep while trying to write. I have felt very much depressed at times over this condition of things, but then the Lord comforts and blesses me.—Letter 10, 1892.

She was ever hopeful of working on the life of Christ, but first she needed to write messages to individuals and institutions as the Lord gave her light. In a letter written March 21, she mentioned the coverage in her correspondence:

> The American mail bore from me a great burden, and I hope my mind will be at rest now that I shall not have to write so many

THE AUSTRALIAN YEARS

letters which I dare not neglect. I have left my testimony for them at the Sanitarium [Battle Creek], at the publishing office, and to the churches. I have left my testimony to the Pacific Press managers, to the health retreat managers, and have left my testimony in regard to Australia and the things that need to be set in order here.

I know not what the next coming mail may bring, but I shall not undertake what I have hitherto done. I shall write, as I have strength, on the life of Christ.—Letter 62, 1892.

A CHEERING INTERLUDE—*STEPS TO CHRIST* RECEIVED

One item of real interest that the mails from America did bring was a copy of *Steps to Christ*, published by Fleming H. Revell and Company, of Chicago. It was announced on the back page of the *Bible Echo* for April 1.

The reception of the book in the United States was phenomenal, as indicated by another back-page note that appeared two months later. An announcement from the publisher, Revell, was reproduced under the title "A Remarkable Book":

> It is not often that a publisher has the opportunity of announcing a third edition of a new work *within six weeks of the first issue*. This, however, is the encouraging fact in connection with Mrs. E. G. White's eminently helpful and practical work, *Steps to Christ*. If you will read this work, it will *ensure* your becoming deeply interested in extending its circulation.
>
> *Steps to Christ* is a work to guide the inquirer, to inspire the young Christian, and to comfort and encourage the mature believer. The book is unique in its helpfulness.

The editor of the *Bible Echo* added that preparations were being made to publish an edition of the book at their office. Theirs was the first edition of *Steps to Christ* to be printed outside North America. Since then, the book has appeared in more than one hundred languages, with an aggregate distribution counted in millions.

PRESSING ON WITH THE WRITING

The task of writing was ever with Ellen White. She described her work in a letter to S. N. Haskell and his wife, written in May:

MINISTRY IN GREAT PAIN AND SUFFERING

I send in this mail sixty pages of letter paper written by my own hand. First, my hair-cloth chair is bolstered up with pillows, then they have a frame, a box batted with pillows which I rest my limbs upon, and a rubber pillow under them. My table is drawn up closer to me and I thus write with my paper on a cardboard in my lap. Yesterday I was enabled to sit two hours thus arranged. My hips will become so painful, then I must change position. She [May Walling] then gets me on the spring bed and bolsters me up with pillows. I may be able to sit some over one hour, and thus it is a change, but I am thankful I can write at all. I have done nothing scarcely on the life of Christ. I am burdened with other matters, so it is all that I can do to keep the mails supplied. I have hoped my arms would be restored, but they are still very painful. I write to you that I wish to have these copied, for if I should wait to have them copied, you would get but very little. I promised articles for the *Instructor*, articles for the *Signs*, *Sabbath School Worker*. Missionary papers and the *Echo* do not trouble me, for they take from other papers; but the will of God be done.—Letter 16c, 1892.

In early July, as she wrote to Dr. J. H. Kellogg in Battle Creek, she mentioned again the conditions under which she worked:

Every mail has taken from one to two hundred pages from my hand, and most of it has been written either as I am now propped up on the bed by pillows, half lying, or half sitting, or bolstered up sitting in an uncomfortable chair. It is very painful to my hip and to the lower part of my spine to sit up. If such easy chairs were to be found in this country as you have at the Sanitarium, one would be readily purchased by me, if it cost $30; but furniture of that style is not manufactured here. All furniture is transported from England, and Boston, Massachusetts. A good, large, roomy chair with soft springs is not obtainable.

It is with great weariness that I can sit erect and hold up my head. I must rest it against the back of the chair on the pillows, half reclining. . . . I am not at all discouraged. I feel that I am sustained daily. . . . I enjoy sweet communion with God.—Letter 18a, 1892.

Occasionally she noted in her diary just what she was sending off in the American mail. On June 12 she wrote:

> Articles written: missionary work, 15 pages letter paper. A. T. Robinson, 13 pages. Sustaining the Cause, letter to Elder Smith, 24 pages; Elder Haskell, 16 pages; Sister Ings, 5 pages; Brother Lockwood, 5 pages; Sara McEnterfer, 2 pages; Ella May and Mable White, 4 pages. Large document to C. H. Jones in regard to publishing and health institutions. J. E. White, 12 pages. Sent Brother Wessels 5 letter pages, to Elder E. J. Waggoner to London; to Elder Washburn, England, 1 page.—MS 33, 1892.

Back of many of these letters were visions in which situations were opened up to Ellen White. After one very restless night she wrote a twelve-page letter to Dr. Kellogg, concerning which she noted:

> I am instructed to caution him to move guardedly, else he will surely lose his bearings. There are many perplexing questions coming up for decision, and he will need great wisdom in order to keep the way of the Lord. . . . He needs a humble, contrite heart, and he needs to walk in constant dependence upon God.—MS 34, 1892.

Sometimes it seemed that the correspondence was a bit one-sided, more going out than coming in. She wrote to S. N. Haskell:

> The coming of the mail is a great event with us. . . . We were so glad to hear from the other side of the broad waters. If our friends only knew how precious are words from them, I think we should receive more communications. But it is a little amusing that nearly all our correspondents assume that others have written all particulars. I thank you for your full letters and that you do not disappoint my expectations.—Letter 10, 1892.

Day after day and week after week the situation was without much change—long winter nights of intense suffering and broken sleep, then days in poorly heated rooms trying to write. Every day it was a battle to keep up courage. Again and again she reviewed in her mind the matter of the invitation from the General Conference

MINISTRY IN GREAT PAIN AND SUFFERING

for her to go to Australia and of the various events of the past year, in America and Australia. On some days it seemed to her to be certain that it was God's will that she was in Australia; at other times she felt her coming might have been a mistake.

On July 5, in her letter to Dr. Kellogg, she mentioned her feelings and attitudes:

> When I first found myself in a state of helplessness, I deeply regretted having crossed the broad waters. Why was I not in America? Why, at such expense, was I in this country? Time and again I could have buried my face in the bed quilts and had a good cry. But I did not long indulge in the luxury of tears. I said to myself, "Ellen G. White, what do you mean? Have you not come to Australia because you felt that it was your duty to go where the conference judged it best for you to go? Has not this been your practice?" I said, "Yes." "Then why do you feel almost forsaken, and discouraged? Is not this the enemy's work?" I said, "I believe it is." I dried my tears as quickly as possible and said, "It is enough; I will not look on the dark side anymore. Live or die, I commit the keeping of my soul to Him who died for me."
>
> I then believed that the Lord would do all things well, and during this eight months of helplessness, I have not had any despondency or doubt.
>
> I now look at this matter as a part of the Lord's great plan, for the good of His people here in this country, and for those in America, and for my good. I cannot explain why or how, but I believe it. And I am happy in my affliction; I can trust my heavenly Father. I will not doubt His love. I have an ever-watchful guardian day and night, and I will praise the Lord, for His praise is upon my lips because it comes from a heart full of gratitude.—Letter 18a, 1892.

ANOINTING AND SPECIAL PRAYER FOR HEALING

Although Ellen White, as well as her husband, had responded a number of times to requests to join others in the service of anointing the sick and praying for their special healing, she deferred making such a request for herself. But after long months of suffering and no evidence of improvement, and although she and her attendants had done all that they could with proper hydrotherapy treatments, she was still almost helpless. Now her mind turned to what it was her privilege to do, to ask the brethren to come and anoint her and pray for her healing. While pondering this, and the whole matter of prayer for the healing of the sick in general, she wrote a statement:

> During my sickness I have thought much in reference to praying for the sick, and I believe that if prayer should be offered for the sick at any place, and it certainly should, it should be offered at the Sanitarium for the relief or restoration of the suffering. But in this matter of praying for the sick, I could not move in exactly the same lines as have my brethren. I have been considering many things that have been presented to me in the past in reference to this subject.—MS 26a, 1892.

She discussed the situation in which individuals pay little heed to the laws of nature, yet when illness strikes they solicit the prayers of God's people and call for the elders of the church. Those called in to pray, with little knowledge of the manner of life of the petitioner, which may be far from what the Lord calls for, petition God to restore health miraculously. Such a prayer, if answered in the affirmative, would open the way for a continuation of a life lived in disregard to nature's laws, which were instituted by God for mankind's own good. She wrote admonishingly:

> Present these thoughts to the persons who come asking your prayers: "We are human, we cannot read the heart, or know the secrets of your life. These are known only to yourself and God. If you now repent of your sin, if you can see that in any instance you have walked contrary to the light given you of God, and have neglected to give honor to the body, the temple of God, . . . [and] by wrong habits have degraded the body which is Christ's property, make confession of these things to God. . . .
>
> If you have sinned by withholding from God His own in tithe and offerings, confess your guilt to God and to the church, and heed the injunction that has been given you, "Bring ye all the tithes into the storehouse." . . .
>
> Praying for the sick is a most solemn thing, and we should not enter upon this work in any careless, hasty way. Examination should be made as to whether those who would be blessed with health have indulged in evil speaking, alienation, and

MINISTRY IN GREAT PAIN AND SUFFERING

dissension. Have they sowed discord among the brethren and sisters in the church? If these things have been committed they should be confessed before God and before the church. When wrongs have been confessed, the subjects of prayer may be presented before God in earnestness and faith, as the Spirit of God may move upon you.—*Ibid.*

In this statement, seemingly intended for herself, as well as others, Ellen White wrote much in the vein presented in the chapter "Prayer for the Sick" in *The Ministry of Healing.* In fact, this manuscript probably formed the basis for the chapter.

After the preparation of heart that accompanied her writing on prayer for the sick, Ellen White called upon the brethren on Friday, May 20, to come to her home and anoint her and pray for her healing. Of this, she wrote in her diary:

> Yesterday afternoon Elder [A. G.] Daniells and his wife, Elder [G. C.] Tenney and his wife, and Brethren Stockton and Smith came to our home at my request to pray that the Lord would heal me. We had a most earnest season of prayer, and we were all much blessed. I was relieved, but not restored.
>
> I have now done all that I can to follow the Bible directions, and I shall wait for the Lord to work, believing that in His own good time He will heal me. My faith takes hold of the promise, "Ask and ye shall receive" (John 16:24).
>
> I believe that the Lord heard our prayers. I hoped that my captivity might be turned immediately, and to my finite judgment it seemed that thus God would be glorified. I was much blessed during our season of prayer, and I shall hold fast to the assurance then given me: "I am your Redeemer; I will heal you."—MS 19, 1892 (2SM, p. 235).

She wrote to Stephen Haskell a few days later: "I did believe the Lord would restore me." She followed with her undaunted confidence in the Lord and His sustaining grace, declaring:

> I can look to Him as one able to help me. One who loves me, who will restore me in His own good time. Will I trust myself in His hands? I will. He has been very nigh unto me the last five months of trial.—Letter 16g, 1892.

CHAPTER 4
(1892)

The Australasian Bible School

ONE of the reasons why the General Conference asked Ellen White and her son to go to Australia was the need there for a school to train the youth in their homeland. The principal item of business at the Australian Conference session that was held immediately after their arrival in Melbourne was the establishment of such a school. Provision was made for a committee on location, to which members representing Australia and New Zealand were named.

The next step was the securing of support from the believers in New Zealand, a conference with a membership about two thirds that of Australia. This was accomplished at the session of the New Zealand Conference held in Napier, April 1 to 14, 1892. Now it was time to move forward with the development of plans and to devise means of financial support. In the General Conference action recommending the school be established, taken in March, 1891, the matter of finances was left to the Australian field. The actions taken at the two conference sessions made no provision for supplying money for the project.

Australia was moving into an economic depression. Not all believers saw the need of a school; nonetheless, they took the first steps in deciding where the school should be located. Some argued for Sydney, others for Melbourne. Ellen White favored the latter.

Work had to begin in rented buildings. As the choice of a location narrowed down to Melbourne, it seemed that the area known as North Fitzroy, about two miles from the publishing house, would serve best. There they found a complex consisting of four buildings,

THE AUSTRALASIAN BIBLE SCHOOL

two of which were available, and the rent was within reason. On either side of the buildings was open land (Letter 13, 1892).

The *Bible Echo* of August 1 carried the announcement of plans for the opening of the school. The arrival of L. J. Rousseau, an educator from the United States, in late July gave assurance that the school could be opened soon. In the *Echo* report, readers were informed of the attractive situation of the school:

> The situation is nearly all that could be desired, on one of the city's most attractive boulevards, and yet enjoying abundance of open space on every side. In connection with the buildings is a nice grass paddock, while across the street are the broad acres and lake of Albert Park.
>
> The place is easy of access from train or boat, and is well known. There is good accommodation in the buildings both for home and school.

The houses rented were so closely connected as to form one house of twenty-three rooms. One large room, about eighteen by thirty-five feet, would serve for chapel exercises and Bible classroom. There were other quite large rooms that would be used in the school work (*ibid.*, Sept. 15, 1892).

THE BIBLE SCHOOL OPENS

At ten-thirty on Wednesday, August 24, opening exercises were held. A. G. Daniells and G. C. Tenney spoke first, then Mrs. White, who had to be carried onto the platform. She seemed to lose sight of the small constituency, of the adverse financial conditions, and the mere handful of students. With a vision of an unfinished task in a world with many continents yet untouched by the third angel's message, she declared:

> The missionary work in Australia and New Zealand is yet in its infancy, but the same work must be accomplished in Australia, New Zealand, in Africa, India, China, and the islands of the sea, as has been accomplished in the home field.—*Ibid.*, Supplement, Sept. 1, 1892 (quoted in LS, p. 338).

W. C. White followed with a review of the development of school work among Seventh-day Adventists and set forth some of

THE AUSTRALIAN YEARS

the conditions of success and some of the elements of danger. L. J. Rousseau, the principal, expressed his appreciation of the cordial reception given to him and his wife. He would teach some of the classes. The other teachers were announced as G. B. Starr, Biblical history and ethics, and W. L. H. Baker and Mrs. Rousseau in the other areas. Mrs. Starr was the matron *(ibid.,* Sept. 15, 1892). Twenty-five students enrolled, more than anticipated.

WHAT MADE THE SCHOOL POSSIBLE

What was not made generally public was how, in the face of adverse financial circumstances and the indifference on the part of a good many, the school actually got under way. Ellen White was to refer to it some months later. In a letter to Harmon Lindsay, the treasurer of the General Conference, she said:

> Last winter when we saw that we must have a school to meet the demands of the cause, we were put to our wits' ends to know where we should obtain the funds. . . . [Ellen G. White tells of expenses.] Some thought it could not be done; yet we knew that it must be started in 1892. Some thought all that could be done was to hold a short institute for the ministers.
>
> We knew that there were many youth who needed the advantages of the school. While we were in such deep perplexity as to how we should be able to make a beginning, the same plan was suggested to Willie's mind that was suggested to mine, and that . . . on the same night.
>
> In the morning when he came to tell me his plan, I asked him to wait until I told him mine, which was that we use the royalty of the foreign books sold in America.
>
> Although in pain, my mind was exercised over this matter, and I prayed earnestly to the Lord for light, and it came. You know that I could not well use the money that is set apart for other purposes.
>
> Of the royalty above referred to, I invested $1,000 to be used when most needed. But $500 must be used as a fund to bring to the school students who cannot and will not come unless they have help. Willie said [that] with this statement to place before the board we shall have their influence to sustain us. Thus our school was begun.—Letter 79, 1893.

THE AUSTRALASIAN BIBLE SCHOOL

As she wrote to another of this, she explained:

> They [the students] would never have been able to enjoy the advantages of the school unless someone did help them, and as no one assumed the responsibility, it dropped on me. I carried several through the first term of school, and am paying the expenses of six during the present term, and the number may swell to eight.—Letter 65, 1893.

A month after the school opened she could report joyfully:

> The school is certainly doing well. The students are the very best. They are quiet, and are trying to get all the good possible. They all like Elder Rousseau and his wife as teachers. He does not show what there is in him, and there is chance for all to be disappointed by his unpretending ways, but when engaged in his work, he shows he has a store of knowledge and is apt to teach. It is so pleasant to see all the students well pleased. This is indeed a harmonious house—no jealousies, no jangling. It is refreshing.—Letter 54, 1892.

Three months later she could write to Elder Olsen:

> The faculty have made few rules, and have not had one case where discipline was required. Peace and harmony have reigned from first to last. The presence of Jesus has been in the school from its beginning, and the Lord has wrought upon the minds of teachers and pupils. Without an exception, all the pupils have responded to the efforts made in their behalf, advancing step by step in obtaining knowledge, by doing their best.—Letter 46, 1892.

CONFRONTED WITH THE COLD OF MIDWINTER

The home in Preston that the staff in midsummer had found so convenient was difficult to heat. Neither the wood they purchased by the hundredweight nor the coke they endeavored to use could raise the temperature in the high-ceilinged rooms to a point of comfort. It was decided to move when the six-month lease expired. Adelaide, in South Australia, offered a more comfortable climate.

But no satisfactory place could be found in Adelaide, popular for

THE AUSTRALIAN YEARS

its winter climate, and the proposed move was delayed. She told Daniells:

> Come what may, we must not for a moment lose courage or hope or faith, because that would give the victory to the enemy. . . . Whatever circumstances may arise, we must remember that the Captain of the Lord's host is leading us.—MS 33, 1892.

THE TIDE BEGINS TO TURN

Beginning with July 10, the entries in Ellen White's diary began to take a new turn. On that day she could write the words "I praise the Lord with heart and soul and voice that I am growing stronger."—MS 34, 1892. Restoration was slow, so slow, but from time to time the entries were brighter. On September 5 she wrote Elder Haskell:

> I am very happy to report that I am much improved in health. . . . In this country we see much to be done. I am anxious to think that it is safe for me to enter upon active labor. Elder Daniells is now in Adelaide. He is much worn, and it is a question whether he should undertake to labor for the church there alone. As the Lord seems to be greatly favoring me with blessings both physical and spiritual, W. C. White and I have decided to go to Adelaide. Emily Campbell and May Walling will accompany us. We are to break up housekeeping, thus saving the rent.—Letter 30, 1892.

TWO MONTHS IN ADELAIDE

The Adelaide church, with a membership of more than one hundred, was second in size only to the Melbourne church. Early in the plans for Australia, Ellen White was to visit Adelaide. The pastor, W. D. Curtis, now returned to the homeland, had engaged in preaching, but neglected personal visiting, and the church was suffering. Just as soon as living quarters could be found, Ellen White was determined to take her helpers with her to join Daniells in his revival meetings and spend two or three months there. Daniells at last found a neat little furnished cottage of six rooms that would cost Ellen White only $25 a month, and sent for her. The group made the trip overnight and settled in on Monday, September 26.

THE AUSTRALASIAN BIBLE SCHOOL

She was pleased with the climate, and found she was in a beautiful city that reminded her much of Copenhagen, Denmark (MS 37, 1892).

The church generously furnished a horse and carriage, Ellen White paying for the care of the horse. She divided her working time between preaching, visiting the church members, and writing. Some of the visiting, because of the neglect of the pastor, was very taxing. Gradually her health improved, and on October 5 she reported that she felt more natural than she had felt during her sickness (Letter 72, 1892). And the time came when on three consecutive mornings she could write:

November 6, 1892: "I praise my heavenly Father for a better night's rest than usual."

November 7, 1892: "I rested well through the night."

November 8, 1892: "I slept well through the night."—MS 38, 1892.

Nearly every day she rode out in the carriage. One Friday she and her companion took their lunch and drove into the hills, where the scenery reminded her of Colorado. Everything was a living green. At noon they ate their lunch under a large tree, then turned homeward to prepare for the Sabbath (MS 37, 1892).

TWO WEEKS AT BALLARAT

Ellen White had her eyes on the closing of the Bible school in Melbourne in mid-December, to be followed by the Australian Conference session in early January. With their work completed in Adelaide, there was just time to squeeze in a two-week visit at Ballarat en route to Melbourne. She and her women helpers stayed at the home of a church member whose family name was James. It was about a mile out of town, surrounded by fruit trees and abounding with beautiful flowers.

On December 12 they returned to Melbourne. Although it was early summer, the weather was cloudy and cold, but the outlook for Ellen White was brighter than it had been for the better part of a year.

CHAPTER 5
(1893)

The Servant of the Lord Could Rejoice

"THE school has been a success!" wrote Ellen White jubilantly to the president of the General Conference on December 13, 1892.

She had just attended the closing exercises of the Australasian Bible School, a simple service held in the chapel room. For almost three months she had been away, working in Adelaide and Ballarat, and had returned to Melbourne for this significant event. She had not forgotten that one of the basic reasons she and her son had been urged to spend a couple of years in Australia was to aid in starting an educational work there. Fighting indifference, financial depression in the country, and prolonged, debilitating illness, her persistence had won out.

The school had been conducted with a limited teaching staff and just a few more than two dozen rather mature students. Her letter to Olsen carried this report:

> The first term of our Bible School has just ended. Today we attended the closing exercises. The schoolroom was well filled with those interested in the school. . . .
>
> Testimonies were borne by the students expressing their gratitude to God for the opportunity they had had of attending the school, saying they had been blessed in their studies. They were especially grateful for the light received from the Word of God. They had been so happy in their associations. Many regretted that the school must close, and this precious season come to an end. . . . All were determined to be present and enjoy the next term.—Letter 46, 1892.

THE SERVANT OF THE LORD COULD REJOICE

Writing a short time later to Dr. J. H. Kellogg in Battle Creek, she went into more detail in reporting the students' comments on the benefits they had received in Bible study:

> How much better they understood the plan of salvation, justification by faith, the righteousness of Christ as imparted to us. This term has been a success; next term we shall have double, I hope treble, the number of students.—Letter 21b, 1892.

Most of the students left immediately to enter the literature ministry in several of the Australian colonies. Church leaders turned briefly to planning for the next term of school, setting the time for opening as June 6. Then the ministers, including the president, scattered to the principal churches to lead out in the newly instituted Week of Prayer.

N. D. FAULKHEAD AND THE CONVINCING TESTIMONY

On the day school closed, W. C. White called a meeting of the available members of the school board. N. D. Faulkhead, treasurer of the publishing house, came to attend. As the meeting closed at about four o'clock, White spoke to him, telling him that Ellen White wanted to see him. As he started down the hall to the room where she was staying, there came to his mind a dream that he had had a few nights before, in which Ellen White had a message for him.

Mr. Faulkhead was a tall, keen, apt, and energetic businessman, genial and liberal in his disposition, but proud. When he became a Seventh-day Adventist, he held membership in several secret organizations, and he did not withdraw from these. As he wrote of his experience some years later in a general letter to "My Dear Brethren in the Faith," he told of these affiliations:

> I was closely connected with the Masonic Lodge, . . . I held the highest positions in the following lodges that could be conferred upon me: first, I was Master of the Master Masons' Lodge (or Blue Lodge); second, I was First Principal of the Holy Royal (of Canada); third, I was Preceptor of the Knights Templars, besides many other minor lodges, the Good Templars, Rechabites, and Odd Fellows, in which I also held high positions.—DF 522a, N. D. Faulkhead letter, Oct. 5, 1908.

As the Faulkhead family—Mrs. Faulkhead was a teacher in the

public school system—accepted the third angel's message, his unusual ability was recognized, and he was employed as treasurer in the Echo Publishing Company. He served well at first, but as time advanced he became more and more engrossed in his lodge work, and his interests in the work of God began to wane.

This was his situation when Ellen White arrived in Australia in December, 1891. As matters involving the publishing house workers were opened up to her in a comprehensive vision a few days after her arrival, she wrote of conditions there in general; she also penned testimonies to a number of the individuals involved, including Mr. Faulkhead and his wife. The document addressed to them dealt with his connection with the publishing house and his affiliation with the Masonic Lodge, and filled fifty pages. When she thought to mail it to him, she was restrained from doing so. She said, "When I enclosed the communication all ready to mail, it seemed that a voice spoke to me saying, 'Not yet, not yet, they will not receive your testimony.' "—Letter 39, 1893.

Ellen White said nothing regarding the matter for almost twelve months, but maintained a deep interest in Mr. and Mrs. Faulkhead and their spiritual welfare. Some of his associates in the publishing house were very much concerned as they observed his growing infatuation with the work of the lodge and his waning spirituality and decreasing concern for the interests of the cause of God. They pleaded with him, urging him to consider the danger of his course. "But," as Mr. Faulkhead states, "my heart was full of those things; in fact, I thought more of them than I did of anything else."—DF 522a, N. D. Faulkhead letter, Oct. 5, 1908.

He defiantly met the appeals with the bold statement "that he would not give up his connection with the Freemasons for all that Starr or White or any other minister might say. He knew what he was about, and he was not going to be taught by them."—Letter 21b, 1892. It was clear to those in charge of the work that unless a marked change came in his attitude, he would soon have to find other employment.

Mrs. White wrote of this experience: "None could reach him in regard to Freemasonry. He was fastening himself more and more firmly in the meshes of the enemy, and the only thing we could see to be done was to leave him to himself."—Letter 46, 1892. His

THE SERVANT OF THE LORD COULD REJOICE

condition was shown to her to be like that of "a man about to lose his balance and fall over a precipice" (MS 4, 1893).

For a period of months Mrs. White held messages for him and thought to send them, but was restrained.

In early December, 1892, J. H. Stockton, one of the first Seventh-day Adventists in Australia, was talking with Mr. Faulkhead. He asked him what he would do if Ellen White had a testimony for him in regard to his connection with the lodge. To this Faulkhead boldly retorted: "It would have to be mighty strong." Neither man was aware that almost a year before, the whole matter had been opened to her.—DF 522a, N. D. Faulkhead to EGW, Feb. 20, 1908.

It was shortly after this, on Saturday night, December 10, that Mr. Faulkhead dreamed that the Lord had shown his case to Ellen White, and that she had a message for him. This, with his defiant reply to Stockton in regard to what would be his attitude toward a message through her, led him to serious thought. At the time of this dream Mrs. White was at Ballarat, but on Monday, December 12, as noted earlier, she had returned to Melbourne. The next day she attended the closing exercises of the first term of the Australasian Bible School.

With this dream vividly in his mind, Faulkhead found Ellen White, who greeted him cordially. He asked her whether she had something for him. She replied that the burden of his case was upon her mind, and that she had a message for him from the Lord, which she wished him and his wife to hear. She called for a meeting in the near future, when she would present that message. Faulkhead eagerly asked, "Why not give me the message now?"—Letter 46, 1892.

Although she was weary from her journey and her work that morning, Ellen White went over to a stand and picked up a bundle of manuscripts. She told Faulkhead that several times she had prepared to send the message, but that she "had felt forbidden by the Spirit of the Lord to do so"*(ibid.)*, for the time had not fully come that he would accept it.

She then read and talked. A part of the fifty pages that were read that evening was of a general nature, relating to the work in the Echo Publishing Company and the experience of the workers employed

THE AUSTRALIAN YEARS

there. But the major part dealt more particularly with Mr. Faulkhead's experience and his connection not only with the work in the office but also his affiliation with the Masonic Lodge. She pointed out that his involvement with Freemasonry had absorbed his time and blunted his spiritual perception. She read to him of his efforts to maintain high principles for which the lodge claimed to stand, often couching her message in Masonic language. She also told him where in the lodge hall she had seen him sitting and what he was endeavoring to do with his associates. She spoke of his increasing interest in the work of these organizations and of his waning interest in the cause of God; of her seeing in vision his dropping the small coins from his purse in the Sabbath offering plate and the larger coins into the coffers of the lodge. She heard him addressed as "Worshipful Master." She read of scenes of drinking and carousal that took place in the lodge meetings, especially after Mr. Faulkhead had left.—DF 522a, G. B. Starr, "An Experience With Sister E. G. White in Australia."

"I thought this was getting pretty close home," he later wrote, "when she started to talk to me in reference to what I was doing in the lodges."—*Ibid.*, N. D. Faulkhead letter, Oct. 5, 1908.

ELLEN WHITE GIVES THE SECRET SIGNS

She spoke most earnestly of the dangers of his connection with Freemasonry, warning that "unless he severed every tie that bound him to these associations, he would lose his soul." She repeated to him words spoken by her guide. Then, giving a certain movement with her hand that was made by her guide, she said, "I cannot relate all that was given to me."—Letter 46, 1892.

At this, Faulkhead started and turned pale. Recounting the incident, he wrote:

> Immediately she gave me this sign. I touched her on the shoulder and asked her if she knew what she had done. She looked up surprised and said she did not do anything unusual. I told her that she had given me the sign of a Knight Templar. Well, she did not know anything about it.—DF 522a, N. D. Faulkhead letter, Oct. 5, 1908.

They talked on. She spoke further of Freemasonry and the

impossibility of a man being a Freemason and a wholehearted Christian. Again she made a certain movement, which "my attending angel made to me" (MS 54, 1899).

Again Mr. Faulkhead started, and the blood left his face. A second time she had made a secret sign, one known only to the highest order of Masons. It was a sign that no woman could know, for it was held in the strictest secrecy—the place of meeting was guarded both inside and outside against strangers. "This convinced me that her testimony was from God," he stated.—*Ibid.*

Speaking further of his reaction to this, he wrote:

> I can assure you . . . this caused me to feel very queer. But, as Sister White said, the Spirit of the Lord had come upon me and taken hold of me. She went on talking and reading as if nothing had happened, but I noticed how her face brightened up when I interrupted her again and spoke to her about the sign. She seemed surprised that she had given me such a sign. She did not know that she had moved her hand. Immediately the statement that I had made to Brother Stockton, that it would have to be mighty strong before I could believe that she had a message for me from the Lord, flashed through my mind.—DF 522a, N. D. Faulkhead letter, Oct. 5, 1908.

When Mrs. White finished reading, tears were in the man's eyes. He said:

> I accept every word. All of it belongs to me. . . . I accept the light the Lord has sent me through you. I will act upon it. I am a member of five lodges, and three other lodges are under my control. I transact all of their business. Now I shall attend no more of their meetings, and shall close my business relations with them as fast as possible.—Letter 46, 1892.

He also stated, "I am so glad you did not send me that testimony, for then it would not have helped me."—MS 54, 1899.

> Your reading the reproof yourself has touched my heart. The Spirit of the Lord has spoken to me through you, and I accept every word you have addressed especially to me; the general matter also is applicable to me. It all means me. That which you

THE AUSTRALIAN YEARS

have written in regard to my connection with the Freemasons, I accept. . . . I have just taken the highest order in Freemasonry, but I shall sever my connection with them all.—Letter 21b, 1892.

When Mr. Faulkhead left Ellen White's room, the hour was late. He took the streetcar to the railway station, and while traveling up Collins Street he passed the lodge hall. It suddenly dawned upon him that he should have been there attending a Knights Templar encampment that very evening. As he neared the station, he saw the train for Preston pulling out, so he was obliged to walk the rest of the way home. He chose an unfrequented road so that he might have opportunity for meditation. The walk he enjoyed very much, for there had come to him a new experience. He so much wanted to meet Daniells, Starr, or W. C. White and tell them that he was a new man, and how free and how happy he felt in his decision to sever his connection with all secret societies. It seemed to him that a ton of weight had rolled from his shoulders. And to think that the God who rules the universe and guides the planets had seen his danger and sent a message just for him!

FAULKHEAD RESIGNS FROM THE LODGES

The next morning found Mr. Faulkhead at his office. Word quickly spread to the group of workers of his experience the night before; over and over again he recounted with one after another how God had sent a message to arrest him from a course of action that would have led him to destruction. As his first work he called in his assistant and dictated his resignation to the various lodges. Then A. G. Daniells came in, and Mr. Faulkhead told him of his experience. While the two were talking, his letters of resignation were passed to Mr. Faulkhead for his signature. He signed and enclosed them and handed them to Daniells to mail. In telling of it, Faulkhead says, "How his eyes did sparkle with pleasure to think that the Lord had gained His point at last, and that his prayers had been answered."—DF 522a, N. D. Faulkhead letter, Oct. 5, 1908.

But no sooner had Faulkhead given the letters to Daniells than a feeling of mistrust came over him; he felt that he should have mailed the letters himself. Then he thanked the Lord for what he had done, for he felt that he could not have trusted himself to mail the letters.

THE SERVANT OF THE LORD COULD REJOICE
ANOTHER INTERVIEW WITH ELLEN WHITE

On Thursday, December 15, Mr. Faulkhead, accompanied by his wife, had another interview with Mrs. White. A number of pages of new matter were read to the two of them, and it was all accepted. "I wish you to know," he told Mrs. White, "how I look upon this matter. I regard myself as greatly honored of the Lord. He has seen fit to mention me, and I am not discouraged, but encouraged. I shall follow out the light given me of the Lord."—Letter 21b, 1892.

The battle was not entirely won with the sending in of the resignations. His lodge friends refused to release him, so he had to serve out his terms of office, another nine months. Most determined efforts were put forth to hold him to their society, but he had taken a firm position and stood by it. At times his church associates trembled for him. Ellen White wrote encouraging letters in support of his stand. He was victorious at last.

With the expiration of his term as officer of several of the lodges, the complete victory was won, and Mr. Faulkhead was able, on September 18, 1893, to write to Ellen White and her son.

Dear Brother and Sister White:
It gives me much pleasure to tell you that my term of office as Master of the Masonic Lodge expired last month. And I feel to thank God for it. How thankful I am to Him for sending me a warning that I was traveling on the wrong road. I do praise Him for His goodness and His love shown toward me, in calling me from among that people. I can see now very clearly that to continue with them would have been my downfall, as I must confess that my interest for the truth was growing cold. But thanks be to God, He did not let me go on with them without giving me warning through His servant. I cannot express my gratitude to Him for it. . . .
I can praise God with all my might, and then I cannot express my gratitude to Him for the love that He has shown me.
N. D. Faulkhead
—DF 522a.

This experience brought great confidence to the hearts of church members in Australia, and it was ever a source of encouragement

THE AUSTRALIAN YEARS

and help to Mr. Faulkhead. With the renewal of his first love and interest in the cause of God, he continued to serve the publishing house for many years, giving his time and strength and life to the spreading of the message.

In the testimony that was read by Ellen White to Mr. Faulkhead were recorded counsel and instruction of general application regarding the relation of Christians to organizations of the world. This was selected for publication and was issued at the time in Australia, and a little later in the United States, in a pamphlet under the title "Should Christians Be Members of Secret Societies?" (see 2 SM, pp. 121-140).

WRITING MESSAGES TO ENCOURAGE AND INSTRUCT

The Australian Conference session would convene in Melbourne beginning Friday, January 6, and continue to Sunday, January 15, 1893. Ellen White, with gaining strength, took up residence in the now nearly deserted school building and devoted her time to writing and speaking in the intervening weeks.

She wrote several letters to leading men in Battle Creek who stood in some peril. One was to Dr. J. H. Kellogg at the Battle Creek Sanitarium. In a twenty-one-page communication she urged him to maintain confidence in his brethren in the gospel ministry and called upon him to uphold Christian principles in his medical ministry. Then turning to a discussion of conditions and needs in Australia, she wrote:

> My brother, our stay here must be prolonged. We cannot leave the field as it is. We will be compelled to add the third year to the two we specified. Poverty and distress are in our large cities in Australia. Seventeen thousand persons have moved out of Melbourne to keep from perishing with hunger. Some of our own people can find nothing to do. Some who have commanded $30 and $40 per week as tailors or cutters have nothing to do. The brethren and sisters have found them sick, and suffering for bread to eat.—Letter 86a, 1893.

There was a twenty-two-page letter to the manager of the Review and Herald, a man of experience and ability who felt he could no longer continue in denominational employment. He found

THE SERVANT OF THE LORD COULD REJOICE

it difficult to live on the salary he received, and proposed leaving his work for a more lucrative position elsewhere. The first five pages of the letter were devoted to a report of her activities in Australia. Expressing her gratitude for the opportunity to serve, she wrote:

> I am so grateful for the privilege of being connected with God in any way. I feel highly honored. All I ask is that the Lord, in His great mercy and lovingkindness, will give me strength to use in His service, not to minister to my own ease or selfish indulgence, but that I may labor for Christ in the salvation of souls. I am waiting and believing, and receiving His rich blessing, although I am unworthy.

Then she came to the burden of her message:

> The word of the Lord has come to me in clear lines in reference to the principles and practices of those connected with the Review office. There has been need of self-examination on the part of the workers. Every man who has to do with sacred things should perform his work in a Christlike manner. There must be no sharp practice.

"In your letter," she wrote, "you speak of leaving the Review office. I am sorry that you can be willing to separate from the work for the reasons you mention. They reveal that you have a much deeper experience to gain than you now have." She reminded him:

> Other families, much larger than yours, sustain themselves, without one word of complaint, on half the wages you have. We have been over the ground, and I know what I am talking about.—Letter 20a, 1893.

She likened his course of action to that of deserters from the army of the Lord and urged that, rather than to take such a course as he proposed, he bring about changes in his home that would make it possible to live within his means. The heart of this testimony may be found in *Selected Messages*, book 2, pages 210 to 218. This promising leader failed to heed the counsel.

She wrote several messages that would be of service in the coming General Conference session, some of which have served to remind the church that God was at the helm.

CHAPTER 6
(1893)

Influence at Administrative Convocations

THROUGHOUT the churches of Australia the newly introduced Week of Prayer was an inspirational experience, and made an excellent prelude to the fifth session of the Australian Conference, which opened on January 6, 1893.

Meetings of the session were at first held in the tent pitched for use during the Melbourne Week of Prayer, but this was not a satisfactory arrangement for the session, so the work was moved to a rented hall.

Ellen White spoke Sabbath afternoon, and although she was weary and exhausted, she could write later, "I never spoke with greater ease and freedom from infirmity. The hearers said my voice was clear and musical, and the congregation could . . . but know that the Spirit and power of God was upon me."—Letter 23a, 1893. As her writing allowed time, she attended meetings addressing the conference almost every day. Wednesday she spoke on the publishing work; and Friday she spoke on tithing, a subject not too well understood by all in the colonies. She declared the session itself to be "by far the best that has ever been held in this country," and she wrote:

> All listened to me respectfully a year ago, but this year my message means far more to them.—*Ibid*.

The main items of business taken up at the session dealt with advancing the cause through the personal ministry of the church members in missionary work, the developing of the literature ministry, and the newly started school. The committee on the

INFLUENCE AT ADMINISTRATIVE CONVOCATIONS

permanent location of the school reported that study would be given to a climate that would be appropriate for students coming from Polynesia.

MESSAGES TO THE 1893 GENERAL CONFERENCE

During the ten-day session of the Australian Conference Ellen White's mind was much on North America and the forthcoming General Conference session, to be held in Battle Creek from February 17 to March 7. Preceding this would be a three-week institute, which would be attended by most of the delegates to the session and scores of ministers, colporteur leaders, Bible instructors, and laymen. The two gatherings, each three weeks long, were so closely related that a separation can hardly be made. The *General Conference Bulletin* for 1893 carried full reports of both in its 524 double-column pages.

The president of the General Conference, O. A. Olsen, was in frequent correspondence with W. C. White, who represented the General Conference as the superintendent of District Number 7, which comprised all of Australasia. On November 1, 1892, Olsen wrote to him concerning some proposals being made by certain key workers in the field that called for dismantling certain phases of organization of the church. His letter stated:

> Now about the matter, or rather, question, of organization. . . . I have had some fears that this question might come up and take a shape in the coming General Conference that much precious time would be wasted in discussing something that was not practical. . . . I received a letter from Elder Holser after he had been with Dr. [E. J.] Waggoner on that tour in Scandinavia that gave me some uneasiness. Others, too, have written and spoken in a way that has given me the idea that this matter was being discussed at some considerable length in some places. But I think that the question can be kept within proper limits.—O. A. Olsen to WCW, Nov. 1, 1892.

At issue was a greater centralization of the work and the elimination of some familiar features. This would involve turning from "plans of working that the Lord has seen fit to bless."

W. C. White shared his letter with his mother, as was fully

expected by Olsen. On December 19 she wrote a fifteen-page communication titled "Organization." The entire communication dealt with the organization of the Seventh-day Adventist Church. On its first page, Ellen White reminded church leaders that she knew the history well from firsthand contact:

> It is nearly forty years since organization was introduced among us as a people. I was one of the number who had an experience in establishing it from the first. I know the difficulties that had to be met, the evils which it was designed to correct, and I have watched its influence in connection with the growth of the cause. At an early stage in the work, God gave us special light upon this point, and this light, together with the lessons that experience has taught us, should be carefully considered.
>
> From the first, our work was aggressive. Our numbers were few, and mostly from the poorer class. Our views were almost unknown to the world. We had no houses of worship, [and] but few publications and very limited facilities for carrying forward our work. The sheep were scattered in the highways and byways, in cities, in towns, in forests. The commandments of God and the faith of Jesus was our message.

She then wrote of the inception of the various enterprises that were developed within the church, the educational work, and the establishment of health institutions, "both for the health and instruction of our own people and as a means of blessing and enlightenment to others." She asked,

> What is the secret of our prosperity? We have moved under the orders of the Captain of our salvation. God has blessed our united efforts. The truth has spread and flourished. Institutions have multiplied. The mustard seed has grown to a great tree. The system of organization proved a grand success.

She decried situations in which the machinery had become too complicated and conference sessions at times "burdened down with propositions and resolutions that were not at all essential." This, she pointed out, was an argument against, not organization, but the perversion of it.

It was in this setting she penned the unforgettable words:

INFLUENCE AT ADMINISTRATIVE CONVOCATIONS

> In reviewing our past history, having traveled over every step of advance to our present standing, I can say, "Praise God!" As I see what the Lord has wrought, I am filled with astonishment and with confidence in Christ our Leader. We have nothing to fear for the future, except as we shall forget the way the Lord has led us, and His teaching in our past history.—Letter 32, 1892.

President Olsen chose to present this message at the very opening of the institute, bringing it before the assembly of some three hundred workers and visitors on Sunday afternoon, January 29. As Olsen presented Ellen White's letter to the workers gathered at the institute, he broached the question of an administrative organization that would serve between the local conference, missions, and organizations, and the General Conference, thus planting the seeds for the union conference plan that was adopted in 1901. "What can be the objection," he asked, "to organizing district conferences? . . . It would seem that the problem of unity of effort in many distant fields, such as Australasia, South America, et cetera, could not be solved so well in any other way as to provide such fields with district conferences."—GCB 1893, pp. 24, 25.

Some months later Ellen White referred to this subject. She wrote:

> Elder Waggoner has entertained ideas, and without waiting to bring his ideas before a council of brethren, has agitated strange theories. He has brought before some of the people ideas in regard to organization that ought never to have had expression.
>
> I supposed that the question of organization was settled forever with those who believed the testimonies given through Sister White. Now if they believed the testimonies, why do they work contrary to them? Why should not my brethren be prudent enough to place these matters before me, or at least to enquire if I had any light upon these subjects?
>
> Why is it that these things start up at this time when we have canvassed the matter in our previous history, and God has spoken upon these subjects? Should not that be enough? Why not keep steadily at work in the lines that God has given us? Why

THE AUSTRALIAN YEARS

not walk in the clear light He has revealed in place of tearing to pieces that which God has built up?—Letter 37, 1894.

ELLEN G. WHITE'S MESSAGE TO THE DELEGATES

Four days after penning the message to church leaders quoted above, she wrote a message to be delivered to the delegates at the session. It read:

Dear Brethren of the General Conference:

I am rejoiced to report to you the goodness, the mercy, and the blessing of the Lord bestowed upon me. I am still compassed with infirmities, but I am improving. The Great Restorer is working in my behalf, and I praise His holy name.

After writing briefly of her prolonged illness and her relation to it, she declared:

Since the first few weeks of my affliction, I have had no doubts in regard to my duty in coming to this distant field; and more than this, my confidence in my heavenly Father's plan in my affliction has been greatly increased. . . .

I have since leaving America written twenty hundred pages of letter paper. I could not have done all this writing if the Lord had not strengthened and blessed me in large measure. Never once has that right hand failed me. My arm and shoulder have been full of suffering, hard to bear, but the hand has been able to hold the pen and trace words that have come to me from the Spirit of the Lord.

THE USE OF ANOTHER'S LANGUAGE

As her heart overflowed with the sense of the goodness of God to her and to His church, she chose to express her feelings in phrases from God's Word and also in the wording of a book she had recently read, *The Great Teacher*, by John Harris, published in 1836. Such a procedure was not uncommon in her work. She found the language choice and the truth well expressed.* Speaking of God's tender care for His church, Ellen White wrote:

---

*In his introduction to the volume from which Ellen White drew some expressions, Harris wrote:
"Suppose, for example, an inspired prophet were now to appear in the church, to add a

INFLUENCE AT ADMINISTRATIVE CONVOCATIONS

I have had a most precious experience, and I testify to my fellow laborers in the cause of God, "The Lord is good, and greatly to be praised." I testify to my brethren and sisters that the church of Christ, enfeebled and defective as it may be, is the only object on earth on which He bestows His supreme regard. While He extends to all the world His invitation to come to Him and be saved, He commissions His angels to render divine help to every soul that cometh to Him in repentance and contrition, and He comes personally by His Holy Spirit into the midst of His church.

. . .

Consider, my brethren and sisters, that the Lord has a people, a chosen people, His church, to be His own, His own fortress, which He holds in a sin-stricken, revolted world; and He intended that no authority should be known in it, no laws be acknowledged by it, but His own.

After writing at some length of the church, its authority, and its resources and facilities, she penned the following, again couching her message in part in the words of Harris:

The Lord Jesus is making experiments on human hearts through the exhibition of His mercy and abundant grace. He is effecting transformations so amazing that Satan, with all his triumphant boasting, with all his confederacy of evil united against God and the laws of His government, stands viewing them as a fortress impregnable to his sophistries and delusions. They are to him an incomprehensible mystery.

The angels of God, seraphim and cherubim, the powers commissioned to cooperate with human agencies, look on with astonishment and joy that fallen men, once children of wrath, are through the training of Christ developing characters after the divine similitude, to be sons and daughters of God, to act an important part in the occupations and pleasures of heaven.— Letter 2d, 1892 (GCB 1893, pp. 407-409; see also TM, pp. 15-19).

supplement to the canonical books—what a Babel of opinions would he find existing on almost every theological subject! And how highly probable it is that his ministry would consist, or seem to consist, in a mere selection and ratification of such of these opinions as accorded with the mind of God. Absolute originality would seem to be almost impossible. The inventive mind of man has already bodied forth speculative opinions in almost every conceivable form, forestalling and robbing the future of its fair proportion of novelties and leaving little more, even to a divine messenger, than the office of taking some of these opinions and impressing them with the seal of heaven."—John Harris, *The Great Teacher*, pp. xxxiii, xxxiv.

THE AUSTRALIAN YEARS
"TESTIMONY NO. 12"

While Ellen White's message to the session was appreciated, and parts have often been quoted, neither church leaders nor Bulletin editors attached words of special comment. Not so with an eighteen-page document titled "Testimony No. 12," which was read on two occasions to those assembled.

Olsen read the message at the first hour of the Friday-morning institute session, February 3. He designated it as "a testimony received from Sister White for this conference." The notice describes it as "a solemn, searching appeal to the ministry to set about the work of cleansing and purification with terrible earnestness." The response is also noted:

> The reading was followed by testimonies from quite a number who confessed failures with brokenness of heart and accepted the testimony as personal to them, and laid hold of the promises in it, as well as the corrections. The Spirit of the Lord brought a spirit of deep earnestness and solemnity into the meeting.—GCB 1893, p. 115.

Ellen White opened her message by relating an incident that had just taken place. One who was attending the Australian Conference session had related to her his perplexity and discouragement in finding in the *Review and Herald* articles by two leading brethren, A. T. Jones and Uriah Smith, one in disagreement with the other. She described the effect:

> He saw in the *Review* the articles of Brother A. T. Jones in regard to the image of the beast, and then the one from Elder Smith presenting the opposite view. He was perplexed and troubled. He had received much light and comfort in reading articles from Brethren Jones and Waggoner; but here was one of the old laborers, one who had written many of our standard books, and whom we had believed to be taught of God, who seemed to be in conflict with Brother Jones.
>
> What could all this mean? Was Brother Jones in the wrong? Was Brother Smith in error? Which was right? He became confused. When the important laborers in the cause of God take opposite positions in the same paper, whom can we depend on?

INFLUENCE AT ADMINISTRATIVE CONVOCATIONS

Who can we believe has the true position?

She pointed the troubled inquirer to the Bible, and urged that he be not confused by the differences of opinion he had observed. And she admonished church leaders and ministers that "the zeal that leads to this kind of work is not inspired of God." She gave counsel on dealing with such situations:

DEALING WITH DIFFERENCES

I have received letters from different points telling the sad, discouraging results of these things. We have opposition enough from our foes, and we shall have conflicts fierce and strong; let us not now cause Satan to glory because of the pitched battles within our own ranks. The unity for which our Saviour prayed should be brought into our practical life.

After devoting several pages urging unity, in the words of the apostle Paul she urged: "I beseech you, brethren, by the name of our Lord Jesus Christ, that ye all speak the same thing." She admonished that "this is not a time for brother to cherish prejudice against brother. Put not into our enemies' hands anything that bears the least suggestions of differences among us, even in opinion."

Then she put her finger on what appears to have been the cause behind the situation she was dealing with:

The conference at Minneapolis was the golden opportunity for all present to humble the heart before God and to welcome Jesus as the great Instructor, but the stand taken by some at that meeting proved their ruin. They have never seen clearly since, and they never will, for they persistently cherish the spirit that prevailed there, a wicked, criticizing, denunciatory spirit. Yet since that meeting, abundant light and evidence has been graciously given, that all might understand what is truth.

Those who were then deceived might since have come to the light. They might rejoice in the truth as it is in Jesus, were it not for the pride of their own rebellious hearts. They will be asked in the judgment, "Who required this at your hand, to rise up against the message and the messengers I sent to My people with light, with grace and power? Why have you lifted up your souls against God? Why did you block the way with your perverse spirit? And afterward when evidence was piled upon evidence, why did you not humble your hearts before God, and repent of your rejection of the message of mercy He sent you?" The Lord has not inspired these brethren to resist the truth.

In this communication Ellen White addressed herself to the loss that had come to the cause of God because of the resistance on the part of some at the Minneapolis General Conference session to the presentations of truth made there, and the burden thus placed on the Lord's messengers that tended to divert them from aggressive work in the field.

Ellen White had just written of her amazement of what God had wrought in the advancement of the cause, and that we have nothing to fear for the future unless we forget. Yet she sensed the presence of situations that gave her concern:

> The Lord designed that the messages of warning and instruction given through the Spirit to His people should go everywhere. But the influence that grew out of the resistance of light and truth at Minneapolis tended to make of no effect the light God had given to His people through the testimonies. *Great Controversy* . . . has not had the circulation that it should have had, because some of those who occupy responsible positions were leavened with the spirit that prevailed at Minneapolis, a spirit that clouded the discernment of the people of God. . . . The dullness of some and the opposition of others have confined our strength and means largely among those who know the truth, but do not practice its principles.

Then she penned the following startling words—words that answer in part the question as to why Christ has not yet come:

> If every soldier of Christ had done his duty, if every watchman on the walls of Zion had given the trumpet a certain sound, the world might ere this have heard the message of warning. But the work is years behind. What account will be rendered to God for thus retarding the work?

She appealed to the church for sacrifice and dedication: Eternity

INFLUENCE AT ADMINISTRATIVE CONVOCATIONS

is to be kept in view; troublous days are ahead.

The appeal closed with the words "Our work is plainly laid down in the Word of God. Christian is to be united to Christian, church to church, the human instrumentality cooperating with the divine, every agency to be subordinate to the Holy Spirit, and all to be combined in giving to the world the good tidings of the grace of God."—MS 1, 1893 (see also GCB 1893, pp. 419, 420).

THE WHOLEHEARTED RESPONSE

The message as given in the manuscript was probably read in its entirety at the institute. Perhaps, though, only the latter half, which did not deal with personalities and issues so sharply, was read four weeks later, Monday morning, February 27, during the session. That is indicated by the fact that the *General Conference Bulletin* for the Monday-meeting recorded only the last half of the message; it is also indicated by the description that was given of the response to the reading. The editors of the Bulletin reported:

> Following the reading of this, a most excellent social meeting occurred, a number of brethren responding with hearty confessions and expressions of determination to walk in unity and love and the advancing light. The good Spirit of the Lord came in in marked degree, tears flowed freely, and expressions of joy and thankfulness seemed to well up from every heart.—GCB 1893, p. 421.

Such reports of the influence of the testimonies indicate that even with the messenger of God thousands of miles away, her influence was felt in a marked manner. Other reports, in more than five hundred pages of the *General Conference Bulletin* for 1893, show clearly the pervasive influence of the Spirit of Prophecy in the remnant church.

RELATION TO DOCTRINES

One of these pages carries remarks made by S. N. Haskell concerning the relation of the Spirit of Prophecy to the doctrines of the church. In answering a question raised in one of his meetings, he referred to the Scripture argument and then read some extracts from the Spirit of Prophecy throwing light upon the subject.

THE AUSTRALIAN YEARS

Alluding to the use of that which had been given to the church by the Spirit of Prophecy, he said he never attempted to establish doctrine from the testimonies.

> The testimonies have not been given to establish new doctrine. The doctrine is established by the Word of God, and the Spirit of Prophecy comes in to bring out the light, revealing new beauties in it, and bringing out here and there details which help in the understanding of the Word of God. . . .
>
> [A voice: "Isn't it safe to say that the testimony reveals no new doctrine?"]
>
> Yes. Some of our old brethren know that in the East and New England it is a great place for battles over the testimonies. . . . I happened to be born in the East, and embraced the truth there, and so have battled in this line a good deal. Nothing pleased me more than to get those who opposed the visions together and have a Bible reading on the testimonies. And before we began we always made this statement: that if they could find any line in the testimonies that pertained to a doctrine that I could not establish from the Bible, I would give up the testimonies. And second, If they could ever find a line in the testimonies giving a prophecy or prediction which should be fulfilled, and which had not been fulfilled, I would give up the testimonies. There I will stand today. So I believe the testimonies.—GCB 1893, p. 233.

Thus while Ellen White was helping to pioneer the work in Australasia, battling what seemed to be almost insurmountable difficulties, stalwart leaders at the home base of the church functioned as if she were in their presence, and benefited from her pen.

In January, 1893, longstanding plans for Ellen White to visit New Zealand were coming to fruition. These plans called for visiting the churches and for a camp meeting to be held in Napier in March. A conference session would be held in connection with it. Ellen White, W. C. White, and G. B. Starr and his wife would attend. The tour was expected to take about four months.

CHAPTER 7
(1893)

On to
New Zealand

ELLEN WHITE looked forward to spending a week with the Parramatta church while en route to New Zealand. Parramatta was a beautiful community, a suburb of Sydney. Robert Hare and David Steed had held evangelistic meetings there, beginning in March, 1892, and a church of fifty members had been raised up, with a Sabbath school of seventy. Those accepting the message were described as "no mean citizens," representing "excellent families and possessing some means" (Letter 34, 1892).

The congregation was determined to have a house of worship. Beginning with donations amounting to £420 ($2,100),* a good lot and building materials were purchased. Within three weeks' time of the laying of the foundations, the building was erected with donated labor, and Sabbath meetings were being held in it. It was dedicated on Sabbath, December 10. The next day, 480 people crowded into the new church at what was called its opening meeting (BE, Jan. 15, 1893). This was the first church building owned by Seventh-day Adventists in continental Australia. A little chapel had been erected in Bismark, Tasmania, in 1889.

As funds were being raised in September, Ellen White, who had received a gift from friends in California of $45 with which to buy a comfortable chair for use during her illness, appropriated the money to aid in building the Parramatta church. She explained to her friends who had given her the money that she wished them to

---

* Note: The exchange rate held steady throughout the years Ellen White was in Australia, very close to five dollars to the British pound. Ellen White moved easily from one to the other.

69

THE AUSTRALIAN YEARS

have something invested in the Australian missionary field (Letter 34, 1892).

Leaving Melbourne on Thursday, January 26, the party arrived in Sydney on Friday. Ellen White met with the church at Parramatta on Sabbath morning, and this introduced a full week of meetings. There was a question in the minds of some as to whether she was well enough to speak in the town hall on Sunday night and also take the Sabbath-morning service as planned. She determined in the strength of God to go forward with the Sabbath-morning worship service, and spoke with great freedom from John 14 to an audience that filled the house (Letter 127, 1893).

Sunday night she spoke in the Parramatta town hall. It was well filled also, and she reports:

> The people listened with great attention, and the people here, believing the truth, are much pleased. But I do not feel satisfied. I needed physical strength that I could do justice to the great and important themes that we are dealing with. What a work is before us!—*Ibid.*

In addition to speaking in the church on Tuesday and Thursday nights, she visited in the community, as well, where she was well received. She was told that the wife of a local minister had declared: "Mrs. White's words are very straight; she has gone deeper than any of us in religious experience. We must study the Word to see if these things be so."—DF 28a, "Experiences in Australia," p. 316.

For the Seventh-day Adventist pastor, Robert Hare, she had words of counsel and instruction that she arranged to read to him and his wife. After listening for a time, with a troubled look he declared that he might as well give up preaching. Ellen White tells the story:

> I said to him, "That is what I expected you to say, for it is your way to take reproof in just this spirit. Your past experience has been presented to me. You think you are humble, but if you were so in truth, you would not act as you are doing. The Lord reads your heart. He is acquainted with our dangers. He loves you, and He wants to save you.
>
> "It is because you do not understand your errors, and the

ON TO NEW ZEALAND

defects in your character, that He sends you warnings and encouragements. You should receive these as blessings, the most to be appreciated of anything He sends you.

"I have done my duty in setting before you your true situation. . . . Brother Hare, study the lessons that Christ gave to His disciples, and let their simplicity charm you. Seek to have the mind of Christ, and you will teach as He taught."—*Ibid.*, pp. 317, 318.

Ellen White wondered how the testimony would be received. She was pleased when she met him in the evening to find him seemingly a changed man.

But in all this Ellen White herself struggled with discouragement. On the second Sabbath morning, before taking the church worship service, she felt depressed and wished that she had not promised to speak. But when she stood on her feet to address the congregation, she reports:

> The Lord gave me special help. Ideas came to me when speaking that had not before been in my thoughts. I was instructed, as well as instructing others. I spoke from the words of Christ in Matthew 13:12-17, and dwelt especially on the last verse: "Verily I say unto you, That many prophets and righteous men have desired to see those things which ye see, and have not seen them; and to hear those things which ye hear, and have not heard them."
>
> I showed them that those now living on the earth are favored above all people in the possession of precious advanced light. I felt the importance of my subject, and I know that I had the Holy Spirit's help in bringing things to my remembrance in an impressive manner. I praised the Lord that He gave power to the weak, and that to me who had not strength He increased strength.—*Ibid.*, pp. 322, 323.

Then she opened up her heart in a way she seldom did. She questioned whether the time had not come to cease her public labors. She wrote:

> I have seasons of temptation, when infirmities press so heavily upon me, and at such times I ask myself, "Am I really in

THE AUSTRALIAN YEARS

the way of my duty? Is it not time I retired from active labor?"

Then when I stand before the people after such a battle with the enemy, the Holy Spirit comes to me as a divine helper. I have the assurance that my work is not to close yet. My mind is clear, and I am able in words to make truth forcible, because the Lord is my helper.

Let us be of good courage in the Lord, lift up Jesus at all times, grasp His might by faith, for He is our strength and our efficiency. "Bless the Lord, O my soul: and all that is within me, bless His holy name."—*Ibid.*, p. 323.

VOYAGE TO NEW ZEALAND

At two o'clock that Sabbath afternoon Ellen White, together with her son William, her secretary, Emily Campbell, and G. B. Starr and his wife, boarded the *Rotomahanna* for Auckland, New Zealand. She describes the ship as a "beautiful steamer, and one of the fastest on these waters" (RH, May 30, 1893). She had a convenient and pleasant stateroom on the upper deck, and endured the journey well. Arriving at Auckland on Wednesday morning, February 8, she and her companions were taken to a comfortable furnished cottage arranged for by the church. The next twelve days were devoted to meetings in the Auckland church; on two evenings she spoke to attentive audiences in a well-filled theater. In all she spoke eight times while there.

ON TO KAEO AND THE JOSEPH HARE HOME

Among the very first in New Zealand to accept the third angel's message, as S. N. Haskell began work in Auckland in late 1885, were Edward Hare and his wife. As soon as he accepted the Sabbath he was eager that his father, Joseph Hare, who resided in Kaeo, should also hear. So Haskell made a visit to Kaeo, 160 miles north of Auckland. Of this visit he wrote:

> We became deeply interested in Father Hare and his family. For twenty years he had been a schoolmaster in the north of Ireland. By his present and his former marriage, and by the former marriage of his present wife, he has a family of twenty-four children. Sixteen of these are married and have

ON TO NEW ZEALAND

children. Many of them are men of means, and hold honorable positions in society. They are persons of more than ordinary ability, and have an extensive influence. Father Hare himself is local preacher for the Methodists.—HS, p. 103.

Many members of the family accepted the third angel's message, including Father Hare. Now, eight years later, Ellen White was in New Zealand and was urged to visit Kaeo. She recorded:

> Here is a company of interesting people—a father, and his children and grandchildren. Father Hare is now in the seventies. . . . He is a man much respected. The community was so anxious to see us that we consented to take this trip from Auckland to Kaeo.
> They have a little chapel which was built by the Hare family. One son is in Auckland, one son obtained his education at our college in Healdsburg, California. We feel pleased that we can visit this church consisting mostly of the members of this one large family.—Letter 55, 1893.

Kaeo was a twenty-four-hour journey from Auckland by coastal boat, which made several stops en route. There was just time to squeeze in comfortably a two-week visit to Kaeo before entering into preparations for the camp meeting scheduled to open in Napier on Thursday, March 23.

So on Monday the White party, the same that had come from Australia, boarded the *Clansman* at Auckland for its weekly trip north. Once on shipboard Mrs. White soon discovered that it would be unwise for her to go into the cabin below. She reported, "It was close, and the berths in staterooms narrow and hard as a board."—MS 77, 1893. She described the journey in a letter written to her older sister Mary Foss, who resided in Maine. Ellen White was still suffering a good deal of pain in her hips and could walk but little. A comfortable chair had been purchased for her in Auckland; this, along with a folding spring bed, was brought on board. The chair, she said, suited her as if made especially for her. There was a stiff breeze as they started on their journey, and Ellen White was wrapped up "like a mummy" to shelter her from the wind. She continued:

THE AUSTRALIAN YEARS

My chair was the easiest I ever had; but after about two hours my hip began to pain me, and I knew I must lie down. When Willie came to see if all was well with me, I told him I could not endure to sit up any longer.

The only place open to me on deck was the smoking room, but all said if I could not do better they would empty that room and put my spring bed in there; but lo, the bed would not go in. Then the steward and W. C. White went off by themselves to get things fixed. After a while they came and helped me to the other side of the boat, where a shelter had been made with rugs, and I lay down on a good spring cot, oh, so grateful for the privilege. . . .

The arrangement made for me on deck was a great comfort, and I felt so thankful for the change from chair to cot. Emily lay in a steamer chair next to me. Willie had a steamer chair on the other side of me. Brother and Sister Starr were below in a stateroom.—Letter 55, 1893.

During the trip Ellen White had a long visit with the captain, who had suffered severely from rheumatism but had been cured, according to him, by spending some time at a hot sulfur spring near Auckland. The captain's wife urged Ellen White to visit these springs. She thought she might do so. As they made their way up the east coast of the North Island of New Zealand, the scenery was exquisite. She wrote as they traveled:

I think it is not possible for anyone who is not a Christian to understand and enjoy the works of God and the precious things in nature. When we behold the evidences of His matchless love, in the lofty trees, the shrubs and opening flowers, our minds are carried up from nature to nature's God, and our hearts overflow with gratitude to the great Master Artist who has given us all these beautiful things to delight our senses.—*Ibid.*

When they arrived at their destination, Whangaroa Harbor, at seven in the evening, Joseph and Metcalfe Hare were there to meet them. The men had come three miles from Kaeo in their skiff. Travelers and baggage were transferred to the little boat, and they started on the two-hour trip to Kaeo. The water was smooth, the air

ON TO NEW ZEALAND

was mild, and the new moon gave just enough light to outline the mountains (RH, May 30, 1893). Ellen White describes the trip in her diary:

> Willie sat at the end of the boat at the helm, his back to my back to give me support and to guide the boat. Brethren Hare stood up in the boat, each with an oar, and were guided by word and motion of head when the boat should go veering to right and left in the narrow passage, shunning rocks and dangerous places.
>
> The view on this passage must be grand when it can be seen, but it was night and we were deprived of the privilege of viewing the scenery. The water was as smooth as a beautiful lake. . . . The landing place was close to Joseph Hare's backyard. We stepped, with help, on the embankment and passed through the gate, and a few steps brought us to the back piazza [porch]. We climbed the steps and entered the open door and were welcomed by Sister Hare.—MS 77, 1893.

In the morning Father Hare came with his carriage and took them the three miles to his home. As they traveled, Ellen White became ecstatic by what she saw: fern trees in abundance, mountains "closely linked one to another, rounded or sharp at the top, and precipicelike at the sides; then uniting with this was still another and another, peak after peak presenting itself like links uniting in a chain" *(ibid.)*. Father Hare's home was well located, close to a high, wooded mountain. A passing stream supplied pure water. There was a flourishing orchard of apples, pears, peaches, plums, and quince trees, and beyond, beautiful, fragrant pines.

Wednesday Ellen White spent in writing letters for the American mail. Early Thursday it began to rain, and how it did rain! By afternoon the little creek was a swollen roaring torrent, bringing down driftwood and logs. The lower part of the Kaeo Valley was flooded, houses were destroyed, horses and sheep were drowned, and hundreds of huge logs were floated over fields and orchards (RH, May 30, 1893). But the rain was soon over, and the weather improved.

Sabbath morning Ellen White spoke in the little meetinghouse the Hare family had built. As she stood before her audience, she recognized faces she had previously seen in vision, as had happened to her many times. She was well aware of the experiences and attitudes of some present (MS 77, 1893). Sunday afternoon she addressed about two hundred of the community folks at the Wesleyan church. George Starr spoke in the same church Sunday evening. Thus began a busy stay at Kaeo.

Some members of the Hare family had not yet confessed Christ, and one had grown harsh and sharp in his dealings with neighbors and in his efforts to win people to the message. This left them with but little influence. Yet, Ellen White reported, the people in the community seemed anxious to hear the Word of God. Souls were asking, "What is truth?" Of the youth she wrote that "there are some in Kaeo whom God has been calling to fit themselves for labor in His vineyard, and we rejoice that several are preparing to go to the Bible school" in Australia (RH, May 30, 1893). Because of bad weather and irregular boat schedules, the visitors stayed an extra week in Kaeo. They filled the time with meetings, and in earnest visiting from family to family. Near the time for them to leave, Minnie and Susan Hare, ages 20 and 14, respectively, youngest daughters of Father Hare, were baptized.

Thursday morning, March 16, the visiting group caught the steamer for Auckland. Ellen White and the Starrs were taken to Whangaroa Harbor on Wednesday afternoon so that Ellen White could speak in the town hall that evening. W. C. White and Emily Campbell came with the baggage early Thursday morning, and they were soon on the *Clansman* en route to Auckland.

At Auckland they changed to the *Wairarapa*, bound for Napier. Here the first Seventh-day Adventist camp meeting in the Southern Hemisphere was scheduled to open on Thursday, March 23. Again the trip meant Sabbath travel, and while waiting for the two-o'clock (Friday) departure Ellen White wrote letters. In one she stated, "I am sorry, so sorry, that again we will travel on the Sabbath."—Letter 32b, 1893.

At Auckland, ten church members joined them on board, bound for the same meeting. There was a stop en route on Sabbath at Gisborne, where A. G. Daniells and Robert Hare had raised up a church (RH, June 6, 1893). The ministers went ashore and met with the believers in their Sabbath service.

CHAPTER 8
(1893)

The New Zealand Camp Meeting

As THE passengers of the *Wairarapa* woke up Sunday morning, they discovered that they were at anchor off Napier. Ellen White describes the little city as "a beautiful place, the resident portion of the town being built on a series of high hills overlooking the sea" (RH, June 6, 1893). She, W. C. White, and Emily were taken to the comfortable home of the Doctors Caro,* not far from where preparations were already under way for the camp meeting. They were to be entertained there for the full time. A two-wheeled horse-drawn rig was made available for Ellen White's use in getting to the meetings.

Arrangements had been made for her to speak Sunday evening in the Theater Royal, and she presented her favorite theme, "The Love of God," to an attentive audience. The next three days were devoted to getting ready for the meeting. Two large tents were pitched. Notice had been sent to the churches weeks before, but the response was poor, so plans for a dining tent and a reception tent were dropped. Only a few family tents were pitched. It was expected that the restaurant in town could serve whatever food was needed.

However, by midweek boats and trains brought delegations from the churches, fully doubling the number expected. The camp meeting planners faced a minor crisis.

From the time plans were under way, Ellen White had urged that this first camp meeting must be a sample of what future camp

---

*The husband, a physician, was cordial but not an Adventist. The wife, a dentist, corresponded often with Ellen White.

meetings should be. Over and over again she declared: " 'See, saith he, that thou make all things according to the pattern shewed to thee in the mount.' As a people," she said, "we have lost much by neglecting order and method." She commented, "Although it takes time and careful thought and labor, and often seems to make our work cost more, in the end we can see that it was a paying business to do everything in the most perfect manner."—*Ibid.* For the people to go uptown for their meals would, she pointed out, "break into our program, waste precious time, and bring in a haphazard state of things that should be avoided" *(ibid.).*

The camp was enlarged; more tents were procured, a reception tent was fitted up, and also a dining tent.

The food provided was plain, substantial, and plentiful. Instead of the dozen people first expected, about thirty took their meals in the dining tent.

The first meeting held in the big tent was on Tuesday evening, in advance of the opening, and Stephen McCullagh spoke. On the first Sabbath afternoon Ellen White was the speaker. At the close of her address she extended invitations for a response, first from those who had never taken their stand for Christ and then from those "who professed to be the followers of Christ, who had not the evidence of His acceptance." The responses were encouraging. A hard rain had come up, and the big tent leaked in many places, but this did not worry the audience, for the interest in "eternal matters" was too deep to be affected by the surroundings. As the rain continued, George Starr gave precious instruction and exhorted the people. The meeting continued until sundown *(ibid.).*

Sunday evening, six were baptized. Monday was devoted to business meetings.

In the evening McCullagh spoke on phrenology. The next morning in the six-o'clock testimony meeting, phrenology and spiritualism were seen to be topics in which there was great interest, so that morning, in place of the meetings that had been planned, Ellen White spoke on phrenology and its perils.

A day or two later one of the literature evangelists brought to Starr a pamphlet containing the sermon of an influential Wesleyan minister in New Zealand in which he defended "higher criticism" of the Bible and scoffed at the idea that all portions of the Bible were

THE NEW ZEALAND CAMP MEETING

inspired. When it was announced that there would be an address on the subject, the people of Napier flocked out to hear. Many Adventists residing in the city where they were employed attended the early-morning and evening meetings. Ellen White was at most of the early meetings, but much of her time was spent writing in the Caro home.

The messages presented at the camp were very practical, she joining the ministers in their work. One morning she spoke on Sabbath observance, at another time on John 14 and the Christian's heavenly home, then on sanctification and transformation of character. The subject of "dress" was presented, and one evening the subject of the school in Australia was introduced and a call made for means. Ellen White spent thirty minutes recounting the establishment of Battle Creek College. It was a most profitable meeting. At a number of the meetings, only about half of the audience were Adventists.

One morning Ellen White, wanting to attend the early-morning meeting, found there was no transportation readily available. She tells the story in her diary:

> The horse is in the pasture, and I decide to make an experiment of walking. I start on my way, but I see W. C. White behind me with a two-wheeled cart. He is between the fills, trotting along on the descending grade to overtake me. He insisted upon my taking my seat as usual and he drew the conveyance himself.
>
> As he approached the encampment, Elder Starr saw him and came out to help him, and they drew up the vehicle to the very tent entrance. After the meeting opened, I spoke to the people.—MS 78, 1893.

The camp meeting was scheduled to close on Wednesday, April 5, but boat transportation was delayed, and so meetings continued another day. A meeting for literature evangelists followed over the weekend. Ellen White remained for still another week in Napier; she and associate workers visited families and churches nearby. But much of her time was devoted to writing. She devoted one entire day during the camp meeting to getting materials off to Fanny Bolton and Marian Davis in Melbourne.

THE AUSTRALIAN YEARS

Two or three weeks after the camp meeting was over she wrote of its success to Harmon Lindsay in Battle Creek:

> Our camp meeting in Napier was excellent from the commencement to the close. Several decided to observe the Sabbath for the first time, and some who had left the church came back.
>
> One man named Anderson said, "The testimonies of Sister White drove me out of the church. I have been disconnected from the church three years. I bless God I came to this meeting, for I have heard the testimonies and believe them to be of God. It is the testimonies that have brought me back to the church."
>
> He requested baptism and was as happy a man as there was upon the ground all through the meetings.—Letter 79, 1893.

MEETING OFFSHOOT TEACHINGS

The day before the camp meeting opened, Ellen White addressed a letter to a Mr. Stanton in America, who had begun to teach that the Seventh-day Adventist Church had, through apostasy, become Babylon. She wrote:

> Dear Brother Stanton,
>
> I address to you a few lines. I am not in harmony with the position that you have taken, for I have been shown by the Lord that just such positions will be taken by those who are in error. Paul has given us a warning to this effect: "Now the Spirit speaketh expressly, that in the latter times some shall depart from the faith, giving heed to seducing spirits, and doctrines of devils."
>
> My brother, I learn that you are taking the position that the Seventh-day Adventist Church is Babylon, and that all that would be saved must come out of her. You are not the only man whom the enemy has deceived in this matter. For the last forty years, one man after another has arisen, claiming that the Lord has sent him with the same message. But let me tell you . . . that this message you are proclaiming is one of the satanic delusions designed to create confusion among the churches. My brother, you are certainly off the track.—Letter 57, 1893.

Mr. Stanton had published a pamphlet titled "The Loud Cry of

THE NEW ZEALAND CAMP MEETING

the Third Angel's Message." In this he quoted freely from the Spirit of Prophecy messages of reproof and rebuke, forgetting that God had said, "As many as I love, I rebuke and chasten" (Rev. 3:19). He concluded that the testimonies of reproof constituted a message of rejection, and that those who would join in sounding the loud cry must withdraw from the Seventh-day Adventist Church. The church, he asserted, had become Babylon, and those who would finish God's work in the earth and meet their Lord in peace must separate from the body. His pamphlet of more than fifty pages was made up largely of misapplied E. G. White messages pieced together with the compiler's comments. It also contained a personal testimony from her that somehow had come into Stanton's hands. This he had employed in a less-than-honorable fashion.

As she wrote most earnestly to him, she touched on several points:

> Do not seek to misinterpret and twist and pervert the testimonies to substantiate any such message of error. Many have passed over this ground, and have done great harm. As others have started up full of zeal to proclaim this message, again and again I have been shown that it is not the truth. . . .
>
> God has a church upon the earth, who are His chosen people, who keep His commandments. He is leading, not stray offshoots, not one here and one there, but a people. The truth is a sanctifying power, but the church militant is not yet the church triumphant. . . .
>
> It is our individual duty to walk humbly with God. We are not to seek any strange, new message. We are not to think that the chosen ones of God who are trying to walk in the light compose Babylon. The fallen denominational churches are Babylon. Babylon has been fostering poisonous doctrines, the wine of error. This wine of error is made up of false doctrines, such as the natural immortality of the soul, the eternal torment of the wicked, the denial of the preexistence of Christ prior to His birth in Bethlehem, and advocating and exalting the first day of the week above God's holy, sanctified day.—*Ibid.*

In the weeks that followed, Ellen White wrote at length warnings to the church concerning this new "message." They appeared in a series of four articles published in the *Review and Herald*, from August 22 to September 12, under the title "The Remnant Church Not Babylon." The first opened with these words:

> I have been made very sad in reading the pamphlet that has been issued by Brother Stanton and by those associated with him in the work he has been doing. Without my consent, they have made selections from the testimonies, and have inserted them in the pamphlet they have published, to make it appear that my writings sustain and approve the position they advocate.
>
> In doing this, they have done that which is not justice or righteousness. Through taking unwarrantable liberties, they have presented to the people a theory that is of a character to deceive and destroy. In times past, many others have done this same thing, and have made it appear that the testimonies sustained positions that were untenable and false. . . .
>
> In the pamphlet published by Brother Stanton and his associates, he accuses the church of God of being Babylon, and would urge a separation from the church. This is a work that is neither honorable nor *righteous*. In compiling this work, they have used my name and writings for the support of that which I disapprove and denounce as error. The people to whom this pamphlet will come will charge the responsibility of this false position upon me, when it is utterly contrary to the teaching of my writings, and the light which God has given me. I have no hesitancy in saying that those who are urging on this work are greatly deceived.—RH, Aug. 22, 1893 (see also TM, pp. 32-36).

It was in this connection that Ellen White made a statement that has brought assurance and comfort to many:

> Although there are evils existing in the church, and will be until the end of the world, the church in these last days is to be the light of the world that is polluted and demoralized by sin. The church, enfeebled and defective, needing to be reproved, warned, and counseled, is the only object upon earth upon which Christ bestows His supreme regard.—*Ibid.*, Sept. 5, 1893 (see also TM, p. 49).

THE NEW ZEALAND CAMP MEETING

Ellen White closed the series of articles by publishing in full her letter of March 22 to Mr. Stanton, quoted at the beginning of this section. As the clear-cut warnings and assurances reached Seventh-day Adventists through the *Review and Herald,* the threatening offshoot movement was checked and soon forgotten.

THE W. F. CALDWELL MISSION TO AUSTRALIA

Before receiving Ellen White's testimony written March 22, Mr. Stanton commissioned one of his newly acquired disciples, W. F. Caldwell of Pennsylvania, to hasten to Australia to spread the message there and to gain Ellen White's support for the new movement. The two men of kindred minds, Stanton and Caldwell, had met in Battle Creek. They had spent three days together and had agreed on the urgency of Caldwell's Australian trip.

So eager and earnest was Caldwell, an Adventist of somewhat fluctuating experience, that when Stanton dispatched him to Australia he did not even return to his Pennsylvania home to bid his wife and two children goodbye. He never saw them again; his wife, not a Seventh-day Adventist, divorced him for deserting her, and refused to allow him to see the children.

In San Francisco another of Stanton's disciples gave Caldwell money and a steamship ticket, and he hastened on his way. Reaching Hobart, Tasmania, he was informed by George Starr that Ellen White was in New Zealand; he was further told that she had written a testimony to Stanton pointing out that he was "off the track." Caldwell was eager, of course, to see a copy of the testimony. Upon learning that a copy could be found at Melbourne with Sister White's papers, he was soon there and read the message.

The testimony unsettled him, but he was not convinced. Frustrated by the fact that Ellen White was in New Zealand and that he was without funds to travel there to see her, and feeling that she misunderstood the Stanton message on the loud cry, he wrote a letter to her and settled down to wait for a reply. "Then came the real struggle." He recounted his experience in the following words:

> None but God knows how hard Satan and his emissaries worked for me during those few days of idleness; but Christ is able to save all who trust Him.

THE AUSTRALIAN YEARS

One Sunday I strolled down to the park where the Socialists were holding an open-air meeting. After listening to a part of three speeches, I turned away in disgust. You know how they talk, "Down with the government, down with the judges, away with these oppressive laws," et cetera, always trying to tear down, but never having any idea of a better way, or in fact, of any substitute.

The Spirit of the Lord was by my side, and showed me that I was doing the same kind of work. I could not silence that voice. The similarity of their work and mine opened before me more clearly every time I tried to excuse myself, until finally I gave in and confessed, like David, "I am the man." I went to my lodgings, and after much prayer, decided to give up the message, although still more than half believing that it was true, in part at least.—DF 463a, "A Confession," W. F. Caldwell to "Dear Brethren and Sisters," July 7, 1893 (RH, Sept. 19, 1893).

Caldwell had about made up his mind to give up his mission and return to the United States—he had sufficient money for a passage by steerage—when he received a response from Ellen White in New Zealand. It was tender, understanding, motherly:

Dear Brother Caldwell:

Your letter addressed to me was received at the beginning of the Sabbath. . . . I should advise you to attend the school, and not to leave this country until you become thoroughly settled in your mind as to what is truth. I sincerely hope that you will attend this term of school and learn all you can in regard to this message of truth that is to go to the world.

The Lord has not given you a message to call the Seventh-day Adventists Babylon, and to call the people of God to come out of her. All the reasons you may present cannot have weight with me on this subject, because the Lord has given me decided light that is opposed to such a message.

I do not doubt your sincerity or honesty. . . . You think individuals have prejudiced my mind. If I am in this state, I am not fitted to be entrusted with the work of God.—Letter 16, 1893 (2SM, p. 63).

In a kindly way she reviewed a number of experiences,

THE NEW ZEALAND CAMP MEETING

somewhat similar to Caldwell's, in which individuals felt they had some special message for the Seventh-day Adventist Church. (These may be read in *Selected Messages*, book 2, pages 64 to 66.) In this letter a most enlightening statement is made, identifying the "Laodiceans" whom Christ will spew out of His mouth:

> God is leading out a people. He has a chosen people, a church on the earth, whom He has made the depositaries of His law. He has committed to them sacred trust and eternal truth to be given to the world. He would reprove and correct them.
>
> The message to the Laodiceans is applicable to Seventh-day Adventists who have had great light and have not walked in the light. It is those who have made great profession, but have not kept in step with their Leader, that will be spewed out of His mouth unless they repent. The message to pronounce the Seventh-day Adventist Church Babylon, and call the people of God out of her, does not come from any heavenly messenger, or any human agent inspired by the Spirit of God.—2SM, p. 66.

Caldwell accepted Ellen White's advice, abandoned the so-called new light, attended the Australasian Bible School in Melbourne, and then engaged in the literature work. A little later Ellen White employed him to assist with the work about her residence; he even copied on the typewriter some of her manuscripts. Some years later he returned to the United States and worked in the Pacific Northwest in the literature ministry. Thus the messenger of the Lord, while filling her assignments in somewhat pioneering work in local fields overseas, was ever ministering to the church throughout the world.

GOOD NEWS FROM AMERICA

Mail, both going and coming, was an important part of the program of Ellen White and those who were with her in New Zealand.

Sunday, April 23, she arose early—at half past three—to prepare the mail bound for Melbourne, expecting it to leave on Monday.

That same Sunday, in came a large stack of letters. There was a long letter from O. A. Olsen, president of the General Conference, giving a full summary of the General Conference session and

THE AUSTRALIAN YEARS

reporting on the confession of a number of prominent men who had taken a wrong position at the 1888 General Conference session.

Another letter was from Leroy Nicola, a prominent pastor in Iowa. It was the Nicola letter that brought her special rejoicing. It was a confession, "a most thorough confession of the part he acted in Minneapolis." Of this Ellen White wrote: "It is thorough, and I praise the Lord for the victory he has gained over the enemy who has held him four years from coming into the light. Oh, how hard it is to cure rebellion! How strong the deceiving power of Satan!"—MS 80, 1893.

Ellen White could scarcely sleep that night. She writes:

> The good news from America kept me awake. Oh, how my heart rejoices in the fact that the Lord is working in behalf of His people—in the information in the long letter from Elder Olsen, that the Lord by His Holy Spirit was working upon the hearts of those who have been in a large measure convinced of their true condition before God, yet have not humbled their hearts before to confess!
>
> The Spirit of the Lord moved them to the point at this conference. Elder Morrison, who has been so long president of the Iowa Conference, made a full confession. Madison Miller, who has been under the same deceiving power of the enemy, made his confession, and thus the Lord is indeed showing Himself merciful and of tender compassion to His children who have not received the light He has given them, but have been walking and working in darkness.—*Ibid.*

As she wrote the next day of Leroy Nicola's experience to Harmon Lindsay, treasurer of the General Conference, she said, "I knew if he walked in the light that this must come. . . . My heart is rejoiced that he has yielded to the influence of the Holy Spirit. It has taken four years of striving of the Spirit of God to bring him to this."—Letter 79, 1893.

THE VAN HORN CONFESSION

But Nicola was not alone in resisting light in 1888. Another was Isaac Van Horn, who labored in Battle Creek and to whom on January 20 Ellen had written a testimony filling eleven pages: "I

THE NEW ZEALAND CAMP MEETING

want to say a few words to you," she wrote, "to tell you some things which burden my heart. You are represented to me as not walking and working in the light as you think you are doing." She continued:

> Again and again has the Lord presented before me the Minneapolis meeting. The developments there are but dimly seen by some, and the same fog which enveloped their minds on that occasion has not been dispelled by the bright beams of the Sun of Righteousness. Notwithstanding the evidences of the power of God which attended the truth which was shining forth at that meeting, there were those who did not comprehend it.
>
> In the blessings that have since accompanied the presentation of the truth, justification by faith and the imputed righteousness of Christ, they have not discerned increased evidence from God as to where and how He is and has been working.—Letter 61, 1893.

She pleaded with Van Horn: "Why did you not receive the testimony the Lord sent you through Sister White? Why have you not harmonized with the light God has given you? . . . Elder Van Horn, you need the quickening influence of the Spirit of God. . . . I plead with you, dear brother, take off thy shoes from off thy feet, and walk softly before God."

The earnest testimony was used of God to save the man. In a four-page handwritten letter he reviewed his experience in receiving and accepting the testimony. He said:

> This communication by your hand to me I heartily accept as a testimony from the Lord. It reveals to me the sad condition I have been in since the Minneapolis meeting, and this reproof from the Lord is just and true. Since it came, I see more than ever before the great sin it is to reject light. And this is made doubly sinful by my own stubborn will holding out so long against the light that has shone so brightly upon me.

He then related how, a few days before receiving the testimony, he began to see his true condition and on a Sabbath morning at the General Conference confessed his great wrong at Minneapolis and since then. He felt this experience was but paving the way for the testimony he was about to receive. Three days later, and still during the General Conference session, the testimony came. He told Ellen White what took place on receiving it:

> Late in the evening I went to my room where all alone I read it three times over with much weeping, accepting it sentence by sentence as I read. I bowed before the Lord in prayer and confessed it all to Him. He heard my earnest plea, and for bitterness of soul He gave me peace and joy. . . .
>
> I could but thank Him for sending me this message, for it is a token of His love. "For whom the Lord loveth he chasteneth, and scourgeth every son whom he receiveth."

The next morning he went into the ministers' meeting and made a most earnest and extended confession of his wrong before the men who knew of his course. It brought light and blessing to his soul. He could exclaim, "I am now a free man again, thank the Lord, having found pardon and peace."

Before closing his letter to Mrs. White, he wrote:

> I shall need counsel and instruction. If you have anything further that would give me more light, showing me more clearly my true condition, I shall be very glad to receive it.—I. D. Van Horn to EGW, March 9, 1893.

In her five-page reply Ellen White declared:

> I do accept your letter fully, and am very, very thankful your eyes have been anointed with the heavenly eyesalve, that you may see clearly and give to the flock of God meat in due season, which they do much need.—Letter 60, 1893.

When the testimonies were wholeheartedly received and accepted, joy came to Ellen White's heart. In addition to Isaac Van Horn and Leroy Nicola, word from O. A. Olsen told of others who were moved to confess at the 1893 General Conference session (MS 80, 1893). A week later George I. Butler, residing in Florida, made a public confession through the *Review and Herald* (June 13, 1893) of wrong attitudes on his part and of his coming into line with his brethren. This left but very few holdouts among men of particular significance in the cause.

CHAPTER 9
(1893)

The Winter in New Zealand

WITH the Napier camp meeting over, Ellen White and her party moved on to Wellington, at the southern tip of North Island, New Zealand. Wellington was the headquarters of the New Zealand Conference—if a book depository and the president's residence together could be called a headquarters. M. C. Israel served as president. The trip by train would take them through Palmerston North, and it seemed convenient to stop over there for a long weekend.

Ellen White, accompanied by W. C. White and Emily Campbell, left Napier Thursday morning, April 13. George and Mrs. Starr were to follow the next day. Of the five-hour train trip she wrote:

> I rode with Emily and Willie in the second-class cars for the first time since my severe illness. We could make me a comfortable seat with cushions, and I think I did not suffer any more in the second class than I should in the first, and we would have to pay one pound, one shilling extra for us three if we rode in first class. We left Napier at half past eleven o'clock and arrived at Palmerston at half past four.—MS 79, 1893.

For the first two or three hours of the trip they traversed rich farming country dotted with villages. Nearer Palmerston North the land was level with much heavy timber here and there and large fertile pastures. It reminded Ellen White of the newer portions of Michigan, Canada, and New York State in the 1850s. Evangelistic meetings had been held at Palmerston four years earlier, but the town had doubled in population, and further work was due. She

THE AUSTRALIAN YEARS

and Emily were invited to stay with a couple named McOlivors, local church members. Sabbath morning Elder Starr spoke in the little hired hall and Ellen White in the afternoon. She reports in her diary that "I . . . led out with words of comfort and encouragement for the little few who had met together to worship God."

Noting that a large part of the audience were children and youth, she adapted her remarks accordingly. Of this she says:

> I addressed words to them, to instruct and help them in doing right, in loving the Lord Jesus in the early years of their life. "Those that seek me early shall find me." Proverbs 8:17. I think the lambs of the flock are left or passed over with but little effort to have them understand they may give their hearts and lives to Jesus in their childhood and youth. The simplicity of the lessons of Christ could be understood by children.—*Ibid*.

Sunday, services were held in the Theater Royal. She reports that there was a good congregation who listened attentively as she presented before them the love of Christ, speaking from 1 John 3:1-4.

Monday morning, she was up at three to get ready to catch the six-thirty train to Wellington. She was accompanied by W. C. White, Emily Campbell, and M. C. Israel. They traveled through what seemed to be newly developed country, wooded land and burned-over land, and, as they neared Wellington, sections abounding in tree ferns. At Wellington they were driven to what was to be their home for the winter months. It was now mid-June, and the weather was turning cold.

As she looked back since leaving Australia, she wrote:

> It is now three months since we left Melbourne. We have traveled about twenty-five hundred miles by sea and by land, and I have written over three hundred pages of letter paper. I have spoken to the people forty-one times, and am gaining in health and strength, for which I render thanksgiving and praise to God every day, and in the night season.—RH, June 13, 1893.

She had occasion to rejoice, for while she had suffered so painfully through most of 1892 she could now travel, speak, and write. Yet she confided, "Infirmities are still my companions by night and day." She was thankful that the Lord gave her grace to bear the pain. She explained:

> Sometimes when I feel unable to fill my appointments, I say, In faith I will place myself in position. I will go to the meeting, and stand upon my feet, although feeling unable to say a word; and whenever I have done this, I have had strength given me to rise above all infirmities, and to bear the message the Lord has given me for the people.—*Ibid.*

HER WELLINGTON HOME

Her temporary home in New Zealand was the mission building secured for use primarily as a book depository. Mrs. M. H. Tuxford carried the responsibility of management, which was no small task considering that it served all of New Zealand. Ellen White described her as "a businesswoman and capable, pleasant, and active" (MS 80, 1893). One room of the building was devoted to the book depository, Mrs. Tuxford resided in another, and three rooms were made available to Ellen White and Emily Campbell.

It was planned that she would reside there for a month or six weeks, but it turned out to be the four months of the winter.

It was Tuesday, April 18, when they moved in, and she closed her diary entry for that day with the words: "Now comes the taxing part of our work—preparing not only the American mail, which closes Thursday, but mail for Melbourne, which leaves every week."—*Ibid.*

As there was no church in Wellington, the whole worker group would drive six miles to Petone for Sabbath services. Ellen White tells of how it worked out:

> Last night the stars shone like diamonds in the heavens, but this morning is cloudy and rainy. Elder Israel, W. C. White, and Sister Brown go to Petone about nine o'clock. Sister Tuxford, Sister Israel, and I go this afternoon, as soon as we shall take an early dinner. But rain, rain, rain is the order of the day. . . . Brother Simpson, who bears the responsibilities of the meetings when he is at home, said to Willie, "I do not think your mother will come." Willie said, "We will see. It would be an exceptional occurrence for my mother to fail to meet her appointments." . . .

THE AUSTRALIAN YEARS

When we drove up to the place of meeting, there were about one dozen in all assembled, but when that carriage drove through the village and it was known I had come, the house was well filled, and . . . best of all, we had the heavenly Guest. The Lord gave me words to speak to the people. John 14. I was surprised myself at the words given me.—*Ibid.*

The reason for her surprise was that she had intended to speak on a different topic, but when she stood to speak, that subject was taken from her mind and another pressed itself forcibly upon her.

DIFFICULTIES IN ADVANCING THE MESSAGE IN NEW ZEALAND

The workers in Wellington, both those long in the field and the newcomers, took a good look at the state of the cause and the prospects for the future. In Wellington there was no tangible work. D. M. Canright's books—as well as the activities of some of the church members, which were less than honorable but were quite widely known—had closed the eyes and ears of those who should hear and respond. A consistent opposition of Protestant ministers also had a strong influence.

The Adventist leaders studied the map of New Zealand and could see that "only a little portion of it has yet heard the proclamation of the truth. The very best and more favorable fields have not yet been entered."—*Ibid.* They felt the dire need of experienced workers. Wrote Ellen White:

A deep, deep sleep seems to be upon the people. Pleasure-loving, something new to attract the mind, something startling, and a dish of fables from the pulpit are relished, but the truth that would arouse and disturb their self-complacency is the very thing they do not want. The people seem encased, as though nothing can penetrate the armor of self-deception and stolid indifference.

Our cry is to God for help, for strength and power. He alone can work upon the hearts of the people of Wellington. Elder Daniells has had good congregations, but no souls have been brought into the truth. Elder Israel has been here much of the time for four years, but nothing has been successful to create an interest. *The Great Controversy* and other books have been taken

THE WINTER IN NEW ZEALAND

in this city, yet no souls have been added as the result. What can be done? O Lord, lead and guide!—*Ibid.*

Determined to make a break, the workers decided to rent the skating rink, which would seat about a thousand, for evangelistic meetings. Even though the rent seemed high, they would go forward in the name of the Lord and do something. At three o'clock Sunday afternoon, April 30, Ellen White spoke there on temperance to a good audience. She reported deep interest on the part of the hearers. In the evening Starr addressed an audience of about the same size on the inspiration of the Scriptures. An interest was created, and meetings continued for some time in the skating rink on Sabbath and Sunday and some evenings.

WRITING ON THE LIFE OF CHRIST

Ever since crossing the Pacific nearly two years earlier, Ellen White had been watching for an opportunity to write on Christ's life. Now in the winter months in New Zealand, when travel would be somewhat curtailed, she determined to push the work forward as her strength and her program would allow. Letters she should have answered remained unanswered, in some cases, for months, as she tried to make room for work on her book. A diary entry for May 19 reads: "Before breakfast, wrote seven pages on the life of Christ." The next Tuesday she wrote in her diary: "It is cloudy and raining this morning. I have been writing upon the life of Christ since four o'clock." She added a prayer, "Oh, that the Holy Spirit may rest and abide upon me, that my pen may trace the words which will communicate to others the light which the Lord has been pleased in His great mercy and love to give me."—*Ibid.*

In mid-June W. C. White, writing for the *Bible Echo*, reported on his mother's activities:

> Mrs. E. G. White was enduring the damp and windy weather of Wellington very well, and having found at the Tract Society Depository a quiet and comfortable place to reside, is engaged in writing on some of the unfinished chapters of her forthcoming "Life of Christ." At the close of the camp meeting in Napier, she felt a great desire to attend another general meeting in New Zealand. The appointment of the next annual conference early in

THE AUSTRALIAN YEARS

the season may enable her, if she can endure the dampness of the climate, to remain and attend this meeting, before the next annual conference and first camp meeting in Australia.—July 1, 1893.

From time to time through the winter—June, July, and August—she mentions, in her letters and her diary, writing on the life of Christ.

Thursday, June 15, 1893: I do not flatter myself that very much progress can be made on the life of Christ. I am writing on it as fast as I possibly can. . . . The days are short and are gone before we really know it.—Letter 131, 1893.

Monday, June 19: I am trying to write on the life of Christ, but I am obliged to change my position quite often to relieve the spine and the right hip. Sister Tuxford and I had our season of worship alone—only two to claim the promise.—MS 81, 1893.

Thursday, June 29: This morning there was some frost. I have a fire in my room today. Have not had a fire before for several days. Am writing on life of Christ.

We have secured a wheelchair, that I can be wheeled in the open air when I cannot ride in carriage.—*Ibid.*

Friday, July 7: I wrote some today. Pain is making me very nervous, but I keep this to myself. . . . Letters are constantly coming for an answer, and should I write to the many that I desire, I should not find any time to write on the life of Christ.—*Ibid.*

AN AGONIZING LETTER TO EDSON

Letters from James Edson White brought little comfort to his mother. While she was in New Zealand, he was in Chicago in the printing business, and quite involved in debt, which was not unusual for him. In one letter he stated, "I am not at all religiously inclined." There had been times when, with a heart dedicated to God, he had served in the Lord's work—Sabbath school, hymn book preparation, publishing, et cetera. Now his letter, with these words, nearly crushed her. Her response opened:

Dear Son Edson: Why should you express yourself as you have done? Why use such firm language? Why do you have any satisfaction in this selfish independence? If you were a man unacquainted with truth, I could address you in a different way, approach you by presenting the truth in all its beauty and attractive loveliness, but this would not move you. The answer would be, "I knew all that before. I am not as ignorant as you suppose."

She wrote to him of the "qualities of character" that he might have displayed and of how different it would have been if he had "surrendered to God and brought Christ and His instructions into" his business. Then she laid her pen down until the next day. When she picked it up again to continue the message, she wrote:

June 21: I awoke quarter past one o'clock full of terror.

I had a scene presented before me. You and four other young men were upon the beach. You all seemed too careless—unconcerned, yet in great danger. Many had collected on the beach to observe your movements, and this seemed to make you more determined and venturesome.

The waves were rolling up nearer and still nearer and then would roll back with a sullen roar. Gestures and warnings were given by the anxious ones looking on, but in answer to all their warnings you were more presumptuous.

Someone placed his hand on my shoulder. "Did you know that is your son Edson? He cannot hear your voice, but he can see your motions. Tell him to come at once. He will not disobey his mother."

I reached out my hands. I did all I could do to warn. I cried with all the power of voice, "You have not a moment to lose! The undertow! The undertow!" I knew that once you were in the power of the treacherous undertow no human power could avail.

A strong rope was brought and fastened securely around the body of a strong young man who ventured to risk his own life to save you. You seemed to be making light of the whole performance. I saw the merciless undertow embrace you, and you were battling with the waves. I awoke as I heard a fearful shriek from you. I prayed most earnestly in your behalf and arose and am writing these lines.

THE AUSTRALIAN YEARS

The undertow! I have had opportunity to watch the movements of the waves as I have often visited Island Bay, four miles from Wellington. In Napier, I had a chance to see its more powerful movements.

Continuing the letter, she told of having a few weeks before read the experience of four young men, "experts in the water," who were caught in the undertow. "Only one was saved," she wrote, "and not by his own energies."

As she continued her letter, which filled ten double-spaced typewritten pages, she contemplated, "The undertow—what does it represent? It represents the power of Satan and a set, independent, stubborn will of your own which has reached even against God. You have not preserved a surrender to God."

Then in graphic terms she pictured changes that had come over a period of a few years:

> You are no more a child. I would that you were. I would cradle you in my arms, watch over you as I have done. But you are a man grown. You have taken the molding of your character out of the hands of your mother, out of the hands of God, and are placing defective, rotten timbers in the building. Evil influences are accepted; the good and saving influences refused.
>
> You would almost fail to recognize yourself should your present picture of character be presented by the side of the former one when you tried to walk in the fear of God. And you . . . coolly state you will not change your course—that is, as I understand it, come into submission to God—until your debts are paid and you have a reliable competency.
>
> Your religious history need not have been vacillating, but firm and true; but you would be independent and take your own course. You have been strong one hour, vacillating the next. I am now determined to press upon your notice and make you hear: "This is the undertow."

"Several times has the Lord heard and answered prayer in your behalf and raised you up when your case was apparently hopeless," she wrote, referring to some of his childhood experiences. "And now I see that invisible foe, lurking, alluring and deceiving your

THE WINTER IN NEW ZEALAND

soul to your ruin. I know your only hope is to cling to God and to your mother and brother." The tearful mother closed her letter with the words:

> I cannot save you; God alone can save you. But work, while Jesus invites you, in harmony with God. Mother.—Letter 123, 1893.

The letter, written in such anguish, was attended by the winning and softening influence of the Spirit of God; Edson, yielding his hard heart, experienced a reconversion. His immediate response and his experience of the next two or three weeks are not recorded in the files, but on August 10, 1893, he wrote to his mother:

> I have surrendered fully and completely, and never enjoyed life before as I am [enjoying it] now. I have for years been under a strain, with so much to accomplish, and it has stood right in my way. Now, I have left it all with my Saviour, and the burden does not bear me down any longer. I have no desire for the amusements and pleasures that made up the sum of my enjoyments before, but have an enjoyment in the meetings with the people of God such as I never had before.

As to his future, he declared he wanted to connect with the work of the church in some way. Later in the month he wrote his mother: "I have been thinking of going down into Tennessee to work among the colored people. . . . I shall go into the work somewhere in the spring. . . . I still hope and trust in God, and am sure He will care for me. I have proved my own way and it is a poor way. I now want God's way, and I know it will be a good way."

His mother's call and beckoning, heard and seen above the roar of the tumbling ocean waves, had been heeded. The answer—which could not come then to Ellen White in the vivid representation in the hours of the night, for only Edson could determine the response—came shortly in joyous reality. Through the next decade Ellen White thrilled to Edson's vivid reports of God's blessings as he pioneered the work among the blacks in the great Southland of the United States.

DENTAL PROBLEMS

Ellen White's teeth were causing her a good deal of trouble.

THE AUSTRALIAN YEARS

Some were abscessing, and she concluded it was time to get rid of them. She had only eight left, and she wrote to Dr. Caro, the dentist in whose home she had stayed in Napier, inquiring whether she could not come down to Wellington and have them pulled out. They settled on the date, Wednesday, July 5.

That Wednesday morning after breakfast she wrote to her son William, "Sister Caro is here; leaves at half past one o'clock. You will know what will take place. I am not afraid. My teeth are troubling me a little too much for comfort."—Letter 132, 1893.

At the end of the day she told the story in her diary:

> Sister Caro came in the night; is in the house. I met her in the morning at the breakfast table. She said, "Are you sorry to see me?" I answered, "I am pleased to meet Sister Caro, certainly. Not so certain whether I am pleased to meet Mrs. Dr. Caro, dentist."
>
> At ten o'clock I was in the chair, and in a short time eight teeth were drawn. I was glad the job was over. I did not wince or groan. . . . I had asked the Lord to strengthen me and give me grace to endure the painful process, and I know the Lord heard my prayer.
>
> After the teeth were extracted, Sister Caro shook like an aspen leaf. Her hands were shaking, and she was suffering pain of body. She had felt sick, she said, on the cars during her ten hours' ride. She dreaded to give pain to Sister White. . . . But she knew she must perform the operation, and went through with it.—MS 81, 1893.

Ellen White took nothing to deaden the pain, for she suffered adverse aftereffects of such medication.

Then the patient turned attendant. She led Dr. Caro to a comfortable chair, and found something to refresh her. As Ellen White looked ahead, she could see that she would have to give up public work for a while, perhaps for two months, when Dr. Caro would fit her for a new set of teeth. She pushed ahead with her writing.

CHAPTER 10
(1893)

Evangelism—
The Struggle for
a Foothold

OF WELLINGTON, and of New Zealand in general, Ellen White cried out almost in despair: "God has a people in this place, and how can we reach them?"—Letter 9a, 1893. Writing to the churches in America, she said:

> The city abounds in churches; and I have never seen a place where prejudice was stronger or opposition so perseveringly and determinedly carried on. I was reminded of the prejudice of the priests and Pharisees in the days of Christ.
>
> At Wellington a branch of the International Tract and Missionary Society had been established, but there was no house of worship. We were dependent upon halls, and the people did not attend meetings in these halls. . . . We tried to hold meetings in Elder Israel's house. We did everything possible to get the people out. We circulated notices, leaflets, tracts. Workers went from house to house, sowing the seed upon ground that had hitherto proved unfruitful.
>
> To the utmost of our ability we labored to create an interest in this place, and at no small outlay of means; and yet the prejudice seemed like a granite wall. A few times we had a moderately large congregation, but the people seemed afraid of us. We worked on, however, trying to do our part as faithful messengers, for we had a message to bear of the utmost importance. Though our efforts showed no manifest results, I remembered that of Christ it was said, "He shall not fail nor be discouraged." We need the mind of Christ to enable us to work in His lines.—DF 28a, "Experiences in Australia," pp. 424, 425.

THE AUSTRALIAN YEARS

She explained how the ministers had told their congregations that there was danger in going to hear the Adventists. " 'These people,' they said, 'have no special interest in Wellington. Few will believe in their doctrines. They have no one to represent them here. If they make you believe in their doctrines, where will you go to worship? They have no place of worship. They are only adventurers.' "—*Ibid.*, pp. 425, 426. They characterized the teachings of Seventh-day Adventists as "satanic doctrines" that would mislead the people.

A FEW DAYS AT LONG POINT

On July 26, Ellen White felt that she needed a break in her work. "Our stay here is too monotonous," she exclaimed. "One cannot keep upon one strain continuously without breaking down. It has been one steady strain early and late, but there must come a halt."—MS 81, 1893.

At half past six in the morning Ellen White was writing, and the rain was coming down in torrents. The wind, which had been blowing all night, was shaking the house, and even shook the bed. As the clouds broke away in midmorning, she thought of the invitation she had just received from Martha Brown, who, when Ellen White had first come to Wellington, had helped with the cooking. Martha Brown was inviting her to bring Emily Campbell, who was badly worn, and come to Long Point for a few days' rest and change. "We cannot well leave this week, but we will be off next week, if the Lord wills," Mrs. White noted, and repeated, "We need some change."—*Ibid.*

It was not the next week but the next day that they were off for the little change. M. C. Israel accompanied them on the train to Paremata and Long Point, an hour and a half from Wellington. Describing the trip, she wrote:

> We passed through eight tunnels. The scenery was odd and romantic. Much of the road on this line is through a gorge, very deep in many places. Then we would see nice little farms in the valleys, and then again steep mountains and waterfalls.—MS 59, 1893.

At the station Martha Brown, a young woman in her late 20s,

EVANGELISM—THE STRUGGLE FOR A FOOTHOLD

was awaiting them with a horse and gig to take them the mile to the Brown home. Situated on a rise of ground with a good view of the bay, and surrounded by flowers, shrubs, and trees and encircled by hills and high mountains, the large house was most inviting. Ellen White and those with her were given a hearty welcome and felt quite at home. Martha's mother, a congenial woman, had been a widow for eight years and was the mother of thirteen living children. She had had a rather hard life, and of course a busy one. In addition to the children at home, three unmarried children lived on a farm rented to them by their mother at quite a distance from Long Point.

Martha was the first member of the Brown family to become a Seventh-day Adventist, followed by her mother. At this point they stood alone in that faith. Ellen White found herself in the midst of a needy mission field. She determined to let her light shine. "I labored with the family," she wrote, "every morning and night."—Letter 138, 1893.

"Monday morning [August 7], at 1:00 A.M.," she recorded in her diary, "I was awakened repeating these words, 'While it is called To day . . . To day if ye will hear his voice, harden not your hearts, as in the provocation.' Hebrews 3:13-15."

> In the night season I had been in different companies bearing a message to them. I was in the family of Sister Brown, and was instructed by the angel of God to call them to a decision by speaking to each one of the children by name.

Isabella was 22 years old and had a strong influence with the younger members of the family. She was very worldly, with a love for parties and dancing. At family worship that Monday morning Ellen White addressed her:

> "Will you give your heart to Jesus? Will you cut the cords binding you to the world, its pleasures and attractions, and leave the service of Satan and be a follower of Christ?"
> She said, "I will."
> Next was Alex, the only boy at home, and who was obliged to bear heavy responsibilities for a boy of 16. He was of quick understanding. I addressed myself to Alex. I said, "Will you decide this morning to confess Jesus Christ? . . . Will you this

very morning choose to be a child of God and engage to serve the Lord Jesus to the best of your ability?"

He responded, "I will."

Victoria was quite grown up for a girl of 14 years. Turning to her, Ellen White addressed her by name:

> "Jesus says to you this morning, 'Victoria, follow Me.' Will you obey His voice? Will you enter the school of Christ to learn of Him?"

She responded decidedly, "I will."

Then it was Charlotte to whom Ellen White spoke:

> "I am sure you wish to be a child of God. You wish to learn of Jesus. You love the Lord Jesus. Will you confess that you love Him?"

She responded.

"And now my heart was broken before the Lord, melted with His love," wrote Ellen White, "and we had a thanksgiving morning service. It was a precious season to us all."—MS 59, 1893.

But that was not the full extent of the fruitful missionary endeavors. On Thursday night, August 3, a vivid scene had been presented to her, and at four o'clock in the morning she arose and began to write:

> The angel of God said, "Follow me." I seemed to be in a room in a rude building, and there were several young men playing cards. They seemed to be very intent upon the amusement in which they were engaged and were so engrossed that they did not seem to notice that anyone had entered the room. There were young girls present observing the players, and words were spoken not of the most refined order. There was a spirit and influence that were sensibly felt in that room that was not of a character calculated to purify and uplift the mind and ennoble the character. . . .
>
> I inquired, "Who are these and what does this scene represent?"
>
> The word was spoken, "Wait."
>
> I had another representation. There was the imbibing of the

liquid poison, and the words and actions under its influence were anything but favorable for serious thoughts, clear perception in business lines, pure morals, and the uplifting of the participants. . . .

I asked again, "Who are these?"

The answer came, "A portion of the family where you are visiting. The great adversary of souls, the great enemy of God and man, the head of principalities and powers, and the ruler of darkness of this world, is presiding here tonight. Satan and his angels are leading on with his temptations these poor souls to their own ruin."—Letter 1, 1893.

The communication addressed to the mother and the children and sent to them after Ellen White returned home was blessed by God in leading these young men to the Lord. Among the eventual grandchildren were two who served the church as ministers and editors, and others as teachers and in other capacities.

The visit to the home was to be for a week, but when Thursday came it rained so hard that they could not leave. Friday morning they went in the rain to the railway station and waited an hour for the train, only to learn that a landslide had occurred and there would be no train. Of the experience Ellen White wrote:

We decided our work was not done and felt reconciled to the delay. We spent Sabbath with the family, and I labored hard to present before them the important crisis that is just before us, when there will be two distinct parties—the one elevating the standard of truth, the other trampling under foot the law of God and lifting up and exalting the spurious Sabbath. . . . It is God's great plan that the Sunday question shall be agitated and the Sabbath of the fourth commandment be exalted as the Lord's memorial sign of the creation of the world, and that a knowledge of truth upon the Sabbath question shall be brought before many minds as a witness.—MS 59, 1893.

The service in the Brown home that Sabbath morning commenced at 11:00 A.M., and did not close until 2:00 P.M. Monday, August 7, promised to be a good day, and Ellen White and Emily decided that they must return to Wellington. They felt they could reach the station between showers, and started out.

THE AUSTRALIAN YEARS

"We did," wrote Ellen White, "almost." Bedding and trunks got wet, but the train was on time. The second-class car was full, and men were lighting their pipes. The three ladies (Martha Brown was with them) felt they must find some other provision. They were allowed to ride in the freight car, a more compact car than those in America. With her spring seat on a freight box and the bedding roll at her feet, Ellen White was quite comfortable. There was a box of dogs nearby, some rather smelly fish, and plenty of boxes of freight. At subsequent stops, they were joined by other passengers, until there were seven women sitting on boxes of freight, and about as many men were standing. "We were thankful to get home anyway," she wrote, "after making this third trial."—*Ibid.*

AT HASTINGS AND NAPIER

Doors seemed closed in Wellington. Ellen White was still waiting for her much-needed dental plates, but was feeling quite well and had found she could talk so as to be understood, even without teeth. She, M. C. Israel, and Mr. Mountain studied plans for the immediate future. They thought it would be well to join G. T. Wilson, now the conference president, and his wife, who were working in Napier and Hastings. There, several people were just in the balance of decision, for or against the message of the church.

Tuesday morning, August 15, they were off early for Hastings, a ten-hour trip by train—Ellen White, Emily Campbell, and Nina Piper, whom they took with them to assist in the home duties. They were to be in Hastings for several weeks, and they wanted to avoid being a burden wherever they might stay.

On the train were many Maoris, natives of New Zealand, a people among whom Mrs. Caro was beginning to do missionary work with some favorable response. At one station Ellen White and her traveling companions had a unique experience: "We saw for the first time the ceremony of salutation—the rubbing of noses." She commented, "It was a novel sight."—MS 84, 1893. At Hastings they were taken to the Wilson home, where they were to stay. It was a large home, and the visitors were easily accommodated.

Wednesday evening twenty-five people gathered in the home. Ellen White spoke with great freedom. Three in the audience were not members of the church. One of them was a woman who, by

EVANGELISM—THE STRUGGLE FOR A FOOTHOLD

reading *Daniel and the Revelation* and *The Great Controversy* sent to her by her son in Wellington, was deeply interested. Following Ellen White's remarks, there was a social meeting in which the people bore their testimony to God's providences. "These social meetings," she commented, "do more than preaching to ripen off the work."

It was here that Ellen White wrote in her diary:

Wednesday, August 16, 1893: I see so much to be thankful for in my case. The Lord is my Restorer. I am able to kneel down now.

I feared I might not ever be able to bow upon my knees in prayer. For more than one year I was unable to bend the knees to kneel down, but I am gaining all the time in health, for which I praise the Lord who is so good to me. His mercies are seen every day.—*Ibid.*

W. C. White, after three months in Australia, was now back in New Zealand, and joined others in a special interest in the Maoris, who rather thickly populated this area. One 16-year-old Maori lad, who attended a nearby school and who had begun to keep the Sabbath, came to talk with the workers in Napier about attending the Australasian Bible School in Melbourne. Some others would soon be going to Battle Creek College. Mrs. Caro gave freely to aid them, and Ellen White promised support for one Maori student at the Melbourne school. For nearly two months she divided her time between Hastings, Napier, and Ormondville.

Here and there baptisms were reported, and things were beginning to look up. It was thought, as the brethren counseled together, that the time had come when Mrs. White could return to Australia, by way of Auckland. But just then a telegram came informing them that the missionary brigantine *Pitcairn** would be in Auckland in a few days. There was trouble on board, and it seemed essential that W. C. White should spend a little time with the crew. Another telegram informed them that O. A. Olsen, president of the General Conference, would be arriving from Africa in time to attend the camp meeting that was scheduled to open in Wellington November 23 (DF 28a, "Experiences in Australia," pp. 499, 500).

---

* A hundred-foot sailing vessel built in 1890 for use as a missionary ship in the South Pacific, paid for by Sabbath school offerings.

THE AUSTRALIAN YEARS

Plans for an early return to Australia were dropped, and their minds turned to preparing for the meeting.

A NEW APPROACH IN GISBORNE

There would be several weeks before camp meeting would open, and it was now planned that Ellen White and Emily Campbell would accompany G. T. Wilson and his wife to Gisborne for an evangelistic thrust. For years a little company had been worshiping in Gisborne, but the work very much needed a boost. Prejudice against Seventh-day Adventists was strong there. The question was "How to approach the people?"

So far, except in a few places, almost every conventional means of reaching the people in New Zealand in a favorable way had failed. As the little worker group counseled together, they decided to try a new approach to arrest the attention of the public. Ellen White described what took place in letters to her son W. C. White, and to her niece Addie Walling:

> We thought we would strike out on a new line. We would have Sunday-afternoon services in an open-air meeting. We did not know how it would come out. . . . Brother Wilson and Brother Alfred Wade secured the paddock just back of the post office. There was one large willow tree. Under this a platform was made and the organ and stand placed on the platform. Lumber for seats was right in the yard, costing nothing for their use.—Letter 140, 1893.

> There were seats without backs in abundance, and a dozen taken from the church with backs. . . . The weather was favorable, and we had an excellent congregation. The mayor and some of the first people in Gisborne were in attendance.

> I spoke upon temperance, and this is a living question here at this time. Hundreds were out to hear, and there was perfect order. . . . Mothers and any number of children were present. You would have supposed that the children had had an opiate, for there was not a whimper from them. My voice reached all over the enclosure (paddock is the name they give it here).

> Some of the hearers were very enthusiastic over the matter. The mayor, the policeman, and several others said it was by far

EVANGELISM—THE STRUGGLE FOR A FOOTHOLD

the best gospel-temperance discourse that they had ever heard. We pronounced it a success and decided that we would have a similar meeting the next Sunday afternoon.—Letter 68, 1893.

They did hold just such a meeting the next Sunday afternoon. It, too, was a decided success. Ellen White commented: "One thing we have learned, and that is that we can gather the people in the open air, and there are no sleepy ones. Our meetings were conducted just as orderly as if in a meetinghouse."—*Ibid.* A church member declared, "It is altogether the best advertisement of our people they have ever had in Gisborne."—Letter 140, 1893.

Prejudice was broken down, and from that time on, the meetings in the church and the Theater Royal were well attended. At last they had witnessed a breakthrough.

It was while in Gisborne that Ellen White received a letter from Edson telling of his reconversion after reading her agonizing admonition to beware of the undertow.

Immediately she acknowledged the good news:

October 21: Edson, the Lord Jesus is of tender, pitying loving-kindness. This day we received your letter and were very glad that you had indeed made the surrender to God. I am glad more than I can express that you have, in the simplicity of faith, accepted Jesus, and I am not surprised that you found something to do at once. . . .

Never fail or be discouraged. It is that which you ought to have done long ago, and your mother will give you encouragement and her prayers and so will your brother. Years that have passed into eternity are beyond your power to recall, but through the grace of Christ you may labor in the vineyard for the Master.—Letter 120, 1893.

COUNTDOWN TO CAMP MEETING

As the fall camp meeting in Napier had come to a close in early April, the believers had been promised that the next such meeting would be conducted at Auckland in the spring. But now as the time neared it seemed very important to hold it in Wellington instead, to make, if possible, a breakthrough in that most difficult place. W. C. White was dispatched to Auckland to explain matters to the

THE AUSTRALIAN YEARS

believers there and get their wholehearted support for the Wellington meeting.

Just before leaving Gisborne, Ellen White addressed a letter to "Dear Brethren and Sisters in New Zealand," urging a strong attendance. It opened:

> I have an appeal to make to our churches to attend the coming camp meeting in Wellington. You cannot afford to lose this opportunity. We know that this meeting will be an important era in the history of the work in New Zealand. There should be particular efforts made to get a representation of those who believe the truth to this meeting, for the very reason we are so few in numbers, and the additional help of everyone is called for. The enemies of truth are many in number. On such an occasion as this we want to present as good a front as possible. Let not your business detain you. You individually need the benefits of this meeting; and then God calls you to number one in the ranks of truth.—Letter 8a, 1893.

In the meantime she journeyed to Napier; W. C. White, who would travel on the *Pitcairn*, left Gisborne for Wellington. When a full week later no word had reached Wellington of the arrival of the *Pitcairn*, Ellen White, at the Caro home, was concerned. Then the long-awaited telegram came:

> *Pitcairn* arrived in Wellington Sabbath afternoon, November 11. Encountered calm and tempests. All well.—MS 87, 1893.

Ellen White was fitted with new teeth, and then traveled to Ormondville for the weekend and the dedication of the newly erected house of worship.

On Monday, November 20, they were on their way to Wellington, arriving there at ten o'clock at night. W. C. White was on hand to meet the train. They hastened to hired rooms.

THE WELLINGTON CAMP MEETING

New tents, both large and small, had been shipped from Australia and were now being pitched on high and dry ground in a beautiful fenced paddock within walking distance of the city of Wellington. It was with somewhat bated breaths that church

EVANGELISM—THE STRUGGLE FOR A FOOTHOLD

members and others watched the process. Wellington was well known for its fierce winds. Not long before this, a circus tent had been torn to shreds by the high wind. Church leaders knew well the risks. "Our earnest prayer," wrote Ellen White, "is that this encampment may have the favor of God. The winds and fountains of waters are in His hands, under His control."—MS 88, 1893.

God did hold His sheltering hand over the encampment. An early report to the *Bible Echo* indicated this:

> Every provision is made, and every care taken, to carry out the arrangements with facility and decorum. The tents are arranged in streets. The large tent has seating accommodation for about six hundred.—January 1, 1894.

O. A. Olsen arrived during the opening days of the meeting, and he became the main, and much appreciated, speaker. *Pitcairn* was in port, and her officers and crew were a help to the meeting. Dr. M. G. Kellogg, the medical missionary of the ship, was drawn into service and spoke from day to day on health topics and Christian temperance, which were reported to be one of the most telling and interesting features of the meetings *(ibid.)*.

From the very beginning Ellen White was often on the platform and almost every day addressed the congregation. Sabbath afternoon she spoke and again on the afternoon of Sunday, her sixty-sixth birthday. She felt great freedom as she took pleasure in "showing our colors on which were inscribed the commandments of God and the faith of Jesus." Reporting the response, she wrote:

> I told them that we were Seventh-day Adventists, and the reason of the name which distinguished us from other denominations. All listened with deepest interest.—Letter 75, 1893.

Sunday evening the tent was full when G. T. Wilson was the speaker. Ellen White's disclosure of the identity of the people holding the meetings did not deter a good attendance. In a letter to Edson she told of their concern for the success of the meeting:

> We had much fear lest we would have a very slim attendance, but we were happily disappointed. From the first to the last there was a good appearance of congregation of the best class of our

own people who fed on the bread of life during the meeting. Evenings there were good-sized congregations of outsiders. . . .

We have had good, large, respectful audiences, and a very large number of people now understand what we do believe. The discourses have been close, plain, and thorough upon present truth, appropriate and applicable to our time. The people listened as if spellbound. . . . The citizens were impressed with this meeting as nothing else could have transpired to impress them. When the winds blew strong, there would be many looking with wonder to see every tent standing unharmed.—Letter 121, 1893.

What a victory had at last been gained! Walls of prejudice were crumbling.

As the camp meeting opened, Ellen White observed that Mrs. Brown, of Long Point, only twenty miles distant, was not there. She hastened off a note to her:

Dear Sister Brown and Household:

We sincerely hope that you will not lose this opportunity of attending the meeting brought so near your own door. Come, Mother and children and Sister Lounge. We want to enjoy this holy convocation with you, and bring all the children you can spare from the home place, for this meeting is that which you all need to strengthen and confirm your faith, and you want to hear the message which God has for you. . . .

Be sure and bring the younger members of the family. You will never regret the expense or the trouble. It is seldom you will be favored, and perhaps never with such an opportunity. . . . You can and must come, Sister Brown. You need all the help and all the strength you can possibly gain to help you in your lifework.—Letter 74, 1893.

And she did come, with part of the family attending the earlier days of the camp meeting and the others coming later. How Ellen White rejoiced! She reported to Edson:

The mother and three youngest members of the family came—Alex, 16 years old, and the two girls, one 14 and the youngest 9. . . . These children remained with the mother, were

EVANGELISM—THE STRUGGLE FOR A FOOTHOLD

baptized, and returned to their home and sent the older members—four grown daughters from 17 years of age to 30.

These were all united with the Wellington church after their baptism. They have a church now at Long Point, Paremata, numbering nine of their own household.—Letter 121, 1893.

During the meeting Ellen White wrote in a letter:

> The camp meeting is a success. It is a marvel of wonders to Wellington. Meetings have been held for one week. This camp meeting will give character to our work and do much to counteract the falsehoods that ministers have framed for others to repeat. . . .
>
> The Lord is in the encampment. The Spirit of God is moving upon the hearts of believers and unbelievers. Visitors are pouring in to wonder over and admire the well-fitted-up tents which are to be the homes of those camping on the ground.—Letter 75, 1893.

Others agreed with Ellen White in the success of the meeting and of its far-reaching influence. This was reported in the January 8, 1894, *Bible Echo:*

> Indeed, the whole meeting was a spiritual feast. The people return to their homes rejoicing in the liberty they enjoy in Christ Jesus, and praising God for His goodness and mercy. . . . Twenty-four persons were baptized as a result of the services.

Dr. Kellogg and G. T. Wilson remained in Wellington for a time to follow up the camp meeting interest. In the meantime the tents were quickly dismantled and shipped to Australia for use in their first camp meeting, scheduled to open in a suburb of Melbourne on January 5.

RETURN TO AUSTRALIA

Within a week of the close of the camp meeting, Ellen White had closed up her work and was one of quite a large group, which included W. C. White and O. A. Olsen, on their way back to Australia.*

---

*Ellen White's visit to New Zealand was confined to the North Island. She never labored in Christchurch or other cities on the South Island.

THE AUSTRALIAN YEARS

They boarded the *Wairarapa* at Wellington on Wednesday, December 13, for the seven-day ocean journey. Friday morning they were at Auckland for a stay of a day and a half, which gave the traveling party opportunity to attend services in the Adventist church there on Friday evening and Sabbath morning. The trip was a rough one, with waves at times swamping the deck; none of the travelers fared well. Ellen White was given the privilege of sleeping in the ladies' lounge each night when it was vacated at ten.

The stewardess, Mrs. MacDonald, was very kind to Mrs. White, and the latter gave her *Steps to Christ* and some pamphlets and papers. As Ellen White had opportunity, she talked with her about her soul's salvation and pointed out the perils of any whose life was on the sea. Mrs. MacDonald's response was "If I could, I would be a Christian, but I cannot. It would be an impossibility to serve God on such a vessel as this."—MS 88, 1893. Then she opened up and told of the wickedness of the officers and the crew, and of how she wanted to seek other employment to support herself and four children, but had not done so because the job paid better than others and she needed all she could earn. There was an earnest conversation about the Christian life and prayer, but she held out that "it is no use to pray here, or try to be religious."

Later, one of the crew told Emily Campbell:

> "I have been much impressed that this boat will go down with all hands on board ere long. I have felt so strongly exercised that I shall not, if I can possibly disconnect from it, continue to remain on the boat."—*Ibid.*

A few weeks later the ship was lost in a storm, and the crew member who had predicted its fate was one of only two rescued. The stewardess-nurse was listed among those who did not survive.

Arriving in Sydney Wednesday morning at about nine o'clock, the traveling workers were taken to the International Tract and Mission House. All were hungry for both food and mail. Mail interested Ellen White the most. There was a letter from Edson, and she wrote in her diary for December 20, "It is like the prodigal son returned to his father's house. Edson and wife are obtaining a rich experience."—MS 89, 1893.

CHAPTER 11
(1894)

The Evangelistic Thrust in Australia

WITH the Wellington camp meeting fresh in their minds, the workers looked forward optimistically to plans for the first camp meeting in Australia. They entertained hopes that there would be a response similar to that witnessed in New Zealand. The meeting was scheduled to open in Melbourne on Friday, January 5, 1894, and there was just time to get the tents pitched for this innovation in gospel preaching.

But this was not the only matter on the minds of the workers as they arrived in Sydney. A. G. Daniells, president of the Australian Conference, met their ship Wednesday morning, December 20. He had done some preliminary work in searching for a rural site for the school. For a week after the worker group from New Zealand arrived, they also were busily engaged in searching for a school site. That Thursday, according to Ellen White's diary, they were off by train to visit the Fountaindale Estate, fifty miles in the country. After weekend meetings in Sydney, Kellyville, and Parramatta, in which O. A. Olsen and Ellen White participated, they were off again on Monday morning to visit another tract of land. Again on Tuesday, before taking the night train for Melbourne, they visited other sites. It would be desirable, of course, to have something to report at the coming conference session, which would be held in connection with the camp meeting.

PREPARATION FOR THE CAMP MEETING

For weeks in Melbourne there was feverish preparation for the convocation. At the *Bible Echo* office, not only printing presses were in operation, but sewing machines also. Family tents were being made in three sizes for the camp meeting. Prices and styles of what might be purchased in the city did not fit the plans of the camp meeting committee, so good material was secured, and by early November, thirty-five were ready for sale or for rent.

The committee on location found a ten-acre tract of land, grass-covered and partly shaded by eucalyptus trees (blue gum), in the suburb of Middle Brighton, nine miles from the Melbourne post office. It was south of the city, near the bay, and was served by an excellent railway line that had trains running every thirty minutes from morning till late at night.

The weekly issues of the *Bible Echo* reminded readers, both Seventh-day Adventists and others, of the coming meeting and the excellence of the location—"one of the nicest and most accessible places we have been able to find" (BE, Nov. 8, 1893)—and the plans for tenting on the grounds.

The *Bible Echo* for December 8 carried an Ellen White appeal for an outstanding attendance, as she pointed out the objectives of the meeting. It was to be a time of spiritual refreshing for the church and also an effective means of reaching the city with the third angel's message. "Come to the Feast" was the title of the three-column invitation, which opened with the words:

Dear Brethren and Sisters in Australia:

The first Australian camp meeting among us as a people is about to take place. This meeting will mark a new era in the history of the work of God in this field; it is important that every member of our churches should be present, and I urge you all to come. The enemies of truth are many, and though our numbers are few, we would present as good a front as possible. Individually you need the benefits of the meeting, and God calls upon you to number one of the ranks of truth.

Combining the two strong reasons for everyone to come, she wrote:

God has committed to our hands a most sacred work, and we need to meet together to receive instruction as to what is personal religion and family piety; we need to understand what part we shall individually be called upon to act in the grand and important work of building up the cause and work of God in the earth, in vindicating God's holy law, and in lifting up the Saviour as "the Lamb of God, which taketh away the sin of the world."

Notice was also given of some of the best help the denomination could supply in making the meetings a success. The president of the General Conference of Seventh-day Adventists would be present. Ellen White and W. C. White would be there; and Dr. M. G. Kellogg, ship physician for the *Pitcairn*, would be giving instruction along health lines. One notice especially delighted the believers of a few years:

> Our readers will be pleased to hear that Elder J. O. Corliss, who spent some time in Australia five or six years since, is now on his way back, accompanied by Elder W. A. Colcord. They expect to be with us at our camp meeting.—*Ibid.*, Dec. 1, 1893.

It was announced also that there would be a dining tent on the campgrounds, "furnished with tables, dishes, chairs, et cetera, and with proper waiters to serve the meals" *(ibid.,* Nov. 22, 1893).

A week-long workers' meeting would immediately precede the camp meeting, so the pitching of tents began on Tuesday, December 26. Initial plans called for fifty family tents, but these were taken so early that orders were given for twenty-five more.

Attendance was so large at the workers' meeting that Ellen White exclaimed in her letter to Edson and Emma White: "We are now on the ground, where to all appearances there is a veritable camp meeting."—Letter 86, 1894. And when on Tuesday, January 2, the large pavilion was pitched and she was asked to speak in it in the evening, she wrote that she "was surprised that so large a number of believers were on the ground."

CAMP MEETING OPENS WITH LARGE ATTENDANCE

The camp meeting opened on Friday, January 5, as scheduled. Through buying and renting, the number of family tents had more than doubled during the week of the workers' meeting. Even though they were in stringent economic times, every possible effort had been made to "make all things in the camp meeting after the divine order" (RH, Sept. 25, 1894), so as to leave the right impression upon the people.

THE AUSTRALIAN YEARS

The Sabbath meetings were a feast for the believers, and by then the grounds were being filled with people from the community whose interest had been aroused by the tent city and the distribution of reading matter.

As Ellen White wrote to her son and his wife in America, and also to Dr. Caro, the dentist in New Zealand, she was filled with ecstasy:

> The community is stirred in Brighton—a beautiful town. Places thickly settled stand all about and surrounding the city of Melbourne. People of the finest and noblest of society are coming from all places. The tent is filled in the afternoons and evenings, so there is scarcely room for them to find a seat.—Letter 125, 1894.

> We see nothing like the bitterness of opposition we met in Wellington. A deep interest is developing everywhere. People come twenty and thirty miles, bringing their lunch, and remaining from morning till night. They say, "Never, never, did we hear the Bible made so plain before. We are amazed at what we hear. Strange things are brought to our ears." In the afternoons and evenings throughout the week our congregations number about one thousand. . . .
>
> The congregations surprise us all. The interest is wonderful. The first class of people are searching for truth as for hidden treasures. All who come to the meetings seem astonished beyond measure. They are pleased with everything Elder Olsen presents before them, and express themselves as well pleased with the words I spoke upon temperance Wednesday afternoon, also on Sunday afternoon, and upon education Thursday afternoon, when the subject of our school was up.—Letter 100, 1894.

The visitors made good use of the dining tent. On Sunday, January 14, 190 were served. The cost to the patrons was only six pence, or twelve and a half cents. No meat was served, and the diners really enjoyed their meals (MS 3, 1894).

"This camp meeting is advertising us as nothing else could," Ellen White wrote in her letter to Mrs. Caro. "The people say it is a wonder of wonders, this city of clean, white tents. Oh, I am so

THE EVANGELISTIC THRUST IN AUSTRALIA

thankful that the Captain of the Lord's host is upon the encampment."—Letter 100, 1894.

By Friday, January 12, there were 108 family tents on the grounds, with 445 persons occupying them. Several houses just off the grounds were rented to accommodate families without tents. In the camp were a number of people who had accepted the third angel's message from reading such books as *The Great Controversy, Thoughts on Daniel and the Revelation,* and the missionary journal *Bible Echo,* and were for the first time mingling with fellow Sabbathkeepers. Wrote Ellen White in the midst of the meeting:

> You can hardly imagine the delight of these persons as they feast upon the rich banquet that heaven has prepared for them, and their hungry souls are filled. A holy joy pervaded the encampment. . . . Many voices are heard expressing the gratitude of joyful hearts as men and women contemplate the precious truth of the third angel's message, and come to realize the paternal love of God.—Letter 86, 1894.

Ellen White took some time out on Sunday, January 14, to write to A. T. Jones in Battle Creek. She reported:

> The first Sabbath of the conference meeting [January 6] three commenced the observance of the Sabbath, and yesterday five more took their position on the truth. Two businessmen [A. W. Anderson* and his brother Richard] with their wives and relatives, numbering eight, begged for tents in order that they might remain on the ground and attend early-morning and evening meetings. One of the men will return every day with his horse and carriage to Melbourne, a distance of eight or ten miles, and look after the business, returning at night. These two brothers keep a large music establishment and are convicted of the truth, and we believe will yet take their position. Far and near the sound has gone out concerning this city of tents, and the most wonderful interest is awakened.

Other campers crowded together a bit to make two tents available to the Andersons, who camped there for a few days. "Had

---
*Note: Father of the well-known evangelist and teacher R. A. Anderson, and his brothers, Ormond and Dr. Clifford.

we tents," continued Mrs. White to Jones, "many from the outside would camp with us on the ground who never heard that there were such people as Seventh-day Adventists until this time." She added:

> We have already extended the meeting one week, and may have to extend it still longer. The Lord is among us working to His own name's glory.

Then she told about the weather, which had been delightful until Sabbath, January 13, when a sandstorm overtook them.

> Sentinels were placed at every post of the tent so that there was no flopping of the tent or raising of the poles, for they were held down. Three family tents and two larger tents were blown down. The larger tents were blown down because the center poles broke; but these circumstances did not disturb us, since the Lord is at work.
>
> The Lord is encamped on the ground, and will take care of His own work. The prince of darkness may use his power to annoy and perplex us, but he cannot overthrow us. We gave up our tent to those who were without shelter, and came to the school building.—Letter 37, 1894.

BENEFICIAL CONTACTS WITH CAPT. AND MRS. PRESS

A Capt. Press and his wife, of Williamstown, attended some of the meetings. Mrs. Press was the president of the Women's Christian Temperance Union and for several years had been a vegetarian. She sought an interview with Mrs. White, and visited with her in her tent. Mrs. Press requested Ellen White to address her group and urged participation on the part of Seventh-day Adventists in the work of the WCTU. The WCTU president called for someone to give the union members lessons in hygienic cooking; when told the Adventists had no one in Australia well enough qualified, her response was, "Tell us what you do know."—Letter 88a, 1894. Mrs. Press also urged Ellen White to take an all-out stand to banish all meat from her own table. As to this point Mrs. White wrote: "I have had much representation before my mind in the night season on this subject."—Letter 76, 1895 (CDF, p. 488) but with her travels, with a diversity of cooks of varied skills, and with the pleading of certain of those who ate at her table, she had not taken a stand that would have cleared the table entirely of meat. In this connection, while on the Brighton campground, she wrote:

> As a denomination we are in the fullest sense total abstainers from the use of spirituous liquors, wine, beer, cider, and also tobacco and all narcotics, and are earnest workers in the cause of temperance. All are vegetarians, many abstaining wholly from the use of flesh food, while others use it in only the most moderate degree.—Letter 99, 1894.

A year later she could write, "Since the camp meeting at Brighton, I have absolutely banished meat from my table. It is an understanding that whether I am at home or abroad, nothing of this kind is to be used in my family, or come upon my table."—Letter 76, 1895 (CDF, p. 488).

It was with difficulty that Ellen White found words to speak adequately of the camp meeting and its influence. In her report to Jones she declared:

> This is the first camp meeting that Melbourne has seen, and it is a marvel of wonder to the people. There is a decided interest to hear the truth. This interest we have never seen equaled among those not of our faith. The camp meeting is doing more to bring our work before the people than years of labor could have done. . . . Yesterday the most noted physician in North Fitzroy was here to listen. Some ministers have been here, and a large number of businessmen.—Letter 37, 1894.

Writing to Edson White, she said, "Taking it in on all sides, this is the best camp meeting we have ever attended," and added:

> Many visitors come from long distances, and as it used to be seen in 1843 and 1844, they bring their lunch and remain through the day. A number of the citizens of the place have declared that if they were not living close by, they would hire tents and camp with us on the grounds. They value the privilege of hearing the Word of God so clearly explained, and they say the Bible seems to be full of new and precious things, and will be like a new book to them.—Letter 86, 1894.

THE AUSTRALIAN YEARS

THE BUSINESS SESSION OF THE AUSTRALIAN CONFERENCE

There was conference business to attend to. Eight meetings were held, beginning on Monday morning, January 8, and running through the week. Resolutions were adopted expressing gratitude to God for His blessing in "the progress of the message" and for the excellent help sent to the Australian field, including the visit of O. A. Olsen. Resolutions were also adopted pointing out that in consideration of the times, there should be the faithful reading of *The Great Controversy* and the *Testimonies*, especially the chapters on "The Coming Crisis" and "The Impending Conflict." Issues involving church and state loomed. Steps were taken to increase the circulation and reading of the *Bible Echo*, now a weekly, and other journals of the church.

The school location and future plans for its operation were reviewed, with Ellen White speaking on the subject, but as plans were beginning to take shape for the forming of an Australasian Union Conference, all decisions relating to the school were assigned to that potential organization. The nominating committee brought in the name of A. G. Daniells to continue as president of the Australian Conference, with the Echo Publishing Company, rather than an individual, named to serve as treasurer. Other officers and committees were appointed.—BE, Feb. 5, 1894.

A UNION CONFERENCE IS BORN

As was the case with all local conferences and missions throughout the world, those in Australia were separate units under the direction of the General Conference, with headquarters in Battle Creek, Michigan. Local conferences, when formed, were accepted into the General Conference. The arrangement oftentimes proved awkward.

One problem was the time element. Mail to and from the States took a month each way. Then there was the distance between local conference or mission and the General Conference. Institutions were developing to serve the peoples of the whole South Pacific, and they needed careful supervision. All this led A. G. Daniells and W. C. White to give study to a type of organization that would bind together the local organizations in a given area into an administrative unit, which in turn would be responsible to the General

Conference. In several trips they took together to New Zealand and back, they had time to canvass the matter carefully and to outline a course that might be followed.

But they were not alone in their concerns. O. A. Olsen, as president of the General Conference and chairman of the Foreign Mission Board, had clearly seen the problems. He was now in Australia in close association with White and Daniells, and Mrs. White as well. While the workers were assembled in Brighton for some days together, there was opportunity for united study to the forming of what was called a union conference. With the business of the Australian Conference out of the way by the end of the second week, the key workers turned their attention to the creation of a new type of organization, which would stand between local conferences, missions, and institutions, and the General Conference. In this way matters of local concern could be studied and acted upon by those nearby.

On Monday morning, January 15, with W. C. White, who had been appointed by the General Conference as the "superintendent of the Australasian Field," in the chair, some 250 persons came together to consider the matter of forming a union conference. Olsen was asked to preside at the meetings dealing with the matter. There were nine in all, during the next ten days. Committees on organization, nominations, and resolutions were appointed. Early in the work, the committee on school location gave its report, which was printed in the February 26, 1894, *Bible Echo:*

> The committee on school location reported that diligent inquiry had been made for suitable sites near Melbourne and Sydney; that several places had been found which they thought were worthy of consideration: and they recommended that the executive committee of the conference be authorized to take immediate steps to raise funds, and to purchase land which in their judgment is most suitable, and that their decision be made as early as is consistent.

The committee on organization presented a constitution that would foster the beginning of the new union conference and called for steps to be taken to enable it to hold church and school property. The nominating committee recommended for officers:

THE AUSTRALIAN YEARS

President, W. C. White
Vice-President, A. G. Daniells
Secretary, L. J. Rousseau
Treasurer, Echo Publishing Company

THE WORK OF THE UNION OUTLINED

The committee on resolutions during the ten days of the conference brought forward twenty-seven propositions relating to various phases of the union conference and its work. Among these was a resolution recognizing the responsibility of the union conference in the light of the gospel commission. Ten comprehensive resolutions had to do with the school, its location and development. Six related to the publishing work, the *Bible Echo,* and the production and distribution of literature.

Others had to do with the sending of worthy young people selected by the union conference to Battle Creek for training as medical missionaries and missionary nurses, and the inviting of church members to come to the colonies as self-supporting missionaries, with the Foreign Mission Board of the General Conference giving counsel as to qualifications, locations for labor, et cetera.

Several resolutions gave authority to the executive committee for its various lines of activity in moderating between conferences, arranging for travel, and the transaction of the business of the conference between sessions. Various committees were named to manage and edit the *Bible Echo,* to take care of religious-liberty issues and handle transportation, and to implement the decision reached that the next session of the Australasian Union Conference would be held sometime late in the year 1895.

It was a trailblazing meeting, setting up in essence what the church as a whole would adopt when the appropriate time came. Olsen was strongly in favor of what was accomplished and worked closely with the brethren. The development of the union conference organization would relieve the world headquarters of many administrative details. The union conference plan was well thought through and devised with understanding and care. It opened the door for true advancement throughout the Australasian field and in time the world field.

THE EVANGELISTIC THRUST IN AUSTRALIA
THE SCHOOL—ITS CHARACTER AND LOCATION

The resolutions relating to educational work in Australasia called for securing a permanent site for the school and providing buildings and facilities to expedite the work. Perhaps the most far-reaching and controversial resolution was the one that read:

> *Whereas,* It is desirable that the Australasian Bible School be located away from the large cities, and in a place favorable to simplicity and economy, and where agricultural and manufacturing industries may be developed for the benefit of students, and of families having students in school, and
>
> *Whereas,* A village settlement close to the school would be a desirable place of residence for ministers and canvassers, who must be separated from their families much of the time, and for many persons of various pursuits who wish to fit themselves or their children to be laborers for Christ, therefore,
>
> *Resolved,* That we recommend the purchase of a site suitable for the purposes aforementioned.—*Ibid.*

Not all workers present could envision a school in a rural location where "agricultural and manufacturing industries" would be developed and carried on for the benefit of the students. Australia was in the depths of a depression. Families were losing their homes because they could not meet the most modest mortgage payments. Thousands were out of work. How could the little band of workers in Australasia go into the country, secure a large tract of land, erect buildings, and start a school? On one occasion a prominent member of the Melbourne church, after listening to the proposal to establish an industrial school in a rural region, declared to W. C. White:

> This plan of building such a school is not an Australian plan at all; the demand for having such a school is not an Australian demand. The idea of establishing a school at this time, when our cause is so young and weak, is not an Australian idea.—DF 170, "The Avondale School," WCW to F. C. Gilbert, Dec. 22, 1921.

Other resolutions gave strong support for the summer school about to open in Melbourne, and provided for the continued operation of the Australasian Bible School for another full term.

Every evening during the session, evangelistic meetings continued through the fourth weekend. The meetings held in the large tent were well attended to the last Sunday night, January 28.

BREAKING CAMP

Thoroughly weary but with a sigh of nostalgia, Ellen White wrote on Monday, January 29:

> In a few hours we leave this pleasant spot, where the Lord has manifested His power and His presence in a marked manner. I have spoken sixteen times during this meeting, besides having considerable to say in the ministers' meetings. The meetings that have been held here have drawn heart to heart. A feeling of tenderness and love has been manifested throughout. The discourses have been given with power. Many have seen great light, and there has been manifested a hunger of soul for the truth, precious truth. Some have not missed a meeting. . . . The camp meeting has been in every way a success. We wish there were many more workers to take right hold and follow up the interest.—MS 4, 1894.

FAR-REACHING INFLUENCE OF THE BRIGHTON CAMP MEETING

About a hundred souls were baptized as the immediate fruitage of the Brighton camp meeting, among them the two Anderson brothers (Letter 40b, 1894). Their wives followed a few months later. An evangelistic tent was pitched in North Brighton, and Elders Corliss and Hare continued with a series of meetings that were well attended. Another tent was pitched in Williamstown, across Hobson's Bay from Brighton and twelve miles south of Melbourne. Here M. C. Israel and W. L. H. Baker carried on the evangelistic thrust. Churches were raised up in both communities. Ellen White spoke at both places, several times in Williamstown, either in the tent or a hired hall.—MSS 5, 6, 1894.

Mrs. Press was in the harvest at Williamstown. Almost immediately a private cooking school was conducted by Mrs. Starr and Mrs. Tuxford in the Press home, giving the family helpful guidance in food preparation (Letter 127, 1894). All in all, the first camp meeting held in Australia was a success and served to establish a pattern of fruitful evangelistic camp meetings.

CHAPTER 12
(1894)

The American Mails— Almost Overwhelmed

WITH camp meeting over and school not in session, Ellen White and her assistants found a home in the buildings of the Bible school in Melbourne. It was temporary, as she wrote:

> I take up my abode in the school building for eight weeks. It may be less than that before we leave for New South Wales, where I hope to find a pleasant, retired place in which to complete the "Life of Christ." . . .
> We are now in the school, occupying five rooms. Our family consists of Emily [Campbell] and May [Walling], Marian [Davis], Sister Tuxford from New Zealand, and myself.—MS 4, 1894.

She was weary from labors in connection with the camp meeting and divided her time between visiting the companies where there were new believers, and resting and writing. In mid-February she wrote, "We are usually well, hurrying off the American mail, but my mind has been so taxed recently for three weeks [that] it is a poor, tired mind, and I cannot tax it much more. After this mail is gone, I shall take things easier."—Letter 141, 1894.

THE ANNA PHILLIPS EXPERIENCE

One of Ellen White's concerns at this time was the mishandling on the part of some leading brethren in America of Anna Phillips and her claims to special revelations from God.

Miss Anna Phillips—sometimes spoken of as Anna Rice, for she had been taken into the Rice family—felt she had been called by God to serve as a special messenger to the church, inspired by heavenly visions.

Ellen White first learned of this while in New Zealand in October, 1893. Anna resided with Elder and Mrs. J. D. Rice, workers in northern California, and was at times in Battle Creek.

When both Rice and his wife attributed unusual importance to Anna's dreams and impressions, she came to believe that what came to her mind were the intimations of the Spirit of God, that is, that visions were given to her and that she had the gift of prophecy.

She wrote "testimonies," first to the Rices and then to other husbands and wives, touching on their personal experiences. These were earnest appeals for purity of life, with teachings that went beyond the Bible and the Spirit of Prophecy. Messages were directed to the leaders of the church aimed at giving guidance in administering the work.

Correspondence from America called the matter to Ellen White's attention. On November 1 she wrote to Elder and Mrs. Rice that she had not felt called upon earlier to encourage or condemn so long as she "had no special light in reference to this case."

She continued:

> I now feel constrained to write. Matters have been presented before me which I will now mention. . . . Elder Rice and some others were encouraging this sister to her injury that she had been ordained of God to do a certain work. . . . I will say the Lord has not given you this work to do to impress minds that this is a work which they must receive as from God. You have no duty to present it to the people in this light.
>
> My guide said to you, "Look unto Jesus; receive your light from Jesus; talk of the light He has already given." . . .
>
> It is not the burden the Lord has given you to explain and interpret the words, the works, the writings of Sister Phillips. If you do this, you will mislead the people. . . .
>
> The Lord has not laid upon her the work of accusing, of judging, of reproving, of condemning and flattering others. . . . I will say no more at present on this subject, only this: there will be, I have been shown, many who will claim to be especially taught of God, and will attempt to lead others, and they will undertake a work from mistaken ideas of duty that God has

THE AMERICAN MAILS—ALMOST OVERWHELMED

never laid upon them; and confusion will be the result.—Letter 54, 1893.

Almost two months went by before Ellen White addressed herself again to the matter of Anna Phillips. On her journey back from New Zealand she had a few days in Sydney. There, on December 23, she wrote a general warning in the form of a ten-page letter addressed to "Dear Brethren and Sisters." It opens:

I have a message to you from the Lord. Brother Rice is not engaged in the work which the Lord would have him do. . . . He cannot see the outcome of this work which he has taken up. Anna Phillips is being injured; she is led on, encouraged in a work which will not bear the test of God.

Ellen White then declared:

I have received from God the warning which I now send you. Anna Phillips should not have been given the encouragement she has had. It has been a great injury to her—fastened her in a deception. I am sorry that any of our brethren and sisters are ready to take up with these supposed revelations, and imagine they see in them the divine credentials.—Letter 4, 1893.

Mail each way across the Pacific took a full month, and mail boats ran about once a month. The lack of other data makes it difficult to pinpoint the time of reception and the dispersal of the messages sent. There is evidence that some letters, having missed the boat, were delayed in Australia for several weeks. Ellen G. White letters on file that pertain to this matter carry dates of November 1 and December 23, 1893; and for 1894, January 15, March 15, April 10, April 16, and June 1. Limited space precludes presenting her counsel in detail, but an extensive presentation appears in *Selected Messages*, book 2, pages 85-95, in chapter 10, "The Visions of Anna Phillips."

In the nine-page letter of January 14, written in Melbourne to A. T. Jones, Ellen White discussed several matters. On page 5 she reported that word had reached her that Jones was giving encouragement to Anna Phillips, and even reading some of her messages in public in such a way that people found it hard to discern when he was reading from her writings and when he was reading from Ellen White's pen. She urged, "I want you to consider this carefully, for the Lord has given me light to the effect that the attention of the people is not to be called to Anna Phillips."—Letter 37, 1894.

In the first paragraph of her ten-page letter to Jones written March 15, 1894, she dealt quite fully with the situation. She declared:

> I have a message for you. Did you suppose that God had commissioned you to take the burden of presenting the visions of Anna Phillips, reading them in public, and uniting them with the testimonies the Lord has been pleased to give me? No, the Lord has not laid upon you this burden. He has not given you this work to do. . . . Do not belittle the work by mingling with it productions that you have no positive evidence are from the Lord of life and glory.

She pointed out that God had not called Anna Phillips to follow on after the testimonies. She wrote:

> Many things in these visions and dreams seem to be all straight, a repetition of that which has been in the field for many years; but soon they introduce a jot here, a tittle of error there, just a little seed which takes root and flourishes, and many are defiled therewith.—Letter 103, 1894 (see also 2SM, pp. 85-87).

W. M. Adams, who was a student of Battle Creek College in 1894, has recounted his experience. He heard Elder Jones preaching in the Battle Creek Tabernacle. He intermingled some of the messages of Anna Phillips with those he read from the testimonies, and asked the congregation whether they did not hear the same voice in each. The people were left in confusion.

The next morning Adams was at the post office in the Review and Herald building, writing a postcard home. Jones came in and asked for his mail. He was handed a long envelope with Ellen White's name in the return address. He dropped on the bench, tore the envelope open, and began to read. Adams reports that as Jones read, tears came to his eyes and dropped on the sheets.

Soon A. O. Tait came in, and Jones addressed him: "Oscar, come

THE AMERICAN MAILS—ALMOST OVERWHELMED

here. Sit down. You heard me preach that sermon yesterday?"

"Yes," replied Elder Tait.

"Well, read this," Jones said, as he handed him the testimony he had just received from Ellen White. After Tait had had time to read, Elder Jones asked, "Who told Sister White a month ago that I was going to preach that sermon about Anna Phillips as a prophetess?"

"Ah, you know, Alonzo," Tait answered in his calm yet firm way.

"Yes, I do know. God knew what I was going to do, and He impressed Sister White a month before I preached the sermon to send the testimony that I am wrong. Look at that date."

It was a thoughtful week for the brusque and ever-ready A. T. Jones. Adams reported that the next Sabbath he again preached in the tabernacle and that he read portions of the testimony he received Sunday morning. He said, "I am wrong, and I confess it. Now I am right."—RH, July 7, 1949.

Elder W. W. Prescott also became a supporter of Anna Phillips, but a few hours before he was to address the students at Walla Walla College, intending to introduce some of her messages, he was handed a copy of a letter from Sister White dealing with the matter. It was the first to come to his attention, and he dropped his plans. S. N. Haskell, president of the California Conference, happened to be at Walla Walla at the time. He exclaimed as he wrote of the incident to Ellen White: "I have heard about testimonies coming just in season, but I never experienced such providence before."—S. N. Haskell to EGW, March 31, 1894.

Ellen White was very careful in her approach to both Miss Phillips and the two prominent ministers who gave her support. "Sister Phillips is not to be condemned and denounced" (Letter 4, 1893), she counseled, pointing out that others close to her were largely responsible by giving her encouragement. Ellen White was concerned for Jones and Prescott, fearing that people would take advantage of the fact that they had been misled. She found it hard to understand why neither of these men, along with Rice, had communicated with her before supporting Anna Phillips. Of this she wrote:

> I have expected that some account of these matters would be sent to me, and that counsel would be asked, and thus the way

would be opened for me to let the light from my past experience shine forth. But nothing has come to me, and now I have my commission to speak concerning these things. I am so sorry that brethren in whom our people have confidence should appear in any way to endorse these things that claim to be from God, when no real ground for faith has been given. It is a terrible mistake to present before the people that which we have not had unmistakable evidence is the revelation of God.—*Ibid.*

As warnings became known to leaders in America, acknowledgments of being mistaken were made, and tensions over the Anna Phillips work and writings subsided. On June 1, 1894, Ellen White wrote:

I have been much interested to understand more fully the true condition of Anna Phillips. I feel sorry for her. I feel sorry that our brethren have done her so great an injury as they have, by encouraging her in the work she has been doing. I feel sorry that Brother Rice has not followed the counsel of God. I have nothing but tender feelings toward her.

I am indeed sorry both for Brother Prescott and Brother Jones. I have felt very anxious in regard to them both, but especially in regard to Brother Jones, who is so ardent in his faith and does not manifest the caution he should in his statements by pen or voice. I did pray that these dear brethren would be so completely hid in Christ Jesus that they would not make one misstep.

Heartfelt confession having been made, she could say:

I have more confidence in them today than I have had in the past, and fully believe that God will be their helper, their comfort, and their hope. Like as a father pitieth his children, so the Lord pitieth those who love and fear Him.

She wrote assuringly, and sounded a warning to those who would be critical:

I have the most tender feelings toward our brethren who have made this mistake, and I would say that those who depreciate the ones who have accepted reproof will be permitted

THE AMERICAN MAILS—ALMOST OVERWHELMED

to pass through trials which will make manifest their own individual weakness and defects of character.

Brethren Jones and Prescott are the Lord's chosen messengers, beloved of God. They have cooperated with God in the work for this time. While I cannot endorse their mistakes, I am in sympathy and union with them in their general work. The Lord sees that they need to walk in meekness and lowliness of mind before Him, and to learn lessons which will make them more careful in every word they utter and in every step they take.

These brethren are God's ambassadors. They have been quick to catch the bright beams of the Sun of Righteousness, and have responded by imparting the heavenly light to others.—Letter 27, 1894.

A prominent worker in Battle Creek made this observation on the effectiveness of Ellen White's messages of warning:

> It was your testimony to Elder A. T. Jones which saved us from this terrible calamity. Nothing else could have accomplished that end. I tremble when I think how near the whole denomination came to being sold out bodily to the devil.—W. H. Littlejohn to EGW, March 25, 1894.

When the word from Ellen White concerning her work came to Anna Phillips' attention, she heartily accepted the message and repudiated her claims. She became a trusted Bible instructor, and died after years of faithful service.

In contrast to the way Anna Phillips "bore testimony" to several families regarding intimate matters, Ellen White presented her teaching on moral purity, teachings that linked poor mortals with "the riches of heaven's blessings."

> The purity, the holiness of the life of Jesus, as presented from the Word of God, possess more power to reform and transform the character than do all the efforts put forth in picturing the sins and crimes of men and the sure results. One steadfast look to the Saviour uplifted upon the cross will do more to purify the mind and heart from every defilement than will all the scientific explanations by the ablest tongue.—Letter 102, 1894.

THE AUSTRALIAN YEARS

This is my teaching of moral purity. The opening of the blackness of impurity will not be one half as efficacious in uprooting sin as will the presentation of these grand and ennobling themes.

The Lord has not given to women a message to assail men, and charge them with their impurity and incontinence. They create sensuality in place of uprooting it. The Bible, and the Bible alone, has given the true lessons upon purity.—*Ibid.*

A decade later Ellen White sounded the following warning:

There will be those who will claim to have visions. When God gives you clear evidence that the vision is from Him, you may accept it, but do not accept it on any other evidence, for people are going to be led more and more astray in foreign countries and in America.—RH, May 25, 1905 (2SM, p. 72).

THE NEW EXPERIENCE OF JAMES EDSON WHITE

Responding to his mother's appeal in which she recounted his perils shown to her as one endangered by the undertow, Edson White enjoyed a thorough reconversion and desired again to enter the service of the Lord. She understood well the attacks the enemy would attempt to make to regain his lost prey. She wrote him often.

Edson's heart had been stirred as he read in Battle Creek his mother's appeal for something to be done among the neglected blacks in the Southern States. His exuberant letters told of his plans to build a missionary boat and sail it down the Mississippi River as a base for work among the blacks. Knowing Edson's proclivity for adventure and his weakness in handling business matters, Ellen White entertained misgivings. She wished he and his wife, Emma, could be with her in Australia. She wrote on May 2:

In regard to the boat, I can only say, "The will of the Lord be done." If this is the Lord's plan, I have not a sign of an objection to it; but I feel deeply over the fact that you are not with us in the work. I am more disappointed than I can express. . . . I have not been able to get over this disappointment without tears.—Letter 79, 1894.

She followed with deep interest and many prayers the building,

THE AMERICAN MAILS—ALMOST OVERWHELMED

launching, and sailing of the *Morning Star* and its evangelistic and educational thrust along the rivers flowing through the Southern part of the United States.

THE MONTH-BY-MONTH AMERICAN MAILS

On April 9, she wrote of preparing the American mail while the house was full of visitors. "Elder Starr had to do most of the entertaining," she wrote, "for my letters must be prepared for the American mail."—MS 23, 1894. And on April 16, the day the mail closed, as she finished her letter to A. T. Jones, she, in weariness declared: "I can write no more. This mail carries out more than one hundred pages."—Letter 68, 1894.

The May American mail carried 150 pages, some addressed to the president of the General Conference.

In many cases the communications ran from four or five pages of double-spaced typewritten material to ten or twelve, and the few lines quoted in this volume, although selected as epitomizing the thrust of a respective message, represent but very brief samples of the many, many messages painstakingly penned.

EXPOSING ERRORS AND WEAKNESSES OF GOD'S WORKMEN

In early June as Ellen White was beginning to write for the American mail a member of her family said to her, "Have you read Elder Littlejohn's articles contained in the two issues of the last papers we have received?"

She had not, but she did. They carried the title "Danger in Adopting Extreme Views" and portrayed some of the weaknesses and mistakes of the apostles, the Reformers, and the pioneers of the Seventh-day Adventist Church. Ellen White, either by vision or experience or both, was so closely linked with these noble and fearless men who had been in God's service that to touch them pierced her heart.

She recounted her experience:

> That night, in agony of distress both of soul and body, I groaned in spirit; I feared I should not live. I have had some experience of what is meant when it was recorded of Christ that "being in . . . agony he prayed." Certainly I was helpless. Not one I knew could give me a word to bring relief.

THE AUSTRALIAN YEARS

All the next day my feelings were so intense that I could not write; all the next day I could not do anything. Certainly in my case these articles did not lift up the hands that hang down, or strengthen the feeble knees. The second night was one of sorrow and unspeakable grief. I felt crushed as a cart beneath the sheaves.

I prayed at half-past twelve o'clock at night, "O God, bring not Thine heritage unto reproach. Suffer not the world who hate Thy law to reproach God by reproaching His people who are seeking to present His truth to the world." . . .

I could take in the situation, I knew what would be the sure results, for I have had the movements of the world presented before me, and was aware of the advantage that men would take of unwise statements. All these things forced themselves upon my mind as I considered the points presented in the articles to which I have referred.—MS 27, 1894.

She wrote to Littlejohn on June 3:

Elder Littlejohn, you have undertaken to point out the defects of Reformers and pioneers in the cause of God. No one should trace the lines which you have done. You have made public the errors and defects of the people of God, and in so doing have dishonored God and Jesus Christ. I would not for my right arm have given to the world that which you have written. You have not been conscious of what would be the influence of your work. . . .

The Lord did not call upon you to present these things to the public as a correct history of our people. Your work will make it necessary for us to put forth labor to show why these brethren took the extreme position that they did, and call up the circumstances that vindicate those upon whom your articles have laid suspicion and reproach.—Letter 48, 1894.

LET NO ONE CALL ATTENTION TO THEIR ERRORS

There are twelve pages in the letter to Littlejohn. In words that may well be pondered, the messenger of the Lord wrote:

You were not in the early experience of the people of whom

you have written, and who have been laid to rest from their labors. You have given but a partial view, for you have not presented the fact that the power of God worked in connection with their labors, even though they made some mistakes.

You have made prominent before the world the errors of the brethren, but have not represented the fact that God worked to correct those errors, and to set the objectionable matters right. . . . You have arrayed the errors of the early apostles, the errors of those who were precious in the eyes of the Lord in the days of Christ.

In presenting the extreme positions that have been taken by the messengers of God, do you think that confidence will be inspired in the work of God for this time? Let God by inspiration trace the errors of His people for their instruction and admonition, but let not finite lips or pens dwell upon those features of the experience of God's people that will have a tendency to confuse and cloud the mind. Let no one call attention to the errors of those whose general work has been accepted of God.—*Ibid*.

Before closing the solemn testimony, Ellen White penned these thought-provoking words:

God will charge those who unwisely expose the mistakes of their brethren with sin of far greater magnitude than He will charge the one who makes a misstep. Criticism and condemnation of the brethren are counted as criticism and condemnation of Christ.—*Ibid*.

In a seventeen-page general letter addressed to "Dear Brethren in the Seventh-day Adventist Faith," she declared, "I have been acquainted with everything that has arisen in connection with the work that has borne the appearance of fanaticism." When the Reformers and pioneers saw their mistakes, they "opened their minds and hearts to receive the light that was sent of God, and He forgave the mistakes they made, and through His great mercy cast their mistakes and errors into the depths of the sea." She asked, "Now since God has thus covered their errors, who will presume to uncover them, and to present them to the world?"—MS 27, 1894.

Some argue that in the Word of God the sins and mistakes of

THE AUSTRALIAN YEARS

various Bible characters are presented to all who may read, and does this not provide a pattern for today? The question finds its answer in a paragraph in the same letter, written four days after the testimony was penned to Littlejohn:

> From the light which God has been pleased to give me, the work of calling up the mistakes and errors of sleeping saints, and resurrecting the errors which they have committed (except under the special direction of God), is not a work that God can accept.—*Ibid.*

After presenting the experience brought to view in the Littlejohn articles, Ellen White presented the episode of Joshua and the angel as set forth in Zechariah 3,* quoting extensively.

AN ENCOURAGING EXPERIENCE

To be the messenger of the Lord was no light matter. The work was in no sense routine, and often it bore so heavily on Ellen White that she despaired for her life. Her dedication to the work of God, her love for it, and her love for the workmen in proclaiming the message drew her into heavy involvement when situations were opened up to her in their true light. She wrote:

> When in great burden of soul for the people of God, seeing how many who profess to serve Him are dishonoring His name, seeing the end so near and a great work to be accomplished, I have wept in anguish of spirit; I was sore oppressed; I could not sleep, I could not find peace because of the peril of the Lord's people, especially at the great center of the work. I prayed in great agony of spirit.
> Then I lost myself in sleep, and was in a council in America; I was unburdening my soul to my brethren and sisters.—*Ibid.*

In recounting the experience, she told of a surprising development. While she was speaking she heard a voice behind her. She looked, and exclaimed, "It is Jesus, my Saviour." Jesus repeated words that He told her to read in the fifty-fourth chapter of Isaiah: "Fear not; for thou shalt not be ashamed: neither be thou

---

*Note: She had presented this subject earlier in *Testimonies*, vol. 5, pp. 467-476. Again, a decade later, she gave a chapter to it in *Prophets and Kings*. See pp. 582-592.

confounded; for thou shalt not be put to shame: for thou shalt forget the shame of thy youth, and shalt not remember the reproach of thy widowhood any more. For thy Maker is thine husband; the Lord of hosts is his name; and thy Redeemer the Holy One of Israel; The God of the whole earth shall he be called. For the Lord hath called thee as a woman forsaken and grieved in spirit."

Jesus said reassuringly, "Lay your burden upon Me; I will be your Burden-bearer."—*Ibid.*

"Well," wrote W. C. White, "from that time there was a complete change, and she has been gaining."—4 WCW, p. 463. There was a very noticeable turnaround on her part in spirits and health. He told of her resuming her ministry in the nearby churches, and declared:

> Her labors here seem to lift her up and give her strength and courage. It is the letters from America, and the views she has of some things there, that seem to wear on her mind and pull her down.—*Ibid.*

And Ellen White could at that time report:

> I am now much better healthwise than during my first year in Australia. I can walk better, and am improving in activity. . . . I am so thankful to my heavenly Father for His great goodness and lovingkindness to me.—Letter 13a, 1894.

But in another month, and another month, and another month, there would be "the American mail." In late July she wrote:

> The preparation of mail to send to America, and the reception of mail from America, are stirring times in our history, and if we are not very careful, both the going out of the mail and the coming of the mail has a telling influence upon me that is not the most favorable.—Letter 85, 1894.

CHAPTER 13
(1894)

The Move to New South Wales

IN FEBRUARY, 1894, while in Melbourne Ellen White wrote:

> I am tired, tired all the time, and must ere long get a restful place in the country. I want not a home where all is bustle in city life. I want this year to write and to exercise prudently out of doors in the open air.—Letter 140, 1894.

> I am getting to be very tired of moving. It worries me out, settling and unsettling, gathering manuscripts and scattering them, to be gathered up again.—Letter 102, 1894.

During the two years or so it was expected she would be in Australia, Ellen White had planned to spend some months in Melbourne and also some months in New South Wales, in the vicinity of Sydney. With the next term of the Australasian Bible School scheduled to open on April 4, the time had come when she must close up her work in Melbourne to free for student use the rooms she and her helpers were occupying. Also, the climate of New South Wales, being farther north, gave promise of being more comfortable than that of Melbourne. So in March a house was rented for her in Granville, a Sydney suburb.

Ellen White made the overnight train trip, leaving on Monday, March 26. She was accompanied by six associates and helpers, Marian Davis, May Walling, Mrs. Tuxford, Elder and Mrs. Starr, and a Mr. Simpson from New Zealand. Stephen Belden and his wife and Fannie Bolton had gone on ahead by boat two weeks earlier, accompanying a portion of the household goods along with Ellen

THE MOVE TO NEW SOUTH WALES

White's and the Beldens' horses and the carriages. Emily Campbell was left in Melbourne for a month to rest and catch up on the bookkeeping.

By early afternoon the next day they were surveying the Granville home and its surroundings. The building was large enough, with crowding, for her and her son, Elder and Mrs. Starr, and several of her helpers. Half an hour after their arrival she took her pen to hasten off a letter to Willie, reporting on the trip, describing the unpacked boxes of household goods scattered in different rooms, and announcing that Maude Camp, who was to do the cooking, had just arrived the night before. She added that the house was "better than I had imagined it would be" (Letter 145, 1894).

As do many houses in Australia, it carried a name: Per Ardua. It was of brick and had ten rooms, some oddly shaped. It stood on a three-acre plot with an orchard, a place for a vegetable garden, and a grassy paddock, with some shade from gum trees. There were also shade trees in the front. In her letter Ellen White commented favorably on the fireplaces, the broad porches, and the flower garden; she was pleased with the home generally. The air, she wrote, seemed to give her more freedom in breathing than Melbourne, and she courageously declared: "We all mean to be very cheerful and happy and of good courage in the Lord." She added, "It is just now a struggle for me, but I shall look to the light and not darkness."—*Ibid.*

GETTING SETTLED IN GRANVILLE

With so large a home only six minutes from the railway and two miles from Parramatta, it was inevitable that there would be many visitors. Soon after their arrival, in reporting on a brief trip into the country to buy apples, Ellen White wrote:

> When we returned we found a temporary table made of stable door and boards extending out nearly the whole length of the dining room and three of our brethren sitting at the table in addition to our family, and Brother McCullagh made four.

She commented, "We enjoyed the meal as much as if the table was the best walnut pattern." In the next paragraph she explains how they adjusted to their circumstances:

THE AUSTRALIAN YEARS

We find there are many ways we can spend money and many ways we can save money. We have a skeleton wardrobe of two upright standards, and cross pieces nailed to these, and a shelf put on the top. A very simple cheap lace over blue or red cheap cambric is fastened to the top and back of the shelf. This back is neatly arranged, lifted up and fastened securely to the posts of the head of the bedstead.

Hooks were put in the crossbars, and an adjustable screen hid the washstand. All in all, a nice little dressing room emerged. "I am much pleased with this arrangement," she wrote, and added, "It costs so little. This was the arrangement in our tents at the camp meeting, and it proved such a convenient affair we do not dispense with it in our houses, which are usually destitute of clothes-presses."—Letter 128, 1894. Supplementing their homemade improvisations were inexpensive articles of furniture purchased at auction sales.

Helping in a material way in the food line was the milk from a good cow they purchased soon after their arrival. They planned to secure a second one so they could have "plenty of cream and milk to cook with" (Letter 46, 1894). At the Brighton camp meeting Ellen White had taken a positive stand for a meatless diet. No meat was served in the dining tent at the camp meetings and none was used while they were living in the school buildings, although some roosters in the fowl yard and a calf in the pasture presented some temptations. "Some might have enjoyed it," she wrote to Dr. Kellogg, "but I said positively, 'No.'" No meat appeared on the table at Granville.

> I cannot consent to have flesh meats on my table. If I taste it myself, my testimony against it has no real edge. Some may have thought I was straining the point.—*Ibid.*

IN PERSONAL AND PUBLIC LABOR

Instead of finding a quiet place where she could write on the life of Christ, Ellen White almost immediately found herself drawn into both personal and public labor as evangelistic meetings in the Sydney suburbs yielded new members, and new companies and churches were formed. The *Bible Echo* reported:

THE MOVE TO NEW SOUTH WALES

Mrs. E. G. White, notwithstanding her arduous labors by pen, has entered upon public labor also, speaking to the churches and outside congregations with her well-known energy and earnestness.—April 23, 1894.

In working with these groups she came close to the people and soon discerned their needs. "We see now," she wrote Olsen, "that we must enter into personal labor, and visit from house to house, for great reforms must be made in families before we advance any further."—Letter 62, 1894.

As the results of the united labors of the several workers at Seven Hills, twenty-five accepted the Seventh-day Adventist message. A. S. Hickox held services not only Sabbaths and Sundays but also evenings, and then engaged in personal labor from house to house. By mid-May Ellen White had spoken four Sundays and one Sabbath. George Starr also labored there. "We rejoice," she wrote, "as we have seen family after family embracing the truth."—Letter 50b, 1894.

HELPING DESTITUTE FAMILIES

Not infrequently, as a family took its stand for the Sabbath the wage earner lost his job. Being depression times in Australia, it was almost impossible to find other regular employment.

"Now is a critical time," Ellen White observed.

> You cannot know how we carry the heavy burden as we see these souls tested, thrown out of employment, unable to obtain labor unless they will give up the Sabbath. We must comfort and encourage them; we must help them as they shall be brought into strait places. There are many souls as precious as gold, and every sinner saved causes rejoicing in the heavenly courts.—Letter 30a, 1894.

Several families who were keeping the Sabbath lost their farms. As financial conditions worsened, their mortgaged farms were sold out from under them. Iram James was one who had thus lost his farm (Letter 146, 1894). She noted:

> They are destitute of food and clothing. He keeps up good courage in the Lord. . . . Brother James, I understand, has four children, and some days has had nothing to eat but wild berries.

THE AUSTRALIAN YEARS

But we have sent them flour, beans, peas, cornstarch, cabbages, turnips, and potatoes, enough to last them a little time. Perhaps help will come.—Letter 147, 1894.

The McKenzie family lost everything—farm, home, and furniture. The husband was a real-estate agent and a bookkeeper, earning good wages, but on the acceptance of the Sabbath he lost his position. The failure of the banks climaxed the situation. The man who bought the furniture at auction offered to sell back what pieces McKenzie's friends might help with. The Parramatta church raised what they could for him, and £10 was sent from Melbourne to help. The family was without food for three days, except a little dry bread (Letter 24, 1894). Food was sent from the White home—peas, tapioca, flour (graham and white)—and £1 in money. Mr. McKenzie attempted to sell books, but without success. Ellen White reported that when supplies were taken to the family, she "found Sister McKenzie full of courage and faith" (Letter 50, 1894).

A number of families went through similar experiences, and Ellen White came to their aid in very substantial ways as her means would permit.

MR. RADLEY MAKES HIS DECISION

While many families suffered severely during the financial panic, not all were in the same circumstances. In early May, Ellen White, with another worker or two, visited the Radley family living near Castle Hill. They were just taking their stand for the message. The Radleys owned a large, well-established orchard of orange, lemon, and other fruit trees. At the time of the visit the wife was keeping the Sabbath, and from all appearances the husband and children would soon follow. But Ellen White was told that Mr. Radley, not fully having taken his stand, slipped back. As she recounted the experience at the General Conference session in 1901, she described him as a reading man. "In the night season," she said, "the angel of the Lord seemed to stand by me, saying, 'Go to Brother Radley, place your books before him, and this will save his soul.'"

> I visited with him, taking with me a few of my large books. I talked with him just as though he were with us. I talked of his responsibilities. I said, "You have great responsibilities, my

THE MOVE TO NEW SOUTH WALES

brother. Here are your neighbors all around you. You are accountable for every one of them. You have a knowledge of the truth, and if you love the truth, and stand in your integrity, you will win souls for Christ."

He looked at me in a queer way, as much as to say, "I do not think you know that I have given up the truth, that I have allowed my girls to go to dances, and the Sunday School, that we do not keep the Sabbath." But I did know it. However, I talked to him just as though he were with us.

"Now," I said, "we are going to help you to begin to work for your neighbors. I want to make you a present of some books."

He said, "We have a library, from which we draw books."

I said, "I do not see any books here. Perhaps you feel delicate about drawing from the library. I have come to give you these books, so that your children can read them, and this will be a strength to you."

I knelt down and prayed with him, and when we rose, the tears were rolling down his face as he said, "I am glad you came to see me. I thank you for the books."

As she recounted the experience, she spoke of the fruitage of the work:

> The next time I visited him, he told me that he had read part of *Patriarchs and Prophets.* He said, "There is not one syllable I could change. Every paragraph speaks right to my soul."
>
> I asked Brother Radley which of my large books he considered the most important. He said, "I lend them all to my neighbors, and the hotelkeeper thinks that *Great Controversy* is the best. But," he said, while his lips quivered, "I think that *Patriarchs and Prophets* is best. It is that which pulled me out of the mire."—GCB 1901, pp. 84, 85 (Ev, pp. 451, 452).

Mr. Radley soon took his position firmly, and his whole family united with him. Several of the children later gave their lives to the work of the church.

WORK ON THE LIFE OF CHRIST

The pioneering work in New South Wales did not lend itself well to the writing on the life of Christ she hoped to do. As she picked up

THE AUSTRALIAN YEARS

her diary on April 25, just a month after the move from Melbourne, she wrote:

> I thank and praise the Lord for the precious few hours' sleep I have had. It is now half past one o'clock that I awake and cannot sleep. My mind is troubled. I want every day to write something on the life of Christ.—MS 74, 1894.

THE TRIAL AND SENTENCE OF THE FIRTH BROTHERS

In a letter written May 2, Ellen White describes an interesting new experience in Australia, the enforcement of ancient Sunday laws:

> Two brothers named Firth, who reside in Kellyville, were converted to the truth from the world. The eldest is married. His wife is with him in the faith, and he has one child. He has a small place on a few acres of land upon which he makes his living. He gave the lot on which the church has been built. It is a nice little church, and is a gratification to them, for the people acted a part in building it.
>
> The brothers live quite a distance back from the road in an orchard of orange and lemon trees. We were much surprised to learn that they were summoned last week for working on Sunday. . . . These men are to come before the police authorities today to answer for the charges against them. They say they will refuse to pay the fine.

Later in the letter she reported:

> Our brethren Firth from Kellyville, who were arraigned for breaking the Sunday law, were today sentenced by the court either to pay a fine of five shillings or to be placed in the stocks. They brought an old law made in Charles II's time to bear upon this case of Sundaybreaking. Our brethren refused to pay the fine, and therefore will be put in the stocks.
>
> But as the people have been so well behaved in New South Wales, these instruments of torture have fallen into disuse, and there are no such instruments as stocks at the command of the prosecutors. The stocks will have to be made for the occasion to punish the heinous crime of working on the first day of the week.

THE MOVE TO NEW SOUTH WALES

... There was quite a representation of our brethren and sisters in the courtroom. ... The judge looked at them keenly, as also did his coadjuters.—Letter 79, 1894.

This triggered a whole chain of events. Wide publicity was given to the trial and sentence in the newspapers in the larger cities of Australia under such headlines as "SEVENTH-DAY ADVENTISTS IN STOCKS" (see BE, May 14, 1894). The *Bible Echo* from week to week presented the unfolding story. Elders Daniells and Starr, assisted by J. O. Corliss, held well-attended meetings in the Parramatta town hall, and a growing interest in the teachings of Seventh-day Adventists was generated. On May 14, in a letter to C. H. Jones, Mrs. White dwelt on this point:

The persecution of two of our brethren of one of the neighboring churches, and the sentence requiring them to pay a fine or be placed in the stocks, has created such indignation in the public mind that the people are ready to hear, and are calling for the reasons of our faith. This persecution has resulted for the truth rather than against it. Our brethren refused to pay the fine, and the alternative was the stocks, but the authorities have no such instruments of torture. They forced one brother to pay the fine, by seizing upon his horse and cart, leaving him no chance to get home, so he had to hand over the money. The other brother has no property they can attach, and refuses to pay the fine; so here the matter stands.—Letter 40b, 1894.

W. C. White, now carrying the burdens of the new Australasian Union Conference in addition to his other duties, was engaged in a feverish search for a site for the new school. Ellen White followed each move with keen interest. In his room in the Per Ardua home he not only administered the work of the union conference but also collected samples of soil taken from the different properties that he and other members of the locating committee visited.

CHAPTER 14
(1894)

A Place for the School

THE autumn and winter months of 1894, April to July, were a time of anxiety, disappointment, and discouragement. Overtaxation in April in writing, especially the American mail with the burden of meeting the Anna Phillips situation, brought to Ellen White two months of weakness and illness. The desperate financial crisis in Australia brought almost overwhelming demands that could be met only partially. The proposal of the Foreign Mission Board, pressed by O. A. Olsen, that Ellen White should quickly finish her work on the life of Christ and, with W. C. White, visit Africa and then proceed to America by way of Europe (this at just the crucial time in getting the school started in Australia [4 WCW, p. 463]); the frustration of not being able to make much progress in writing on her book; the lawsuit by Will Walling against Ellen White, for what he claimed was the alienation of the affections of his daughters, Addie and May; the confusion brought about by the many visitors to the White home, and their treating it much as a hotel, even though some members of the family had to bring cots into the dining room at night; and on top of this, the action of the General Conference Committee, because of financial adversity in America, to cut her wages by $2 per week and W. C. White's by $1 per week, when every available dollar was so much needed—all pressed hard upon her. Ellen White was tempted to board the next boat back to America and take up her writing at her Healdsburg home.

But this was not Ellen White's way of meeting difficulties. She would not turn and run, but would face it all courageously. She

A PLACE FOR THE SCHOOL

would put her trust in Jesus and face the issues day by day.

THE EARNEST SEARCH FOR A SCHOOL SITE

When Elders Olsen and White returned with Ellen White from New Zealand to Australia in late December, 1893, the search for school land began in earnest. Following up investigations Arthur Daniells had made, they visited several places during their few days in Sydney. This continued off and on through the late summer and fall. The school had been made a union conference project, which drew W. C. White, the president, very closely into the task. By the time Ellen White had moved to New South Wales, the conviction seemed to prevail that the school should be located in that colony, with its warmer climate, perhaps within seventy-five miles of Sydney.

The suffering of Sabbathkeeping families, not a few of whom lost their homes, led some church leaders in Australia to feel that the land that would be secured for the school should be large enough to provide little farms for some of these families. Thus they thought in terms of a thousand or two thousand acres. The big problem, of course, was the shortage of money. Their dire situation is revealed in a letter W. C. White wrote May 16 to his longtime friend C. H. Jones, who was at the Pacific Press: "We are planning to buy a large tract of land, and we can scarcely get enough money to go and see it."—4 WCW, p. 385.

When W. C. White made the move in early April from Melbourne to Granville, he stopped over at Thirlmere to examine two tracts of land they had heard were available. After the weekend with the churches close to Granville, he and his associates were off Monday morning to Dapto, fifty-six miles south of Sydney, where they found three thousand acres of beautiful land on Lake Illawarra. They got back at midnight, and three hours later started off for Morisset, seventy-six miles north on the coast, to see a tract of land near Dora Creek and Cooranbong. After a day there, they went twenty miles on to Newcastle. Then back to Morisset, where another day and a half was spent examining the Brettville estate on Dora Creek (*ibid.*, p. 254).

The latter consisted of nearly 1,500 acres, which could be purchased for $4,500. After hearing the report of what had been found, Ellen White wrote to Dr. Kellogg in Battle Creek:

> Most diligent search has been made for a tract of land of several hundred acres on which to locate the school, so that the students may have an opportunity to till the soil, and poor families may have a little piece of land on which to grow vegetables and fruit. These would go far toward sustaining them, and they would have a chance to school their children. But money matters are very close. We are all hard pressed for means, and know not just what to do unless money shall come in. We must live, and have means to carry forward the work.—Letter 47, 1894.

While at home in Granville, W. C. White devoted some time each morning to reading the manuscript on the life of Christ. He gave study also to a manuscript prepared by J. O. Corliss for two tracts dealing with some of the D. M. Canright criticisms of Ellen White and Seventh-day Adventists. The most misleading falsehoods were being disseminated in the Melbourne area by the Protestant ministers in an effort to combat Adventism.

A few days later the workers reached the decision that the Brettville estate at Cooranbong was the place for the school. A contract was signed and $125 paid to bind the transaction until a further inspection could be made by the president of the Australian Conference and other workers from Melbourne in mid-May (Letter 40, 1894; 4 WCW, p. 423).

Ellen White reported:

> Brother and Sister Lawrence went yesterday [May 16] with a tent, W. C. White has taken a supply of bedding and provisions, and thus the party will be provided with board and lodging, to save hotel bills. And the fact that they can spend their nights on the ground will expedite business. All will return Monday or Tuesday.—Letter 46, 1894.

The L. N. Lawrence family, father, mother, and daughter, had come from Michigan at their own expense to aid wherever they could with the work in Australia. This was in response to an appeal made by Ellen White in the *Review and Herald* of February 14, 1893 (see also GCB 1893, p. 316), in which she declared:

A PLACE FOR THE SCHOOL

What a great amount of good might be done if some of our brethren and sisters from America would come to these colonies as fruit growers, farmers, or merchants, and in the fear and love of God would seek to win souls to the truth. If such families were consecrated to God, He would use them as His agents.

When Mr. and Mrs. Lawrence reached Dora Creek they found they could rent a small house, three rooms and a kitchen (4 WCW, p. 457). So when the church leaders came in on Thursday and Friday they found a place to stay. Those who came to inspect the land were Brethren Daniells, Smith, Reekie, Humphries, Caldwell, Collins, and White. McCullagh followed early the next week after Sabbath obligations had been fulfilled. Even though she was not feeling well, there came a time when Ellen White could not refrain from joining the group. This she did on Wednesday morning, May 23, accompanied by Emily Campbell, George Starr, and Mr. McKenzie (MS 75, 1894; 4 WCW, p. 457).

By the light of a candle Ellen White wrote of it early the next morning:

> We found a good dinner waiting for us, and all seemed to eat as if they relished the food. After dinner we went to the riverside, and Brethren Starr, McKenzie, and Collins seated themselves in one boat, Brethren Daniells, McCullagh, and Reekie in a still larger boat, and Willie White, Emily Campbell, and myself in another.
>
> We rode several miles upon the water. Though the stream is called Dora Creek, yet it has the appearance of a river, for it is a wide, deep stream. It is somewhat salt, but loses its saltness as it borders the place which we are investigating. It required two rowers to pull the boat upstream. I should judge this is no creek, but a deep, narrow river, and the water is beautiful. . . . On our way we passed several houses upon farms of about forty acres of land. . . .
>
> When we landed on the ground to be explored, we found a blue-gum tree about one hundred feet long lying on the ground. There was a fire in the center, and the smoke came out of the forked ends, and the main trunk, which united together to form three chimneys; several feet of one fork was a burning mass of

glowing coals. The day before, Willie and Brother Reekie had taken their dinner at this place and had kindled a fire in a knot of wood, and it had been burning ever since. There was no danger of setting the woods on fire, and it was a pretty sight.

Willie, Emily, and I rested here for a little while, but the rest of the party took their shovels and went on to examine portions of the land that they had not yet passed over. . . . Around us were immense trees that had been cut down, and parts were taken out which could be used. . . . I cannot for a moment entertain the idea that land which can produce such large trees can be of a poor quality. I am sure that were the pains taken with this land, as is customary to take with land in Michigan, it would be in every way productive.—Letter 82, 1894.

She had most likely read the negative report of Mr. A. H. Benson, the government fruit expert who had examined the land at the request of church leaders. He had declared it for the most part very poor, sour, sandy loam resting on yellow clay, or very poor swamp covered with different species of Melaleuca. According to him the whole of the land was sour, requiring liming and draining (DF 170, A. H. Benson, "Report of the Campbell Tract Near Morisset, N.S.W.," May 21, 1894; see also 4 WCW, pp. 410-412).

It has been told that when Mr. Benson handed the report to a member of the committee he remarked that "if a bandicoot [a marsupial about the size of a rabbit] were to cross the tract of land he would find it necessary to carry his lunch with him." (See DF 170, "The Avondale School," WCW to F. C. Gilbert, Dec. 22, 1921.)

"While sitting on the log," Ellen White recorded, "my mind was actively planning what could be done. . . . I could see nothing discouraging in prospect of taking the land. But our party returned, and broke up my future faith-prospecting." She was escorted to some parts of the land, walking and resting and thinking. As the larger group came together near the boat landing, they brought encouraging reports of their findings.

Wrote Ellen White:

> They came from their investigation with a much more favorable impression than they had hitherto received. They had found some excellent land, the best they had seen, and they

A PLACE FOR THE SCHOOL

thought it was a favorable spot for the location of the school. They had found a creek of fresh water, cold and sweet, the best they had ever tasted. On the whole, the day of prospecting had made them much more favorable to the place than they had hitherto been.—Letter 82, 1894.

But night was drawing on, and the party returned down Dora Creek to the cottage by the light of the stars. As Ellen White pondered the work of the day there was one point that troubled her. She wrote:

> Everything about the place had impressed me favorably except the fact that we were far from the great thoroughfares of travel, and therefore would not have an opportunity of letting our light shine amid the moral darkness that covers our large cities like the pall of death. This seems the only objection that presents itself to my mind. But it would not be advisable to establish our school in any of our large cities.—*Ibid.*

High-priced land they could not buy—this land was only $3 per acre. There were problems of having the school too close to the city, with its many temptations. All in all, Ellen White was well pleased with the prospects.

Ellen White retired early, but the committee earnestly discussed their findings on into the night. There were diverse opinions, for there was considerable variation in different parts of the land, but the majority felt the enterprise could be made to succeed. Added to this was their observation of Mrs. White's confidence in the potentialities of the property. Late that autumn night, the committee voted to purchase the Brettville estate for $4,500.

SPECIAL EVIDENCE IN THE HEALING OF ELDER MC CULLAGH

Although the vote had been taken to buy the acreage, it was felt that to be sure, another day should be spent in further investigation. On Thursday morning before leaving the little cottage at Dora Creek, they met for prayer to seek God's special guidance. As Ellen White prayed, she felt impressed to plead with God for some token, some special evidence, that would make certain to all present that they were moving in God's providence.

THE AUSTRALIAN YEARS

In the group that morning was Elder McCullagh, who, afflicted with diseased lungs and throat, was losing ground physically. In writing to O. A. Olsen, she tells what took place:

> While we were all bowed in prayer, the Lord rolled upon me the burden of prayer for Brother McCullagh, that he should be blessed, strengthened, and healed. It was a most blessed season, and Brother McCullagh says the difficulty has been removed from his throat, and he has been gaining ever since.—Letter 57, 1894.

McCullagh, speaking of it later, said that it seemed as though a shock of electricity went through his body. His coughing ceased and he soon regained his normal weight and strength. Thirty-four years later he was still living.

The further examination of the property on that Thursday confirmed the conviction that they should move forward with plans for the establishment of the school on the Brettville estate.

REPORT TO THE FOREIGN MISSION BOARD

In his report written June 10 to the Foreign Mission Board in Battle Creek, W. C. White describes the tract in considerable detail, filling four single-spaced typewritten pages:

> Much of the land in this section of the country is a clayey gravel with subsoil of shale or rock, or a coarse red sand with a subsoil of red clay. So much of it is of this character that the district is generally spoken against. There is much good land to be found in strips, and some most excellent soil in places.... We estimate two hundred acres fit for vegetables, two hundred fit for fruit, and two hundred good for dairying. The cost of clearing will vary considerably.—4 WCW, pp. 420-422.

Twenty-five years earlier, land in the area had been cleared for agriculture, and orange and lemon orchards had been planted. But the settlers neglected their orchards and turned to the cutting of timber to supply the nearby mines. W. C. White reported:

> We have prayed most earnestly that if this was the wrong place, something would occur to indicate it, or to hedge up the way; and that if it was the right place, the way might be opened up. So far, everything moves most favorably.... We have signed

A PLACE FOR THE SCHOOL

a contract to buy the place, and have paid £25. At the end of this month, June 30, we are to pay £275, and then we have two years in which to pay the balance, with the privilege of paying all at any time.—*Ibid.*, pp. 422, 423.

MAKING A BEGINNING

The first step was to find the funds with which to make the payment of £275 due on June 30. W. C. White reported to A. G. Daniells:

> On Thursday, June 28, I borrowed £150 from Brother Sherwin and £105 from the Australian Tract Society, and scraped up all there was in our house, and made payment of the £275 due on the first payment.—*Ibid.*, p. 488.

Their solicitor (attorney) said the title was good. Two weeks later Mr. Lawrence, the church member who had come from Michigan, rented an old twelve-room hotel in Cooranbong, known as the Healey Hotel, and the furniture at the Bible school in Melbourne was sent for. Arrangements were made for surveying the land (6 WCW, p. 68). The last two weeks of August found quite a company of workers at Cooranbong.

Ellen White was on the lookout for the manner in which the land in the Cooranbong area produced. There were excellent oranges and lemons, but during the depressed times these brought but small returns. Vegetables did well; they bought cauliflower for "a mere song," as she termed it, large bags full for eight or ten cents. At that price they purchased a large quantity and used it for horse and cow feed.

She observed: "The people need to be educated as to how to raise fruit and grains." The letter to Edson and Emma continued:

> If we had several experienced farmers who would come to this country and work up the land and demonstrate what the land would yield, they would be doing grand missionary work for the people. At Melbourne, your Uncle Stephen Belden plowed a piece of land, and worked the soil thoroughly, and raised a most profitable crop of sweet corn for the school. Everyone told him not to undertake it, but he was determined to

show them what could be done. He will come on the school land here, and carry out the same plan.—Letter 89a, 1894.

As soon as it had been decided to purchase the Brettville estate for the school, a horse and cart were purchased in Sydney and dispatched to Cooranbong for the Lawrence family and visitors to use. Mr. Collins, a colporteur leader suffering some eye difficulty, and Jimmy Gregory collected provisions for three days and started out on the seventy-six-mile journey. At Cooranbong the rig proved very helpful. It was put to use by Ellen White and Emily and May while visiting Cooranbong in August.

In describing her thoughts to Marian Davis, her close working companion, she exclaimed:

> The more I see the school property, the more I am amazed at the cheap price at which it was purchased. . . . I have planned what can be raised in different places. I have said, "Here can be a crop of alfalfa; there can be strawberries; here can be sweet corn and common corn; and this ground will raise good potatoes, while that will raise good fruit of all kinds." So in imagination I have all the different places in a flourishing condition.—Letter 14, 1894.

Then Ellen White introduced an intriguing reference to special light on the matter presented to her "at different times":

> In the dream you have heard me relate, words were spoken of land which I was looking at, and after deep plowing and thorough cultivating, it brought forth a bountiful harvest. Having had this matter presented to me at different times, I am more than ever convinced that this is the right location for the school. Since I have been here for a few days and have had opportunity to investigate, I feel more sure than at my first visit that this is the right place. I think any [of the] land which I have seen would produce some kind of crop.—*Ibid.*

THE FURROW STORY

In 1898 she wrote specifically of an experience with which several were familiar:

> Before I visited Cooranbong, the Lord gave me a dream. In

A PLACE FOR THE SCHOOL

my dream I was taken to the land that was for sale in Cooranbong. Several of our brethren had been solicited to visit the land, and I dreamed that I was walking upon the ground. I came to a neat-cut furrow that had been plowed one quarter of a yard deep and two yards in length. Two of the brethren who had been acquainted with the rich soil of Iowa were standing before the furrow and saying, "This is not good land; the soil is not favorable." But One who has often spoken in counsel was present also, and He said, "False witness has been borne of this land." Then He described the properties of the different layers of earth. He explained the science of the soil, and said that this land was adapted to the growth of fruit and vegetables, and that if well worked it would produce its treasures for the benefit of man. . . .

The next day we were on the cars, on our way to meet others who were investigating the land; and as I was afterward walking on the ground where the trees had been removed, lo, there was a furrow just as I had described it, and the men also who had criticized the appearance of the land. The words were spoken just as I had dreamed.*—MS 62, 1898.

As she recounted the experience in a letter to Edson White some years later, she seemed to locate the finding of the furrow at a point in time not so early as her first visit to the property, but rather a little later when serious questions were raised by church leaders acquainted with the soil of Iowa, and the whole matter of the land at Cooranbong hung in the balance. In her dream she had seen the furrow as in an open space "close to where our school buildings now stand." She recounted finding the furrow this wise:

---

* Note: Neither of the two Ellen G. White accounts of this experience fixes precisely the time of the dream and later the seeing of the furrow on the school land. Nor do they pinpoint the exact location, except "close to where our school buildings now stand" (Letter 350, 1907). W. C. White penciled in on a copy of the account as given in MS 62, 1898, the words, in parentheses, "the committee on their last visit." In 1921 he placed the event as following the Ashfield camp meeting when "a large committee were sent up to give the land another careful examination" (DF 170, WCW to F. C. Gilbert, Dec. 22, 1921). An inability to fix precisely the exact timing or point out the exact location cannot undercut the validity of the event.

In 1958 the author was taken by Jack Radley, retired mission boat captain, to the approximate location of the furrow as pointed out to him by his father, John Radley, of Castle Hill. The latter had seen it in connection with one of the inspection trips to Cooranbong as the purchase of the estate was under consideration. Today a granite monument on the college grounds commemorates the furrow experience and reminds all of God's providence in the founding of the college.

THE AUSTRALIAN YEARS

When we came to Avondale to examine the estate, I went with the brethren to the tract of land. After a time we came to the place I had dreamed of, and there was the furrow that I had seen. The brethren looked at it in surprise. "How had it come there?" they asked. Then I told them the dream that I had had.

"Well," they replied, "you can see that the soil is not good." "That," I answered, "was the testimony borne by the men in my dream, and that was given as the reason why we should not occupy the land. But One stood upon the upturned furrow, and said, 'False testimony has been borne concerning this soil. God can furnish a table in the wilderness.'"—Letter 350, 1907.

NORFOLK VILLA, PROSPECT STREET, IN GRANVILLE

When Ellen White and her traveling companions returned to Granville, it was to a different house. Per Ardua, the brick building they had moved into in late March on coming to New South Wales, was at the foot of a hill. It had low, rather small windows, and Ellen White became less pleased with it. On looking around in June, as winter came on, they found a large house, Norfolk Villa, on the top of a nearby hill in a neighborhood known as Harris Park. W. C. White described it as high, light, and dry, and planned more conveniently than where they had been living. It had ten rooms and rented for the same rate as the previous property, $5.00 a week. "It is . . . real homelike," he said, with a "big dining room," which was a real comfort, for the whole family could gather (4 WCW, pp. 459, 489).

Ellen White's tent was pitched as an extra bedroom for the many visitors who came and went (Letter 30a, 1894). The day after they were settled in the new home, July 9, Ellen White wrote to Edson:

> We are now in our new home. The house is the best we have ever lived in. It is two-story. I have the room above the parlor. Both parlor and chamber have large bay windows, and the scenery is very fine. Everything is nice and pleasant here, and it is more healthful. . . .
>
> I shall not write many letters now, but I shall endeavor to put all my time and powers in writing on the life of Christ. I have written very little on this book, and unless I do cut off and

A PLACE FOR THE SCHOOL

restrain my writing so largely for the papers, and letter writing, I shall never have strength to write the life of Christ.—Letter 133, 1894.

RUNNING A FREE HOTEL

With the interest developing at Cooranbong, the White home was a sort of stopping-off place, rather like a free hotel, a situation to which they tried hard to adjust.

She wrote of the heavy burden of entertaining. As preparations were being made to send off Jimmy Gregory and Mr. Collins with the horse and cart to Cooranbong, Ellen White wrote to Willie:

> We are supplying them with provisions for a three-day journey. We are expected to entertain all the saints who come and go, to shelter and feed all the horses, to provide provisions for all who go out, and to lunch all who come in.
>
> This would be all very well if it were only an occasional thing, but when it is continual, it is a great wear upon the housekeeper and upon those who do the work. They are continually tired and cannot get rested, and besides this, our purse will not always hold out so that we can keep a free hotel.

She asked:

> But what can we do? We do not wish to say No, and yet the work of entertaining all who come is no light matter. Few understand or appreciate how taxing it can be; but if this is our way to help, we will do it cheerfully, and say Amen.
>
> But it is essential that we donate large sums of money to the work and that we lead out in benevolent enterprises. . . . Is it our duty also to keep a free hotel, and to carry these other burdens? May the Lord give us His wisdom and His blessing, is our most earnest prayer.—Letter 85, 1894.

Within a few days Ellen White caught herself. She felt remorse and self-condemnation for complaining. Repenting, she bravely wrote:

> I begrudge nothing in the line of food or anything to make guests comfortable, and should there be a change made in the

THE AUSTRALIAN YEARS

matter of entertaining, I should certainly feel the loss and regret it so much. So I lay that burden down as wholly unnecessary, and will entertain the children of God whenever it seems to be necessary. . . . I would not have it otherwise in entertaining, if I could. The Lord has made us stewards of His grace and of His blessings in temporal things, and while writing to Elder Loughborough a letter on this subject, my mind cleared wonderfully on these matters. No! I want not to hoard anything, and, God helping me, those who have embraced the truth and love God and keep His commandments shall not go hungry for food or naked for clothing if I know it.—Letter 135, 1894.

NEW HOME IS BETTER FOR W. C. WHITE

W. C. White, a widower whose growing girls were living at his home in Battle Creek, was driven as it were from pillar to post in his living accommodations. Forced to the strictest of economy by the shortage of means, he contented himself with a room in his mother's home. He traveled the ocean by steerage; took low-fare, slow trains when there was a choice; and as union president often typed his own letters and worked prodigiously.

The new home offered some relief, for his room, which served also as his office, was large, light, and airy. He kept an observant eye on his mother and her welfare, and when at home made it a point to walk with her for a few minutes after breakfast or dinner. Of this he wrote on July 20: "She cannot walk far at a time, but it does her good to walk a little way," sometimes as much as around a block. To go much farther pained her hip (6 WCW, p. 69).

WORK AT COORANBONG BROUGHT TO A STANDSTILL

In late August, as W. C. White, L. J. Rousseau, L. N. Lawrence, and others were at Cooranbong with the surveyor, tramping over the newly purchased land, two letters were handed to W. C. White, one from F. M. Wilcox, secretary of the Foreign Mission Board in Battle Creek, and the other from W. W. Prescott, educational secretary of the General Conference. White read them to Rousseau and Lawrence as they rested in the forest. The two letters carried the same message. The writers of each had just attended a meeting of

A PLACE FOR THE SCHOOL

the Foreign Mission Board at which W. C. White's letter of June 10, with his description of the land at Cooranbong, had been read. Each conveyed the same word, that the board felt, from the description of the land, it would be well to look for other property that was more promising, even if because of a higher price not more than forty acres could be secured. White called a halt to the work in progress, and the surveyor was sent back to Sydney (DF 170, "Report of the Proceedings of the Executive Committee of the Australasian Union Conference for the Year 1894"; 6 WCW, pp. 126, 129).

To Prescott, White wrote on September 3:

> As regards the land, we are acting upon the suggestion of the Mission Board, and have suspended all operations as far as we can. How this will affect our future progress and prospects, we cannot now conjecture. If it were an enterprise of our own, we might have many forebodings, but as we are servants of a King, and as He has power to make light from darkness, and to turn what looks to be failure into success, we shall wait and trust.—6 WCW, p. 126.

Dreaded misgivings swept over W. C. White. He later described the circumstances in the report he prepared to present to the constituency at the camp meeting to be held at Ashfield, near Sydney. After noting the careful inspection of many properties and that there had been twenty-eight meetings of the committee on school location between January 23 and August 29, he reluctantly wrote:

> Letters were received from the secretary of the Foreign Mission Board and the educational secretary of the General Conference acknowledging receipt of the description of the place sent them by W. C. White and intimating their fears that the place was not suitable for our work. The same fears were felt to some extent by W. C. White, L. J. Rousseau, and [A. G.] Daniells; therefore, at a meeting held in Sydney, August 27, White, Daniells, McCullagh, Reekie, and Rousseau being present, the following resolution was adopted:
>
> *Whereas,* The Mission Board has expressed its doubts and cautions regarding our school location, therefore,
>
> *Resolved,* That we delay further proceedings at Cooranbong

until we have time to consider the question of location. —DF 170, "Report of the Proceedings of the Executive Committee of the Australasian Union Conference for the Year 1894."

Somewhat stunned, W. C. White found himself frequently humming the words "Wait, meekly wait, and murmur not" (6 WCW, p. 137), and threw himself into the search for what might be a more promising site for the school. To Ellen White also, the decision of the Foreign Mission Board was a blow, and she waited at Cooranbong for word on what action would be taken by the committee on school location to be held in Sydney, Monday, August 27. On that same day she wrote:

> The more I see the school property, the more I am amazed at the cheap price at which it has been purchased. When the board want to go back on this purchase, I pledge myself to secure the land. I will settle it with poor families; I will have missionary families come out from America and do the best kind of missionary work in educating the people as to how to till the soil and make it productive.—MS 35, 1894.

On Wednesday, August 29, Ellen White received a telegram calling for her to return to Sydney the next morning. Cutting her restful stay at Cooranbong short, she and her women helpers took the morning train, arriving at Sydney about noon. They were met by W. C. White, Daniells, Reekie, and Rousseau, and taken to the mission. Here, after refreshments, the news of the decision of the committee on Monday was broken to Ellen White. That evening she wrote in her diary of it:

> Brethren Rousseau and Daniells had propositions to lay before us that the land selected for the locating of the school was not as good land as we should have on which to erect buildings; we should be disappointed in the cultivation of the land; it was not rich enough to produce good crops, et cetera, et cetera.
> This was a surprising intelligence to us, and we could not view the matter in the same light. We knew we had evidence that the Lord had directed in the purchase of the land. They proposed searching still for land. . . . The land purchased was the best, as far as advantages were concerned. To go back on this and begin

A PLACE FOR THE SCHOOL

another search meant loss of time, expense in outlay of means, great anxiety and uneasiness, and delay in locating the school, putting us back one year.

We could not see light in this. We thought of the children of Israel who inquired, Can God set a table in the wilderness? He did do this, and with God's blessing resting upon the school, the land will be blessed to produce good crops. . . . I knew from light given me we had made no mistake.—MS 77, 1894.

It was clear where her confidence lay, and this was a point that neither the committee in Australia nor the Foreign Mission Board in Battle Creek could put out of mind, yet their best judgment led them to look with misgivings on plans to build a college at Cooranbong.

While to Ellen White the Brettville estate at Cooranbong was the right place, she knew that the final decision must be made by the men carrying the responsibility of leadership, and they must be sufficiently confident of their decision to see the plans through not only in favorable circumstances but also in the face of the most foreboding difficulties.

The course now outlined seemed to her "very much like the work of the great adversary to block the way of advance, and to give to brethren easily tempted and critical the impression that God was not leading in the school enterprise. I believe this to be a hindrance that the Lord has nothing to do with. Oh, how my heart aches! I do not know what to do but to just rest in the Lord and wait patiently for Him."—*Ibid*.

The decision to search further for land held, and the task was begun. Ellen White reluctantly joined the committee in inspecting some new sites.

CHAPTER 15
(1894)

The Ashfield Camp Meeting in New South Wales

So SUCCESSFUL had been the camp meeting held in the Melbourne suburb of Middle Brighton in early January that there was enthusiastic anticipation of a repeat performance in Sydney later in the year. G. B. Starr and Ellen G. White and her staff of workers had journeyed north from Melbourne in late March and, as noted, had very soon been drawn into following up interests in Sydney suburbs. Granville, with easy access to Sydney and a number of rail connections, had become somewhat of a center of evangelistic operations. But all eyes were on the coming camp meeting and the annual session of the Australian Conference that would accompany it in late October.

The Sydney church, with eighty-five members, suffered somewhat from adverse and critical members. The Parramatta church, with a membership of ninety, had its own meetinghouse, one of the first in Australia, but was heavily in debt. At Kellyville there was a small but neat and debt-free meetinghouse, serving a church of twenty-four.

The evangelistic meetings held in a tent at Seven Hills resulted in a congregation of forty, including children. As winter came on, they decided to build a simple, neat church to cost about $300. All members and ministerial workers contributed to this, and Ellen White gave liberally to make the building possible. She insisted, and all agreed, that it should be erected without debt. The elected building committee did good work, securing favorable concessions in purchasing materials, and getting donated labor from the members (Letter 44, 1894).

THE ASHFIELD CAMP MEETING

Sabbath and Sunday, September 15 and 16, were high days for this new church. Elder McCullagh explained why in an article in the *Bible Echo:*

> On Sabbath, September 15, we organized the church, with one elder, two deacons, and a clerk as officers. The blessing of God attended the word spoken, and all felt assured that the Lord set His seal to the work by the presence of His Holy Spirit.
>
> On Sunday the dedicatory services took place. In the morning Dr. Kellogg preached, presenting some practical truths to the edification of all. In the afternoon the special service of the day was held. Mrs. E. G. White spoke to a crowded house, with great energy and freedom. The word spoken was precious.—October 1, 1894.

With a warm heart overflowing with joy and thankfulness Mrs. White looked on the earnest little flock as "babes in Christ." She wrote:

> If there is joy in the presence of the angels over one sinner that repenteth, we know that there is joy over these twenty precious souls who, one after another, have had the moral courage to decide to obey the truth. Now this little flock are babes in Christ, and need to be taught and led along, step by step, into faith and assurance; they need to be educated and trained to do the work of soldiers in the army of the Lord, and to bear hardness, that is, trials and oppositions, contempt and scorn, as good soldiers of Jesus Christ.—Letter 44, 1894.

That very week she received from an energetic and successful literature evangelist in California, Walter Harper, a gift of $1,000 to aid in the work in Australia. She had written to him in July, a man with whom she was well acquainted, telling of the development of the work in what she termed "this region beyond." She pointed out that meetinghouses must be erected, a college founded, assistance must be given to students unable to meet school expenses, and Adventist families, destitute because of Sabbathkeeping, must be helped. She specifically mentioned that "a church must be built at Seven Hills, and we must have means." She asked, "If in the providence of God you have means, will you help the truth to advance in this country?"—Letter 30a, 1894.

This he did, and in her letter expressing her gratitude for the liberal gift she wrote:

> If the Lord has made you a successful canvasser, and by this means you can not only obtain your livelihood but at the same time impart light to others, you have much for which to be thankful. I am thankful you are trading on your Lord's goods, and putting out your money to usury, in order that you may double your entrusted talent.—Letter 31, 1894.

ANOTHER SUNDAY-WORK ARREST

Then came the Shannon case, which was given wide publicity in some of the Sydney newspapers. One carried the headline "SUNDAY-LABOR PROSECUTION—'Two Hours in the Stocks.'" A. G. Daniells opened his front-page article in the *Bible Echo*:

> After an interval of three months and one day, the Seventh-day Adventists have again been brought prominently before the people of Australia. Again one of their members has been summoned to court, prosecuted, fined, and sentenced to the stocks for working on Sunday.—August 20, 1894.

Ellen White gave the details in a letter to S. N. Haskell:

> We are in the midst of stirring times just now. Brother Shannon, who lives in Sydney, has been arrested and prosecuted for working on Sunday. He owns houses, and builds houses. He is a stonemason, and in an out-of-the-way place was stirring up some mortar, in a quiet way that could offend no one, on Sunday, July 29. It seems that spies were watching him, and he was reported to the officers, and arrested. A fine was imposed in accordance with the law made by Charles II, and it was required that he either pay the fine or submit to confinement for two hours in the stocks.
>
> Elder McCullagh and several other brethren were present at the trial. My secretary, Sister Emily Campbell, was also present to take shorthand notes of the proceedings.... The authorities of Sydney find that they have an elephant on their hands, and they are at a loss to know what to do in this affair. They do not covet

THE ASHFIELD CAMP MEETING

the record that it would give them in carrying out a punishment invented under the profligate rule of Charles II.—Letter 30, 1894.

Then she told of how, after McCullagh conversed with the magistrate and the officers in the courtroom, one of the officers left the room saying that "if that man kept on talking, he would convert them all." Judicial officers in high places in the colony, embarrassed by the whole affair, found that an error had been made in imposing the fine (which Shannon had refused to pay, calling for the stocks). He had been sentenced to pay two shillings six pence when the law on the statute books called for five shillings. On this technicality the magistrates called for a remission of sentence under the two-hundred-year-old law.

In the meantime Daniells had hastened from Melbourne to Sydney to fill speaking appointments in two halls. "Just now," wrote Ellen White, "there is a wonderful stir in Sydney."

> This prosecution has awakened an intense interest. The authorities are collecting the statements that were made in regard to the persecution of the Firth brothers in Parramatta, and they say that they will present these things to the next parliament, and work for the repeal of that miserable old law.*—*Ibid.*

Issues of the *Bible Echo* carried reports from time to time of religious persecution elsewhere. Adventists in Tennessee and Georgia were imprisoned for violation of antiquated Sunday laws. H. P. Holser, in Basel, Switzerland, was arrested, fined, and imprisoned for allowing the operation of the publishing house on Sunday (BE, Nov. 26; Dec. 10 and 24, 1894). In one way or another, the work and doctrines of Seventh-day Adventists were coming before the general public.

---

* Note: Consideration was being given at this time to the formation of the Federal Commonwealth of Australia, binding the several colonies together. With regard to a proposed constitution, Seventh-day Adventists pressed in with public meetings calling for religious liberty, and with petitions calling for total separation of church and state. When a constitution was finally adopted in 1898, it contained Clause 116, which read: "The Commonwealth shall not make any law for establishing any religious observance, or for prohibiting the free exercise of any religion, and no religious test shall be required as a qualification for any office or public trust under the Commonwealth."

The thirty-eight thousand signatures gathered by Seventh-day Adventists in Victoria wielded an influence at the propitious time.—See Milton R. Hook, "The Avondale School and Adventist Educational Goals, 1894-1900," pp. 24-26.

THE AUSTRALIAN YEARS

On September 10 the *Bible Echo* carried an announcement that the Australian camp meeting for 1894 would be held at Sydney, October 18-30; there would also be a ten-day workers' meeting preceding the camp. The land selected was a five-acre grassy plot in Ashfield, five miles from the Sydney General Post Office.

To advertise the evangelistic meetings, which was a new thing for that area, a special camp meeting issue of the *Bible Echo*, dated October 15, was published. During the workers' meeting twenty young people distributed it to the homes in the various suburbs of Sydney. As they called on people, they gave a hearty invitation to attend the camp meeting and sold copies of the *Echo*. Some eight thousand copies were sold, and another eight thousand copies of the special cover, carrying an advertisement of the coming meeting, were given away.

Articles in the *Bible Echo* urged attendance of church members. In the September 17 issue, A. G. Daniells, conference president—one local conference at that time took in all of Australia—pointed out to believers, many of them new church members:

> There are many reasons why this meeting should be held, and why we may look for most excellent results.
> When God established His people Israel in the land of Canaan, He knew the temptations that would be brought to bear upon them, and as one of the safeguards against their being led into apostasy, He established three annual gatherings at which they were to meet together for praise and worship, to recount His mercies and His deliverances, and to encourage one another in the way of obedience. . . .
> There are many educational advantages to be enjoyed at these general convocations, which to those persons who wish to become laborers with God in the work of uplifting fallen humanity will be of inestimable value. . . .
> Therefore we say to our brethren, Prepare for the camp meeting; begin at once; work in faith, and let as large a number as possible receive its benefits.

As church members came in on Friday, October 19, they found more than fifty white canvas family tents among and under the shade trees. There were sixty-two by the end of the first week. The

THE ASHFIELD CAMP MEETING

tents were arranged in rows, with streets named after the Reformers, as was often done in America. The large pavilion would seat between six hundred and eight hundred persons.

The opening meeting was held on Friday night with a discourse from J. M. Cole, recently come from Norfolk Island. Sabbath morning there were 125 adults in the senior Sabbath school. These were quickly grouped into twenty-one classes.

A. G. Daniells spoke Sabbath morning, reading as his text, "Draw nigh to God, and he will draw nigh to you" (James 4:8). In the afternoon Ellen White spoke. Far from boasting or calling attention to herself, but ever eager to know whether her ministry was effective, she wrote of her observation to O. A. Olsen concerning this Sabbath-afternoon meeting:

> One man whose hair is white with age said, "I never heard such preaching as that woman gave us since I was born into the world. These people make Christ the complete center and system of truth."—Letter 56, 1894.

A large sign over the entrance to the enclosed grounds read, "WHOSOEVER WILL, LET HIM COME" (MS 1, 1895). In response to the advertising, Sabbath afternoon the attendance began to accelerate, and Ellen White reported to Olsen:

> On Sunday we had an immense congregation. The large tent was full, there was a wall of people on the outside, and the carriages filled with people in the street. The tents are a great surprise and curiosity to the people, and indeed, these white cotton houses interspersed among the green trees are a beautiful sight.—Letter 56, 1894.

Fully a thousand were present as the afternoon discourse began, and, reported W. C. White, "before its close there were upwards of two thousand on the ground." He too noted the drawing features of the experience unique to so many:

> Although many had apparently come from feelings of curiosity, the greater part of this multitude gathered in and about the large tent and listened attentively to Mrs. White as she presented the love of God and its effect upon the heart and character.—BE, Nov. 5, 1894.

THE AUSTRALIAN YEARS

The total conference membership throughout Australia was 872; 170 of these were camping on the grounds. Ministerial workers watched with deep interest the size of the crowds attending the weekend and evening meetings. W. C. White reported at midcamp:

> The evening meetings have been well attended. The large pavilion, which will accommodate from six to eight hundred persons, is filled every night, and sometimes there are two or three hundred standing outside.—*Ibid.*

In her diary Ellen White put it this way:

> On Saturday and Sunday, and during the evenings of the week, the grounds were thronged with interested spectators. The people listened in rapt attention to discourses on the coming of Christ, spiritualism, theosophy, the third angel's message, the love of God, temperance, practical godliness, and themes especially related to our time.—MS 1, 1895.

She listed the principal speakers as Pastors Corliss, Daniells, Cole, Colcord, Hare, Baker, and herself.

THE FRIDAY-MORNING WORKERS' MEETING

But not all was well, and Ellen White sensed this from the first. From observation and from special insights divinely revealed, she understood the nature of the trouble. True, they had beautiful grounds well laid out; they had the best speakers who could be brought together; they had crowds of people exceeding in number their fondest hopes; but there were deep-seated problems not visible to the throngs on the grounds. Jealousies existed between key workers at the camp, and a spirit of criticism prevailed. Sunday night, in vision, she seemed to be laboring with them, "speaking to them under the influence of the Spirit of God, and pointing out the necessity of earnest work in our own individual cases if we would have the deep moving of the Spirit of God in our midst" (MS 41, 1894). What took place Friday morning she reported in several letters and in her diary:

> This morning my work was in the large tent. The enemy seemed determined that I should not bear my testimony; there was not much vitality in the atmosphere, but I thought I would

THE ASHFIELD CAMP MEETING

try. I was so faint that I had to return to my room. I took a little nourishment and again went to the tent, but could not remain.

I then felt that Satan was trying to hinder me, and I went the third time, and the Lord gave me power to bear a decided testimony to those assembled, especially to the ministers. Then there was a break, and a good social meeting followed.

I had directed that the horse and phaeton should be ready for me to ride after breakfast, but Willie was so anxious that I should attend the ministers' meeting that I did so.

The power of the Holy Spirit came upon me, and I gave a decided testimony of reproof because of the lack of love and sympathy and courtesy toward brethren in the ministry. These feelings are positively forbidden by our Saviour. . . .

There is a sad dearth of real courtesy, sympathy, and tender regard and confidence. I presented these things, and the Lord helped me.—Letter 42, 1894.

Writing further of the experience, she related:

After breakfast I met with the ministers in the reception tent, and bore them a decided testimony, addressing them by name. I spoke to Brother A in regard to his treatment of his brother ministers. Brother A confessed in a very tender spirit to Brother B, and Brother B confessed that he had not had that love and tender regard for his brethren that he should have had. . . .

With tears they clasped each other's hands. The Spirit of the Lord came into the meeting, and the hearts of all melted down. From this time there was altogether a purer and more holy atmosphere in our meetings.—MS 41, 1894.

Ellen White's references to the meetings from day to day witness to the fruitfulness of that agonizing Friday-morning session. That afternoon she reported that "Elder Corliss spoke with great power."—*Ibid*. There was an altar call, and seventy-five responded; twelve decided to be baptized.

FAVORABLE IMPRESSIONS

The many visitors who came onto the grounds were very favorably impressed, and expressed their appreciation of the reception tent and the dining tent, with the oilcloth-covered tables set attractively. The cleanliness and order, and the taste in arrangements, added relish to the good meals served. The book tent also attracted many who visited the camp meeting.

Those on the grounds felt that there was more than one way to witness. Observed Ellen White:

> Some of the campers brought their cookstoves and had their tents so arranged that in passing by, one could see the neatly and bountifully set tables, the white beds, and attractive sitting rooms. Those who tented upon the ground were certainly comfortable in their tents.—MS 1, 1895.

In the same manuscript she wrote of the camp meeting near its close:

> The man who has brought the lumber which we have used on the ground has favored us in every possible way. He has attended the meetings and is now convinced of the truth. He is a local minister, and he says that he has tried to get the Ashfield people to attend church, but he could not persuade them to do so. The very people for whom he has been anxious are now attending our meetings, and you could not get them to remain away. Several are under deep conviction, and the interest grows. In conversation with him, Brother Corliss told him that we designed moving the tent to another locality. He remarked that he himself and many others would be sorry to see the tent moved. He also said, "I am with you, for you have the truth."

A good press was given to the meetings, as reported in the *Bible Echo:*

> Many papers in Sydney, in other parts of New South Wales, and even in other colonies, freely opened their columns to reports of the camp meeting at Ashfield, New South Wales.
>
> Two influential and leading papers in Sydney, the *Town and Country Journal* and the Sydney *Mail,* used cuts of the campground in connection with the reports.—November 19, 1894.

Ellen White reported on another interesting development:

> Last Friday the Baptists, of their own accord, offered our

THE ASHFIELD CAMP MEETING

ministers the use of the baptistry of their church, and they wished to have a discourse preached upon baptism to their church members. The favor was accepted, and sixteen believers went forward in baptism. The Baptists say it was the most perfectly conducted service they ever witnessed.—Letter 43, 1894.

During the camp meeting Ellen White spoke eight times to the congregations in the large tent *(ibid.)*. She also attended and participated in almost all the early-morning devotional meetings, in which she on two occasions read from manuscript prepared there on the grounds on the subject of education.

BUSINESS MEETINGS OF THE AUSTRALIAN CONFERENCE

Throughout the week business meetings of the conference were held in the mornings, with various departments of the work given time for reports, discussions, and plans. Officers were elected for the ensuing year. A. G. Daniells was reelected president of the Australian Conference. Among the actions taken were two relating to the school. They were just in the midst of the period of uncertainty over its location, and the resolutions lacked precision and force:

> *Whereas,* Our educational work is of great importance, and
> *Whereas,* We believe a school for the education of workers, and especially of our young people in the colonies, should be maintained, and properly and permanently located, therefore—
> *Resolved,* That we hereby express regret should there be any unnecessary delay in permanently locating the school, and erecting buildings in harmony with the action taken by the union conference last January. And further—
> *Resolved,* That we approve of the school's being located in a rural district away from the large cities.—BE, Nov. 12, 1894.

THE LAST PUBLIC SERVICE

After a second week of good meetings, the Ashfield camp meeting came to a triumphant close on Sunday with 2,500 people present. Ellen White describes the climaxing service:

> The last public service, on Sunday evening, was one long to

THE AUSTRALIAN YEARS

be remembered. The night was a beautiful one. The walls of the large tent were raised, and extra seats were placed around the outside, yet a large crowd was left standing. Elder Corliss preached upon the glorious appearing of our Lord, and it was just the discourse for the occasion.

The Spirit and power of God were manifested through the human agent. At times the whole congregation was held as if spellbound. Truly many had an opportunity of hearing things strange to them. Yet these were old truths, but placed before the hearers with freshness and power the hearers had never known before.—DF 28a, "Experiences in Australia," p. 789g.

POST-CAMP MEETING EVANGELISTIC MEETINGS

Interest was high when the camp meeting closed. Many requested that the services should not close, so it was decided to move the tent to another location, about a mile distant but with rail connections more convenient to several of the suburbs of Sydney. Corliss and McCullagh were commissioned to continue with meetings nightly; these were well attended. Other workers were drawn in to visit the people in their homes and conduct Bible readings (BE, Dec. 3, 1894).

As various individuals took their stand for the Sabbath, the ire of the Protestant ministers, particularly Wesleyan and Church of England, was stirred up. Ellen White wrote of it:

> Most bitter opposition has been manifested, and the ministers put forth an organized effort to visit every family. They were in possession of Canright's books,* and used them to the utmost to turn away the ears of the people from the truth. There was a meeting appointed, and one of their ministers thought that he had exploded the truth concerning the Sabbath. Our brethren were present to take notes.
>
> Another meeting was appointed in which the ministers, church officials, and those who were troubled over the Sabbath question were invited to assemble. . . . The ministers were ridiculing passages from the Bible which had a bearing on the subject. . . . Brother McCullagh asked if he might speak a few

---

* Books written by D. M. Canright, an apostate Seventh-day Adventist minister.

THE ASHFIELD CAMP MEETING

words, and permission was granted. He gave the true interpretation of the Scriptures which they had garbled.

Then a man by the name of Picton, a Campbellite minister, who was a trained debater, and according to his own opinion, a man of intellectual superiority, challenged our people to meet him in debate on the Sabbath question. We felt very sorry to enter into a discussion on this matter, for generally it leaves an excited state of feeling, but there was no evading the matter. The man boasted that he would wipe out the Seventh-day Adventists, and as God would be dishonored if this proud, boasting Goliath was left to defy Israel, the terms of the debate were agreed upon.—Letter 123, 1894.

THE DEBATE ON THE SABBATH QUESTION

According to the terms agreed upon, six nights would be given to the debate, beginning December 11 and closing December 19. J. O. Corliss would represent Seventh-day Adventists; Mr. Picton, the Protestant churches. Each speaker would have a half-hour to speak on each evening. There was to be no applause. The debate would take place in the Wesleyan church (BE, Dec. 17, 1894).

Ellen White was intensely interested in what was to take place, for when the debate was proposed she was given in vision a preview, together with potential hazards. She described Corliss as "an excellent teacher," able to make things "very plain and interesting," a man able to speak with "power and great clearness" (Letters 39, 1895; 130, 1894). She had been acquainted with him since his boyhood days. She knew him also to be a man of quick temper, high self-esteem, and with a proclivity to lash out at an opponent or supposed opponent. Her great concern was that he should put his full dependence on the Lord and speak with great discretion.

She hastened off an earnest letter warning Corliss that if he were not constantly on guard, making Christ his strength, he would reveal the natural temperament of J. O. Corliss. She urged him to keep in mind that the universe of heaven composed his audience (Letter 130, 1894). "Your only safety," she urged, "is in joining yourself to Jesus and keeping close to His side."—Letter 21a, 1895.

She recounted how Jesus met opposition with "It is written." With a grateful heart Corliss accepted the message of caution. Much

THE AUSTRALIAN YEARS

time was spent in earnest prayer for God's special blessing on his work and that truth might conquer. After the second evening of the debate Ellen White reported:

> The Lord has used Elder Corliss. . . . He has spoken with power and great clearness. Truth is indeed bearing away the victory, and light is shining upon many minds.—*Letter 130, 1894.*
>
> The debater is a clear, moderate-spoken man, but he has arguments weak as weakness itself. I felt and still do feel that much is at stake, depending upon the result of this debate.—*Ibid.*

Some days later she added:

> The discussion lasted six nights. Much prayer was offered to God during this time, and the Lord manifested His special grace and power in presentation of the truth. Error appeared weakness; the truth, strength.—*Ibid.*

Midway in the debate the interest was such that the discussion was moved to a large hall, which was well filled every evening. The minister of the Wesleyan church and Elder McCullagh sat on the stand together with the chairman of the meeting and the two speakers in the debate. Describing Corliss' presentation, Ellen White wrote to Edson:

> He [Corliss] went through the discussion trusting in God, not relying upon himself, and the truth was not dishonored in his hands. The man stood before the people as if bathed in the bright beams of the Sun of Righteousness. He was dignified because he was conscious of the fact that he was the mouthpiece for God.

As she continued, she gave a word picture of changing attitudes on the part of the listeners:

> As the debate continued night after night, the minds of the majority of the people were turned in favor of the truth. There were some who allowed prejudice to control them to such an extent that they would not acknowledge truth even though it was as plain as noonday.
>
> Time and again the chairman had to call the meeting to order

THE ASHFIELD CAMP MEETING

as Brother Corliss showed up the inconsistency of Mr. Picton's arguments, for they were so delighted with the keen, cutting truth that they could not restrain the demonstration of their pleasure. These demonstrations on the part of the people in behalf of the truth made the opposing party feel rather crestfallen, and they insisted that the chairman should hold the meeting to the rules of the debate. . . .

All through the debate Brother Corliss kept insisting that his opponent should produce a text in favor of Sundaykeeping, for the question of the debate was "Do the Scriptures teach that Christians should observe the first day of the week as the Sabbath day?"—Letter 123, 1894.

The debate ended with Elder Corliss exhorting the people, arraigning them before the judgment bar where all would be called to give an account of the way in which they had improved their opportunities and valued their privileges. So impressed was the audience with the outcome of the discussion that they could not be restrained from thunderous applause, and the chairman commented that aside from the spiritual benefits of the discussion, they had enjoyed a rare intellectual treat.

As she recounted the experience, Ellen White reported to Edson:

> They did not take an expression of decision on the merits of the debate; but the applause showed that their sympathies were on the side of the truth.—*Ibid*.

And in a final word she wrote: "As a general thing, a debate kills the interest, but in this case it has not had such an effect. There is still a good attendance at the tent, and about twenty-seven persons have signed the covenant, and there are about twenty more who are keeping the Sabbath that have not yet joined the church. . . . We hope for a good church in Ashfield."

CHAPTER 16
(1894-1895)

"Is There Not a God in Israel?"

THE Ashfield camp meeting closed November 5, 1894, with no decisive action concerning the location of the school. This was most disheartening. From the light given to her there was no question in the mind of Ellen White that the estate at Cooranbong was the place, but several members of the locating committee hesitated and questioned. They battled in their minds between their understanding of Ellen White's clear convictions and their judgments supported by adverse soil reports rendered by the government agricultural experts.

Sunday morning, November 4, the last full day of the camp meeting, Ellen White was certain the time had come for action. That day she wrote, in part:

> This morning as I awoke I was repeating these words to my son Willie:
>
> "Be careful that you do not show any distrust of God in your decisions concerning the land upon which our school should be located. God is your Counselor, and we are always in danger of showing distrust of God when we seek the advice and counsel of men who do not make God their trust, and who are so devoid of wisdom that they do not recognize God as infinite in wisdom. We are to acknowledge God in all our councils. When we ask Him concerning anything, we are to believe that we receive the things we ask of Him.
>
> "If you depend upon men who do not love and fear God, who do not obey His commandments, you will surely be brought into very difficult places. Those who are not connected with God

"IS THERE NOT A GOD IN ISRAEL?"

are connected with the enemy of God, and the enemy will work through them to lead us into false paths. We do not honor God when we go aside to inquire of the god of Ekron."—MS 1, 1895.

In harmony with these deep impressions, Ellen White summoned W. C. White, chairman of the locating committee, and A. G. Daniells. In most earnest tones she demanded of them: "Is there not a God in Israel, that ye have turned to the god of Ekron?"—As told to the author by W. C. White.

The records available seem to indicate that the committee planned to return to Cooranbong to take another look at the Brettville estate. Monday, November 5, she addressed a letter to those who would be going:

Dear Brethren:

As you go to Dora Creek, my prayers shall follow you. This is an important mission, and angels of God will accompany you. We are to watch and pray and believe and trust in God and look to Him every moment. Satan is watching to communicate to you through men those things which will not be in harmony with the mind and will and work of God. Only believe. Pray in faith as did Elijah. Let prayer be the breath of the soul. Where will God direct to locate the school? "The effectual fervent prayer of a righteous man availeth much."—Letter 154, 1894.

In the meantime, however, members of the Foreign Mission Board found it difficult to put out of their minds their knowledge of the fact that Ellen White, with the light given her of God, was firm in the conviction that the Brettville estate at Cooranbong was the place for the school. By formal action they removed their objection to plans to establish the college there. Word to this effect brought courage to the committee on school location in Australia. On November 20, the Australian Union Conference committee took the following action:

Whereas, The Foreign Mission Board has withdrawn its objections to our locating the Australasian Bible School in the Brettville estate at Cooranbong, and . . .

Whereas, We believe that the Brettville estate can be made a suitable place for our proposed school. . . .

THE AUSTRALIAN YEARS

Resolved, That we proceed to the establishment of the Australasian Bible School on the said Brettville estate.—Minutes of the Australasian Union Conference, Nov. 20, 1894, in 5 WCW, p. 197.

CANNING TIME AT THE WHITE HOME

When Ellen White returned from the campground to Norfolk Villa, in Granville, flowers were blooming in all their glory, and the fruit season was coming on. When they had moved to New South Wales ten months earlier, it was near the end of the fruit season. They had to gather odds and ends of everything they could find to get them through the winter. It took some doing to feed a family of a dozen or fifteen adults, with two to four visitors nearly every day. Now as the fruit came on, they prepared to move into a heavy canning program. On Thursday, December 20, as she wrote to Edson and Emma she gave a little insight into the involvements:

> Well, we are now in the midst of fruit canning. We have canned one hundred quarts of peaches and have a case more to can. Emily and I rode out five miles in the country and ordered twelve cases of peaches, one dollar a case. A case holds about one bushel. The ones we canned are the strawberry peach, called the day peach here. . . .
>
> Emily has canned fifty-six quarts today of apricots, and we have twelve cases yet to can. We did have such a dearth of anything in the line of fruit desirable, that we are putting in a good supply.—Letter 124, 1894.

A month later she could report, "We have canned no less than three hundred quarts, and no less than one hundred more will be canned"—some from the peach trees in their little orchard. She commented, "If I continue to keep open a free hotel, I must make provision for the same."—Letter 118, 1895. She reveled in the fruit in the Sydney area, especially the peaches and the grapes.

CORRESPONDENCE WITH JOSHUA V. HIMES

Ellen White continued to meet with the new companies of believers, entertaining those who came to her home. And of course, she kept busy with her heavy correspondence. One letter, written January 17, was addressed to Joshua V. Himes, who in the early

"IS THERE NOT A GOD IN ISRAEL?"

1840s worked closely with William Miller in the Great Second Advent Awakening. Himes was now 89 years of age and at the Battle Creek Sanitarium for treatment of a cancer of his cheek. In attending an evening meeting in the Battle Creek Tabernacle in mid-September, he heard the reading of several letters from Ellen White in which she gave a little report of the work in Australia and made an appeal for financial assistance. The next day he took his pen and wrote to her, recounting briefly some of his experience. "It is more than twenty years," he wrote, "since I met you and James in the Sanitarium and had our last conversation on the Adventist movement." He reported that he had returned to the church affiliation of his childhood, Protestant Episcopal, and was serving as a deacon of St. Andrews church in Elk Point, South Dakota, where he had ministered for fifteen years. He wrote:

> I preach the Advent as being near, without a definite time, and I believe it. I do not look far into the future of the present dispensation. You and your associates have done a great work since 1844, and still go on. . . . Well, I finished my work really in 1844, with Father Miller. After that, what I did at most was to give comfort to the scattered flock. . . .
>
> God bless, and guide you to the end. I enclose five dollars for your own use.
>
> Truly in Christ, J. V. Himes.—September 12, 1894.

Ellen White may have hastened off to Himes a handwritten note thanking him for his letter and the gift, but the typewritten file contains no record. However, Himes wrote her a second letter on November 7, reporting that under Dr. Kellogg's care he was improving in health and hoped soon to be able to return home cured. The believers in Battle Creek had many warmhearted conversations with him concerning the Advent movement, with which he had been so intimately connected. In this letter he wrote:

> My visit here has been very pleasant and I hope a blessing to the waiting ones. You know my mission ended in 1844. I did my work faithfully, and have waited faithfully for the Advent and still wait in hope.
>
> You have your mission with which I have no right to interfere.

THE AUSTRALIAN YEARS

He appended a postscript in which he mentioned a second gift of $40, money he had raised in Battle Creek for the work in Australia. To this Ellen White responded on January 17, 1895:

> My Brother in Christ Jesus,
>
> I received your donation of $40. In the name of our Redeemer I thank you. Be assured we shall invest this money in the best possible way to accomplish the most good for the salvation of souls. . . . It costs money to raise the standard of truth in the "regions beyond." . . . We are working upon missionary soil in the most economical manner to make a little means go as far as possible, but the treasury is often drained in order to supply the necessities of the workers.
>
> The spirited participation evidenced by your donation for this field has rejoiced my heart, for it testifies that you have not lost the missionary spirit which prompted you first to give yourself to the work and then to give your means to the Lord to proclaim the first and second angels' messages in their time and order to the world. This is a great gratification to me, for it bears an honorable testimony that your heart is still in the work; I see the proof of your love to the Lord Jesus Christ in your freewill offering for this "region beyond."—Letter 31a, 1895.

The Battle Creek Sanitarium nurse, Mrs. Austin, who attended Himes at the Sanitarium and reported his death, wrote to Ellen White that he treasured dearly her letter and often said that the work being done by Seventh-day Adventists "was but the continuation of the work he and Father Miller had begun," and if he were 25 years younger, he would take hold with the Seventh-day Adventist Church and do what he could (undated letter attached to J. V. Himes's letter).

THE VISIT FROM MOTHER WESSELS AND HER FAMILY

The visit of members of the Wessels family of South Africa in late December brought joy to Ellen White's heart. There were Mother Wessels, with whom she had had some correspondence; two sons, Daniel and Andrew, ages 16 and 14; and her daughter Annie along with Annie's husband, Harmon Lindsay, and their 4-month-old child (7 WCW, pp. 105, 106). The family were on a one-year

"IS THERE NOT A GOD IN ISRAEL?"

around-the-world trip, timed to give opportunity to attend the 1895 General Conference session to be held in Battle Creek.

The women in the White home were in the midst of canning when Mother Wessels and the family reached Norfolk Villa. Writing of their entertainment, Ellen White declared, "I am glad that I can present the party from Africa plenty of fruit, and plenty of good vegetables fresh from the gardens."—Letter 124, 1894.

"It was our good fortune," wrote W. C. White, "that Mother had a large house, so that we could entertain them all, and we enjoyed the visit immensely."—7 WCW, p. 98. Ellen White noted, "They are very social and enjoy company very much."—Letter 124, 1894. After spending a few days in the White home, they were persuaded to go up to Cooranbong to see the school property, spending a day or two there. White describes the fruitage of that visit:

> They were much pleased with many features of the place and after inquiring into our financial situation, Brother and Sister Lindsay gave us £1,000 [$5,000] toward the enterprise. This was accepted with thanksgiving, knowing that it was providential, and especially as it came at a time when we needed some encouragement.—7 WCW, p. 186.

W. C. White averred that the gift was "wholly unsolicited on our part," and commented, "They saw our needs, and gave according to the liberality of their hearts."—*Ibid.*, p. 99. Tuesday, January 8, the Wessels family sailed from Australian shores to Tasmania, New Zealand, and points east, seemingly carrying with them "very pleasant thoughts" (*ibid.*, p. 98).

DEVELOPMENTS AT COORANBONG

Arrangements had been made by the Foreign Mission Board for a builder, W. C. Sisley, who had been giving counsel on the erection of denominational buildings in England, Denmark, Germany, and South Africa, to spend a little time in Australia working with the brethren in the drawing of plans for school buildings and estimating their cost. He came with the Wessels (BE, Dec. 24, 1894) and threw himself wholeheartedly into the challenge of the task. He worked in Melbourne for nearly a week with Adventist builders called from Tasmania and Adelaide, and then he went up to Cooranbong to

THE AUSTRALIAN YEARS

assist in getting things started there.

In the meantime, Ellen White, sensing the need for rest and a change, decided to go up to Cooranbong for a somewhat extended visit. She hoped to ride around the country in the two-wheeled trap and, having two boats available, to row on the water and see the lake, which she understood to be "very beautiful" (Letter 130, 1895). She took with her May Lacey, her new traveling companion and assistant, and Maude Camp, her cook. She was eager that both these young women receive the benefit of instruction in dressmaking from Mrs. Rousseau. Maude, who was unable to continue to carry the heavy load in the White kitchen, was eager to gain new skills, and May would find a knowledge of sewing to be most useful.

A few weeks before, May Walling had been sent back to America to be on hand if the Walling lawsuit were pushed. W. C. White encouraged his mother to bring May Lacey, whom he had met at the Bible school in Melbourne, into the home in May Walling's place. "I have employed her," wrote Ellen White to Edson while she was at Cooranbong, "and she fills the bill nicely." She commented:

> I soon learned why Willie was anxious for May Lacey. He loved her, and she seems more like Mary White, our buried treasure, than anyone he had met, but I had not the slightest thought when she came to my home. . . . You will have a new sister in a few months, if her father gives his consent. She is a treasure. I am glad indeed for Willie, for he has not had a very happy, pleasant life since the death of Mary.—Letter 117, 1895.

The visit to Cooranbong, aimed largely at affording some change and rest for Ellen White, was cut short by constant rains and threatened floods. So, taking Mrs. Rousseau with them, they started back to Sydney on Tuesday morning, January 22.

THE BAPTISM AT A LAKE

With the progress of the evangelistic work in the Sydney area, there were baptisms, many of them. The first two, resulting from work in the tent in Ashfield, had been conducted in the Baptist church at their invitation. But when some of their key members were rebaptized into the Seventh-day Adventist Church, a tender point was reached, and this privilege was cut off. Ellen White saw it

"IS THERE NOT A GOD IN ISRAEL?"

as a blessing and witnessed a baptism of twenty at a lake, attended by about two hundred persons (MS 60, 1895).

BOOKS FOR NEW BELIEVERS

She wanted to do all she could to bring stability to the experience of the new believers. She sent to the Echo office for a good supply of her books to give to the destitute, determined to supply those who wanted to read but could not buy. "The reading matter treating on present truth," she said, "the people must have."—MS 59, 1895. Reaching out further, she wrote to Lucinda Hall in Battle Creek, asking for bound papers and also books, specified by titles that she could lend or give away (Letter 160, 1895).

The aid she gave in clothes, food, literature, education, and the building of meetinghouses drew heavily on her resources, as did her assuming the support of three workers in the Sydney area that the conference, for lack of means, could no longer employ (Letter 110, 1895).

As to meetinghouses, her investments included:

> One hundred dollars in one, and $150 in another; in four other meetinghouses, £5 each. . . . We have purchased a new tent to be erected in Canterbury, a new location to lift the standard of truth. Five pounds I donated to this enterprise. But I shall continue to invest as long as I can command any means, that the cause of God shall not languish.—Letter 46, 1895.

GOVERNMENT FAVORS AND GRANTS

She longed to get on with her book work, but first came the correspondence. On January 30, 1895, W. C. White read to her a letter he had received from S. N. Haskell, who was spending some months in South Africa. It dealt largely with a matter Haskell wished brought to Ellen White's attention, which was giving him and workers and believers in South Africa considerable concern.

The background was found in actions taken by the General Conference at its session of 1893 aimed at dealing with the separation of church and state and their response to the proposition of a gift of land for a mission station. The British South Africa Company was offering grants of several thousand acres each in

THE AUSTRALIAN YEARS

Mashonaland (known later as Rhodesia and now as Zimbabwe) to mission bodies who would go in, take up the land and cultivate it, and educate the nationals. The brethren in Africa saw in this the providence of God for the advancement of the cause. Peter Wessels, from Africa, attended the General Conference session of 1893 and early in the meeting reported that such land was available to the church.

At the same session, propositions thought to be in the interests of separation of church and state were introduced. These would repudiate tax exemption for church property, insist on paying to the government sums equal to past exemptions, and in addition, endeavor to persuade State legislatures to require the payment of taxes on all church properties regardless by whom held. The session had two issues before it simultaneously. Two days were given to animated discussion, only a part of which was recorded in the *General Conference Bulletin*. The president of the General Conference and a number of his associates were perplexed; they felt some things were being carried to extremes by the religious-liberty men. Nonetheless, the actions taken March 3, 1893, revealed the general trend of the moment:

> *Whereas,* In view of the separation which we believe should exist between the church and the state, it is inconsistent for the church to receive from the state pecuniary gifts, favors, or exemptions on religious grounds, therefore,
>
> *Resolved,* That we repudiate the doctrine that church or other ecclesiastical property should be exempt from taxation, and further,
>
> *Resolved,* That we use our influence in securing the repeal of such legislation as grants this exemption.—GCB 1893, p. 475.

These actions were moderated a day or two later by the following amendment:

> *Whereas,* This conference has clearly stated its position on the taxation of church and other ecclesiastical property, and
>
> *Whereas,* There are certain institutions incorporated under the laws of the state which occupy confessedly disputed grounds, therefore
>
> *Resolved,* That matters in which the taxation of such

institutions as do occupy this disputed territory is involved—orphanages, houses for aged persons, hospitals, et cetera—we leave to the action of the legislature, without any protest against their taxation, or any request for exemption.—*Ibid.*, p. 486.

The debate over accepting the South African land grant grew tense. Peter Wessels told the session "that though six thousand acres of land were offered to any denomination who would inaugurate a mission, and that we expected to accept [the] land for our mission, it was not from the government that we looked for the gratuity, but from a company."—*Ibid.* Developments, however, indicated that the disclaimer was not justified. This matter seemingly was left in the hands of the Foreign Mission Board and took several months to develop fully.

The outcome was that the denomination should not accept the twelve thousand acres offered as a gift, but should pay for whatever was felt would be needed for a mission.

This seemed most unreasonable to the workers and laity in South Africa. On January 1, Haskell wrote to both F. M. Wilcox, secretary of the Foreign Mission Board, and W. C. White for Ellen White's attention, protesting the decision taken in Battle Creek and pointing out the position taken in South Africa in accepting the land. When W. C. White received the letter, he took it immediately to read to his mother, along with the enclosed documents. She took her pen and addressed a letter to Haskell:

> You inquire with respect to the propriety of receiving gifts from Gentiles and heathen. The question is not strange; but I would ask you, Who is it that owns our world? Who are the real owners of houses and lands? Is it not God? He has an abundance in our world which He has placed in the hands of men, by which the hungry might be supplied with food, the naked with clothing, the homeless with homes.
>
> The Lord would move upon worldly men, even idolaters, to give of their abundance for the support of the work, if we would approach them wisely, and give them an opportunity of doing those things which it is their privilege to do. What they would give we should be privileged to receive.

Ellen White pointed out that church workers should become

acquainted with men in high places and "obtain advantages from them, for God would move upon their minds to do many things in behalf of His people." She declared that she had letters to write to the workers in Battle Creek, and continued:

> Our brethren there are not looking at everything in the right light. The movements they have made to pay taxes on the property of the Sanitarium and Tabernacle have manifested a zeal and conscientiousness that in all respects is not wise or correct. Their ideas of religious liberty are being woven with suggestions that do not come from the Holy Spirit, and the religious liberty cause is sickening, and its sickness can only be healed by the grace and gentleness of Christ.

She cited Bible illustrations in which God moved on the hearts of kings to come to the help of His people in ancient times. She added:

> I am often greatly distressed when I see our leading men taking extreme positions, and burdening themselves over matters that should not be taken up or worried over, but left in the hands of God for Him to adjust. We are yet in the world, and God keeps for us a place in connection with the world, and works by His own right hand to prepare the way before us, in order that His work may progress along its various lines.—Letter 11, 1895. (For the full message, see TM, pp. 197-203.)

Copies of this letter to Haskell were sent to F. M. Wilcox, of the Foreign Mission Board, and O. A. Olsen, president of the General Conference. With the exception of one or two men in Battle Creek, it was received with deep gratitude and a sigh of relief. The land grant was accepted in South Africa, and any steps being taken in Battle Creek to adjust the tax-exempt status of churches and institutions were promptly dropped. In an article published in the *Southern Watchman*, March 15, 1904 (quoted largely in *Christian Service*, pp. 167-172, 202, 239), Ellen White elaborated further on the principles involved.

THINGS AT HOME

More correspondence delayed Ellen White's book work. In mid-February, diary entries read:

"IS THERE NOT A GOD IN ISRAEL?"

This day [February 17, 1895] we have earnest work to do to prepare the American mail. Oh, that the Lord will make me a channel of light to impart light to those who need it so much in America! My heart takes in the situation, and I am praying and writing to those who need the letters of encouragement and caution.

February 18: Cannot sleep past 2:00 A.M. . . . It was and ever has been a trying time to send off so large a mail to America, to Africa, and to London, England.

I am writing now upon New Testament subjects on the life of Christ. Fannie [Bolton] will prepare the matter for the papers, and Marian [Davis] will select some portions of it for the book "Life of Christ." Some days my head is weary, and I cannot write much.

February 19: Slept until four o'clock. I praise the Lord when I can sleep, for I am aware I do not get the sleep I should. I cannot write much the last part of the day. The subject I am writing upon is of intense interest—"The Call to the Supper."—MS 59, 1895.

In early April, Ellen White could give a good report on her state of health. "I am glad to inform you," she wrote to Edson and Emma, "that my health, strength, and activity are about equal to what they used to be before my long experience with rheumatism. I can get in and out of a carriage with as much activity as a young girl. . . . I always have to be careful of my right hip, or else I have trouble. . . . But this infirmity does not prevent my activity, except in the matter of taking long walks. . . . If I guard myself diligently, I am able to get about with marked alacrity."—Letter 88, 1895.

It was well that this was so, for a few days later she wrote to Edson that she would soon be off to Tasmania to be present at the wedding that would unite her son William in marriage with May Lacey.

CHAPTER 17
(1895)

Tasmania—The Convention and the Wedding

I AM going to the convention in Tasmania," wrote Ellen White to her son Edson, "and to witness and participate in the marriage of my son Willie to a noble Christian woman.... If Providence favors, you will have a sister of whom you will be proud."—Letter 92b, 1895.

The convention, according to an announcement in the *Bible Echo,* would be the first meeting of its kind to be conducted in that colony. It would be held in Hobart, April 26 to May 6, 1895, and would include instruction on the duties of church officers and members, evening discourses on religious liberty, lessons on various lines of missionary work, and practical instruction given by Mrs. White. The announcement urged, "Let no ordinary obstacle keep you from the meeting."—April 22, 1895.

W. C. White was in New Zealand, accompanied by Elder and Mrs. Corliss and W. A. Colcord, conducting a camp meeting and visiting the churches. From there he would go directly to Tasmania. Ellen White hesitated at first as to whether she should accompany May Lacey, her prospective daughter-in-law, to Hobart, her home city, and at the same time assist at the convention. To Edson she wrote on March 21:

> I hope I shall soon feel decided in regard to what my duty is concerning visiting Tasmania. I am still questioning concerning the matter. May and her father both wish that I would go. If the "Life of Christ" were finished, and if my heart had gained its normal strength, I might feel clearer about visiting Tasmania.—Letter 92a, 1895.

TASMANIA—THE CONVENTION AND THE WEDDING

But on April 4 she found her "health, strength and activity" "about equal to what they used to be" (Letter 88, 1895), and soon she was packing for the month-long trip. On April 11 she wrote to O. A. Olsen:

> I have hesitated a long time in reference to leaving this field and visiting Tasmania. The call is very urgent for me to attend the convention to be held in Hobart. . . . I take the cars accompanied by May Lacey for Tasmania by way of Melbourne. May the presence of the Lord go with me is my most earnest prayer. "Send me not up without Thy presence, O God."—Letter 62, 1895.

Sabbath, April 13, she spoke in Melbourne at the North Fitzroy church to a congregation of more than two hundred. It seemed good to her, after an absence of a year, to be with the believers there, but as they met in a rented hall, their needs stood out in bold relief. As yet, Seventh-day Adventists had no meeting place of their own either in this city, the capital of Victoria, or its suburbs. In addition to this church of more than two hundred members, three others had been raised up as fruitage of the Middle Brighton camp meeting.

The cost of a lot on which to build a house of worship seemed astronomical—$7,000—and this was said to be very reasonable for the area. The 1,450 acres of land recently purchased for the school at Cooranbong in New South Wales had cost $4,500, an amount that seemed barely within their reach. How could a local church raise nearly twice that amount for a lot—in addition to the cost of the building itself? "Let everyone who loves God and professes to keep His commandments practice self-denial and walk by faith," declared Ellen White. She continued:

> We cannot see how it is possible to advance the work, to have the truth go in decency and order, unless we arise and build. But every foot of ground costs from £7 to £10, and unless we have trained ourselves to walk by faith and not by sight, it will seem impossible to push forward the work of building. But there are no impossibilities with God. . . . We must have a house of worship erected in Melbourne, so that those who embrace unpopular truth may feel that they have a church home.—Letter 99, 1895.

THE AUSTRALIAN YEARS

The heart of Ellen White rejoiced as she saw the progress of the message made in Melbourne and its surroundings. But what especially encouraged her was to witness the fruitage of the messages God had given her for N. D. Faulkhead, treasurer of the publishing house. She reported to Olsen:

> I was thankful to see that the testimony of warning and encouragement given to Brother Faulkhead more than two years ago had been fully heeded, and that he had separated himself from the secret society of which he was a member. Jesus had spoken to him as He spoke to the fishermen, saying, "Follow me." . . . He called to him as He had called to Matthew sitting at the receipt of customs, and said, "Follow me." The Lord had a work for this brother to do in His cause, and he heeded the word of invitation.—*Ibid.*

Then she referred to the days of Christ when the people called for a miracle, and she declared that "there is a miracle wrought when a man who has been under strong delusion comes to understand moral truth. He hears the voice saying, 'Turn ye, turn ye . . . ; for why will ye die?' . . . Every time a soul is converted, a miracle is wrought by the Holy Spirit."

ON TO TASMANIA

Ellen White intended to spend most of the week in Melbourne, and appointments were made for her to speak Sunday and Tuesday nights. But then she learned that because of a delay in ship movements, the boat they had intended to take on Thursday afternoon for Launceston, Tasmania, would not sail till Friday, arriving on the Sabbath. She recounted her reaction to this in a letter to Elder Olsen:

> I could not consent to go on this steamer when we should thus have to trespass on the Sabbath, if there was any way possible by which we could avoid it. We learned that a boat left Melbourne Tuesday afternoon, and we decided that it would be much better to get this early boat than to travel on the Sabbath.—Letter 58, 1895.

The voyage was a pleasant one. Arriving at Launceston

TASMANIA—THE CONVENTION AND THE WEDDING

Wednesday morning, the travelers were taken to the Rogers home for lunch, and in midafternoon took the train south 125 miles to Hobart. It was nine o'clock in the evening when they arrived. They were met by May's father, David Lacey, and several members of the family, and were taken to the comfortable and hospitable Lacey home in Glenorchy, just north of the city.

In his younger years David Lacey had filled the post of British Police commissioner at Cuttack, in India, near Calcutta. Here May was born. She attended school in London, and on the retirement of her father joined the family in Tasmania. When colporteurs came to Hobart with *Thoughts on Daniel and the Revelation,* the family gained their introduction to Seventh-day Adventists. The careful follow-up work of evangelists Israel and Starr gathered the entire family into the church—Father and Mother Lacey and the four children, Herbert Camden, Ethel May, Lenora, and Marguerite. The mother died in 1890, and the father had by now married a widow, Mrs. Hawkins, who had four lively daughters and two sons. It was a loving and close-knit family that welcomed the daughter May and Ellen White that Wednesday night.

MEETINGS IN HOBART AND BISMARK

On Sabbath afternoon Mrs. White spoke to the little church group in Hobart, then to a large gathering in the temperance hall Sunday night. On Sabbath morning, April 20, the workers from New Zealand arrived by ship, among them W. C. White. It had been three months since he had parted with his fiancée and his mother at Granville in New South Wales, and this was a happy reunion. As the convention would not open until the next weekend, meetings were planned for the little country Adventist church built at Bismark* in 1889 ten or twelve miles up in the mountains in fruit-raising country.

Ellen White outlined a sketchy word picture of the area in her diary:

> I came eight miles from Brother Lacey's home to this place, right in "the bush," as it is called here. In America we call it the forest. This place is right up in the mountains. In appearance it is

---
*During World War I the community changed its name to the less-provoking Collinsvale.

THE AUSTRALIAN YEARS

very much like Colorado, with its hills and mountains and valleys, and there are houses and small farms of cultivated lands right in the forests. The heavy timbers have been cut away and the underbrush cleared out and orchards have been planted.—MS 54, 1895.

She wrote of how Willie and May and Brother Lacey walked a large part of the way, for it was up quite a steep grade, while she rode with the luggage in the two-wheeled cart or trap furnished by the brethren in Bismark for the transportation of the workers through the week. A nearby cottage had been rented, and this became the headquarters for the visiting workers. Each took his turn in speaking at meetings—Corliss, Colcord, and Ellen White. She spoke Tuesday evening, Wednesday afternoon, and again Thursday evening. She noted in her diary that "the church was only a few steps from the house, so I could return home easily. The weather was beautiful—cool and sunshiny—and the air was fragrant with the blue-gum trees." The highlight of the time in Bismark was the Thursday visit through the country. It was market day for the Adventist farmers, so there was no afternoon meeting. In her diary account she wrote down what she found:

> Thursday we were promised a horse and cart, and rode over the hills to call on some of our people. We found then that it was some miles they had to walk—fathers and mothers and children—to the meetings. Most preferred to walk rather than to drive their horses up and down the steep hills. . . .
>
> In the evening I could better appreciate the congregation who had sufficient interest to come out through the woods so long a distance to meeting. When I saw the bright-faced children and youth interestedly listening to the truth, my heart was full of gratitude to God. Those parents bringing their children the long distance to attend evening meetings evidenced their interest and their love for the truth.—MS 55, 1895.

THE TASMANIA CONVENTION

The convention opened Friday evening, April 26, in a rented hall in Hobart. To carry it through, the two ministers working in Tasmania, Teasdale and Baker, were joined by Corliss, Colcord, W.

TASMANIA—THE CONVENTION AND THE WEDDING

C. White, and Ellen G. White. To ensure a maximum attendance of the church members from outlying communities and especially those from Bismark, Ellen White joined her son in creating a little fund, as she explained to O. A. Olsen, "to remove every obstacle and make it possible for the people to attend. . . . The poor must have the gospel preached to them. It is as necessary to them as to those who are in good circumstances."—Letter 59, 1895.

W. C. White reported that the convention "was well attended, and did much good. But it was too short to accomplish all that we desired."—7 WCW, p. 273. The closing meeting was held on Sunday night, May 5. As they tarried on in Hobart awaiting the wedding of May Lacey to W. C. White on Thursday, earnest committee work was done in planning for the advancement of the cause in Tasmania and throughout the union. As W. C. White had been in New Zealand for three months, there was much to do.

IN ANTICIPATION OF THE WEDDING

The anticipated marriage of Willie White to May Lacey had his mother's hearty approval. In the several months leading up to the wedding, she had frequently spoken and written of the qualities of this young woman about to become her daughter-in-law. "May Lacey," she wrote to Edson, "is like a sunbeam all the time. We appreciate her very much, and Willie will be greatly blessed in his union with her."—Letter 119, 1895. In another letter to Edson she bubbles over as she writes a rather glowing description of May:

> May has been three terms in the school and has developed a talent for a worker, giving Bible readings and visiting. She loves the truth and loves the Lord and is content with anything. Everyone acquainted with her loves her, and everyone who knows of this engagement says she is just the one for Willie White. She is a good performer upon the piano or organ, and reminds me of Mary [W. C. White's first wife] as she acts this part in meeting. She has a powerful voice that can be cultivated.
>
> She loves me and I love her. I wish you could see her. She is about as tall as Mary, her eyes the color of Mary's eyes. She has a similar forehead as Mary had, she is of a sweet disposition, will never stir him up and make him nervous. She is just the one I

should choose. I have not seen anyone I have cared to take Mary's place in my family relation before, but this is all right.—Letter 117, 1895.

A few weeks later, ever becoming better acquainted with May, she extolled her qualities in a letter to Willie:

> She is not one of a painfully sensitive nature who will imagine slights and conjecture many things to feel hurt over. Her sound good sense forbids this. . . . You need exactly such a temperament as May.—Letter 145, 1895.

W. C. White wrote to his brother Edson:

> Do not look for a little sallow, pinched-up body, nor for a "stuck-up" lady. She is a good, big, wholesome woman, as full of life and goodness as can be. May is as tall as I am, and weighs a few pounds more. I tip the scale at 148, and she, at 153. Her vitals have not been crushed by corsets, nor her spirits by idle ambitions. Wherever she is, there is sunshine and comfort and peace.—7 WCW, p. 182.

Ellen White learned that her prospective daughter-in-law had some financial obligations, for two ministers had advanced money to assist in meeting the expense of her schooling. She also observed that because of a stringency of means, May's wardrobe was rather limited. "I will pay the bill of the schooling myself," she wrote to a friend.—Letter 107, 1895. May's father, on a fixed pension in a time of rising costs in living, was unable to give the help he would liked to have done. "We are . . . fitting up her wardrobe," Ellen White wrote, "and we hope she will be prepared for her married life with a real becoming wardrobe, but not expensive or extravagant." Characteristically she added, "You know that is not my besetting sin."—Letter 117, 1895.

THE ETHEL MAY LACEY—W. C. WHITE WEDDING

Although the wedding was planned to follow W. C. White's three-month trip to New Zealand, with the two separated so widely there could be little detailed planning. In fact, when W. C. White arrived in Tasmania on April 20, he did not know whether the

TASMANIA—THE CONVENTION AND THE WEDDING

marriage would take place in Tasmania or on the mainland of Australia. In a letter to his daughter, Ella, he told what took place:

> When we found that her father and sisters wished it to be there, at their home, and that Sister Lacey and her daughters all united in wishing us to have the wedding in Glenorchy, we decided to comply with their invitation and so arranged to be married on Thursday afternoon, May 9, 1895.—7 WCW, p. 273.

Ellen White described the wedding in a letter to Edson and Emma:

> Last Thursday, Willie and May Lacey were united in marriage. Everything passed off pleasantly. The children seemed very earnest that Mother should pray on the occasion, and I complied with their request. The blessing of the Lord was present. Every movement was conducted with the greatest solemnity. She was married from her father's house. . . .
>
> All, every member of the family, dote on May, and they feel highly honored to take in Willie to their family circle. They all highly esteem Willie. He is 40 years old and May is 21.
>
> There was no sentimentalism in their courtship and marriage. Immediately after their engagement, Willie was called to Auckland, New Zealand, camp meeting, and he spent three months visiting the churches. . . .
>
> Willie planned for two weeks' vacation, but did not have any at all. They were married in the afternoon, and Willie had to attend a committee meeting in the evening. Packing was done Wednesday and completed after the wedding.—Letter 120, 1895.

In writing to Ella about the great event, the groom told how the service itself was performed by a Methodist minister, Mr. Palfryman, an old friend of the Lacey family. There was no Seventh-day Adventist minister in that area qualified according to the laws of Tasmania. All went off well. The rooms in the Lacey home were nicely decorated with ferns and flowers. There were ten members of the family present, and eleven friends of the bride who were invited guests. As they were in a British country, they were married with the wedding ring.

THE AUSTRALIAN YEARS

This was a point of some concern to the bride before the wedding. She was aware of Ellen White's counsel addressed to American ministers laboring in Australia, written from Melbourne on August 3, 1892, and published in a pamphlet. Ellen White had found a growing feeling among some of the American workers that the wives of Seventh-day Adventist ministers should, in Australia, wear the ring. She said Americans could make their position clear by stating that "the custom is not regarded as obligatory" in their country, and added:

> I feel deeply over this leavening process which seems to be going on among us, in the conformity to custom and fashion. Not one penny should be spent for a circlet of gold to testify that we are married. In countries where the custom is imperative, we have no burden to condemn those who have their marriage ring; let them wear it if they can do so conscientiously, but let not our missionaries feel that the wearing of the ring will increase their influence one jot or tittle.—*Special Testimonies to Ministers and Workers*, No. 3, p. 6 (TM, pp. 180, 181).

In May Lacey's heart there was no problem relative to this counsel. She had no desire to wear the ring, and so she hesitated about having the wedding in Tasmania, where she knew her father would be greatly disturbed if she did not wear the ring, especially over the fact that she would be traveling on ships and trains with an American almost twice her age. Before consenting to have the marriage at her home, she talked it over with Ellen White, and then on February 13, 1895, wrote to William:

> I have talked with your mother on the matter of a wedding ring and showed her what you said on the subject. She says she has no objection whatever to my wearing one.
>
> To tell you the truth, I had not given that matter very much thought, but I believed that it would be better to have one, as without doubt, in the colonies, if I was to travel with you not wearing the sign that I was your wife, people would be led to imagine all sorts of things, and we should in many instances lose our influence for good that we might otherwise have over the minds of others. I am very glad you look at the matter in the way you do.

TASMANIA—THE CONVENTION AND THE WEDDING

I have wondered sometimes what you thought about it. I feel sure that, as you say, God will not be displeased with me for wearing it.*—DF 121.

After the wedding service everyone was ushered into the dining room, where an attractive wedding supper was waiting for them. By six o'clock most of the friends were gone, and the bride and groom changed from their wedding garments. The bride finished packing, and her husband attended a committee meeting. At eight-thirty, with Ellen White, the couple took the train north to Launceston en route home (7 WCW, p. 274). A profitable weekend was spent in Launceston, the traveling workers meeting with the seventeen newly baptized Sabbathkeepers there. With the children, there were about forty at the Sabbath service who listened to Ellen White speak with freedom from the first chapter of Second Peter. She also spoke to the group on Sunday (Letter 59, 1895).

While on the steamer en route to Melbourne she reflected on the work of the past two or three weeks and wrote in a thirteen-page letter to O. A. Olsen:

> I am glad I have visited Hobart and Bismark. We are now planning to keep the work alive in Tasmania. . . . If anything is to

---

* Years later, W. C. White, on Ellen White's request, responded to an inquiry from a minister's wife in Edinburgh, Scotland, on the point:

"Now regarding the question raised in your letter. The wearing of a gold ring as a matter of ornament is a useless practice, and contrary to the Bible instruction regarding the simplicity of dress and apparel. The wearing of a ring as a token of loyalty in those countries and among those people where such a custom is so thoroughly established that departure from that custom will be universally misunderstood is, in my opinion, quite another matter, and I think that if you should follow the counsel of men and women of experience who have labored in Great Britain and in India, the Lord will not count it to you as a violation regarding the simplicity of women's apparel.

"Possibly you may be interested in the story of my wife's experience with the wedding ring. While she was attending Bible school in Australia, I became well acquainted with her, and when the time drew near for our marriage, I proposed that it be in Tasmania at her father's home. Regarding this she was not enthusiastic, and upon inquiry, I learned that her father had very decided opinions regarding the duty of the wife to wear the wedding ring, and my wife, knowing that Americans looked upon this matter differently than the British people, supposed that I would object.

"She did not care for it personally, but I purchased a ring, and we were married with it because her father's family and all her friends regarded it as essential. After we had been married a few months, and had settled down in our home where we were well known, she laid aside the ring, and when I asked her why she took it off, she said it was in the way when she was washing. I don't know what became of the ring, but she has not worn it since. I think that in this experience it was her desire to follow the instruction of Paul when he wrote, 'Whether therefore ye eat, or drink, or whatsoever ye do, do all to the glory of God.'

"By the wearing of the ring during that portion of our experience where its absence would have been wondered at, and caused unnecessary prejudice, and by laying it aside as soon as that experience was terminated, she has felt that she was doing that which would best serve the cause of our Master."—DF 121, WCW to Mrs. W. E. Ingle, April 14, 1913.

result from our work in Tasmania, the people must have patient instruction, line upon line, and precept upon precept, here a little and there a little. What precious light and clear evidences we have concerning the truth for this time!—*Ibid*.

Good weather attended the traveling group as they left Launceston, but in the open ocean they encountered rough seas, and they arrived at Melbourne two and a half hours late. Ellen White was entertained in the Israel home and the newlyweds at the Faulkhead home. Mail from Granville told of the arrival from America on May 5 of W. C. White's two daughters, Ella, age 13, and Mabel, age 8. The fond grandmother wrote: "Both are pronounced pretty, but Mabel is, they say, very pretty. We have not seen them for three years and a half, so they must have changed greatly. I wish to see them very much."—Letter 120, 1895. But the reunion with the girls had to wait until committee work in Melbourne was completed, and speaking appointments were quickly made for Ellen White in Melbourne and its suburbs.

On Wednesday, May 29, the committee work was finished, and the little party of Ellen White and W. C. White and his wife were on the train bound for Sydney and home in Granville. What a happy reunion it was that Thursday when, after more than three years, Ella and Mabel could embrace father, grandmother, and their new mother, May Lacey-White! Exclaimed Ellen White a few days later:

> You cannot think how pleasant it is to have my family once more reunited. I have not seen more capable, ready, willing, obedient children than Ella May and Mabel. . . . They seem to have excellent qualities of character. W. C. White is more and better pleased with his May. She is a treasure. Mabel gets off such strange, original remarks. She says, "When I heard Father was to marry one only 21 years old, I thought I should see a little bit of a woman. But I did not expect to see such a tall, large woman. And I just said to myself, 'Father has picked out just the one I can love and respect.'" Dear little children. May is proud of them.—Letter 124, 1895.

*E*cho Publishing House, 1894. The offices and factory were on the ground floor, Federal Hall above (top left). First Seventh-day Adventist meetinghouse in New Zealand, at Auckland (bottom).

N. D. Faulkhead in his regalia of an officer of the Masonic Order.

Norfolk Villa, rented home of Ellen G. White and her family at Granville, near Sydney (top). First Seventh-day Adventist house of worship built in continental Australia, in Parramatta, a suburb of Sydney (bottom).

Australian camp meeting held in Melbourne, in the suburb of Balaclava, in 1898 (top). Monument, erected in 1958, to the furrow found by those searching for a school site in 1894 (above). Dora Creek landing; in background, sawmill turned food factory (right).

W. C. White family, 1896. Seated: Ethel May and W. C. White, holding the twins. Standing: Mabel (10) and Ella (14).

*T*he sawmill, first structure erected on the school property. To the right is a two-wheeled "gig" or "trap" (top left). Sunnyside, Ellen G. White's home, with her home and office family. E. G. White is seated and W. C. White is to the right (below).

Bethel Hall, the girls' dormitory. To the left are the kitchen and dining room (top). Early view of Avondale school campus (below).

Central Hall, or Administration Building, Avondale school (top). Avondale school faculty, 1899 (above). Back row, left to right: E. H. Gates, F. W. Reekie, O. A. Morse, H. C. Lacey. Center row: Miss N. Wittenberg, Miss B. Harlow, Mrs. J. S. Reekie, Miss R. Ellis, Mrs. T. Thomas, Mrs. L. Lacey. Front row: C. B. Hughes, Mrs. C. B. Hughes, Mrs. E. R. Palmer, E. R. Palmer (principal).

Avondale school students and faculty in 1898 (top). S. N. Haskell and wife, Hettie (bottom).

Arthur G. Daniells

Miss Emily Campbell

Cassius B. Hughes

Herbert C. Lacey

Dr. Caro

John O. Corliss

Joseph Hare

Albert W. Anderson

A. W. Semmens and his wife, Emma (seated); Nurses Pallant and Redward (standing).

Medical and Surgical Sanitarium in Sydney, 1899 (top). Avondale Health Retreat (bottom).

Avondale church building (top). W. C. White home near Sunnyside (bottom).

Avondale orchard (top). Dora Creek train station (bottom left). Tiglath-Pileser, Sunnyside watchdog (bottom right).

Avondale College campus (c. 1960). Sanitarium Health Food factory, with grain elevators (top center). Dora Creek is at the edge of trees, beyond the food factory.

CHAPTER 18
(1895)

The Beginning at Cooranbong

MONDAY morning, August 19, 1895, Ellen White had won at Cooranbong, living in a tent with her granddaughter Ella. She was exuberant as she took her pen to write to Edson. "Oh, I am so glad, so glad that my warfare is now over!" Paragraph after paragraph bubbled with good news:

> Yesterday, August 18, 1895, the first [fruit] trees were planted on the Avondale tract. Today, August 19, the first trees are to be set out on Mrs. White's farm—an important occasion for us all. This means a great deal to me.

The reason for her exuberance was that planting had begun:

> There was so much doubt and perplexity as to the quality of the land, but the Lord had opened up the matter so clearly to me that when they discouragingly turned from the land, I said, "No? You will not take it? *Then I will take it.*" And with this understanding the land was purchased.
>
> Brethren Rousseau [the man sent to serve as principal] and Daniells [president of the Australian Conference] backed as clear out of the matter as possible, but I knew the Spirit of God had wrought upon human minds. After the decision was made unanimously by several men to buy the land, then to back down and hinder its purchase was a great trial to me—not that I had the land on my hands, but because they were not moving in the light God had been pleased to give me. And I knew their unbelief and unsanctified caution were putting us back one year.—Letter 126, 1895.

THE AUSTRALIAN YEARS

Ellen White then told of the turnaround in Professor Rousseau's thinking. He acknowledged that "he was now perfectly satisfied for himself in his own mind this was the place God designed the school should be established." A favorable attitude on the part of the school leaders was highly important. They must put their whole hearts into it. Rousseau pointed out to Ellen White:

> There are advantages here that they could not have in any other location they had visited, and the land they had thought so bad was found, on working it, not to be the best land, but average. Good portions are adapted for fruit, especially peaches, apricots, nectarines, and other fruit, while other portions of land were favorable for vegetables.
>
> The twenty-five acres pronounced worthless because [it was] swampland would, they thought, prove the most valuable land.—*Ibid.*

There was an acquiescence also in Elder Daniells' attitude, expressed to Ellen White there at Cooranbong. He still entertained some misgivings as to the quality of the soil. He confided in a July 17 letter to the president of the General Conference that he would be glad if the soil proved "a hundred times more valuable than it appears to me"(DF 170, "The Avondale School, 1895-1907"). Ellen White wrote to Edson of his visit:

> Elder Daniells came on the land en route from Queensland to Melbourne. He called at Cooranbong and visited the land and expressed great pleasure at every part of the work that has been done in clearing and ditching the swamp that is usually several feet under water.—Letter 126, 1895.

"Now, Edson," she triumphantly declared, "you can judge what relief this gives me, after tugging and toiling in every way for one year to help them to discern the mind and will of God, and then after abundant research finding nothing on the whole as good as this, they accept it. Oh, I am so glad, so glad!"—*Ibid.*

HOW THE BEGINNINGS WERE MADE

After spending the month of June at her Granville home, assisting in the work with the new companies of believers being

THE BEGINNING AT COORANBONG

raised up, planning for the evangelistic thrust in Sydney, and writing energetically, Ellen White felt much worn and was eager for a change that could come by being at Cooranbong. So Monday morning, July 1, with W. C. White and his family, she took the train for Cooranbong, and stayed for three weeks, at first in the home of Herbert Lacey, newly come from America. They found twenty-six boys and young men living in the rented hotel building, and some sleeping in tents. They were clearing the land and building roads and bridges, making a beginning for the school. On February 25, Professor Rousseau had sent a letter to the churches announcing plans and inviting young men to come to the school and engage in a program of work and study. Each student would work six hours a day, which would pay for board, lodging, and tuition in two classes.

On March 5 the manual training department opened, but it was without much support at first. In his efforts to get things moving at the school, W. C. White had been talking of such a plan for several months, and he wrote:

> You would be surprised to learn of the criticism, the opposition, and the apathy against which the proposition had to be pressed. The board said it would not pay, the teachers feared that it would be for them much labor with small results, and in many cases, the friends of those for whom the department was planned criticized severely, saying that young men would not feel like study after six hours of hard work.—8 WCW, p. 32.

THE MANUAL TRAINING DEPARTMENT SUCCEEDS

But after watching the program in operation for six weeks, Ellen White could report:

> About twenty-six hands—students—have worked a portion of the time felling trees in clearing the land, and they have their studies. They say they can learn as much in the six hours of study as in giving their whole time to their books. More than this, the manual labor department is a success for the students healthwise. For this we thank the Lord with heart and soul and voice. The students are rugged, and the feeble ones are becoming strong. Such wild young lads as _____ _____, under the discipline of labor, are becoming men. He is becoming a

THE AUSTRALIAN YEARS

Christian, transformed in character. Oh, how thankful are his parents that he is blessed with this opportunity!—Letter 126, 1895.

A week later she wrote enthusiastically to Dr. Kellogg:

These students are doing their best to follow the light God has given to combine with mental training the proper use of brain and muscle. Thus far, the results have exceeded our expectations. At the close of the first term, which was regarded as an experiment, opportunity was given for the students to have their vacation and engage in whatever work they chose to do. But everyone begged that the school might be continued as before, with manual labor each day, combined with certain hours of study. . . .

The students work hard and faithfully. They are gaining in strength of nerve and in solidity as well as activity of muscles. This is the proper education, which will bring forth from our schools young men who are not weak and inefficient, who have not a one-sided education, but an all-round physical, mental, and moral training.

The builders of character must not forget to lay the foundation which will make education of the greatest value. This will require self-sacrifice, but it must be done. . . . Under this training, students will come forth from our schools educated for practical life, able to put their intellectual capabilities to the best use.—Letter 47a, 1895.

METCALFE HARE JOINS THE STAFF

Carrying heavy responsibilities was Metcalfe Hare, of Kaeo, New Zealand. Hare had attended the New Zealand camp meeting held in February at Epsom. There W. C. White pushed the school matter hard. He found Hare deeply interested. Of Hare's eagerness to be a part of the program, White wrote to his mother:

I am very much pleased at the interest that Brother Metcalfe Hare takes in the school work. He is ready, if we think best, to close up his business in Kaeo, and move to Avondale. He will move on his own responsibility, and hold himself ready to act a

THE BEGINNING AT COORANBONG

part in our work of preparing for the school, erecting the buildings, or anything that may be needed. But if we do not wish to employ him, he will engage in work on his own account till school opens, and then he will enter as a student. . . .

It seems to me that he is the right sort of man to stand by the side of Rousseau as a worker and counselor. . . . His whole heart seems to go out to the school, and I believe that the Lord has been fitting him up to help us in this time when we need a man that can do many things at once.—7 WCW, p. 160.

Reporting to the Foreign Mission Board, White wrote in rosy terms of Hare's qualifications:

He has had lots of experience clearing land, and also in handling timber. He has had full experience in running a sawmill. He can build a house or a boat, and has had much experience as salesman, and can keep books. He is a close, conservative man, and may lack breadth in his plans. But he has a high regard for Brother Rousseau, and this would help him some. It appears to me that Rousseau and Hare would make a good team to work together in clearing, making roads, putting up the workshop, and getting material for the girls' hall ready for the builder.—*Ibid.*, p. 188.

At the New Zealand camp meeting White also found a number of young men eager to enter the industrial department. One was a brickmaker, another a tentmaker, still another, a stonecutter.

When Ellen White and W. C. and his family came onto the school grounds in early July, Metcalfe Hare was there managing a team of a dozen or more young men, Rousseau was managing a similar group in their work on the land, and good progress was being made.

On July 6, 1895, the church service was held in the long, narrow dining room of the hotel. Ellen White spoke, and then they organized a church of twenty-five members and chose two elders and two deacons (Letter 88a, 1895; MS 61, 1895).

ELLEN WHITE BUYS ACREAGE FROM THE SCHOOL

From the very first, as the plans began to develop for the use of the 1,450 acres of the Brettville estate, it was calculated that some of

THE AUSTRALIAN YEARS

the land would be sold to Adventist families. By July, 1895, there was talk of some 120 acres being thus disposed of. On Sunday morning, July 7, Ellen White negotiated for the first of such land to be cut off from the estate, forty acres on the north side of the tract. For this she paid $1,350. "The reason I purchase now," she wrote, "is that I may furnish money which they [those connected with the school] need so much just now."—MS 61, 1895.

She planned to leave some of the land as woodland, use some for grazing, and some for orchard and garden. Of course, a select spot would go for the homesite (Letter 88a, 1895).

For some time she had felt that she should have her home in a location more conducive to her writing than the large rented house at Granville. There it seemed inevitable that she must run what seemed to be a "free hotel," with people coming and going almost every day. Now she determined to build a little cottage where such demands could not be made upon her; she also determined to develop a portion of her land in such a way as to provide an object lesson of what could be done in agricultural lines in that area. It was mid-July, and on inquiry she learned that whatever was to be done in planting an orchard must be accomplished in the next few weeks.

As the forty acres came into her possession, the first step in developing her little farm was the clearing of the land for the orchard. Soon there were three good-sized tents on her land. She and her granddaughter Ella lived in one, and also much of the time one of her woman helpers. Another of the tents was used for cooking and dining, and the third was occupied by some of the men working on her land (8 WCW, p. 31).

Mr. Caldwell, somewhat of an all-round man who assisted at her Granville home, was instructed to come, bringing her team and the platform wagon. It was a seventy-five-mile trip, but it was convenient to have the transportation she needed at Cooranbong (Letter 88a, 1895).

On a quick trip to Granville late in July, with Hare, Rousseau, and W. C. White, she spent a day driving around seeking information on securing fruit trees and orchard planting. The tour included stops at the Radley place, where there was a fine, well-kept orchard, and the Whitman home. It turned out to be a missionary visit as well, for Whitman was losing his grip on the message, and

THE BEGINNING AT COORANBONG

Radley had only partially received the truth. Tuesday, July 30, she went into Sydney. Here is her description of the day's activities as found in her diary:

> I went into Sydney to see if I could find anything for the poor families, cheap. Money is so scarce we hardly know what to do and which way to turn to supply the demands in a variety of lines. The calamity of failure of banks has been and still will be keenly felt. We watch our chances where goods are offered for half price and purchase most excellent material to give to those who cannot buy that which they need. We are oft distressed at the sight of our eyes. I never have seen anything like it.—MS 61, 1895.

On Wednesday, the last day of July, they were shopping again:

> All day, W. C. White, Emily, and I spent in Sydney purchasing the things essential for our use in camp life. We thought it wisdom to select an outfit of granite ware [enameled cooking utensils] that will bear transporting and handling.—*Ibid.*

Royalty income and some borrowing made it possible for Ellen White to do what others could not do in missionary lines.

PLANTING AND BUILDING AT COORANBONG

Two things were on Ellen White's mind as she hastened back to Cooranbong—the planting of the orchard and the construction of a humble dwelling. The preparation of the land and planting had the priority. Right after she returned, W. C. White learned that J. G. Shannon, a good Adventist builder from Tasmania, was in Sydney looking for work. For the Whites it seemed most fortunate, for they were at a loss to know who to get to put up the home on the land just purchased. For eight shillings ($2) a day, this master builder was employed and dispatched to Cooranbong to begin work on a five-room cottage (8 WCW, p. 46). Ellen White wrote of the activities at her place:

> Today [Sunday] I am rushing the workmen on preparing ground for the orchard. We have today captured a part of the

students' manual training company to clear the land for fruit trees which must be set this week and next, or give up the matter and lose one year.

Emily and I are driving a span of horses hither and thither and are hunting for cows and gathering all the information possible in regard to planting, growing, et cetera. . . .

Log heaps are burning all around us. . . . Immense trees, the giants of the forest, lie cut up by the roots all around us. It takes days to cut out one big tree. We are indeed in the very midst of clearing and burning the greatest trees I ever saw.

I came up here really sick, but I am giving orders to my hired businessman . . . to rush the work . . . , for the trees must be planted without delay. Every other business stands aside now. I wish to provoke the workers on the school grounds to do something and do it *now* and not lose one year by delay.—Letter 125, 1895.

COUNSEL AND HELP FROM AN EXPERIENCED ORCHARDIST

In search for information and guidance in putting in the orchards on her little farm and on the college estate, they were directed to a Mr. Mosely, a successful fruit grower. In a letter written Sunday, August 4, Ellen White told of how he was "coming in one week to see all the trees set properly and staked properly" and observed, "I shall have most careful work done."—*Ibid.* Feverishly they pushed the work of clearing the land for the orchard and garden—three acres (Letter 126, 1895). Ellen White picks up the story on Tuesday and writes of what was ahead:

Brother Lawrence's hands are helping to clear the land, and good work is being done. The trees are ordered of Mosely, and he will be here on Sunday and he wants every student to be on hand to see how he does the setting of the trees, and help him, and he says he will give talks to the students in the evening upon the subject of fruit raising and vegetable raising, if they wish him to. . . .

I shall have the privilege of experimenting in reference to Mr. Mosely, who promises to look after the trees. I think he will have a determination to do his best for me. . . . We will do our best, and

THE BEGINNING AT COORANBONG

if we make some mistakes we will know better next time. The men work for me with decided interest.—Letter 149, 1895.

On several occasions Mr. Mosely came over to plant trees and give instruction on orchard planting and care. The virgin land was well prepared. It took six span of bullocks pulling an immense plow to break up the unworked soil. As she watched, Ellen White marveled, and wrote that the bullocks were "under discipline, and will move at a word and a crack of a whip, which makes a sharp report, but does not touch them" (Letter 42, 1895). At an early point in the tree planting, she had some input, about which she reminisced a little more than a decade later:

> While we were in Australia, we adopted the . . . plan . . . of digging deep trenches and filling them in with dressing that would create good soil. This we did in the cultivation of tomatoes, oranges, lemons, peaches, and grapes.
>
> The man of whom we purchased our peach trees told me that he would be pleased to have me observe the way they were planted. I then asked him to let me show him how it had been represented in the night season that they should be planted.
>
> I ordered my hired man to dig a deep cavity in the ground, then put in rich dirt, then stones, then rich dirt. After this he put in layers of earth and dressing until the hole was filled. . . . He [the nurseryman] said to me, "You need no lesson from me to teach you how to plant the trees."—Letter 350, 1907.

On through August the tree planting went. The men working on Ellen White's "farm" vied with the men at the school to see who could get the trees in first. The men at the school won out by one day, but it was not Ellen White's fault that her work lagged. At school they had been working for weeks clearing the land and getting ready. At her place, it had to be done in days. The school planted twelve acres of trees; Ellen White planted two (Letter 42, 1895). On August 19 she reported to Edson:

> Mr. Smith [not an Adventist], who has recently moved to Cooranbong, is interested in the truth. He was on the ground receiving all the instruction possible from the lessons given by Mr. Mosely, the fruit grower. The keeper of the police station

was on the ground, and both these lookers-on begged for Brother Rousseau to sell them a few trees—on Sunday, mind you—which he did. We are seeking to be friendly with all.—Letter 126, 1895.

Thus from the very start, Ellen White was able to accomplish one of her objectives: to teach the people in the community what could be done by employing intelligent agricultural procedures. This was not just her own determined, ambitious plan. "The light given me from the Lord," she told Edson, "is that whatever land we occupy is to have the very best kind of care and to serve as an object lesson to the colonials of what the land will do if properly worked."—*Ibid.* And she wrote a few days later to Dr. J. H. Kellogg:

The cultivation of our land requires the exercise of all the brainpower and tact we possess. The lands around us testify to the indolence of men. We hope to arouse to action the dormant senses. We hope to see intelligent farmers, who will be rewarded for their earnest labor. The hand and head must cooperate, bringing new and sensible plans into operation in the cultivation of the soil.—Letter 47a, 1895.

In another communication she wrote:

We shall experiment on this land, and if we make a success, others will follow our example. . . . When right methods of cultivation are adopted, there will be far less poverty than now exists. We intend to give the people practical lessons upon the improvement of the land, and thus induce them to cultivate their land, now lying idle. If we accomplish this, we shall have done good missionary work.—Letter 42, 1895.

She was on the lookout for the best of seeds, most of which had to come from Sydney, but choice tomato seed she secured from one of her neighbors. She recognized that they would at times err, working as they were in unfamiliar territory:

Mistakes will often be made, but every error lies close beside truth. Wisdom will be learned by failures, and the energy that will make a beginning gives hope of success in the end. Hesitation will keep things back, precipitancy will alike retard,

THE BEGINNING AT COORANBONG

but all will serve as lessons if the human agents will have it so.—Letter 47a, 1895.

Rather jubilantly she could write to Dr. Kellogg in late August of the influence of her work at Cooranbong, and of the appraisal of one expert on the quality of the land, a point her ears were attuned to:

> I came to this place, and began work on my place so earnestly that it inspired all with fresh zeal, and they have been working with a will, rejoicing that they have the privilege. We have provoked one another to zeal and good works.
>
> The school workers were afraid I would plant the first trees, and now both they and I have the satisfaction of having the first genuine orchards in this vicinity. Some of our trees will yield fruit next year, and the peaches will bear quite a crop in two years. Mr. Mosely, from whom we bought our trees, lives about twenty miles from here. He has an extensive and beautiful orchard. He says that we have splendid fruitland.
>
> Well, the school has made an excellent beginning. The students are learning how to plant trees, strawberries, et cetera.—Letter 47a, 1895.

BUYING COWS

Mrs. White also needed cows to provide a supply of milk and cream. In a letter written to friends in the United States she described the venture to supply the needs in this line:

> I drive my own two-horse team, visit the lumber mills and order lumber to save the time of the workmen, and go out in search of our cows. I have purchased two good cows—that is, good for this locality.
>
> Almost everywhere in the colonies they have a strange custom of confining the cow at milking time. They put her head in a fixture called a bail, then tie up one of her legs to a stake. It is a barbarous practice.
>
> I told those of whom I bought my cows that I should do no such thing, but leave the creatures free, and teach them to stand still. The owner looked at me in astonishment. "You cannot do this, Mrs. White," he said; "they will not stand. No one thinks of

doing it any other way." "Well," I answered, "I shall give you an example of what can be done."

I have not had a rope on the cows' legs, or had their heads put into a bail. One of my cows has run on the mountains till she was 3 years old, and was never milked before. The people have not the slightest idea that they can depart from their former practices, and train the dumb animals to better habits by painstaking effort. We have treated our cows gently, and they are perfectly docile. These cows had never had a mess of bran or any other prepared food. They get their living by grazing on the mountains, and the calf runs with the cows. Such miserable customs! We are trying to teach better practices.—Letter 42, 1895.

A START WITH BUILDINGS FOR AVONDALE COLLEGE

Land had been cleared on a high rise in the ground with the hope that when funds were available, a beginning could be made in putting up school buildings. The master plan worked out by W. C. Sisley and adopted by the union conference committee called for three buildings as a beginning—the central building for administration and classrooms, flanked on either side at a distance of one hundred feet by dormitories for the young men and the young women. These were to be erected on what L. J. Rousseau described in his letter to the churches, dated February 25, 1895, as "one of the prettiest elevations that could be found in the whole vicinity."—DF 170, "The Avondale School, 1895-1907."

But before there could be buildings, there had to be lumber, milled from trees cut from their forest. This called for a sawmill. W. C. White, writing to his brother Edson on August 3, described plans for the building to house the mill. He reported:

> Brethren Rousseau and Metcalfe Hare have been in Sydney for two weeks buying building materials, horses, wagons, farming implements, fruit trees, et cetera, et cetera. . . . Last night we advertised for a boiler, engine, circular saw, planer, turning lathe, and for a brickmaking plant.—8 WCW, p. 31.

He commented, "We shall have very busy times at Avondale for the next few months."

THE BEGINNING AT COORANBONG
ELLEN WHITE CONTINUES TO WRITE

As the work of clearing land and planting trees on "Ellen White's farm" continued in the weeks of early spring, and the construction of her little home progressed, she stood by to serve in running errands for the workmen to save their time. Yet she pressed in a little writing.

Starting almost from scratch, as it were, in early August, the men made considerable progress on "the farm," and the foundation was in for the house (Letter 156, 1896). Her August 28 description of the little camp at Sunnyside is revealing:

> I am seated on the bed writing at half past 3:00 A.M. Have not slept since half past one o'clock. Ella May White and I are the sole occupants of a large, comfortable family tent. Close by is another good-sized tent, used as a dining room. We have a rude shanty for a kitchen, and a small five-by-five storeroom. Next is another tent, which accommodates three of my workmen. Next is a room enclosed but not finished, for washhouse and workshop. This is now used as a bedroom by two men, Brother Shannon, my master builder, and Brother Caldwell. These five men we board. Several others are at work on the land who board themselves. Fannie Bolton occupies another tent, well fitted up with her organ and furniture. You see we have quite a village of tents.—Letter 42, 1895.

She could write to Elder Olsen, "I have been enjoying tent life for four weeks."—Letter 64a, 1895.

But tent life for her and some of her helpers ended in early September as she returned to her Granville home.

CHAPTER 19

(1895)

Travels in the Last Few Weeks of 1895

"LORD, help me," Ellen White cried out in prayer Friday morning, October 11, 1895, as she tossed sleeplessly on her pillow in her Granville home. She was suffering weakness, physical and mental exhaustion. Discouragement swept over her. She was wrestling with the decision as to whether she should attend the third Australian camp meeting to be held in Melbourne a week later. Would she be able to go? Would she be able to preach if she did go? It was past the midnight hour, and she had just conversed with God:

> Lord, help me. I am determined to cast my helpless soul upon Thee. Satan is the destroyer. Christ is the Restorer. This is Thy word to me. I will try to walk by faith.
>
> The appointments have been made for me to go [on Sabbath] to Sydney, and in order to do this I must go with my horse and carriage, to save any confusion and unfit me to speak. If it is Thy will that I attend the Melbourne meeting, strengthen me to ride twelve miles to Sydney and bear my testimony and strengthen me to give the dedicatory talk [at Ashfield] on Sunday.—Letter 114, 1895.

As she had done so many times before, she decided to move out by faith. Sabbath morning, feeling confident in making this test that the Lord would be her helper and that strength would come, she started on the twelve-mile drive to the city. A day or two later she wrote of the experience to Edson:

> The way was long, but I went trusting in God, and while

speaking I received special strength. A change came to nerve and muscle, and to my soul.

After I had ceased speaking in regard to grace being always proportioned to the trial God gives us to bear, I was led out to speak upon the faith given all who talk faith and encourage faith. They will have faith and increasing faith that will not waver, but remain steadfast, immovable.—*Ibid.*

With strength newly imparted, she was able Sunday afternoon to give the dedicatory address in the newly built Ashfield church. Since the camp meeting held there the last October, more than one hundred had embraced the message, and a new house of worship had been built. It was a growing church; six more were to be baptized on the day of dedication. Evangelistic camp meetings had again proved the most fruitful thrust in building up the cause in Australia. Now Ellen White, having the evidence that she called upon God to give her, turned to preparation for the journey to Melbourne for the camp meeting. From there she would go on to Tasmania for a similar but smaller gathering. She would have to leave Sydney the coming Thursday afternoon. Accompanying her would be her son W. C. White; his wife, May; a secretary, Maggie Hare; and Sara McEnterfer, who that very week had arrived from the United States to assist Ellen White. She had traveled with her and assisted her both in America and Europe and had just come to Australia at Ellen White's request.

THE ARMADALE CAMP MEETING

The camp meeting in Melbourne, scheduled for October 17 to November 11, opened in the suburb of Armadale on Friday, the day the Whites arrived, and Ellen White spoke Sabbath afternoon. Sunday the interest was good and the attendance large, J. O. Corliss speaking in the morning, Mrs. E. G. White in the afternoon, and Prof. W. W. Prescott in the evening (BE, Oct. 28, 1895).

In the initial plans for this, the third Australian camp meeting, it was thought it might be held at Ballarat, some ninety miles north of Melbourne. The conference was in debt, and it would be less expensive to hold a meeting there than in Mebourne. But in response to light given to Ellen White that the message must now go to the people in the large cities, it was decided to select an appropriate site in Melbourne where they would benefit from the work at Middle Brighton the year before. It seemed that they were providentially led to Armadale, declared to be "one of the most inviting suburbs of Melbourne," and a choice site was found on which to pitch the tents. In advance of the meeting, a special "camp meeting edition" of the *Bible Echo* was published and widely distributed. The issue carried notice of the speakers who would address the crowds:

> Professor [W. W.] Prescott, educational secretary of the denomination, who is on tour through Australasia, South Africa, and Europe, in the interests of the school work, will be present, and will take an active part in this meeting.
>
> Mrs. E. G. White, a speaker and writer of rare experience, is to be present. . . . Among her published works, *The Great Controversy Between Christ and Satan, Patriarchs and Prophets,* and *Steps to Christ* are widely circulated in all English-speaking countries, and translated into many foreign tongues. Her long and wide experience makes her labours of special value. Mrs. White will probably speak each Saturday and Sunday afternoon during the meeting.
>
> Pastor J. O. Corliss, one of the first to introduce the views and work of the denomination in the colonies, will take a prominent part in the evening discourses on the prophecies of the Bible and the signs of the times.—September 23, 1895.

Others mentioned in this sheet, advertising the meeting were W. A. Colcord, editor of the *Bible Echo,* and Dr. M. G. Kellogg, who had been spending some time in the South Pacific.

A UNIQUE AND SUCCESSFUL CAMP MEETING

Ellen White was provided with a little rented cottage about three minutes' walk from the campground, where she could rest and work (8 WCW, p. 363). She wrote a report of the camp meeting for the January 7, 1896, *Review and Herald* in which she declared:

> During the meeting we have had abundant evidence that the Lord has been guiding both in the location and in the work of the meeting. A new field has been opened, and an encouraging field it appears to be. The people did not swarm upon the ground

from curiosity, as at our first meeting in Brighton, and as at Ashfield last year. The majority came straight to the large meeting tent, where they listened intently to the Word, and when the meeting was over, they quietly returned to their homes, or gathered in groups to ask questions or discuss what they had heard.

As she continued, she wrote of the topics of the evening discourses delivered by Prescott, Corliss, and Daniells:

> All presented the truth as it is in Jesus Christ. . . . In every sermon Christ was preached, and as the great and mysterious truths regarding His presence and work in the hearts of men were made clear and plain, the truths regarding His second coming, His relation to the Sabbath, His work as Creator, and His relation to man as the source of life appeared in a glorious and convincing light that sent conviction to many hearts.

There were not sufficient seats in the tent to accommodate the people who came to the evening meetings, and many stood outside.

Having discovered the great value of the evangelistic camp meeting as held in New Zealand and Australia in 1893 and 1894, the initial plans for this meeting called for a convocation of three weeks' duration. During the mornings of the first week, sessions of the Australian Conference and the Australasian Union Conference were held.

Writing in the very midst of the camp meeting, W. C. White reported to Abram La Rue working in Hong Kong:

> Yesterday afternoon our large eighty-foot tent was crowded full, and about four hundred stood outside. Mother spoke with power, and many were deeply impressed. In the evening also the tent was packed as full as it could be, and some scores stood around outside. Elder Prescott spoke. "Christ and the Sabbath" was his theme. Some whom I have met today say he was inspired. Certainly he spoke with great clearness and power, and never in my life did I see an audience listen as his audience listened last night.
>
> During the week the attendance averages about one hundred in the afternoon and three hundred in the evening. Everything

about the management of the ground is moving along pleasantly. Quite a large number are spending their afternoons visiting the people and inviting them to the meetings. My wife is out engaged in this kind of work this afternoon.—8WCW, p. 368.

PRESCOTT'S EFFECTIVE PREACHING

Again and again in her report Ellen White mentioned the effectiveness of W. W. Prescott's meetings, stating that "the Lord . . . has given Brother Prescott a special message for the people," the truth coming from human lips in demonstration of the Spirit and power of God. Those attending, she said, exclaimed:

> You cannot appreciate the change of feeling about your meeting and work. It has been commonly reported that you do not believe in Christ. But we have never heard Christ preached as at these meetings. There is no life in our churches. Everything is cold and dry. We are starving for the Bread of Life. We come to this camp meeting because there is food here.—RH, Jan. 7, 1896.

"On every side," she wrote, "we hear discussion of the subjects presented at the camp meeting." She told the readers of the *Review* of how Corliss, stepping out of a train, was stopped by the conductor, who hurriedly asked him to explain certain Scripture texts. While the crowd rushed by, Corliss gave the conductor a hasty Bible study. By earnest and urgent request the three-week camp meeting was stretched into a successful five-week evangelistic series. Ellen White spoke twenty times at length and many times twenty or thirty minutes (Letter 105, 1895). It was difficult for her to find words to describe her ecstasy as it related to the meetings and the response. To S. N. Haskell she wrote:

> The Word is presented in a most powerful manner. The Holy Spirit has been poured out upon Brother Prescott in great measure. . . . Brother Prescott has been bearing the burning words of truth such as I have heard from some in 1844. The inspiration of the Spirit of God has been upon him.
>
> Unbelievers say, "These are the words of God. I never heard such things before." Every evening the tent is full, and even on weekdays there is an intense interest to come out and hear the truth.—Letter 25, 1895.

TRAVELS IN THE LAST FEW WEEKS OF 1895

In the light of the above, Ellen White's urging in 1909 that Prescott enter evangelistic work in the large cities is easily understood.

In another communication Ellen White made an interesting observation: "We cannot now gather in the sheaves. It takes the people in the colonies a long time to make up their minds to obey; but while the interest is at its height, we cannot move our place of meeting."—Letter 51, 1895. "Three weeks this meeting has been in session," she wrote to Haskell, "and the camp meeting proper will not close until next week, Tuesday or Wednesday. Then if the same interest is manifested, the tent will remain on the ground two weeks longer, and as many as choose may remain in their tents to attend the meetings. At the close of the two weeks, Professor Prescott and my family, W. C. White and wife, and my two workers will go to Tasmania."—Letter 25c, 1895.

THE BUSINESS MEETINGS

Important advances were made in the business meetings of the Australian Conference and also in the business meetings of the new Australasian Union Conference in its first biennial session, all held during the extended camp meeting. One action called for an outreach in Australia in medical missionary lines, a project in which Ellen White would become rather deeply involved. Early in the meeting, the six churches in New South Wales were organized into a separate conference, with a church membership of 321. Their petition to the union conference read:

> Dear Brethren:
> A conference having been organized for the colony of New South Wales, we respectfully request that it be received into the union conference, to be under its care and to be represented in its councils.—9 WCW, p. 6.

The request was granted. This was the first local conference in the history of Seventh-day Adventists to be admitted into a union conference instead of the General Conference. The work in Australia was taking shape.

Another important action had to do with the development of the educational work and the new school at Cooranbong. Among the

THE AUSTRALIAN YEARS

resolutions adopted was one calling for the name of the educational institution to be the Avondale School of Christian Workers.

After the close of the camp meeting proper, Ellen White remained in Melbourne writing and occasionally speaking. Maggie Hare and Sara McEnterfer were both with her. Sunday, November 24, with Sara's help they got off the American mail. She opened her heart in her letter to Edson: "Since coming to this meeting I have felt that unless the Lord shall help me, I shall utterly fail. I have been brought into great trial and perplexity and distress of soul through others."—Letter 82, 1895. One of her helpers, Miss Fannie Bolton, sent with her to Australia to assist in the preparation of Ellen White's materials for publication in the journals of the church, had insisted on coming to Melbourne and was not acting as a faithful, trusted helper. More will be said about this in the next chapter.

THE TASMANIA CAMP MEETING

On Tuesday, November 26, her sixty-eighth birthday, which she entirely forgot until a day or two later, Ellen White took the train and then the boat for Hobart, Tasmania, where the camp meeting was to open on Thursday, November 28. The camp was pitched across the street from the post office in Newtown, a suburb two miles from the center of Hobart. Pleased with the campground, Ellen White gave a description in her report to the *Review and Herald:*

> It was elevated considerably above the surrounding streets, and was reached by a flight of steps. A hawthorn hedge formed the enclosure, so that the encampment was hidden until we reached the entrance. Then the white tents, in their orderly arrangement in that grassy retreat, were an attractive sight.
>
> Hobart is surrounded by hills, rising one above another, and stretching away in the distance. Often they brought to our minds those precious words, "As the mountains are round about Jerusalem, so the Lord is round about his people from henceforth even for ever."—February 11, 1896.

There were thirty-two family tents on the grounds. Attendance grew from sixty when the meeting opened, to 107 at the close, representing fully half of all the Sabbathkeepers in Tasmania. With no conference business to divide the time, the ten days were spent in the study of the Word of God. On the first Sabbath Ellen White spoke and felt it was a precious opportunity for the people to especially seek the Lord. She made an altar call inviting "all who were afflicted and troubled in mind, all who were in sorrow and despondency, all who had lost their first love . . . to come forward, that we might unite with them in sending up a prayer of faith for the manifestation of the Holy Spirit" (*ibid.*).

A large share of the congregation came forward. Then Ellen White went down into the audience, right back to the last row of seats in the tent, to speak to several young people, and invited them to give their hearts fully to Jesus. All five of them went forward and were joined by several girls whose hearts were tender.

"I knew that the angels of God were in that assembly," she wrote, "and my heart, that for the past five weeks had been sadly burdened and oppressed, seemed at rest, full of peace and trust in God."—*Ibid.* She stated:

> There were those who had been living in unbelief, doubting their acceptance with God. This distrust had made them miserable, but the Lord revealed Himself to their souls, and they knew that He had blessed them. . . . Many others testified that they had realized more of the presence of the Lord than ever before, and their hearts were filled with thankfulness.—*Ibid.*

Ellen White spoke from time to time through the ensuing week, eleven times in all (Letter 128, 1895). The work of the Spirit of God was manifest on the grounds. W. W. Prescott joined the force of workers in midweek, and the Lord richly blessed his ministry. The people flocked to hear him, and Sunday, the last day of the ten-day meeting, fourteen were baptized in the bay. It was decided to continue evening meetings in the large tent for a week or two, for there was a growing interest in the community.

When it had been proposed that there be a camp meeting in Tasmania, the believers felt they could not sustain it financially. Ellen White offered to give several pounds—she gave twenty-five—to help make the meeting possible. She asked the believers in Tasmania to match her gift with funds of their own. They did so, and the meeting was a success (Letters 83 and 127, 1895).

As her mind turned homeward, she wrote:

THE AUSTRALIAN YEARS

These camp meetings in Melbourne and Tasmania have been the best we have ever attended. We have had precious unity among our ministers and workers. Our hearts seem to be knit together as the heart of one man, and this is worth everything to us. I praise the Lord for this. . . .

These meetings cost money, and yet we must have them. I am, as I have told you, investing all the means I can command, but when you are entering new, poverty-stricken districts, it requires strong purpose and strong faith to push forward where there seems so little means to use. . . .

We leave here on the seventeenth. Shall arrive in Sydney the nineteenth of December, if the Lord prospers us with favorable passage.—Letter 127, 1895.

The ship arrived in Sydney, Thursday, December 19, at midnight. Mr. Caldwell was at the wharf with a carriage to meet the travelers, taking Ellen White, Sara McEnterfer, and Maggie Hare the fourteen miles home to Granville. They arrived at 3:00 A.M. W. C. White and May remained to care for the baggage.

"I was so pleased to be home," wrote Ellen White (Letter 128, 1895), but she was exhausted. The Lord had sustained her in a remarkable manner, but the distressing experience with Fannie Bolton well-nigh drained her life forces and her courage.

Nonetheless, Ellen White took the church service in the Parramatta church on Sabbath, December 21, and she felt God had given her a message for the people.

THE MOVE TO COORANBONG

These were exciting days and there was no time to lose, for it was expected that soon she would move to her new home, Sunnyside, now almost ready for her and her family.

The move came on Wednesday, Christmas Day. The work of construction was not yet finished, and another week would be needed before they could settle. So members of the family moved from room to room through the last days of December. How glad they were that they could greet the new year in their own new home.

CHAPTER 20
(1895)

Fannie Bolton and Her Witness— True and False

ALTHOUGH Ellen White ministered successfully at the camp meetings in Melbourne and Hobart, it was against great odds. Her health had been so poor through the preceding four months that only in the strength God gave her did she dare to venture to attend. There were also problems she was called to face of which others had little knowledge, problems within her working family. "I could not possibly relate," she wrote to Edson, "the suffering of mind while attending the camp meeting at Melbourne."—Letter 123a, 1895. The problem lay in the changeable moods, erratic course, and unfaithfulness of Miss Fannie Bolton, the secretary who had replaced Sara McEnterfer at the last minute as the Whites left America; she assisted in preparing Ellen G. White articles for the journals of the church.

Ellen White had not thought to take Fannie with her on this camp meeting tour, but Fannie insisted on going and promised that the trip would bring very little break in her work. Reluctantly, her employer consented. But things did not work out as Fannie had promised. Soon she became involved in the children's meetings, and then there followed a resumption of an old attitude that in her work for Ellen White she was not being given proper recognition. Added to this was a courtship developing between Fannie and W. F. Caldwell, the man who in 1893 had come from America with the message that the Seventh-day Adventist Church had become Babylon. After a change of heart he had been employed by Ellen White, but with his long stay overseas, his non-Adventist wife had divorced him on grounds of desertion.

THE AUSTRALIAN YEARS
ELLEN WHITE EMPLOYS FANNIE BOLTON

Fannie had been invited to join Ellen White's staff in 1887. The daughter of a Methodist minister, Fannie was brought into the Seventh-day Adventist Church in Chicago through the evangelistic efforts of G. B. Starr and his wife. At the time, she was a correspondent for the Chicago *Daily Inter Ocean*. She received her literary training at the ladies' seminary at Evanston, Illinois (DF 445, G. B. Starr to L. E. Froom, March 19, 1933), and seemed well fitted for a promising future. Starr and others gave her a hearty recommendation for work on Ellen White's staff, and although she was just barely acquainted with Ellen White and W. C. White, she was employed upon Ellen White's return from Europe. She was to fit in where needed, but her work was to be largely in preparing Ellen White's materials in article form for the *Review and Herald, Signs of the Times,* and the *Youth's Instructor*. She traveled west with the White group and resided with them in the White home in Healdsburg, California. W. C. White reported that Fannie "proved to be brilliant and entertaining, and although somewhat erratic at times, was loved by the other members of the family." He and a later secretary, D. E. Robinson, explained the character of her work:

THE CHARACTER OF FANNIE BOLTON'S WORK

It was explained to Miss Bolton, as was made clear to other workers who shared a part in the copying and correcting of Mrs. White's writings for publication, that the matters revealed to Mrs. White in vision were not a word-for-word narration of events with their lessons, but that they were generally flashlight or panoramic views of various scenes in the experiences of men, sometimes in the past, and sometimes in the future, together with the lessons connected with these experiences. At times views were revealed to her of the actions of men in groups, of churches, conferences, and of multitudes in action, with a clear perception of their purposes, aims, and motives. Sometimes verbal instruction was given regarding what was thus revealed. Very prominent among these revelations were precious truths and facts relating to the duty, privileges, and the dangers and errors of the church, of committees, or of individuals.

Miss Bolton learned that the things revealed to Mrs. White

were sometimes written out immediately after the vision, and that other things were not spoken of or written out till a long time afterward.

She was told that Mrs. White, in her earnest endeavor to present all that had been shown her on the great number of important subjects, was often led to repeat portions of the matter she sought to present; also that the grammatical construction of sentences was sometimes faulty, for in her haste in writing, she often paid little attention to spelling, punctuation, and capitalization. She expected these imperfections to be carefully corrected by the copyist.

In cases where paragraphs and sentences lost some of their power because of imperfect arrangement, Mrs. White's secretaries were instructed to make transpositions, leaving out what was clearly a repetition, when preparing matter for the printer. In the cases of letters to individuals, the repetition of important thoughts would often tend to make them more effective.

It was made emphatic that only Mrs. White's thoughts were to be used, and also her own words as far as grammatically consistent in expressing those thoughts. In no case was the copyist given the privilege of introducing thoughts not found in Mrs. White's manuscripts.—*Ibid.*, WCW and D. E. Robinson, "The Work of Mrs. E. G. White's Editors," pp. 3, 4.

With enthusiasm Fannie entered into her work on the E. G. White periodical articles, editing and copying. But in time she became restless and entertained the thought that she was not being given proper credit for what she was doing. The records of just what took place are sparse, but it is clear that again and again feelings of discontent and dissatisfaction swept over her that unfitted her for her assigned task.

After engaging in this work for a year or two, she told Ellen White that "she desired to write herself, and could not consent that her talent should be buried up in the work of preparing" E. G. White's "articles for the papers or books. She felt she was full of matter and had talent she must put to use in writing which she could not do" while connected with her present work (Letter 88, 1894). She was released, and attended classes at the university at Ann Arbor.

THE AUSTRALIAN YEARS
ELLEN WHITE TOOK FANNIE TO AUSTRALIA

Learning in 1891 that Ellen White was to go to Australia, Fannie Bolton contacted her former employer, who reported:

> In Battle Creek, Fannie pleaded hard with tears to come with me to engage with me in the work of preparing articles for the papers. She declared she had met with a great change, and was not at all the person she was when she told me she desired to write herself.—*Ibid.*

As Sara McEnterfer was ill when the White party was to leave, and could not go, Ellen White rather reluctantly accepted Fannie Bolton to accompany her, to report her sermons and assist in preparing her articles. Writing of this later, she recounted:

> Just before coming to this country, in order to help Fannie, I consented to make another trial after she had given me the assurance . . . that her feelings in regard to the work had wholly changed. I followed my best judgment, hoping she had gained wisdom from God and would really love the work.
>
> I knew that she was naturally unbalanced in mind, but thought that through the light given of God, the appeal constantly made presenting definite reproofs to some and general reproofs to others, she would learn the lessons that it was her privilege to learn, and become strengthened in character. Thus she would obtain wisdom to prepare the precious matter placed in her hands, so that it might work for the saving of her soul as well as the souls of others.—Letter 7, 1894.

Unfortunately, after working for a while in Australia, the old feelings that she was not receiving proper public acknowledgment of her contributions in Ellen White's work returned, and relationships between the two became strained.

E. G. WHITE WARNED IN VISION

Late in 1893, during the last month of her stay in New Zealand, Ellen White was shown in vision Fannie Bolton and certain temptations along the line of personal ambition and pride to which she was succumbing. Of this she wrote:

> Not long before I left New Zealand, while in camp meeting, it

was represented to me. We were gathered in a room of quite a company, and Fannie was saying some things in regard to the great amount of work coming from her hands. She said, "I cannot work in this way. I am putting my mind and life into this work, and yet the ones who make it what it is are sunk out of sight, and Sister White gets the credit for the work." . . .

A voice spoke to me, "Beware and not place your dependence upon Fannie to prepare articles or to make books. . . . She is your adversary. . . . She is not true to her duty, yet flatters herself she is doing a very important work."—Letter 59, 1894.

Fannie had apparently been talking in this vein over a period of a number of months (Letter 88, 1894).

A few weeks later at the Brighton camp meeting held early in 1894, Fannie Bolton talked with her friends and at times with new believers concerning the difficulties attending her work, and of the faulty way in which some of Ellen White's manuscripts were written. She dwelt upon the "great improvements" made by the editors as they handled the materials, and belittled Ellen White's work. Again she expressed her decided conviction that the talents of the copyists should receive public recognition.

Writing of this to her son W. C. White on February 6, 1894, Ellen White declared:

> I want not her life, or words, or ideas in these articles. And the sooner this bubble is burst, the better for all concerned. . . . I have now no knowledge of how we shall come out, and what I shall do. I am afraid that Fannie cannot be trusted. . . .
>
> If she has done the work as she has represented to other minds she has done, so that she thinks credit should be given her for her talent brought into my writings, then it is time that this firm is dissolved.
>
> If she has done this work, which she has represented to others has been as much her talent, her production of ideas and construction of sentences, as mine, and in "beautiful language," then she has done a work I have urged again and again should not be done. . . . And she is unworthy of any connection with this work.—*Ibid.*

The day before, in writing to O. A. Olsen, who was just then in

THE AUSTRALIAN YEARS

Australia, Ellen White told of how a voice spoke to her:

> Beware and not place your dependence upon Fannie to prepare articles or to make books. She cuts out words that should appear, and places her own ideas and words in their stead, and because she had done this she has become deceived, deluded, and is deceiving and deluding others. She is your adversary.—Letter 59, 1894.

In a letter to Fannie February 6, Ellen White declared:

> Every time I can distinguish a word of yours, my pen crosses it out. I have so often told you that your words and ideas must not take the place of the words and ideas given me of God.—Letter 7, 1894.

DISCHARGED FROM ELLEN WHITE'S SERVICE

The situation was so critical that Ellen White found she must discharge Miss Bolton from her employ, and do so at once. She wrote Fannie:

> The writings given you, you have handled as an indifferent matter, and have often spoken of them in a manner to depreciate them in the estimation of others. . . .
>
> I mean now for your own good that you shall never have another opportunity of being tempted to do as you have done in the past. From the light given me of the Lord, you are not appreciating the opportunities which you have had abundantly, to be instructed and to bring the solid timbers into your character building. The work in which you have been engaged has been regarded as a sort of drudgery, and it is hard for you to take hold of it with the right spirit, and to weave your prayers into your work, feeling that it is a matter of importance to preserve a spirit wholly in harmony with the Spirit of God. Because of this lack, you are not a safe and acceptable worker. . . .
>
> You have come to think that you were the one to whom credit should be given for the value of the matter that comes from your hands. I have had warnings concerning this, but could not see how I could come to the very point to say, "Go, Fannie," for then you plead, "Where shall I go?" and I try you again.—*Ibid.*

FANNIE BOLTON AND HER WITNESS

On receiving this letter from Ellen White, Miss Bolton wrote a humble confession in which she acknowledged:

> The bottom of all my trouble has been self, and that is satanic. I would keenly regret ever having had an association with the work, only that I still believe that God will work it for good. . . .
>
> It is very clear that I did not have the exalted sense of its sacredness which I should have had. I have felt that I needed human sympathy and recognition, and this has led me to talk to others what I had to do to the work. This was self, of course, yet I must say what is only the truth, that I never cast a doubt upon the inspiration of the work. I have always declared and believed the testimonies, and have never felt to doubt their divine origin. . . .
>
> My faith in the testimonies is stronger today than ever, and I feel that I want to put my whole influence on the side of upbuilding the faith of God's people in this great and sacred work.—DF 445b, Fannie Bolton to EGW, Feb. 9, 1894.

On the advice of her fellow workers, Ellen White consented to give Fannie another trial. Later she wrote that Fannie's repentance was "short-lived" (Letter 102, 1895).

Now, almost two years later at the Armadale camp meeting, with old friends and acquaintances, history repeated itself. This time Ellen White dismissed Fannie Bolton from her employ. In a letter to Marian Davis back at Granville, she reported:

> Fannie represented that she and Marian had brought all the talent and sharpness into my books, yet you were both ignored and set aside, and all the credit came to me.
>
> She had underscored some words in a book, *Christian Temperance*, "beautiful words," she called them, and said that she had put in those words, they were hers. If this were the truth, I ask, Who told her to put in her words in my writings? She has, if her own statement is correct, been unfaithful to me.
>
> Sister Prescott, however, says that in the providence of God that very article came to them (Brother and Sister Prescott) uncopied and in my own handwriting, and that these very words were in that letter. So Fannie's statement regarding these words is proved to be untrue.

THE AUSTRALIAN YEARS

She added:

> If after this meeting Fannie shall come to Granville, you must not put one line of anything I have written into her hands, or read a line to her of the "Life of Christ." I would not have any (advice) from her. I am disconnected from Fannie because God requires it, and my own heart requires it. I am sorry for Fannie.—Letter 102, 1895.

To her son Edson she wrote:

> Fannie Bolton is disconnected with me entirely. I would not think of employing her any longer. She has misrepresented me and hurt me terribly. Only in connection with my work has she hurt me.
>
> She has reported to others that she has the same as made over my articles, that she has put her whole soul into them, and I had the credit of the ability she had given to these writings. Well, this is the fifth time this breaking out has come.
>
> It is something similar to the outbreak of Korah, Dathan, and Abiram, only she has not those to unite with her because they know me and my work. She goes not only to those who believe and know me to tell her story but she goes to those newly come to the faith and tells her imaginative story. The same sentiment is expressed as in Numbers 16:3.—Letter 123a, 1895.

Again Fannie wrote a heartfelt confession to Ellen White, five pages of contrition and repentance that closed with the appeal "O do let me be a channel, if it be ever so hidden. Do let me be a worker, if it be in ever so humble a spot. Now, while I make this request, I do it with all submission to the will of God. I am not worthy to ask anything of the kind. Do with me as it seems best."—DF 445a, Fannie Bolton to EGW, Oct. 31, 1895. But writing of Fannie to Marian Davis, Ellen White declared:

> I am now relieved from this fitful, skyrocket experience. She seems to swell up into such large measurements of herself, full of self-sufficiency, full of her own capabilities, and from the light God has been pleased to give me she is my adversary, and has been thus throughout her connection with me.—Letter 22a, 1895.

FANNIE BOLTON AND HER WITNESS

She recounted former warnings regarding Fannie's connection with her work, and her mistaken judgment in the course she should follow. She wrote somewhat in finality:

> Two years ago He revealed to me that Fannie was my adversary, and would vex my soul and weaken my hands, but I was so anxious to get out things that I thought the people needed. Then came other trials in New South Wales, one after another [so] that I was not able to bear it.
>
> Oh, if I had only heeded the instruction given of God and let no other voice or influence come in to leave me in uncertainty, I might have been saved this last terrible, heart-sickening trial. . . . I hope the Lord will forgive me and have mercy upon me, but to try this matter again is out of the question. I am willing her talent shall be exercised for all it is worth, but it will never be in connection with me. I have served my time with Fannie Bolton.—*Ibid.*

So she conjectured. But there was a factor she had not taken into consideration. Some months later the Lord called it to her attention.

Fannie planned to return to the United States, but was prevented from doing so by a rather prolonged illness. She stayed for a while at the home of Pastor Stephen McCullagh in Melbourne, and then decided to visit Cooranbong. In response to a telegram from her, Ellen White arranged to have her met at nine o'clock at night at the Morisset railway station and taken to the Shannon home. There, under the tender and discerning care of Sara McEnterfer, who gave her hydrotherapy treatments, Fannie's health began to improve. A whole year had passed since the Melbourne experience.

A UNIQUE VISION

Then while Ellen White was visiting Elder and Mrs. Starr in Sydney, a very unusual experience came to her. Not only the message given to her merits a place in this account, but also the manner in which Ellen White received the light—a vision in which she was fully conscious. Of this she wrote:

> Friday, March 20, I arose early, about half past three o'clock in the morning. While [I was] writing upon the fifteenth chapter

of John, suddenly a wonderful peace came upon me. The whole room seemed to be filled with the atmosphere of heaven. A holy, sacred presence seemed to be in my room. I laid down my pen and was in a waiting attitude to see what the Spirit would say unto me. I saw no person. I heard no audible voice, but a heavenly watcher seemed close beside me. I felt that I was in the presence of Jesus.

The sweet peace and light which seemed to be in my room . . . is impossible for me to explain or describe. A sacred, holy atmosphere surrounded me, and there was presented to my mind and understanding matters of intense interest and importance. A line of action was laid out before me as if the unseen presence was speaking with me. The matter I had been writing upon seemed to be lost to my mind and another matter distinctly opened before me. A great awe seemed to be upon me as matters were imprinted upon my mind.

The question was, "What have you done with the request of Fannie Bolton? You have not erred in disconnecting with her. This was the right thing for you to do, and this would bring to her mind conviction and remorse which she must have. She has been tempted, deceived, and almost destroyed. Notwithstanding her perversity of spirit, I have thoughts of mercy and compassion for her. . . .

"Take this poor deluded soul by the hand, surround her with a favorable influence if possible. If she separates now from you, Satan's net is prepared for her feet. She is not in a condition to be left to herself. . . . She feels regret and remorse. I am her Redeemer; I will restore her if she will not exalt and honor and glorify herself. If she goes from you now, there is a chain of circumstances which will bring her into difficulties which will be for her ruin. . . .

"You are not to wait for evidence of transformation of character. The Holy Spirit alone can do this work, and mold and fashion this child's experience after the divine similitude. She has not power, if left to herself, to control a temperament that is always a snare to her, unless she keeps in the love of God, unless she humbles herself under the hand of God, and learns daily the meekness and lowliness of Christ."—MS 12c, 1896.

FANNIE BOLTON AND HER WITNESS

To this instruction Ellen White responded:

> I . . . shall work accordingly. I have taken Fannie to my home here at Sunnyside, Avondale, Cooranbong. I shall do all I can to help her heavenward.—*Ibid.*

FANNIE GIVEN ANOTHER TRIAL

Ellen White fitted up a room for Fannie in her new Sunnyside home and took her in. There, with continued treatment, her health improved. Then in response to the instruction outlined in the vision that she should be given another trial, Mrs. White put copy in her hands as in the past. She began on an article and then brought it back to Ellen White, telling her that she could not possibly do the work, and expressed the conviction that she should return to America. When she said this, Ellen White felt she now was free. It was Fannie's decision. Of the experience, she later wrote:

> I now see why I was directed to give Fannie another trial. There were those who misunderstood me because of Fannie's misrepresentations. These were watching to see what course I would take in regard to her. They would have represented that I had abused poor Fannie Bolton. In following the directions to take her back, I took away all occasion for criticism from those who were ready to condemn me.—Letter 61, 1900.

On May 10, 1896, Fannie Bolton took passage on the *Victoria* of the P. & O. S.S. Line, from Sydney to London. On shipboard she wrote to Ellen White:

> I realize to some degree how unworthy I am, but "Jesus Christ came into the world to save sinners," and this comforts me, and by the power of His grace alone, I hope for salvation. I know your prayers will follow me. Thank you again for your patience and kindness and mercy to me. I go home with much lighter heart than I could have done before this.—DF 445, Fannie Bolton to EGW, May 14, 1896.

FANNIE BOLTON EXPLAINS HER EDITORIAL WORK

In letters, one to an acquaintance written in Australia and another a "confession" addressed to "Dear Brethren in the Truth," penned after returning to the United States, Fannie Bolton spoke truthfully concerning the work done by those who assisted Ellen White in her work. Here are a few paragraphs from the two statements. The first was written November 11, 1894, to a Miss Malcolm:

> Concerning the matter of which I have written to you before, I will say that there is no reason why you or anyone else should be thrown into perplexity. Sister White is the prophet of the Lord for the remnant church, and though the Lord has seen fit to choose one for this work who is not proficient in grammar and rhetoric, and this lack is supplied by others, yet she is responsible for every thought, for every expression, in her writings. Every manuscript that is edited goes back to her for examination, and this work committed to those who have been called to labor in this branch is not done without prayer and consecration.
>
> "The word of the Lord" comes to her; but if in [the word's] passing through the human channel, the human imperfection in education leaves its impress, why should it be a perplexity if God should lay upon another the trifling duty of putting the subject of a sentence in harmony with its verb, or the number or gender of a thing mentioned in harmony with the fact that determines the number and gender? There are many ways of expressing the same thought. We may say, "Sit down," "Take a chair"; "The sun shines," "It is a bright day," "The atmosphere is illuminated," and not mar the thought in using different words.
>
> Now as far as changing Sister White's expressions are concerned, I can say that just as far as it is consistent with grammar and rhetoric, her expressions are left intact.—DF 445b, Fannie Bolton to Miss Malcolm, Nov. 11, 1894.

Seven years later, in 1901, she wrote:

> The editors in no wise change Sister White's expression if it is grammatically correct, and is an evident expression of the evident thought. Sister White, as human instrumentality, has a pronounced style of her own, which is preserved all through her books and articles, that stamps the matter with her individuality.
>
> Many times her manuscript does not need any editing, often

FANNIE BOLTON AND HER WITNESS

but slight editing, and again, a great deal of literary work; but article or chapter, whatever has been done upon it, is passed back into her hands by the editor, and the Spirit of Prophecy then appropriates the matter, and it becomes, when approved, the chosen expression of the Spirit of God.—DF 445a, "A Confession Concerning the Testimony of Jesus Christ," written in early 1901 to "Dear Brethren in the Truth."

THE LONG-RANGE HARVEST OF FALSEHOOD AND MISREPRESENTATION

But the seed had been sown in Australia. Of the harvest, Ellen White wrote on April 11, 1897, to Fannie, who was in Battle Creek:

> My Sister Fannie Bolton:
> The work which you have done here in Australia has yielded a harvest which is widespread. . . . You claimed that it was your superior talent that made the articles what they were. I know this to be a falsehood, for I know my own writings. . . .
>
> Brother McCullagh has reported your words of information given him from house to house, saying that I have very little to do in getting out the books purported to come from my pen, that I had picked out all I had written from other books, and that those who prepared my articles, yourself in particular, made the matter that was published. . . .
>
> You can see by this what a harvest your leaven of falsehood and misrepresentation have produced. . . . I will say that much of the time that you were in Australia, you surely did not know what manner of spirit you were of. Satanic agencies have been working through Fannie Bolton.—Letter 25, 1897.

In response to this very plain message, Miss Bolton replied to Ellen White on July 5, 1897, and, following an extended confession, declared:

> My eyes are open to the way in which I hurt your work, for my spirit was not right. The enemy had magnified my supposed difficulties, and though I did not realize what I was doing, he knew exactly what he intended to do through me, but by the grace of God he has lost his tool. . . .

THE AUSTRALIAN YEARS

> As to the testimony you sent of my feelings, faults, errors, and ignorance of my attitude, I say it is true, true to the core.

In her closing paragraphs she asked a question and made a statement:

> Do you think it can be possible for you to give me a place in your heart now? Can you think kindly toward me? Will you ever be able to repose any confidence in me as a friend? . . .
>
> I do not know whatever made me make such a blunder as to insist on going with you to Australia, or of insisting over and over after repeated failures; but I am warned not to undertake a place of so great responsibility. I dare not do it, for it has been proved over and over that I am as weak as water, and I think the decision of the testimony [that Fannie should never work for her again] was wise.—DF 445a.

This pattern of falsifications and subsequent confessions continued for a number of years, including statements circulated particularly in Battle Creek that she had written *Steps to Christ* and, at Ellen White's bidding, certain of the testimonies she sent out.* Such reports brought perplexity and concern to those unfamiliar with the facts in the case. The fears expressed by some who knew her well, that Fannie Bolton was unbalanced in mind, were confirmed when she was admitted to mental institutions on several occasions.

In 1900, four years after Fannie returned to the United States, Ellen White made the following cogent observation:

> Wherein do my articles in the papers now differ from what they were when Fannie was with me? Who is it that now puts in words to supply the deficiencies of my language, my deplorable ignorance? How was this done before Fannie Bolton had anything to do with my writings? Cannot people who have reason see this? If Fannie supplied my great deficiency, how is it that I can now send articles to the papers?—Letter 61a, 1900.

---

* Note: Those desiring further information regarding Fannie Bolton's connection with Ellen White may secure it from the Ellen G. White Estate at the cost of duplication and mailing.

CHAPTER 21
(1895-1896)

Bearing Testimony by Voice and Pen

THE year 1895 was not an easy one for Ellen G. White. She had hoped to devote a good deal of time to writing on the life of Christ, but her plans in this respect were only infrequently carried through. The developments at Cooranbong and the uncertainty surrounding the establishment of the school; the home situation, with a constant stream of visitors; a shift in workers, as Emily Campbell and May Walling returned to the United States; and then the extended camp meetings in the suburbs of Sydney, Melbourne, and Hobart in October, November, and December were a heavy drain on her strength. All this was topped off by the course of Fannie Bolton.

GIVING COUNSEL IN IMPORTANT INTERVIEWS

A good many pages came from her pen in articles, general manuscripts, and letters. The file carries 188 letters aggregating 1,230 pages of double-spaced typewritten material. Some of these opened with comments such as these: "I have a message from the Lord for you"—Letter 91, 1895. "I am burdened over your case. In the night season I was in your company, and was listening to your words."—Letter 2, 1895. "I was conversing with you in the night season, and I was saying to you . . ."—Letter 33, 1895. "I cannot sleep. I was awakened at one o'clock. I was hearing a message borne to you."—Letter 21a, 1895.

Her work also included interviews such as one held during the Armadale camp meeting. The purpose of the meeting is stated in an introductory paragraph:

THE AUSTRALIAN YEARS

On the morning of November 20, 1895, a council meeting was called at the large tent on the Armadale campground to consider some questions arising from the discussions of our brethren regarding the religious liberty work. The positions recently taken by some of our brethren indicated that there was necessity for a more thorough understanding of the principles which must govern our work.—MS 22a, 1895 (see also SW, p. 66).

At such meetings a record was made of those present. In this case there were W. W. Prescott, A. G. Daniells, W. C. White, M. C. Israel, L. J. Rousseau, W. A. Colcord, M. G. Kellogg, W. D. Salisbury, James Smith, Ellen G. White, and Eliza Burnham.

Several letters were read regarding the questions at issue. The workers were invited to discuss the points treated in the letters, but they wanted to hear further from Ellen White. The questions had to do in part with how black believers in the Southern States should relate to Sunday laws. Should they insist on working on Sunday to demonstrate their attitude toward the sacredness of the day? The counsel given by Ellen White, now found in *The Southern Work*, pages 66-71, discouraged any attempt to defy Sunday laws. She declared:

> From the light that I have received, I see that if we would get the truth before the Southern people, we must not encourage the colored people to work on Sunday. There must be a clear understanding regarding this, but it need not be published in our papers.—*Ibid.* (see also SW, p. 68).

The counsel and information that developed from these discussions were passed along to those carrying the burden of the work in the Southern States. In 1902, Ellen White again gave counsel in the same vein. It is found in *Testimonies*, volume 9, pages 232-238.

BATTLE CREEK DEVELOPMENTS

In 1895 and 1896, with growing frequency and accelerating force visions were given to Ellen White in the hours of the night regarding conditions at the headquarters of the work of the church.

Early in 1895 a General Conference session was held in Battle Creek. O. A. Olsen was reelected president for another term of two years; Harmon Lindsay, General Conference treasurer, was also reelected. This posed some occasion for misgivings on Ellen White's part, for Lindsay was not gaining ground in his spiritual experience; his principles were becoming tainted, and he was inclined to approach the business of the General Conference with calculation, and often without spiritual discernment. He stood close to A. R. Henry, treasurer of the Review and Herald, a man of finance who had long served in Battle Creek, and a man whose principles also were becoming tarnished. She saw these two men swaying the General Conference president. The overall situation gave her great concern.

On May 12, 1895, Ellen White wrote a thirteen-page letter to Olsen, reporting on her work in Australia and Tasmania, and the W. C. White—May Lacey wedding. She then expressed some concerns and gave counsel. She introduced this by writing:

> I had no other idea than that you would be selected as president of the General Conference. We pray earnestly for you, that the Lord will give you a healthful experience and clear understanding of His mind and will, and that you may be continually imbued by the Holy Spirit. Both Willie and myself understand your perplexities and difficulties. I have a most intense desire that you shall keep an eye single to the glory of God, and that you will not allow any man's judgment to control you. The Lord lives and reigns, and He is to be glorified in those that come near unto Him. I have nothing but the most tender, pitying sympathy for you, my brother.

Then she came more directly to the point of concern:

> In the night season I am speaking and writing clear words of admonition. I waken so burdened in soul that I am again driven to take up my pen. In various ways matters are opened up before my mind, and I dare not rest, or keep quiet. I fear and tremble for the souls of men who are in responsible places in Battle Creek.
>
> If their works had no further influence than simply upon themselves, I could breathe more freely; but I know that the enemy is using men who are in positions of trust, and who are not consecrated to the work and who know not what manner of spirit they are of. When I realize that men who are connected

THE AUSTRALIAN YEARS

with them are also in blindness, and will not see the harm that is being done by the precept and example of these unconsecrated agents, it seems to me that I cannot hold my peace. I have to write, for I know that the mold that these men are giving to the work is not after God's order.—Letter 59, 1895.

There were serious defects in the management of the publishing house and the General Conference. The Battle Creek Sanitarium also stood in peril. Basic to the problem, it seemed, were the keen-minded businessmen, Harmon Lindsay and A. R. Henry. Both were very much involved in nearly all of the financial interests of the church.

When A. R. Henry became a Seventh-day Adventist in 1882, he was president of a bank in Indiana. Soon he was called to Battle Creek to assist in the financial management of the publishing association. A review of the responsibilities he carried, as presented in the *SDA Encyclopedia*, helps to an understanding of the strong influence he exerted in 1895 and 1896:

Henry, Archibald R. (1839-1909). Treasurer of the General Conference (1883-1888) and a financial officer and adviser of many early SDA institutions. . . .

In 1882, shortly after he joined the SDA Church, he was called to assist in the financial management of the SDA Publishing Association at Battle Creek, Michigan. He held this position of treasurer continuously until 1897, except between 1885 and 1887 when he was vice-president of the association. Between 1893 and 1895, he was both treasurer and manager of the institution.

In 1883 he was elected to serve also as a treasurer of the General Conference. In 1889 he was president of the General Conference Association of SDA's, in 1890-1891, its vice-president, in 1892, its auditor, and in 1893, its treasurer. Simultaneously he was a member of governing boards of nearly all early SDA medical and educational institutions in the Central and Western States.—*SDA Encyclopedia*, p. 581.

On May 25, 1896, Ellen White wrote to Olsen:

My mind has been so wrought upon by the Spirit of God that

the burden upon me was very great in regard to yourself and the work in Battle Creek. I felt that you were being bound hand and foot, and were tamely submitting to it. I was so troubled that in conversation with Brother Prescott I told him my feelings. Both he and W. C. White tried to dissipate my fears; they presented everything in as favorable a light as possible. But instead of encouraging, these words alarmed me. If these men cannot see the outcome of affairs, I thought, how hopeless the task of making them see at Battle Creek. The thought struck to my heart like a knife.—Letter 87a, 1896.

Of course these men did not have the insights that the visions gave her. She then pointed out to them that at Battle Creek "things are being swayed in wrong lines."—MS 62, 1896.

The significance of her concern surfaced in a letter written July 5, to her son Edson, in which she declared:

I dare not think my own thoughts, for indignation comes upon me at times when I think how men in Battle Creek have supposed they could take the place of God and order and dictate and lord it over men's minds and talents—an endowment given them in trust from God to improve every day, trade upon—and if these talents cannot be placed to the control of men to be in service to do their will, then they make those men have a difficult path to travel. They act just as though they were in God's place, to deal with their fellow men as if they were machines. I cannot respect their wisdom or have faith in their Christianity.

And then, writing more directly:

The Lord has presented to me his [A. R. Henry's] dangers. I expect nothing else but he will say, as he has always done, "Somebody has been telling Sister White." This shows that he has no faith in my mission or testimony, and yet Brother Olsen has made him his right-hand man.—Letter 152, 1896.

Four days later she again wrote about the distressing situation in Battle Creek:

I feel sorry for Elder Olsen. He thought if he should manifest confidence in A. R. Henry and keep him traveling about from state to state, he would be converted, but the conversion has been the other way. We are safe only as we make God our trust. He is our sufficiency in all things, at all times, and in all places.—Letter 153, 1896.

With the confidence Elder Olsen had in the skill and ability of A. R. Henry, it seemed to Olsen that he was unable to stem the tide and fend off propositions and developments that would prove a serious detriment to the proper management of the affairs of the church.

As Ellen White opened her heart to Elder Olsen and presented her feelings, she wrote:

> It has been hard for me to give the message that God has given to me for those I love, and yet I have not dared to withhold it. I have to make my face as flint against the faces of those who set themselves so stubbornly to carry out their own way and to pursue their own unrighteous course.
>
> I would not do a work that is so uncongenial to me if I thought that God would excuse me from it. When I have written one testimony to the brethren, I have thought that I should not have any more to write; but again I am in travail of soul, and cannot sleep or rest.—Letter 59, 1895.

Elder Olsen was a man loyal to the message, a deeply spiritual man, a church leader who leaned heavily on God and had respect for and confidence in the messages and work of Ellen White. It was her suggestion in 1888 that had an influence in his being called to the presidency of the General Conference, an office to which he was four times reelected. But as is common to all humanity, he suffered some weaknesses. He made no attempt to hide these weaknesses from either Ellen White or his brethren. As during the last few years of his administration, which terminated in 1897, communication after communication came from Australia pointing out the dangers that at that time threatened the ministry of the church and its administration, he called his associates together and read the messages directed to him. Many of the messages of counsel sent to him for ministers and executives he had printed in envelope-size leaflets or pamphlets. These were distributed to the working force of the denomination under the title *Special Testimonies to Ministers and Workers*. Many of these are to be found in *Testimonies to Ministers and*

BEARING TESTIMONY BY VOICE AND PEN

Gospel Workers. It was a dark period for the church. Of it Ellen White declared:

> We know not what the developments will be in Battle Creek. There will be a turning and overturning, but God is our Ruler; God is our Judge. The Lord is soon to come, and when the Lord cometh "shall he find faith on the earth?"—Letter 153, 1896.

Worsening conditions at the heart of the work of the church was a topic often touched on by Ellen White in her correspondence with leaders in Battle Creek through the last four years of her stay in Australia.

ELLEN WHITE DESIRES TO REMAIN IN AUSTRALIA

While on several occasions Olsen urged Ellen White to return to the United States, this she declined to do. "I shall write to you," she told him in her letter of May 31, 1896, "but should I return to Battle Creek and bear my testimony to those who love not the truth, the ever-ready words would arise from unbelieving hearts, 'Somebody has told her.'" And she added, "Even now unbelief is expressed by the words 'Who has written these things to Sister White?'"—Letter 81, 1896.

It was in this connection that W. C. White on May 29, 1896, wrote to F. M. Wilcox, secretary of the Foreign Mission Board:

> Mother feels more and more the fact that she has but a short time to work, and she is very desirous of getting out her books. . . . Yesterday I had a long talk with her, and she expressed very emphatically the opinion that the Lord had permitted her to come over here, and make a home in a quiet place, that she might be free to present in writing what the Lord has shown her, without personal conflict with those whose course is an offense to God and who are so persistent and determined in their opposition to the instruction God has given His people, but which is contrary to their feelings and plans.—9 WCW, p. 493.

LIGHT ON A LONGSTANDING MYSTERY

For several years it was a mystery to Ellen White why the Lord had not given specific light to her on the matter of the request of the

THE AUSTRALIAN YEARS

General Conference that she go to Australia. While she recognized that the work there had certainly benefited by her presence, there were some questions that again and again came to her mind. Now, in the setting just described, the situation opened up to her, and the picture grew clear. On December 1, 1896, in writing to the head of the church she spoke of God's intent:

> The Lord designed that we should be near the publishing houses, that we should have easy access to these institutions [so] that we might counsel together.—Letter 127, 1896.

She wrote in contrast of the devisings of men:

> That the people of Battle Creek should feel that they could have us leave at the time we did was the result of man's devising, and not the Lord's. The sum of the matter is proved, and its figures are before you. We are here. The Battle Creek matters have been laid before me at this great distance, and the load I have carried has been very heavy to bear. . . .
>
> There was so great a willingness to have us leave [America] that the Lord permitted this thing to take place. Those who were weary of the testimonies borne were left without the persons who bore them. Our separation from Battle Creek was to let men have their own will and way, which they thought superior to the way of the Lord.
>
> The result is before you. Had you stood in the right position, the move would not have been made at that time. The Lord would have worked for Australia by other means, and a strong influence would have been held at Battle Creek, the great heart of the work. There we should have stood shoulder to shoulder, creating a healthful atmosphere to be felt in all our conferences.
>
> It was not the Lord who devised this matter. I could not get one ray of light to leave America. But when the Lord presented this matter to me as it really was, I opened my lips to no one, because I knew that no one would discern the matter in all its bearings. When we left, relief was felt by many, but not so by yourself, and the Lord was displeased, for He had set us to stand at the wheels of the moving machinery at Battle Creek.—*Ibid.*

Though the topics covered in the letter were not of a pleasant

BEARING TESTIMONY BY VOICE AND PEN

nature, Ellen White wrote it in a spirit of love and tenderness:

> He [God] understands all about the mistakes of the past, and He will help you. But wherever you may be, never, never tread over the same ground.—*Ibid.*

DOING THE WORK OVER AND OVER AGAIN

Another matter that concerned Ellen White was the necessity of doing much the same work over and over again. She would write letters or lead out in meetings in a church, presenting earnest messages and sometimes direct testimonies to individuals to which there was an earnest heartfelt response. But the work did not always last. In writing to S. N. Haskell of her experience in the Parramatta church she pinpointed the problem as the lack of daily conversion:

> Last Sabbath I spoke in Parramatta. The Lord has been giving me His Holy Spirit in rich measures, and I had a message for the church. I called for those who desired to give themselves wholly to the Lord to come forward, and quite a number responded. Our labor continued from eleven o'clock; but there was good accomplished.
>
> But oh, what a task it is to try to lift a church whose individual members do not experience daily conversion. It nearly takes every particle of strength that is in me. The same work has to be done again and again, because the church members do not live in Christ, do not meditate on His Word, and walk apart from Him. I have far greater influence and much better success in working for unbelievers however ignorant they may be, than I have in working for those who know the truth, and are not being sanctified through the truth.
>
> But we are not to fail nor be discouraged. That which I grieve over is the fact that the Lord Jesus is dishonored and that many will lose eternal life, because they do not seek heaven with earnestness, and Satan finds their hearts ready to respond to temptation.—Letter 28, 1895.

To stand as the messenger of the Lord to the remnant church was not an easy assignment.

CHAPTER 22
(1896)

1896—A Year of Good News and Bad News

T HE day has opened beautifully," wrote Ellen White in her diary on the morning of January 1, 1896. "Eighteen hundred ninety-five has passed into eternity with its burden of record. A new year has opened upon us, and there are no changes we can make in the old year."—MS 61, 1896.

It was midsummer as the year opened in the Southern Hemisphere, and some of the days were oppressively hot. The land breeze seemed as from a furnace.

Work on the Sunnyside home was nearing completion, but the hammering, sawing, and painting were not conducive to writing.

W. C. White, in writing to O. A. Olsen on January 19, described the Sunnyside residence as constructed so it could eventually serve as an office building for Ellen White's staff:

> Mother's house, when completed, will contain eleven rooms. The main building is 32 x 32, with a veranda in the front, and a hall running through the center. There are four rooms about 12 x 12, and upstairs there are four more nearly as large. Back of the main building there is a lean-to, 14 x 22, intended for a kitchen. This much of the house is plastered and therefore will be quite cool and comfortable. Mother decides to use the back room for a dining room, and so is having an addition 16 x 22 feet attached to the dining room, which will be divided up into a kitchen, bathroom, and storeroom. We expect the carpenters to complete their work this week, then we shall get settled.—9 WCW, p. 117.

Her often repeated resolution to have a small cottage and to live somewhat in isolation was largely wishful thinking for her literary work demanded that she be surrounded with helpers, and she must provide for their housing and working space.

THE CONTENTED WORKING FAMILY AT SUNNYSIDE

In a letter to Miss Emily Campbell, W. C. White described the situation at Sunnyside:

> Mother is comfortably located in her new house, and has the best corps of workers that has ever been grouped around her.
> Sister Davis is working on the "Life of Christ," and smaller books which will come out in connection with it. Sister Burnham is working on *Christian Temperance,* and articles for the papers. Sister Maggie Hare is working on letters and articles for the papers. Sister May Israel divides her time between bookkeeping and copying for Miss Davis. Sister Belden is housekeeper, with Edith Ward as assistant. Sister Lucas is dressmaker, and Minnie Hawkins has just begun regular work as copyist for Miss Burnham, and to learn other lines of the work. Brother M. A. Cornell is man of all work, with Edgar Hollingsworth as assistant and chore boy.
> Mother is getting along nicely with her book work, and I am more and more thankful that she is located in a quiet place, where she will not be so much interrupted as heretofore.—9 WCW, p. 503.

She closely watched agricultural developments. As summer wore on, she was able to write on February 3 of the garden, which she reported was doing well. She added:

> We have the testimony that with care taken of the trees and vegetables in the dry season, we shall have good results. Our trees are doing well. . . . I can testify by experience that false witness has been borne of this land. On the school ground, they have tomatoes, squashes, potatoes, and melons. . . . We know the land will do well with proper care.—Letter 10, 1896.

There was also the flower garden. On February 10 she got up at half past four, and at five o'clock was at work "spading up the ground and preparing to set out my flowers. I worked one hour alone, then Edith Ward and Ella May White united with me, and we planted our flowers."—MS 62, 1896. Then followed the setting out of twenty-eight tomato plants. The bell ringing for morning prayers and breakfast brought these activities to a close. In her diary she wrote: "I think I have received no harm from my vigorous exercise, but feel better for the work done." She added, "After breakfast I read manuscript—two short chapters on the life of Christ."—*Ibid.* In fact, she was devoting a good deal of time to her last reading of the finished chapters that would soon be sent to the publishers. The next morning she was in the orchard, "tying up the trees. A tuft of grass is put between the stake and the trees so that the tree shall not be marred."—*Ibid.*

CONSULTING WITH W. W. PRESCOTT

Professor Prescott made an extended visit to Cooranbong, invited there to give counsel about establishing the new school. On Tuesday afternoon, February 11, he came to Sunnyside to see Ellen White. "We had a long talk," she wrote. "We would see some matters in a clearer light. The problem of studies in our school was canvassed."—*Ibid.* The diary record indicates that this visit was followed by others:

Wednesday, February 12: Rode to Cooranbong. . . . Brother and Sister Prescott rode up with us.

Thursday, February 13: Awoke in the morning at four o'clock. Commenced writing. Found some special writings dated 1874 [the year the first SDA college was established]; very important instruction in them. I am writing out some things upon education to go in the next mail. . . .

In the afternoon Professor Prescott and wife again visited me in my room. We had a long talk in regard to the management of school matters.

As questions were asked, the Holy Spirit revived many things in my mind, and I could tell them the way many matters concerning our educational interest had been presented to me.

We are to lay the situation of dearth of means before the whole school and then make known the Lord's plan as presented to me. In place of devoting time to inventing amusements to use their muscles, they can strengthen nerves and muscles to good advantage in the work that needs to be done on the school grounds. If we shall be compelled to hire the work done, the price of tuition must be increased.

Every student may consider it to be his privilege to have a part in saving means they would pay for hiring work done that [they] themselves can do. Earning their expenses is to be considered a part of their education. Every student is to exercise brain and bone and muscle. Here is the education of the whole man, right on the ground—an education essential for all, for there is work for all to do.—*Ibid.*

The Prescott visit to Cooranbong buoyed up Ellen White's spirits, and in mid-March she wrote to Edson: "I am only too thankful to report that Professor Prescott's testimony is that of all the places where our schools have been located, none seems to be as favorable as this place."—Letter 147, 1896. Yet with the scarcity of money—and with litigation unnecessarily instigated by a legal firm employed in obtaining proper registration of the transaction that would put the land in the name of the General Conference Association—time went on with little visible progress in getting the school under way.

One means of getting the enterprise under way while conserving funds was the purchase of a sawmill. They found it idle in Sydney, available for £300, or about half its value. It was now cutting lumber from timber on the estate, and tallow wood for floors (9 WCW, p. 201).

The principles under which they hoped to start the new school in Australia were a little different from those commonly held. It was therefore desirable to orient the thinking of those who would carry on the educational program when the school finally opened. W. W. Prescott was an experienced educator and in full sympathy with the principles set forth in the Spirit of Prophecy. He was also an effective evangelist. So it was decided to hold a month-long institute for teachers at Avondale. Notice for it was given in the March 23 *Bible Echo* under the heading "An Institute at Avondale for Teachers, Ministers, and Bible Workers."

A forty-foot camp meeting tent was brought onto the ground, and institute work began on Thursday, March 26. Many who came brought their own tents, bedding, and cooking utensils. Ellen White

THE AUSTRALIAN YEARS

had the Sabbath-morning service and spoke frequently through the four weeks of the institute, emphasizing fundamental principles of Christian education.

The large round tent on the Avondale grounds, with the six family tents neatly pitched nearby, gave the appearance of a small camp meeting and attracted the attention of the community. Not a few came in, especially to the evening meetings, which were given an evangelistic turn. Ellen White reported:

> Those not of our faith were in attendance all through the meeting. After the first meeting they came with their Bibles and answered the questions with the rest. I generally spoke once in the day. Unbelievers say they knew more about what the Scriptures contained, and they were highly pleased.—Letter 168, 1896.

As the institute progressed, attendance increased, and Ellen White reported in a letter to Haskell: "The very best class of the community have come out to hear. We have been made glad to see families attending these meetings. They are as sheep without a shepherd." She continued:

> Last Sunday night the constable came to the meeting. He saw some of the brethren and told them that some boys designed to cut the ropes of the tent, and he was watching them. But the constable and the boys listened with deep attention, as if afraid they would lose one word, as did also the postmaster, the schoolteachers from Cooranbong and Dora Creek, and a number of other outsiders.—Letter 36, 1896.

As the institute came to a close, it was decided to leave the large tent standing for a time and to hold weekend meetings, in which Elder Starr and Ellen White led out. On June 1 she could write of one family at Dora Creek that had embraced the truth from attending the meetings and reading *The Great Controversy* (Letter 167, 1896). Others were deeply interested in the message.

THE BIRTH OF TWIN GRANDSONS

If W. C. White and even Ellen White had their attention diverted from the institute for a few hours, it was not to be wondered at, for

1896—A YEAR OF GOOD NEWS AND BAD NEWS

on Sunday night, April 6, May White gave birth to twin sons. We will let the proud grandmother give the report:

> Last night about ten o'clock, Sara came into my room full of excitement and glad surprise. Mrs. May Lacey White presented to her husband a pair of twin boys. The mother is doing well. She had a midwife—a good, intelligent, motherly woman—and Sara McEnterfer. . . . Both mother and babies are doing well.—Letter 137, 1896.

Ellen White rejoiced, for "at one time," she wrote, "it appeared that the White family, if time lasted much longer, would become extinct, but when these two boys came into the family, the prospect seemed more encouraging."—Letter 119, 1896.

In the days and weeks that followed, Ellen White made frequent mention of the healthy babies, "hearty, hungry little fellows" (Letter 121, 1896), and their steady development.

AN APPEAL TO THE WESSELS FAMILY FOR MONEY

The work at Avondale was at a standstill, mainly for lack of funds. On April 29 Ellen White wrote to the Wessels family in Africa, pleading for help:

> I wish to write you a few lines, asking you to lend me £1000. At the present time we are greatly in need of a building for school purposes. On account of the lack of means, we may not be able to carry out the plans designed by Brother Sisley, but if you will lend us the money I ask, we can commence at once to erect a plain, economical building. . . . It would be a great mistake [to stop] the work on the school building for a year. . . . Are you able to loan us £1000, and can you send it direct to us? . . . If you can send the money, I will give you my note for the same, only asking you to make the interest as low as you can afford. . . . Would you know how you can best please your Saviour? It is by putting your money to the exchangers, to be used in the Lord's service and to advance His work.—Letter 107, 1896.

In another letter she told of how "the word of the Lord" came to her, " 'Send to Africa for help. I have entrusted my stewards there with means, and I will move upon their hearts to trade upon My

THE AUSTRALIAN YEARS

entrusted talents.' "—Letter 114, 1896.

Although money was scarce, the land yielded its crops in such abundance and good quality that Ellen White could write, "We are all convinced that this is the place where we should locate."—Letter 107, 1896. Now she would wait for a response, a response that could assure progress.

In the meantime the program of writing and of ministering in the community continued. "I am so glad I am here," she wrote on May 3. They were calling for her to return to America, but "Not yet, not yet" was her word.

> I have important writing to do, and this must be done before I can leave this locality. The school must be started, a meeting house must be built before we can leave the work. I feel forbidden to go now. We must not leave, for the people here would be utterly discouraged if we did. Poverty binds them about in this country. They say, If you had not been able to help us, what would we have done. I tell them that all the gold and silver in the world belongs to the Lord. The cattle upon a thousand hills are His, and He will not let His work come to a standstill. It must go. "Go forward," saith the Lord; and if we move, the way will open. The work here must not stop.—Letter 111, 1896.

ELLEN G. WHITE STOOD AS A BANK TO THE CAUSE

"I have to stand as a bank," Ellen White wrote to Dr. Kellogg in Battle Creek, "to uphold, borrow, and advance money." She added, "I turn and twist every way to do the work. Others will take hold and do something when they see that I have faith to lead out and donate." Then she stated:

> Here are all our workers that must be paid. I am heavily in debt in this country to those in other countries. Eighteen hundred dollars from one person; this money has been used up. Five hundred dollars from one in Africa, which is a loan and has been applied in different ways that demanded means to forward the work. I move by faith.—Letter 58, 1896.

THE STAGGERING BLOW

But the staggering blow came a few days later. Unexpectedly the

1896—A YEAR OF GOOD NEWS AND BAD NEWS

court hearing the case involving the holding of the school property, for which payment had been made, ruled unfavorably in a suit that arose from disputed interest in the amount of $40. The cost to the school enterprise for the judgment and attorney's fees was $1,750, and this at a time when funds were extremely short. To W. C. White, president of the union and chairman of the school board, it was staggering, and drained him of his courage and strength. It was all so unnecessary. Gladly would the school board have paid the £8 of interest, but the chairman was in New Zealand when the matter came up, and the attorneys handling the title to the property, confident they could win, filed suit without proper authorization. They lost, and Australia lost. The church lost not only the money but also nearly a year in getting the school under way. Depression overwhelmed the few who had a full knowledge of the facts.

On May 31 W. C. White wrote to his longtime friend W. C. Sisley, who had drawn the plans for the buildings and was now in Battle Creek:

> To us this decision [against us] means a great deal. Our work has been delayed nearly a year, and now we have about £350 to pay. This is the severest disappointment and misfortune I have ever experienced in connection with our work, and for a time I was almost paralyzed with discouragement. . . .
>
> While we have been waiting for our lawsuit to terminate, we have not felt free to say much to our brethren about what was delaying us.—9 WCW, p. 496.

The W. C. White family was living at this time in what was known as the "convent," a two-story building formerly occupied by the Sisters of St. Joseph. He rented this from the Catholics in early May, and it provided not only living quarters for his family of six but office space as well. He wrote of it to Emily Campbell, now in the United States:

> This is a pleasant house of nine rooms. We are now fairly settled. Some furniture I had, some Mother loaned me, and some I have bought from the school. We have very little that is new. . . .
>
> Brother Francis Tucker is boarding with us. Sister Nora Lacey is chief housekeeper, with Ella as assistant. Brother and Sister H.

THE AUSTRALIAN YEARS

C. Lacey are boarding with us, so you see we have a family of ten, counting the twins. Ella takes care of the cow; Mabel fills the lamps, cuts kindling wood, and takes care of the babies. Everybody is busy.—*Ibid.*, p. 503.

THE SAWMILL LOFT PUT TO USE

It was midwinter as Ellen White wrote on July 5, 1896:

One week ago yesterday I spoke in the upper room of the mill, partially enclosed, to eighty assembled, mostly our own people. . . . It is rather a rustic place in which to meet, but when the sun shines in this country no other heating apparatus is needed.

I spoke again yesterday. We had a good meeting. We shall be glad to get a meetinghouse and a school building. We are praying for means. We cannot advance until means shall come in from some source.—Letter 152, 1896.

The sawmill loft was often mentioned as a place of meetings that were held from week to week. It also became an assembly room for many of the young people at Cooranbong in a temporary school conducted by Prof. Herbert Lacey and his wife, Lillian. The Laceys had come from America to assist in what was to be the Avondale school. Eager to get on with school work, and finding quite a number of young men and women eager to attend classes, Lacey saw an opportunity to make a beginning. On his own responsibility but with the consent of the school board, he began a night school in the mill loft. Some of the furniture and equipment sent up to Cooranbong when the Bible school in Melbourne closed, was taken out of storage and put to use. Securing textbooks in Sydney and with his wife to help, Lacey conducted classes and collected tuition, with the understanding the school board would not be held in any way responsible for any expense connected with the project, for the board had no money. Some twenty-five young people attended.

SETTLEMENT OF THE WALLING LAWSUIT

On July 9, 1896, Ellen White conveyed in a letter to her niece Mary Watson what was good and bad news. The lawsuit Mr. Will Walling instituted against Ellen White in 1891, for the alienation of

1896—A YEAR OF GOOD NEWS AND BAD NEWS

the affection of his two daughters whom Ellen White had taken at his request and reared and educated, was finally brought to a close. But it cost her money hard to spare, $1,500 for a settlement and $2,000 for attorney's fees. Those familiar with the matter felt certain that if the case had been brought to court, Walling would have lost. In the July 9 letter, she explains why it was not handled that way:

> I could have decided to go into court, but this would have brought the children where they would have been obliged to testify on oath against their father, and would have led to endless trouble. The mother would have been brought into court, and you would probably [have] had to act a part. There is no knowing what lies might have been sworn to, or how much disgrace might have been brought upon us all.—Letter 128, 1896.

GOOD NEWS! MONEY FROM AFRICA! BUILDING BEGINS!

Through August and September the development of the Avondale school was dormant. Poverty abounded, and Ellen White for a time gave employment to five men working on her grounds so that they might have something with which to supply their families.

For three or four months she had not been able to pay her helpers, yet they were willing to suffer inconvenience. Grocery bills accumulated, and then with a draft of $600 from Battle Creek, representing royalties on book sales, she could settle with workers and grocers. Late in September the mail from Africa brought $5,000 on loan to Ellen White from Mother Wessels. Her prayer had been answered, money was in hand, and they could start building. "We praised the Lord for this favor," she wrote. "The building had been delayed for want of means, and the faith of our people had almost come to a standstill. Many, I fear, had lost faith. But I knew that God would work in our behalf."—MS 55, 1896. He did!

In a very few days Ellen G. White and W. C. White would be leaving for the camp meeting scheduled in Adelaide. Surely Ellen White should lay the cornerstone. She tells the glad story:

> On October 1, 1896, we assembled on the school grounds to lay the cornerstone of our first school building. . . . The Lord had moved upon the hearts of Sister Wessels and her sons to grant my request for a loan of £1,000 at 4½ percent interest.

THE AUSTRALIAN YEARS

This was an important occasion, but only a few were present. It had been hurriedly planned that I should have the privilege of laying the cornerstone, as I was to leave the following day for Sydney, en route for Melbourne and Adelaide.

We had a season of prayer and singing, and then I took the stone in my hand and laid it in position. My heart was filled with gratitude to God that He had opened the way [so] that we could erect this first building. We praised the Lord for this favor.—*Ibid.*

Plans for the building, Bethel Hall, as drawn by W. C. Sisley, had long been in hand. Work began immediately.

THE ADELAIDE CAMP MEETING

Friday morning, October 2, accompanied by Sara McEnterfer and her son W. C. White, Ellen White went to Sydney and spent a profitable weekend with the churches in the city and its vicinities. Monday afternoon they boarded the train for the overnight trip to Melbourne en route to Adelaide, where another successful camp meeting was conducted.

She returned to Cooranbong on Wednesday, November 4, and rejoiced to see the progress made in her orchard, where fruit would soon ripen. She was also delighted with the progress being made in erecting Bethel Hall. It would be ready in March. But she could remain for only a few days, for the second session of the New South Wales Conference was called for Thursday, November 12, to Sunday, November 14. It was to be held in the Ashfield church, and she felt she should attend.

SUNNYSIDE IN EARLY SUMMER

Ellen White enjoyed her Sunnyside home, situated on what had now become a tract of sixty acres (she bought more land to help furnish money to the school). "The climate of New South Wales," she wrote, "is as good as any I have knowledge of, and you know, I have traveled nearly round the inhabited world. We came here to get the benefit of this climate." She commented, "My health has improved very much lately. During the last two years I have done more writing than I have ever done before in the same period of time. I am now writing largely."—Letter 128, 1896. She pointed out, no time clock was kept, and when not under the pressure of a crisis,

1896—A YEAR OF GOOD NEWS AND BAD NEWS

the workers were free to find relaxation and diversions.

On the Sunnyside farm she had four horses and three cows. Three of her women helpers, Sara McEnterfer, May Israel, and Minnie Hawkins, each had a saddle horse. In a letter to Edson she wrote of her workers and their recreation:

> The garden is the exercise ground for my workers. Early and late the girls are at work in the garden when they are off duty. It is better for them, and more satisfactory than any exercise they can have.
>
> I could not persuade Marian to ride, could not get her [free] from her writings; but now she has her interest awakened and I have no fears but that she will get out of her chair and work in the garden. This garden of flowers is a great blessing to my girls, and they are working with the tomato raising, planting and caring for the tomatoes.—Letter 162, 1896.

As to the food served in her Sunnyside home, she wrote:

> My table is furnished with fruit in its season. . . . Vegetables, fruit, and bread form our table fare. As we are educating colonials in health principles, we do not under any circumstances place meat on the table. Some of our present company are as pupils in a school, and therefore, precept and example must be harmonious. Each year we put up not less than six or eight hundred quarts of canned fruit. We have peaches, apricots, nectarines, grapes, plums, and tomatoes canned.—Letter 128, 1896.

On Friday morning, December 4, 1896, she discovered a ripe peach in her orchard. She wrote in her diary:

> Today I picked the first ripe peach, deep red in color, from my orchard. These peach trees were planted one year ago the last September. We have several nectarine trees, bearing red-cheeked, fine-looking fruit, some of which is nearly ripe. Next year we will have quite an abundance of fruit if the blessing of the Lord rests upon our trees.—MS 44, 1896.

The demonstration at Sunnyside was working well.

CHAPTER 23
(1896-1897)

Meeting Doctrinal Error and Apostasies

NEAR the close of 1896, on November 8, Ellen White wrote a five-page document titled "Testimony Concerning the Views of Prophecy Held by Brother John Bell." Bell held divergent views regarding the location in time of the three angels' messages of Revelation 14. The testimony opens:

> I have not been able to sleep since half past one o'clock. I was bearing to Brother John Bell [of Melbourne] a message which the Lord had given me for him. The peculiar views he holds are a mixture of truth and error. If he had passed through the experiences of God's people as He has led them for the last forty years, he would be better prepared to make the correct application of Scripture. The great waymarks of truth, showing us our bearings in prophetic history, are to be carefully guarded, lest they be torn down, and replaced with theories that would bring confusion rather than genuine light.

Ellen White likened John Bell's work to some met in the past:

> Some will take the truth applicable to their time, and place it in the future. Events in the train of prophecy that had their fulfillment away in the past are made future, and thus by these theories the faith of some is undermined. From the light that the Lord has been pleased to give me, you are in danger of doing the same work, presenting before others truths which have had their place and done their specific work for the time, in the history of the faith of the people of God.
>
> You recognize these facts in Bible history as true, but apply

MEETING DOCTRINAL ERROR AND APOSTASIES

them to the future. They have their force still in their proper place, in the chain of events that have made us as a people what we are today, and as such, they are to be presented to those who are in the darkness of error.

GOD'S LEADING IN PIONEER DAYS

The five-page testimony closes with a review of early Seventh-day Adventist history in the establishment of doctrinal truth:

Many theories were advanced, bearing a semblance of truth, but so mingled with Scriptures misinterpreted and misapplied that they led to dangerous errors. Very well do we know how every point of truth was established, and the seal set upon it by the Holy Spirit of God.

And all the time voices were heard, "Here is the truth." "I have the truth, follow me." But the warnings came, "Go not ye after them. I have not sent them, but they ran." The leadings of the Lord were marked, and most wonderful were His revelations of what is truth. Point after point was established by the Lord God of heaven. That which was truth *then* is truth today.

Then Ellen White drives the matter home, addressing the words of warning to John Bell:

According to the light God has given me, you are on the same track. That which appears to you to be a chain of truth is in some lines misplacing the prophecies, and counterworking that which God has revealed as truth. The third angel's message is our burden to the people. It is the gospel of peace and righteousness and truth. Here is our work, to stand firmly to proclaim this. We need now to have every piece of the armor on.—MS 31, 1896.

THE THREE ANGELS' MESSAGES PLACED IN THE FUTURE

Bell apparently was placing the three angels' messages as future. Ellen White wrote out in a document of twenty-one pages a more detailed presentation dealing with Bell's position. This, too, carried the title "Testimony Concerning the Views of Prophecy Held by Brother John Bell." Its opening words sound the keynote of warning:

THE AUSTRALIAN YEARS

The proclamation of the first, second, and third angels' messages has been located by the Word of Inspiration. Not a peg or pin is to be removed.—MS 32, 1896.

Not only was Bell altering the position of the three angels' messages, but he was also introducing time-setting elements. She met both points squarely. Her statement may be read in *Selected Messages*, book 2, pages 104 to 117. Here and there in this exposure of error and confirmation of truth are timeless, thought-provoking expressions, such as:

> God's people, who in their belief and fulfillment of prophecy have acted a part in the proclamation of the first, second, and third angels' messages, know where they stand. They have an experience that is more precious than fine gold. They are to stand firm as a rock, holding the beginning of their confidence steadfast unto the end.
>
> A transforming power attended the proclamation of the first and second angels' messages, as it attends the message of the third angel. Lasting convictions were made upon human minds. The power of the Holy Spirit was manifested. There was diligent study of the Scriptures, point by point. Almost entire nights were devoted to earnest searching of the Word. We searched for the truth as for hidden treasures. The Lord revealed Himself to us. Light was shed on the prophecies, and we knew that we received divine instruction.—2SM, p. 109.
>
> The Lord will not lead minds now to set aside the truth that the Holy Spirit has moved upon His servants in the past to proclaim.—*Ibid.*, p. 110.
>
> The Lord does not lay upon those who have not had an experience in His work the burden of making a new exposition of those prophecies which He has, by His Holy Spirit, moved upon His chosen servants to explain. According to the light God has given me, this is the work which you, Brother F. [Bell], have been attempting to do.—*Ibid.*, p. 112.

John Bell read thoughtfully and prayerfully the two communications, and accepted them as messages of warning from God to him. He dropped his fanciful and misleading teachings and embraced

MEETING DOCTRINAL ERROR AND APOSTASIES

without reservation the doctrinal teachings of the church. Of this experience A. G. Daniells wrote to W. C. White on May 6, 1897: "John [Bell] has taken a splendid position on the testimony concerning his book. He has set aside his erroneous views altogether, and stands in the best position I have known him at all."—A. G. Daniells letter in 11 WCW, p. 435.

THE MCCULLAGH APOSTASY

Following close on the Bell experience was the apostasy of Stephen McCullagh. Ellen White was more saddened than surprised when she received a telegram late in March, 1897, from A. G. Daniells that Elders McCullagh and C. F. Hawkins had turned away from the message. Hawkins, a relatively new believer who had come from the ministry in the Wesleyan Church, had been led away by McCullagh, with whom he had been assigned to work. McCullagh had a background of nine years in the Adventist ministry and was a dedicated and efficient evangelist, working both in New Zealand and Australia. Now he had repudiated the Seventh-day Adventist Church and was drawing with him other members of the Adelaide church, which he pastored. In situations of this kind, there is usually no one cause to which such actions can be assigned. In this case it would seem that the home situation figured largely; it could be traced back to the time Ellen White first met him and his wife in New Zealand.

On August 16, 1893, at Hastings, New Zealand, while Ellen White was working with the McCullaghs, she picked up her pen and wrote them a letter:

Dear Brother and Sister McCullagh,

It is with sadness that I learn of your affliction. I sympathize with you in your daughter's illness, and we all pray for you. But, my brother and sister, there is a work that must be done for yourselves, as well as for your child, and I have hope that this work will be done. But let me tell you that unless you are willing to learn, you will not, cannot, obtain that Christian experience which it is so essential for every one of us to have. I have been much pained as I have thought of your family.

She wrote of right impulses that often motivated Mrs. McCullagh, and also of a very critical attitude toward others in the church, and the negative influence she exerted on her husband. She cited an instance of this kind, in the experience of another couple, that had taken place within the decade. The Lord allowed the accusing and critical tongue of the wife of a prominent minister to be forever silenced by paralysis, limiting her vocabulary to a word or two. Mrs. White observed: "Thus a talent, which if rightly employed would have done good to the church and to the world, was laid in ruins." Both husband and wife were left almost useless in the work of the Lord.

Referring to the same couple, she mentioned also that "neither he nor his wife accepted the principles of health reform, chiefly because of her insinuations and misinterpretations." She referred to still another case of a husband-and-wife team engaged in evangelism; he was a powerful speaker and his wife possessed unusual ability and influence.

She wrote of the indulgence and mismanagement in the family that led to sad results, and told of how "today this family have no connection with the truth. Because of mismanagement, father, mother, and children are lost to the cause of God.—Letter 40, 1893.

THE TESTIMONY NOT SENT

But the testimony in which these points were made to Elder and Mrs. McCullagh was not sent. Three years later she explained why:

> I intended to give it to you [Elder McCullagh], but did not do so because I gave a discourse there in which I took up very plainly the principles stated in this letter. You both heard my words, spoken under the power of the Holy Spirit, and Sister McCullagh told me that she received this message as given to herself, for she needed it. She said that she had never seen the case presented in that light before, and that she would make a decided change in her course of action in regard to her child. But this work has been strangely neglected.

Then Mrs. White explained the procedure often followed in her work, which many times proved effective and avoided a confrontation that could repel rather than win:

> It is my first duty to present Bible principles. Then, unless

there is a decided, conscientious reform made by those whose cases have been presented before me, I must appeal to them personally. I have often spoken in the presence of you both on these important subjects, but have never felt that the time had come for me to address you personally, for I could not be sure that you would understand the warning, and work diligently to reform, and I feared that you would both make a wrong use of the matter sent you.—Letter 69, 1896.

McCullagh, and possibly his wife, were present at the Monday-morning workers' meeting in October, 1894, at the Ashfield camp meeting when Ellen White was led by the Spirit of God to present a very close testimony to the workers present. Soon after this meeting she noted in her diary:

I must write that Elder Corliss and Elder McCullagh are in greater danger than they or anyone suppose. Elder McCullagh is tempted, and is gathering darkness to his soul.—MS 41, 1894.

Five months before this, McCullagh had been miraculously healed at the council meeting at Dora Creek. Ellen White mentioned this on several occasions:

We had had a most precious season of prayer while at Dora Creek for Brother McCullagh. The Lord graciously heard our prayers, and the inflammation left his throat and lungs, and he was healed. He has been improving ever since, and the Lord has sustained him in doing a large amount of work.—Letter 29, 1894.

While residing for the year or more at Granville, Ellen White worked very closely with McCullagh in his evangelistic ministry in the suburbs of Sydney. He often ate at her table. It would be most unlikely that with such opportunities as they conversed, she would not endeavor to give guidance on some of the points where he and his wife showed weakness. Both McCullagh and Ellen White wrote of their close working relationship. A letter to her written February 15, 1895, opens:

My Dear Mother:
I hope that you will not think me presumptuous in addressing you thus, but your great interest in me and the many

THE AUSTRALIAN YEARS

blessings the Lord has sent me through you, and the counsel and encouragements which I have received, seem to make you a mother to me.

But matters in the McCullagh home did not rise to the point God would have them. He was ill in the early weeks of 1896, and as plans were laid for the institute to be held at Avondale for a month beginning March 26, Ellen White invited him and his wife to attend. This was followed by a letter dated March 25. In this she pointed out that there was need of a different atmosphere in their home life and there was a deficiency in the cooking, calling for a remedy.

After describing her experience in following the health reform principles, she wrote in tender terms:

> I did not ask you to come here to hurt you in any way, but to change the order of things, which your wife will not properly do unless the Holy Spirit of God shall mold and fashion her character. When this is done she can be a much greater help to her husband, spiritually and physically, than she ever has been; and you will have order and system in your family management.—Letter 66, 1896.

Elder and Mrs. McCullagh responded to the invitation and went up to Cooranbong, but instead of staying at Ellen White's home they chose to stay with a family living at some distance from the school.

A SIGNIFICANT TESTIMONY

At two o'clock Monday morning, March 30, Ellen White was aroused to write, as she said, "those things which force themselves upon my mind." She penned these words:

Dear Brother and Sister McCullagh:

> I have been glad to receive encouraging letters from you. I am anxious that in every respect both of you shall meet the approval of God.... The Lord has given you talents for His service, and He longs to see you reveal Him to others. You have an influence with people; your speaking is acceptable to them. But you need to give more time and more earnest study to the Bible.—Letter 67, 1896.

After writing in this vein for a time, she turned to health reform

MEETING DOCTRINAL ERROR AND APOSTASIES

and the influence ministers exert, and then to the McCullagh home. She called for a change to be made in their experience and in the experience of their daughter. "Your daughter," she wrote, "has not had proper training; she has not been brought up with the careful restraint that God requires." She admonished, "In the home and in the world the love of God must occupy the first place. God must be enthroned in each heart." She called for Elder McCullagh to set his own home in order. In stark words she declared, "If this is not done, you will be more trammeled by the wrong influence felt there than by any other power that can be brought against you." Near the close she wrote:

> Think me not your enemy because I tell you the truth; let not the words I have written discourage you, but let them restore, strengthen, and uphold you. I respect and love you both, and for this reason, I entreat you to heed the message God has given me for you. Do not lightly esteem the voice of the Holy Spirit. God wants you to have liberty in Him, and by placing yourself in His hands, you may abound in every good work, and represent Him to the world. In much love.—*Ibid.*

At the time of writing, Ellen White did not put this message in their hands, even though the McCullaghs were at Cooranbong. Either she felt the time had not come or she did not have a suitable opportunity. On July 28 she mailed the testimony to them in Adelaide. Her hope that it might be received wholeheartedly was not fulfilled. The reproof, though spoken kindly, roiled their hearts, and during the Adelaide camp meeting held in October, Fannie Bolton freely sowed seeds of falsehood, questioning, and doubt about Ellen White's work, which bore a dire harvest. The accumulation led Elder McCullagh on March 23, 1897, to turn from the message and in bitterness tender his resignation as a minister of the Seventh-day Adventist Church.

This sparked a line of action: an immediate and hurried trip by Daniells and Colcord from Melbourne to Adelaide to meet with and attempt to save the two ministers, McCullagh and Hawkins, and the church. Calls were made for S. N. Haskell, now at Cooranbong, and G. B. Starr in Queensland to go to Adelaide also, and to expect to spend some time there. Of course, there were communications from

THE AUSTRALIAN YEARS

Ellen G. White to the parties concerned and to the church.

Daniells and Colcord found that McCullagh and Hawkins had brought the tent meetings at Adelaide to a close, but the tent was still standing. Announcements were out that the two ministers would be speaking in the Knights Templars' hall on Sunday evening. The church members were confused. As Haskell and Starr took up work in the city, they found, as Daniells did, that the prime point at issue was Ellen G. White and her messages. Following closely was the advocacy of a holiness experience and the calling in question of the sanctuary truth.

THE SPIRIT OF PROPHECY A PRIME POINT OF TRUTHS REJECTED

In his letter of resignation McCullagh declared: "I utterly reject Mrs. E. G. White's claims that 'in these days God speaks to men by the testimonies of His Spirit' through Mrs. White."

> I also regret Seventh-day Adventists' views of the atonement. I dare not believe that the blood of Christ had no real efficacy until 1844. I have found by observation that the views of the sanctuary placing the atonement of Christ at 1844 takes from the people their confidence in the perfection of the most glorious gospel of full salvation, made perfect by the offering of the blood of Jesus Christ once and for all.—DF 504b, "Apostasies, McCullagh and Hawkins," S. McCullagh resignation, March 23, 1897.

> [You] yourselves know also that a minister in your connection would not be tolerated as such if he should express his unbelief in the plenary inspiration in every word of Mrs. White's writings.

> The same is true of the doctrine of discrimination between meats and drinks—commonly termed amongst us "Health Reform." The rigid rules of diet as a test in religious standing, and further, in being made a final test for heaven, are a very decided article of faith. Members have been turned out of the churches on account of their unbelief in these, in the sanctuary question, and other lines of creed.—*Ibid.*

C. F. Hawkins, who had been only a few months in the faith but was ordained to the ministry at the camp meeting in Adelaide in

MEETING DOCTRINAL ERROR AND APOSTASIES

October, was less explicit as he wrote his letter of resignation. He declared that he could not harmonize with the Word of God much of the writings of Mrs. E. G. White, or her claim to inspiration (*ibid.*, C. F. Hawkins resignation, March 23, 1897).

ELLEN WHITE'S REACTION

Writing from Sunnyside, Cooranbong, March 30, 1897, to "Dear Brethren," Ellen White, after expressing her feelings of sadness over the developments, declared:

> This is no sudden movement. The enemy has been at work for a long period of time. I knew that Brother and Sister McCullagh would be strongly tempted in the very direction in which they are now. I knew that a crisis would come, that they would either see the defects in their home management, or else that Satan would blind their perception, so that the sin of Eli would become their sin. These things must be kept before the people, whether men will hear or refuse the warnings.
>
> I have not to study the consequences which may be the sure result to me. I have put myself in the hands of God. If He shall permit the enemy to do to me as he did to my Saviour, shall I complain?

In her closing lines of the six-page communication, she wrote:

> You may inquire, "What effect does this have upon you?"
>
> Sorrow only, sorrow of soul, but peace and perfect rest, and trust in Jesus. To vindicate myself, my position, or my mission, I would not utter ten words. I would not seek to give evidence of my work. "By their fruits ye shall know them."

She added, "We have never made meat eating a test of fellowship, *never.*"—Letter 14, 1897.

On April 5 she addressed a communication to the church at Adelaide. It opened with words that may offer a basis for using the names of individuals in the recital of this experience:

> It is your privilege and duty to stand firmly in the faith. I wish you now to see *that which I never meant to be made public*. It will explain to you the reason of this wonderful apostasy.
>
> Brother Haskell, I think, has the matter in clear lines, written

THE AUSTRALIAN YEARS

to Brother McCullagh after he had received a special blessing at the Cooranbong Bible Institute. Brother McCullagh thanked me for reading this to him. . . .

As he has poured out his tirade against me publicly, when I was not present to answer for myself, I think it just and right that his accusations shall be presented in writing or before others, that we may be able to answer them, point by point, and thus to disappoint the enemy in his determined efforts to accuse. This accusing spirit will continue till the close of time, but let none suppose that the Holy Spirit prompts them to work out Satan's attributes. *They are working under another leader.* We have seen this acted over and over again in our experience.—Letter 4, 1897. (Italics supplied.)

S. N. Haskell, soon after reaching Adelaide, listed in a letter to Ellen White the charges being made by McCullagh in his public meetings and in his visiting the church members from house to house. Some of these points were:

1. That you are worth from £10,000 to £20,000.
2. That all your testimonies are written upon the testimony you received from others.
3. That you have tried to separate Brother and Sister McCullagh.
4. That tea drinking and flesh eating are made tests among us and especially among the ministers.
5. That ministers have been disfellowshiped because they would not give them up.
6. That you have spent $3,000 on a sixteen-room house and have an awful household expense, and yet profess to believe the Lord is coming soon.
7. That your books are prepared by others and that you only give them ideas and books to select from.
8. That we do not educate people for the ministry, only for the canvassing work, and that your being located where you are is only to build up a school to educate canvassers to sell your books.
9. That in some meeting where a number of the brethren were, myself [Haskell] included, you saw that we all would live

MEETING DOCTRINAL ERROR AND APOSTASIES

till the Lord would come and that we would all be saved, but many are dying, to our confusion.

Haskell added: "And now their burden in name is Christian perfection, but in reality it is to attack positions on the sanctuary."—S. N. Haskell to EGW, April 5, 1897.

Ellen White's assessment of the situation on Monday, April 6, is mentioned in her letter to Edson:

> By the letters enclosed, you will learn that Brethren Hawkins and McCullagh, who were laboring in Adelaide, have given up their position on the truth, and are going in for holiness altogether. They have come out against the testimonies of the Spirit of the Lord. Elder Daniells telegraphed this to us, and we at once made arrangements for Brother Starr and wife to go to Adelaide. . . .
>
> Brother Haskell has left us for a week or two to visit Adelaide. We deemed it advisable for him to go. . . . We thought that as Brother Haskell had ordained both Brethren McCullagh and Hawkins, he might possibly save these poor, deluded men. He left us last Wednesday.—Letter 152, 1897.

Both Haskell and Starr gave frequent reports to Ellen White of the progress in their attempts to reclaim the men who were departing from the church. They labored hard with the two couples, but without success. Most of the members of the Adelaide church were soon standing firm, however. The hall meetings of McCullagh and Hawkins collapsed. Both men, with their wives, gave up the Sabbath. Hawkins found a position as pastor of a Baptist church in the little town of Mannum about forty miles east of Adelaide.

Reports came in occasionally of McCullagh filling appointments in Baptist churches; in July he was reported to have gone to a little Baptist church about fifty miles from Adelaide.

MC CULLAGH RETURNS TO THE FAITH—BRIEFLY

Two years went by, and little was heard of McCullagh. Then on January 7, 1899, having apparently made a complete turnaround, he wrote a rather extended confession to Ellen White at Cooranbong. On January 24 he carried it with him to the Ballarat camp meeting to show to A. G. Daniells and confer with him concerning the

THE AUSTRALIAN YEARS

possibility of his return to the Adventist ministry. As Daniells took the sheets, he read the opening sentence:

> Dear Sister White:
> Ever since my mysterious and unjustifiable fall about two years ago, we have been in a state of spiritual unrest.—S. McCullagh to EGW, Jan. 7, 1899.

Daniells read the extended confession thoughtfully, and after his visit with McCullagh he wrote Ellen White, mentioning the experience:

> Now I must tell you about Brother McCullagh. He is here with us; arrived this morning by the Adelaide express. I have had a long talk with him, and have read a letter that he wrote to you nearly three weeks ago. He says that he has had two years of solitude, captivity, and anguish, during which time he has reflected a great deal upon his situation.
> He has studied over the different features of the message, and he and his wife have become thoroughly satisfied that this work is of God, and that their only hope of eternal life rests upon their connection with it and faithful obedience to its requirements. He says that he wants to come back to the house of his Father. He wants to again unite with us as a people and devote his life to the proclamation of this truth. He blames himself altogether for his mysterious course. He says that he has not one single thing to justify that course. He tells me that the Lord has taken out of his heart every bit of hard feeling that he has held toward any of our people and every feature of our work.

Daniells told Ellen White of the rejoicing of heart this experience brought to him, and added:

> So far as I can see, he seems to have got hold of the Saviour, and feels greatly humbled. I feel to receive him with open arms and a warm heart. I stood strictly against the course he took when he left us, but now I wish to take hold of his hand and help him all that I possibly can. He says he cannot see how you can have any confidence in him or love for him. He feels that he has wounded you, and the cause that is dearer to you than life, to

such an extent he can never be worthy of your confidence. I tell him there is no one who will forgive him more quickly and heartily and will do more to help him find the solid Rock and stand there forever than you will do.—A. G. Daniells to EGW, Jan. 24, 1899.

Ellen White, as was fully expected, rejoiced in the return of the McCullagh family, but with her experience and insights she approached the matter with some caution, which is seen in her letter of response written February 12, 1899. She made it clear that she fully forgave him and his wife for the strange and malignant attitudes they had taken against her, but pointed out that under the circumstances, most earnest work must be performed by them not only in confession but in attempting to counter the evil work that had been done so publicly in bringing injury to the cause of God. It was not vindictiveness on her part, but only what must be done to be right with God and his erstwhile fellow workers. She wrote:

> As far as I am concerned, I can forgive everything where I have been held personally before the people as a fraud. When by confession you make things right with God, He will abundantly pardon. Be sure that in this work with God you realize that you have greatly dishonored the Lord. Every principle, every action, heart, life, and character, are put into the golden scale and weighed. Infinite Justice watches the beam, and weighs accurately every imagination of the heart, determining the value of the whole man—his thoughts, his words, his works.

The letter was a long one, and she employed some interesting illustrations as she wrote:

> Were you only a common soldier, instead of a captain in the army of the Lord, it would not be necessary to make these statements. But as your future may be spent in opening the Scriptures to others, it is of the greatest importance that you understand your position. It is not possible that we can come to you, but you can come to us.
> There is need of the deep moving of the Spirit of God, that if the word shall come to you, "Put on the armor, and fill your appointed place," you will not serve with eye service, but as the

THE AUSTRALIAN YEARS

servant of Christ.—Letter 33, 1899.

As McCullagh moved back into the work of the church, he wrote a deep-feeling confession that was published in the May 20 issue of the *Union Conference Record*. In this he emphasized his renewed confidence in the message and his relationship to Ellen G. White and her work.

He was one of the delegates sent to the union conference session held at Cooranbong in July, 1899, and continued with his ministry for another year or two. Then it happened again. Independent in spirit and restless in his work, while in the midst of an evangelistic tent meeting, probably in early 1902, he withdrew from the work. He declared, in an undated statement addressed to the conference committee of the Victorian Conference, that he considered a salaried ministry to be a curse to the ministry and to the church, a machine of the devil for the manufacture of hypocrites (S. McCullagh, in "Received Correspondence File," 1900-1901).

He expressed the desire to close his labors as an employee at the end of the month. On the sheet bearing his resignation, the conference president, G. B. Starr, added this note:

> McCullagh had done no work in the tent meetings for about a fortnight before writing this. He said he was sick. Sick in his mind. He was paid in full to the end of the month. The committee acted upon his resignation at once, accepting it and dismissing him from conference employ.—G. B. Starr, in "Received Letter File," S. McCullagh.

McCullagh's later years were spent quite apart from any religious interests. Ellen White had declared in one of her letters dealing with the McCullagh apostasy (Letter 1, 1897, and found in her comments in *The SDA Bible Commentary*, on Numbers 16:1-50, page 1114):

> I question whether genuine rebellion is ever curable. . . . Rebellion and apostasy are in the very air we breathe.

CHAPTER 24
(1897)

The Avondale School— Working Toward the Target Date

As THE new year, 1897, dawned, most activities at Cooranbong were geared to the proposed opening of the Avondale school, announced for April 28, 1897. On New Year's Day Prof. Herbert C. Lacey, who had returned to Australia to assist with the new school, was, with the help of his wife, Lillian, deep into the canning of fruit for the institution—starting with apricots. A donation of $60 just received to aid "where . . . most needed" was applied toward the purchase of other fruit, peaches, plums, et cetera, as they ripened. "There must be ample provision of fruit," declared Ellen White.

On New Year's Eve, Lacey had been dispatched to ride horseback through the community to call the Adventists together for a meeting planned by Ellen White. She was determined that as they neared the target date dedicated enthusiasm for the school enterprise should not wane. It was an excessively warm evening, with the air "close and stifling," so instead of meeting in the loft of the sawmill, chairs were brought out to seat the crowd on the "green sward." Ellen White spoke, seated in her carriage with Sara to her right, holding a lantern, and Herbert Lacey standing on her left, also with a lantern. She reported that "all listened with interest" as she read from a manuscript and then spoke for a time, telling of "the establishment of the work in different localities, where buildings had been erected for schools, sanitariums, and places of worship."

Then she introduced a point of particular concern, the fruitage of the criticism and tale-bearing of two of the carpenters, who because of the limited school finances could not be paid wages they felt they were entitled to receive. To Daniells she reported the evening meeting held under the stars:

> I told the people plainly that those who were not putting their whole heart into the work to be carried on in Cooranbong were only a hindrance to the work, and I heartily wished they would go to some other place.—Letter 44, 1897.

A few weeks later she wrote more specifically of the problems:

> We have been passing through a severe crisis here. Trials have come through Brethren _____ and _____, and their talkative wives.—Letter 57, 1897.

She explained that "when the work was started here, it was not carried forward in all wisdom." More horses had been purchased than were needed, incurring extra expense, and there were some ill-advised steps taken in connection with setting up the sawmill.

The defectors complained of this, but the principal problem lay in the wages paid to the workmen, five shillings a day, instead of the six they demanded. She wrote:

> Because they could not receive the highest wages, notwithstanding the means in the treasury were so low, they would not work. For three months Brother _____ sat on the devil's idle stool, tempting the devil to tempt him.—*Ibid.*

THE WORK AT THE SCHOOL

Progress in erecting the school buildings was steady. Professor Rousseau, who had been connected with the school enterprise from the start of the Bible school in Melbourne, had returned to the United States. The chairman of the school board, W. C. White, who also served as the president of the Australasian Union Conference, had been sent to America to attend the General Conference session and to take care of Australian interests, among them, the production of health foods. Being on the grounds, Ellen White was expected to lead out. She felt quite alone in having to make decisions concerning the school enterprise. There was one ordained minister of experience in the whole colony of New South Wales, whose time was much taken up with the general interests of an advancing work.

THE AVONDALE SCHOOL—WORKING TOWARD THE DATE

Metcalfe Hare, the business manager of the school, leaned heavily on Ellen White, and when important decisions had to be made she was looked upon as the senior officer in charge—a role she did not choose or covet. But those about her recognized that she had insights and experience others did not have. Writing on February 4 to W. C. White in the States, she bemoaned:

> I am left here to carry as heavy a load as I have ever carried in my life, to deal with men who think that they know everything when they know nothing as they ought to know it.—Letter 186, 1897.

Of course she continued with her writing, mostly correspondence, but at times she could get in a little on the life of Christ. She neglected her diary for weeks. "I could not possibly spend time," she wrote in mid-January, "to write in my book."—Letter 166, 1897. She filled speaking appointments on the Sabbath, standing in the pulpit the first five Sabbaths of the new year (Letter 186, 1897).

Willie's family, May, the two older girls, and the twins, on New Year's Day moved from the convent back to Sunnyside, into the washhouse where the twins had been born. As the weather grew colder, they were given the living room at the Sunnyside home. Letters tell of planning some kind of a cottage for the W. C. White family.

Medical work was just getting a start in Australia. A. W. Semmens, a graduate nurse from Battle Creek, opened the Health Home in Sydney. A large residence was rented, and Ellen White notes, "As he had no money, I furnished him with £25 to make a beginning."—Letter 70, 1897. To this was soon added £10 more. The *Bible Echo*, on January 18, 1897, carried an advertisement for the newly developed Battle Creek health foods. The public was informed that "some of these valuable foods are already being shipped to this country, and that a proposition is on foot for their manufacture here at an early date." This was a significant project that was to take on large proportions in Australia.

THE GARDEN AT SUNNYSIDE

The vegetable garden at the Sunnyside home was now yielding its harvest, and Ellen White wrote to the Lindsays, who with Mrs.

THE AUSTRALIAN YEARS

A. E. Wessels, Mrs. Lindsay's mother, had been such benefactors to the school enterprise:

> We have been living off our vegetables this year. Last year we had but few tomatoes, but this year we have enough for ourselves and a good supply for our neighbors also. So we testify that the school land will yield abundantly this coming year if the Lord's blessing shall attend our labors. We are now eating sweet corn that this land has produced, and we enjoy it much.
>
> I wish I could pass around to Mother Wessels and your family the products of our experiments in farming this first year in the bush. The Lord has prospered us indeed. . . . We are seeing the exact fulfillment of the light the Lord has given me, that if the land is worked thoroughly it will yield its treasures.—Letter 92, 1897.

What they grew was supplemented somewhat by what they could glean from the countryside, such as wild blackberries. "This day," she wrote to Willie on February 4, "Sara, Maggie, Minnie Hawkins, Edith, Ella May, and Mabel went . . . to gather blackberries. . . . Our party brought back about twenty-five quarts. . . . All were glad that they went."—Letter 186, 1897.

THE NEED OF COMPETENT LEADERS

But the great need was for competent men to lead out in the work at Cooranbong. To S. N. Haskell, a seasoned minister of long experience who had recently come from Africa and was in New Zealand, Ellen White in her weariness wrote of the progress of the work and the needs:

> You inquire about school buildings. (Dropped asleep.) The first building is progressing well. We have heard of no trouble. The roof is on, and everything moves satisfactorily. . . .
>
> I cannot carry the heavy load of writing, and also of speaking. I must not put in so much labor. . . . I want your help here in New South Wales. What a dearth there is!—Letter 70, 1897.

On a Monday in early February a letter came from Haskell, who had just arrived in Sydney. He urged Ellen White to hasten to the city so they could counsel together. She dropped everything and,

THE AVONDALE SCHOOL—WORKING TOWARD THE DATE

with Sara, within three hours was "speeding to the train with" their "fastest team, conjecturing all the four miles and a half whether or not we would be able to catch the train to Sydney" (Letter 82a, 1897). They did, and at 11:00 P.M. were at the Health Home at Summer Hill, where he was staying. There they joined in planning. To help keep the Health Home afloat financially, Haskell rented and furnished one room. If the home proved a success he would be paid back from earnings. Ellen White rented one room for $1 a week. She and Sara bought furniture in Sydney for this room so that she might have a place to stay when she was in the city. It could also be used by other workers as they passed through the city. Elder and Mrs. Baker took two rooms, for which they paid ten shillings a week (Letter 82a, 1897; Letter 171, 1897). After explaining these steps to help get the enterprise going, Mrs. White noted, "I hope this Health Home will prove a success, but it is an experiment."—Letter 171, 1897. And to W. C. White she wrote on the same day:

> In regard to the Health Home, I cannot see anything very flattering in patients as yet. But it is no use to look on the discouraging side. We must walk by faith. We must talk faith and act faith and live faith.—Letter 188, 1897.

Dr. Kellogg had sent from Battle Creek a shipment of the newly developed health foods, apparently as a donation to the enterprise, and Ellen White reported to him:

> I have learned that Brother Semmens is doing well selling the health foods. . . . We feel thankful that you could give them this timely assistance. They appreciate it very much, for they have been in most straitened circumstances.

In mid-February the mail brought £50 from Peter Wessels. As Ellen White acknowledged the gift she declared:

> It came exactly at the right time. We were at the Health Home, trying to get means to furnish some rooms in the humblest style. . . . When our means gave out, we had to wait; and when that money came, we rejoiced, and were glad. Now we can finish furnishing the rooms.—Letter 130, 1897.

The enterprise did succeed. By advertisements in each issue of the *Bible Echo* and in other media, the public was informed that at the Health Home they were prepared to "treat by the most approved rational methods paralysis, rheumatism, sciatica, neuralgia, and other disorders of the nervous system, also all manner of stomach and bowel disorders."

> These diseases will be treated by the most approved methods of hygiene, hydrotherapy, electrotherapy, massage, manual Swedish movement, diet, et cetera. Electric baths, electric vapour baths, sitz baths, salt glows, hot packs, wet sheet packs, massage, et cetera, can be had.—BE, Jan. 11, 1897, and throughout the year.

After some months the *Bible Echo* on November 15 carried a back-page note to effect that "the Sydney Health Home is having a good patronage at present—about all it can do."

THE SUCCESSFUL TREATMENT OF A VERY CRITICAL CASE

The little struggling health institution soon proved its worth as Professor Herbert Lacey, having contracted typhoid fever during a visit in school promotion in Tasmania, was nursed back to health. On Friday, February 28, a telegram was received by his wife, Lillian, at Cooranbong to the effect that Lacey, desperately ill, would arrive by train in Sydney that day. Lillian hastened to Sydney and arrived just as her husband was arriving from Melbourne. They went immediately to the Health Home, where his case was thought to be typhoid fever. He had lost twenty pounds in one week, and his wife wrote that he was "very poor, nothing but skin and bones." At the Health Home Elders Haskell and Baker were joined by Mr. Semmens in praying for his recovery (Letter 189, 1897). Semmens began using hydrotherapy treatments. Lillian reported to her husband's father, who resided at Cooranbong, that "Brother Semmens was using ice on his bowels" *(ibid.)*. His vitality was low, and when Ellen White learned of the ice remedy, she hastened off a telegram to Semmens, "Use no ice, but hot applications."—*Ibid*. Of course there was a reason for this, as she explained in a letter to W. C. White:

> In several cases light had been given me that the ice remedy

was not as efficacious as the hot water. I was afraid. His vitality, I learned, was very low and to put ice on head and chest I knew was a mistake. It would tax his vitality. . . .

There must be no risk run over Herbert's case. I was not going to be so delicate in regard to the physician as to permit Herbert Lacey's life to be put out. . . . There might be cases where the ice applications would work well. But books with prescriptions that are followed to the letter in regard to ice applications should have further explanations, that persons with low vitality should use hot in the place of cold. . . . To go just as the book of Dr. Kellogg shall direct without considering the subject is simply wild.

Hot fomentations in fever will kill the inflammation in nine cases out of ten where ice applications will, according to the light given me, tax the vitality unsafely. Here is where the danger comes in of not using judgment and reason in regard to the subject under treatment.—*Ibid.*

A week later in reporting to her son, she mentioned the steps being taken in connection with Lacey's illness:

The case is critical, but I believe the Lord will raise him up. We are praying for him. He is having everything done for him possible. . . . Brother Semmens gives his whole time to the sick man, and they are having Dr. Deek, who is watching the case of the hygienic methods of treatment with great interest. He says he is doing just as well as he could possibly do under this attack.—Letter 181, 1897.

In her diary she noted:

We have made his case a special subject of prayer. We wrote a few lines to him each day to call his attention to that which the Lord was ready and willing to do for him. The angels of God have presided over him all through his sickness.—MS 172, 1897.

Ellen White rejoiced when on Friday, April 9, she could send her carriage to the railway station to meet Herbert Lacey and his wife. She reported, "He is feeling real well and means to engage in the school at its beginning. I am so pleased." And she added:

Brother Herbert walked from his father's to the meeting in

the new building. He feels so well and we are so very thankful that the Lord wrought in his behalf, making Brother Semmens His human agent. He carried through the case without drugs.* W. C. White, the Lord has opened to me why so many cases are lost who have typhoid fever. They are drugged, and nature has not strength to overcome the drugs given them.—Letter 190, 1897.

MARRIAGE OF S. N. HASKELL AND HETTIE HURD

S. N. Haskell, a widower, while visiting Africa for some months en route to Australia, renewed acquaintance with Miss Hettie Hurd, a mission worker teaching there. Arrangements were made for them to marry in Australia. While Haskell waited rather impatiently in Sydney, his bride-to-be was held in quarantine for three weeks on shipboard in Melbourne because one passenger came down with smallpox just on the ship's arrival. The wedding finally took place at the Health Home on February 24, 1897. The Haskells proceeded to Cooranbong, for arrangements had been made for them to join the teaching force at the new school. Ellen White had her camp meeting tent pitched near her home and fitted up with floor covering and appropriate furniture. This provided a temporary place for the Haskells to reside.

Mrs. White had felt so alone and in need of help at Cooranbong, but even before the Haskell wedding she was given the encouraging word, "I have provided help in My servant." The Lord also revealed to her that in Haskell's wife He had "provided a matron and teacher" (Letter 99, 1897). "I rejoiced that I had the help of Brother and Sister Haskell. These God appointed to be my companions in establishing the school in this place."—Letter 77, 1897.

The coming of the Haskells to Cooranbong gave a real lift to the sagging spirits of the forces there. Ellen White wrote of it:

> We have appreciated Elder Haskell here at this time very much. He is a great help and strength to us all, especially to Brother Hare. The men working on the second building, some of whom are working out their pledges, are doing very indifferent

---

* Note: The reader should keep in mind that the medications referred to here were poisonous substances that when taken into the body left lasting, harmful effects and were quite unrelated to many of the medications employed now in the treatment of the sick.

THE AVONDALE SCHOOL—WORKING TOWARD THE DATE

work.—Letter 152, 1897.

COUNSEL AND ENCOURAGEMENT

One day Ellen White went over to see the progress being made in this second building, which would provide a dining room, kitchen, and storeroom for the school (Letter 33, 1897). Taking in the overall situation, she had some questions to ask!

"What place have you prepared for the boys to room in?" I asked.

"The chamber above the sawmill," they answered. "Many students can sleep there, and we will also secure tents."

"Is that the best plan you have?"

"It is the best we can do. When the building is enclosed, our money will be expended."

"Have you thought of how much money it would take to run this building up another story?"

Several were present. "We cannot do that," Brother Hare said, "but I wish we could." "You must do it, Brother Hare," I said. "What would the cost be?"

"Not less than £100," he answered.

"Then I advise you to put up the second story, and so provide sleeping rooms for the boys, and a meeting room for the church." . . .

"What shall we do?" they asked.

"Why," I said, "am I too late with my suggestions? Have the preparations gone so far that it would be a sacrifice to change now?"

"As to the matter of that," was the answer, "had your suggestions been a day later, we would have been at some loss." . . .

I said, "I will be responsible for the change made. If any censure comes, let it fall on me. You will be at expense of getting tents, and to the labor of pitching them. The students should not be put in the room over the mill. The influence would be demoralizing."—Letter 141, 1897.

"Now," she wrote, "we have this two-story building nicely enclosed." The expansion provided "a room for Sabbath meetings"

THE AUSTRALIAN YEARS

and "sleeping rooms for the young men" (Letter 33, 1897).

She confided in a letter to Willie:

> Be sure that Brother Hare is consulted in everything, and he will not move out in anything without consulting me. We move harmoniously in all our plans. Brother Haskell says it will not do for anyone to speak questioningly of anything I propose, for Brother Hare raises his right arm and says, "What Sister White advises to be done shall be done, without any ifs or ands about it."—Letter 141, 1897.

She also stated:

> All who see the upper story of the second building say, "Whatever could you do without it?" Brother Hare says he would not have taken the responsibility of changing anything if Sister White had not been right on the ground to say what was most needed. But that added story does Brother Hare lots of good.—*Ibid.*

ELLEN WHITE CALLS A WORK BEE

Just when they were within three weeks of target date for the school to open, Haskell was suddenly called to Adelaide to assist in meeting the crisis in the church there, brought about by the apostasy of the pastor, Stephen McCullagh. With Haskell's leaving, even if for only a couple of weeks, Hare's courage sank to an all-time low. He could see there was no hope of meeting the April 28 deadline for the opening of school. Taking in the situation, Ellen White began to plan a strategy, for she held that the school must open on time. She was not able to attend church on the Sabbath, but she sent an announcement to be read appointing a meeting for all who would, to attend on Sunday morning at six o'clock. She had something to say to them. She sent word to Metcalfe Hare to come to her home after the Sabbath to meet with Mrs. Haskell, Sara, and herself.

Mrs. White told the story to Willie as to what took place:

> On Saturday evening we had our interview. Our means were gone, and the school building could not be finished to open school at the appointed time. Sister Haskell asked just how many hands could be put on to the building, how many on outside

work, how many on the cistern, and how many inside. She wrote these down on paper, and after everything had been stated, she and I said, "We will have every position filled." Brother Hare argued that it was impossible.

We opened the morning meeting with singing and prayer, and then we laid the situation before them all. I told them that I would let them have Brethren Connell, James, and Worsnop, and pay them hire.

Brother Connell said that he had a two weeks' pledge to work out. Brother James said he would give one week's work in any line or place where they might put him. Brother Anderson also had pledged two weeks, and so one and another volunteered until men, women, and children were accepted.

I told them that I would give Sara to work in union with Sister Haskell, and they agreed to lay the floor with the help of Brother James to place the boards and press them into position, while Sister Haskell and Sara should drive the nails.

Our meeting lasted from six until eight o'clock. After [the] meeting the brother from Queensland made some depreciatory remarks about "lady carpenters," but no one to whom these words were addressed responded.

Every soul was put to work. There were over thirty in number. The women and children worked in the first building, cleaning windows and floors. Sister Worsnop came with her baby and children, and while she worked on the inside of a window, her eldest girl of 10 years worked on the outside. Thus the work in the first building was nearly completed in the first day.

Sister Haskell and Sara completed nearly one half on the dining-room floor. Brother Hare says everyone was enthusiastic. The women who engaged in the various branches of the work did well. Brother Richardson was putting the brick in the floor of the cellar. Some of the girls passed the brick from outside, while others inside passed them to Brother Richardson.

In the afternoon I was sent for to consult with Brother Hare in regard to making changes in the divisions of the dining room. . . . Then Brother Hare conducted me over the immediate premises, and we decided on the trees that must come down, one of which went down yesterday. . . . We left all the acacia trees, wattle trees they are called here. They are a very beautiful green, and bear a fragrant yellow blossom. . . .

Yesterday all the furniture in the mill loft was washed and cleansed from vermin, and prepared for the new building. One more floor is to be laid this afternoon. . . . The carpenters are siding up the building. Both ends are done, and quite a piece of the lower part on both sides. . . .

Monday, April 6, the workers, men, women, and children are all at work. . . .

The sisters had put the first coat of paint on the window frames. Brother Hare said that the women's diligent work had done more to inspire diligence in the men at work than any talk or ordering. The women's silence and industry had exerted an influence that nothing else could do. These women have worked until their hands and fingers are blistered, but they let out the water by skillful pricking, and rub their hands with Vaseline. They are determined to get at the work again. . . .

Brother Hare is full of courage now. Brother Haskell will be back in a week or two at most from the time he left. . . . His wife and Sara are heart and soul in the work. They make an excellent span just at this time. They will be in readiness to lay the upper floor after today, I think. Everything that is needed has come from Sydney and is right at hand, so that there will be no delay.

School will be opened April 28, 1897.—Letter 152, 1897.

About the time the work bee began, word was received from W. C. White that at the General Conference session action was taken to send Prof. C. B. Hughes, principal of the school in Texas, to assist at Cooranbong. He was a well-qualified and experienced educator and would bring good help to Avondale. The word brought courage to all (11 WCW, p. 276).

Entering fully into the spirit of things, Sara McEnterfer set out to raise money to buy a school bell. From the families in the community she collected about £6, and what Ellen White declared to be "an excellent sounding bell" was put in operation (Letter 141, 1897).

ANNOUNCEMENT OF THE OPENING OF THE SCHOOL

The good word reached most believers in Australia and New

THE AVONDALE SCHOOL—WORKING TOWARD THE DATE

Zealand through the April 5, 1897, issue of the *Bible Echo*. S. N. Haskell signed the article that informed constituents that school was opening at last. He promised:

> The Avondale school will give a liberal education to its pupils. Its founders are decidedly in favor of this. And at the same time the Scriptures will hold a prominent place in the school. It will aim to give that education in the sciences that will fit those who attend for the practical duties of life.

Haskell mentioned also that connected with the school would be manual training and scientific cooking. In addition, the students would receive instruction on how to care for the health, "believing a sound body contributes largely to a sound mind."

Those who had been in Australia longer, who knew well the general financial conditions, entertained some misgivings as to how many students would show up. W. C. White had alluded to this in his letter to O. A. Olsen written March 13, 1896:

> You will see from my article for the *Echo*, a copy of which I enclose, what my expectations are about the opening of our regular school. These are hard times, and if our buildings were ready, it would be difficult to get a paying patronage.—9 WCW, p. 342.

Two months after White wrote this letter, Professor Rousseau felt that because of his wife's failing health, he must return to the United States for a year, and requested a leave of absence. The board granted this, and in early July, 1896, having packed their household goods for storage, Rousseau and his wife took ship for San Francisco. His responsibilities as school manager were left with W. C. White, and his responsibilities as accountant were placed on the shoulders of Mrs. Lillian Lacey. The latter, a capable young woman but without experience in these lines, was hastily tutored by Rousseau before he left. As the church members saw the strong pillar of the teaching team departing and leaving the newly come Laceys to stand almost alone, their courage plummeted.

Now, in early 1897 Ellen White's undaunted faith was a steadying influence. School would open on April 28, 1897, and her brethren tried hard to exercise faith and to plan wisely. Wrote

THE AUSTRALIAN YEARS

Daniells to W. C. White on May 6: "I believe God is giving us the victory, though the devil is fighting this phase of our work very hard."

Daniells went on to say that they could not learn of one person in New South Wales and knew of only one in New Zealand who was planning to attend the school as a boarding student. He knew of only three or four from his conference. The matter became the subject of prayer, and his secretary, a woman named Graham, came up with a suggestion that he says "worked like a charm."

The suggestion was to ask the members in all the churches to each pledge sixpence a week for twenty weeks toward the students' aid fund. Twenty-seven persons making such payments would meet the tuition of one student for the term of twenty-two weeks. This was to be a revolving fund, the student in time paying it back to aid another. The assignment of the students to be benefited would be in the hands of the conference committee. The people were pleased, and enfused with a new spirit. The North Fitzroy church pledged itself responsible for two students, and other churches responded well. Daniells reported:

> One week ago tonight we sent six young men and women off by Cook's excursion. This morning at six o'clock we sent six more. One went alone in the middle of the week. This makes thirteen who have gone from this conference, and we are expecting to send four more.—11 WCW, p. 435.

Plans called for the literature evangelists to sponsor one student, and the scattered believers another. Daniells wrote rather jubilantly:

> If these plans work, and from the way things are going I have reason to believe they will, we shall have a pretty good attendance after all. We shall pull hard to have from thirty-five to forty boarding students by the time Professor Hughes arrives. These with the day students will give us an attendance of about sixty students.—*Ibid.*, p. 436.

THE QUESTION OF A PRIMARY SCHOOL

In the meantime there were some tense moments at Cooranbong brought on by an ill-advised action of the school board. It was

THE AVONDALE SCHOOL—WORKING TOWARD THE DATE

decided that there would be no primary school. Ellen White learned of this only after some announcements had been made, and she felt impelled to step in and take a firm position. She wrote of this, too, in her May 5 letter to Willie:

> The board met, and . . . decided that for this term there would be no primary school. On the next Sabbath morning, I told them that the primary school would commence when the other school did.—Letter 141, 1897.
>
> When Brother Lacey made the statement that there would be no primary school this term, Brother Hare felt much disappointed, for he wanted both of his children in the school. The officers are on his track, telling him that his children must attend the public school. . . .
>
> But in the first Sabbath meeting we held in the upper room, I presented this matter and called for a response, and you should have heard Brother Gambril's remarks. He came forward to the front seat, so that I could hear him. He spoke of the influence of the public schools on his children, of the education they were receiving.—*Ibid.*

It was in this setting that Ellen White made the rather familiar statement (found in *Testimonies*, vol. 6, p. 199), "In localities where there is a church, schools should be established if there are no more than six children to attend."—*Ibid.*

Steps were taken to again rent the convent for use in educating Adventist children in Adventist principles. Some of the children would be coming up Dora Creek by rowboat; Gambril's 15-year-old daughter would bring two Gambril children and two others to the primary school, which by mid-May had an enrollment of fifteen (*ibid.*; Letter 126, 1897).

THE AVONDALE SCHOOL OPENS

For some unknown reason, no official report of the opening of the Avondale school graces the pages of the *Bible Echo*. However, Metcalfe Hare stated in a report:

> The school opened the twenty-eighth of April, Mrs. E. G. White, Elder S. N. Haskell, and the teachers being present, with

THE AUSTRALIAN YEARS

all those who had been associated with the work. The buildings were dedicated to their sacred mission by Elder Haskell.—DF 170, "The Avondale School, 1895-1907."

Ellen White furnished a few more details in a letter to W. C. White a few days later:

> April 28 our school opened. At the opening exercises the upper room of the second building, above the dining room, was quite full. Brother Haskell opened the meeting by reading a portion of Scripture. He then prayed, and made a few remarks. I then followed.—Letter 141, 1897.

"The Spirit of the Lord was present," she wrote to Edson (Letter 149, 1897), and in her diary for the opening day she wrote:

> We had the opening exercises in the last building erected. We had more in attendance than we had expected. We felt very thankful to make so good a beginning. We were very much pleased to have Brother and Sister Haskell with us. Brother Herbert Lacey and his wife were with us.—MS 172, 1897.

So with a staff of six (of which four were teachers) and with ten students (LS, p. 365) the Avondale school commenced, and on the very day appointed. When some expressed the opinion that the buildings could not be completed on time, Ellen White had declared:

> There must not be one day's postponement. . . . If there is but one student present, we will begin the school at the appointed time.—Letter 149, 1897.

She understood well the far-reaching psychological effect if they failed. But they did not fail. She wrote on May 5:

> School had been delayed so long that we knew that no matter what our condition was in the way of preparation, it must start on time. But no one believed that it would. Now, when they see that we are in earnest, they will have some confidence and interest in the school.—Letter 141, 1897.

One week after school opened, Ellen White reported forty students. The *Bible Echo* dated June 7 reported that "about fifty students are in attendance at the Avondale school," rather more than expected. The next issue declared that they were "happy to revise these figures this week and state that there are sixty-two."

Ellen White felt comfortable with the Haskells at the school taking a leading role. She wrote of them as experienced laborers, who "were a great help to us in the work of preparation, in devising and planning to get things in order" (Letter 149, 1897). Prof. and Mrs. C. B. Hughes were on their way from Keene, Texas. After the school was quite well organized and had continued for two months, the faculty was described in a report by G. T. Wilson in the *Bible Echo:*

> Prof. C. B. Hughes and wife arrived two weeks ago from America. He has been chosen by the school board as principal of the school, and is to have the general management of things on the place. He teaches the history class, who are now studying "Empires of the Bible." His wife teaches grammar, rhetoric, elocution, penmanship, and one Bible class.
>
> Prof. H. C. Lacey is teacher of mathematics, physiology, geography, singing, and voice culture; and his wife teaches the primary department.
>
> Pastor S. N. Haskell is the principal instructor in Bible study; and Mrs. Hettie Hurd Haskell, his wife, has charge of one Bible class, and acts as the matron of the school.
>
> Mr. T. B. Skinner, a graduate of St. Helena Sanitarium Nurses' Training Department, has charge of the kitchen and dining room, and on one day in the week gives practical instruction in cooking. The students are taught how to make bread, can fruit, and the other arts of healthful cookery.—June 21, 1897.

In concluding his report, Wilson observed that "the students are mostly young men and women, of good, intelligent class, besides whom there are a few persons of more mature years." About one half were below the age of 16.

The school at Avondale was off to a good start.

CHAPTER 25
(1897)

Avondale—
A New Start in
Christian Education

"WE EARNESTLY desire to have this school such as the Lord shall approve," wrote Ellen White on June 9, 1897 (Letter 33, 1897). For twenty-three years Seventh-day Adventists had been engaged in operating educational institutions, commencing in Battle Creek in 1874. Through those years a good deal of experience had been gained, and the Lord had many times given special instruction to guide in the founding and operation of schools. Mistakes had been made from the start; oftentimes, courses were set that were not for the best and were hard to alter. Now it seemed appropriate and possible, as a new beginning was being made in a new land, to establish a course more in keeping with God's will. Mrs. White wrote:

> We must all work earnestly and intelligently to do the utmost to make this school as God would have it. No man's notions are to be brought in here. No breezes from Battle Creek are to be wafted in. I see I must watch before and behind and on every side to permit nothing to find entrance that has been presented before me as injuring our schools in America.—Letter 138, 1897.

In the same vein she wrote in her diary on July 22:

> This is not to be a school after the common order of schools. It is such a school as the Lord has marked out should be established. We have to demonstrate that we have not followed cunningly devised fables.—MS 174, 1897.

Some members of the faculty contributed to these desirable ends

AVONDALE—A NEW START IN CHRISTIAN EDUCATION

more than others. There was the steady and experienced Elder Haskell, of whom Ellen White could write:

> His experience and knowledge of the truth, commencing in so early a stage of our history as Seventh-day Adventists, was needed in this country. From his youth upward, he has been a self-denying, self-sacrificing man. And now his age and gray hairs give him the respect of all who know him.—Letter 126, 1897.

There was Prof. C. B. Hughes and his wife. Of them Ellen White wrote:

> We are pleased with the principal of the school and his wife. They are determined to carry out the testimonies. . . . He is the right man for the place.—Letter 164, 1897.

And there was the more youthful Herbert C. Lacey, with his wife, Lillian. Twenty-five years of age, he was just out of Battle Creek College, having completed the classical course. He was one of the young men sent from Australia to the United States to gain training to enter the Lord's work. It was expected he would make a strong contribution. Ellen White had met a portion of his school expenses both at Healdsburg and in Battle Creek. Although Lacey was in time to grow and develop to become one of the most able and respected Bible teachers in the denomination, at this point he was described by Ellen White:

> Brother Herbert Lacey has the impulsive temperament to move out after the education received in Battle Creek and would feel perfectly competent to manage everything, when he will have to obtain as a learner how things ought to be managed.—Letter 182, 1897.

Matters became complicated when Prof. Rousseau left for the United States. Herbert Lacey was chosen by the Avondale school board to serve as principal. He was without experience in lines of management and in finance, yet he readily accepted the position. It was difficult for Ellen White to understand why not one member of the school board sought her counsel about the matter. She wrote Daniells that "all these things had been opened before me," and

THE AUSTRALIAN YEARS

commented, "It was a large pill for me to swallow."—Letter 185, 1897. She felt she must act, distasteful as it might be. To W. C. White she wrote on June 6:

> The board . . . elected Brother Herbert Lacey as principal without counseling with me. This brought me to the front to speak.—Letter 140, 1897.

PROF. C. B. HUGHES CHOSEN TO LEAD

Just how the switch was brought about was not recorded, but the same letter reports:

> Brother Hughes is principal, and he will, I think, do well in this position. He has had experience in managing. I think there will be no trouble. But I have had to speak plainly, and keep out the breezes coming from Battle Creek.—*Ibid.*

She reported that "Herbert and Brother Hughes get along nicely together."—*Ibid.* In this, Lacey showed his true mettle; three days later, June 9, she could write: "Brother Herbert Lacey and his wife are teaching in the school, and are doing good work."—Letter 33, 1897.

But changes in attitudes and relationships and even in the understanding of principles come slowly. On July 15 Ellen White noted in her diary:

> Brother Herbert Lacey called and made a short visit. We engaged in profitable conversation. He stated that while in America at Healdsburg, he engaged in Bible studies. After going to Battle Creek, he went deeper into study but did not take Bible studies at all. Here he has lost much, for the most important of all education is to understand what saith the Scriptures—and yet he was ordained for the ministry when he had not fitted himself at all for such a position. . . . The Word of God is our lesson book, lying at the very foundation of true education.
>
> He is just beginning to understand that he has everything to learn. The Lord gave me a message for him and he says every word of it is truth and he wants to know himself.
>
> May the Lord mold and fashion him. The very first work he needs is thorough conversion. He is ignorant of the Scriptures

AVONDALE—A NEW START IN CHRISTIAN EDUCATION

and the power of God. This is the great mistake that has been made in this young man's education. Oh, that as a teacher in this school, he may be a learner.—MS 174, 1897.

Lillian Lacey fitted into the school program nicely as the teacher handling the fifteen children in what today would be called the grade school. "I understand," wrote Ellen White on June 6, "that the children in the primary division are highly pleased with their teacher."—Letter 140, 1897.

S. N. HASKELL'S DEEP KNOWLEDGE OF GOD'S WORD

If Herbert Lacey, trained at Battle Creek College, was deficient in a deep knowledge of the Word of God, Stephen Haskell, somewhat a self-made man, was not. Of this, Ellen White wrote on June 6:

> Brother Haskell is the Lord's servant, a man of opportunity. We appreciate his experience, his judgment, his thoughtful care and caution. He is indeed a mighty man in the Scriptures. He opens the Word of God in such a simple manner, making every subject reveal its true importance. He urges home practical godliness.—*Ibid.*

Nearer the opening of school she wrote of his speaking each morning at six o'clock, leading out in a Bible lesson.

> This is free to all, and there is a goodly company out each morning, for it is a blessing to all. This study lasts for one hour. These meetings are intensely interesting. The subject thus far has been the sanctuary question, and we are highly gratified to see the interest manifested.
>
> All are much interested in the way he presents the subject. He speaks in a clear, simple style, and brings in much Scripture to sustain every point. He feels that altogether too little has been said upon this subject, for it is the central pillar that sustains the structure of our position at the present time.—Letter 126, 1897.

Nor did his talented wife, Hettie, a teacher of experience, come far behind. Writing on June 9 to an old friend in New England, Mrs. White mentioned both Haskell and his wife:

> Brother and Sister Haskell fill very important places in our

THE AUSTRALIAN YEARS

school in giving Bible lessons. Sister Haskell is matron, and also teaches a Bible class. Brother Haskell also teaches a Bible class. . . . His wife is a woman of rare ability as a manager. She takes hold most earnestly, not afraid to put her hand to any work. . . . We have had most precious instruction from the Word from Brother and Sister Haskell.—Letter 33, 1897.

School was well underway when Professor and Mrs. Hughes arrived in late May. Several weeks later, Ellen White wrote of how well he took hold of the work. As she watched him move into his responsibilities as principal and manager, she wrote on July 4 of the student-principal relationship: "Brother Hughes does not say, 'Go, boys,' but pulls off his coat and says, 'Come, boys.' He works with them. He is the right man for the place. All take hold with a will, cheerfully."—Letter 164, 1897.

A CLOSE LOOK AT ELLEN WHITE'S PARTICIPATION

Ellen White's diary for the month of July reveals that she was deeply engrossed in the work of the school, its triumphs and its problems. As the pioneer school for the Australasian field, it needed to succeed, to form a pattern that would have wide influence. On Monday, July 5, she reported:

> I had a long interview with Brother Martin in regard to many important matters in reference to the school orchard, and my own orchard, and in reference to the best methods so to manage the land that it shall produce sufficient for the consumption of the school and thereby no expenditure of money for fruit and vegetables. We expect good crops this year, and we shall have, we expect, all that the school will demand on their own land and all that our own family will require on our little farm. . . .
>
> *Tuesday morning, July 6:* I brought before the students the most important matters in regard to an all-round education. May the Lord bless the effort made to bring before the school the necessity of physical culture combined with the mental taxation. The Lord has pointed out the deficiencies in our ideas, and the true education that is essential in our school here in Cooranbong. . . .
>
> *Thursday, July 8:* I arose at two o'clock A.M. and commenced

AVONDALE—A NEW START IN CHRISTIAN EDUCATION

my writing. My prayer is, O Lord, teach and lead and guide me. Help me to feel my responsibilities in regard to my committed trust. . . . Quarter before 9:00 A.M. I again visited the school and read to them important matter in regard to the relation of diet and health and morals—words that had been written years ago for the book *Christian Temperance.* It is just what is needed now for the students in our school. I occupied about fifty-five minutes.

Sabbath, July 10: I spoke to the people. . . . I felt the deep movings of the Spirit of God upon me. Brother Lacey, a young man, stood up before the people to pray. That act so pained my heart I said, "Brother Lacey, get down upon your knees," which he did. I knew if any human being knew whom he was addressing—the great and holy God, who dwelleth in light inapproachable, before whom angels veil their faces and cry, "Holy, holy, holy"—he would not stand erect before his students and present his petitions to God.—MS 174, 1897.*

She did not speak at the school every day, but frequently she wrote instruction regarding school matters and often went over to address the faculty and students. There stood out clearly in her mind the contrast between God's ideal in the education of Adventist youth and the training being given in some of the older colleges of the church in America. After the experience in requesting one of the faculty members to kneel while addressing God in the formal Sabbath-morning worship prayer, she wrote:

> I feel very sad when I consider that young men come from Battle Creek with a deficient education in spiritual godliness. After devoting years of study in the school at Battle Creek, some have stated they had an education that was of little use to them. I see more and more the folly of five years in succession devoted to the education of any student. Let them learn common hard work, in exercising the muscles and their hands, and let them learn from books that have not one grain of infidelity sprinkled in through their brilliant productions. It is like the sugarcoated pills that are used—a drug to destroy rather than to restore.—*Ibid.*

---

* See 2SM, pp. 311-316, for counsel given in connection with this experience.

THE AUSTRALIAN YEARS
A VISION CONCERNING THE SCHOOL

On Tuesday morning, July 13, Ellen White arose early, heavily burdened in heart. The state of things in the school had, a few days before, been presented to her in vision. Things at the school, she was shown, were "not meeting the mind of the Spirit of God. His heart of love is grieved," she stated, and she felt impelled to present a message to the students. She wrote in her diary:

> There is a spirit of levity and recklessness that should not be tolerated. There are some who have not stood in the counsel of God, but have by their words and by their attitude given more or less encouragement to the students to suppose they were under too much restraint. I knew from the light given me it was time for me to speak.
>
> I went to the school this morning and found Brother and Sister Hughes and Brother and Sister Haskell counseling together as to what they should do to change the order of things. . . . The foolish talking, the jesting, the joking, the low, cheap talk, and the unruly spirit were contaminating the youth. I presented to them that both principal and teachers were held responsible, and were under condemnation of God while these things existed. They are to watch for souls as they that must give an account. . . .
>
> I read before the school that a change must come. No longer should any such deportment be tolerated in the school. After I had read the matter written, there were some testimonies borne by the students, which were to the point.—*Ibid.*

In her July 12 entry she stated:

> While we are not to be gloomy, but cheerful and happy, there is to be no silliness, but a sobriety in harmony with our faith. Words and actions form character. Therefore our words should be clean, pure, simple, yet elevated. The gift of speech is a valuable talent, and the Lord has no pleasure in having low, cheap, degrading nonsense which tastes strongly of vice and revelry. No Christian should condescend to imitate and catch such habits from another student. These evil, silly words are discordant notes and contribute to the happiness of no one. They

AVONDALE—A NEW START IN CHRISTIAN EDUCATION

are a detriment to spirituality. The Word of God forbids them.—*Ibid*.

On July 14, with this experience in mind, she declared:

> It is often not pleasant to speak the plain words of reproof and counsel; but I dare not hold my peace, lest the . . . wrongdoer, not warned, shall go on in heedless indifference until the Lord shall cut him down like a tree that is as a cumberer of the ground.—*Ibid*.

A CALL FOR SOUND FINANCIAL POLICIES

A month later, Ellen White had something to say about the tuition rates and balancing the school budget:

> There is a very great mistake made in setting the price of tuitions so low. It cannot be thus. It is a wild movement.
>
> If I had known it before the matter had gone out, I would not have consented to have any such prices. I have had the matter presented to me that one cause of the debts accumulated in Battle Creek has been low tuition and rates for rooms and board, and then not proper management to bring the outgoes to harmonize with such prices.
>
> The Lord would have His people act sensibly. They cannot possibly keep from sinking under the outgoing expenditures. When they have tested this way of management long enough to see the outcome, why do they repeat the same thing term after term? You will have less students—that may be and may not be. But whichever way it shall turn, there must be wise managers in every school who understand the practical workings of the expenditures and the income, and the outgoes must harmonize with the income. Therefore, do not dishonor the educational interests with mismanagement.
>
> Let there be careful tact and wisdom in all our school arrangements and place the tuition sufficiently high to make ends meet. The Lord is not glorified by any such unwise managing. If the correct management of the school in setting the tuition at a figure to clear expenses shall bring in less students, then let the risk be run on the safe side, and there will be a better class of students.—Letter 193, 1897.

THE AUSTRALIAN YEARS
CONFRONTED WITH THE PROBLEM OF ASSOCIATION

When Battle Creek College was started, no provision was made for housing the students. They found lodging with families in Battle Creek and made their own boarding arrangements. There were many problems linked with this plan. Later, of course, the need was clearly seen, and provisions were made. On the establishment of Healdsburg College, it was felt that a real advance was made by the erection of a school home. One floor was allotted to the girls and another to the young men. Even this was not without its problems. Now at Cooranbong they were facing the question of association of the students and the housing problem. Ellen White mentioned this in her letter of July 23 to W. C. White. School attendance exceeded their expectations, housing facilities were crowded, and more students were expected. She wrote:

> There are now to be about five more students, so there is no more room for an increase until we shall have means to put up buildings.
>
> One thing we are seriously considering, that the building for the boys shall be entirely separate from that of the girls, a distinct building. . . . I have spoken and read five mornings in succession in the school, and after talking with the whole school, I then took the girls by themselves and talked with them seriously and charged them to keep themselves sacredly to themselves. We would not, could not, allow any courting or forming attachments at the school, girls with young men and young men with girls. This I said before the whole school, and then to the young ladies. I entreated them to be reserved, to be delicate and refined and not to be forward and bold and inviting the attention of young men; [I told them] that they should consider it an honor to cooperate with their teachers and seek to please them in everything.—Letter 193, 1897.

The records indicate that nearly half the student body were 16 years of age or younger. Restraints of a more rigid character were called for than in dealing with a normal college-age group. On another occasion she wrote:

> We have labored hard to keep in check everything in the

AVONDALE—A NEW START IN CHRISTIAN EDUCATION

school like favoritism, attachments, and courting. We have told the students that we would not allow the first thread of this to be interwoven with their schoolwork. On this point we are as firm as a rock.—Letter 145, 1897.*

FACTORS THAT ENCOURAGED ELLEN WHITE

In the midst of the struggle to make the Avondale school all that God designed it to be, there appeared in an E. G. White letter written July 9, to a friend, some interesting observations:

> All the determined opposition that we have met has only strengthened, stablished, and settled me in the belief that this is the location we should occupy. Were it not, Satan would not labor with such intense energy to discourage us, and drive us from the ground. All who truly love God will prove strong enough to stand the strain. Temptations will come to teachers and to students. Will we conquer them, or will we be conquered?
>
> Christ is testing every soul on this ground. He demands loyalty. Who will be true to Him? Who will stand on guard day and night, maintaining a vital connection with God? The underlying principle of heart-life and home-life and church-life is supreme love to God and love to our neighbors.—Letter 77, 1897.

She then spoke of the battles that had had to be fought during the past fifty years and declared that they would have to be fought over and over again. She urged that God's people must stand constantly on guard, and reminded that "it is he that endures to the end that will be saved."

THE CONFESSION OF A. G. DANIELLS

As workers came to visit the school in progress, they were well pleased. Of one such occasion she wrote:

> I am very glad that these brethren came up. All who had not before seen the grounds were delighted with the situation. Elder Daniells was surprised at the improvement that had been made

---

* See *Ellen G. White: The Later Elmshaven Years*, pp. 382-386, for Ellen White's approach to this matter when preparing a book manuscript for general use. See also CPT, p. 101.

THE AUSTRALIAN YEARS

in the buildings and on the land. All were free to acknowledge that this was the place where the school should be located.—Letter 149, 1897.

In connection with this visit, Daniells promised to work for the school with all his power (Letter 140, 1897). But that which brought the greatest satisfaction to Ellen White was what took place a few weeks later as he again visited the school. Of this she wrote on June 24:

> Brother Daniells made a most thorough acknowledgment to me. He confessed that he had not helped at all, either by his faith or his influence, but had permitted Willie and me to drag the load uphill. He said he saw that he had been wrong, and he now had to confess that the Lord had been leading step by step, but that he had had no part in it. "I am thoroughly convinced," he said, "that this is the place for our school, and I am going to work with all my heart and strength to advance and build up the school interest, and I may repair, as far as possible, that harm I have done."—Letter 132, 1897.

> Elder Daniells has had little faith that a school would ever be in successful operation here, but he has been thoroughly converted on this subject.—*Ibid.*

As winter gave way to spring and the end of the first school year at Avondale was in sight, Ellen White entertained one growing concern—the need of a house in which to worship God. Could one be built by the close of the school year, now only seven weeks away? Such an accomplishment would crown this year that marked a new start in Christian education.

CHAPTER 26
(1897)

The New Church Building at Avondale

ON SABBATH, January 2, 1897, in the loft above the sawmill, Ellen White spoke to the believers comprising the Cooranbong church. It had become a place for general storage as well as a place for meetings. The audience filled the room, but, she wrote, "It did appear so badly." "There was, well, I need hardly describe it—almost everything but money." She exclaimed, "I am fully decided that we must have a meeting house."—Letter 70, 1897.

With the construction, just before school opened, of the second story over the kitchen and dining hall, a room of limited space became available for meetings, and everyone was thankful for this. But as more students came in and the community grew, this proved to be too limited.

On Wednesday morning, August 11, Baker and Daniells, the presidents of the two leading conferences, were on the campus to counsel with Ellen White and others concerning school matters and the coming camp meetings. Word had just been received at Cooranbong of the discovery of an accounting error in Melbourne. Eleven hundred pounds on deposit for the school had been lost track of—six hundred from the Wessels family and five hundred from the General Conference (Letter 177, 1897)—but was now available. Construction of a dormitory for the men could now be undertaken, and £100 was allotted toward a church building. In reporting the interview, Ellen White wrote: "We feel the need of a church very much."—MS 175, 1897.

Friday morning, August 13, Daniells and Baker again met with

THE AUSTRALIAN YEARS

Ellen White. The subject was "ways and means—how to build the meetinghouse" (*ibid.*). A few days later she wrote of it:

> We took matters up quite fully, and decided that a meetinghouse must be built. We decided to start the work at once, and then in a few weeks we would have a place of worship.—*Letter 90, 1897.*

She saw that the faith of the brethren was limited. They felt they should build small, to accommodate possibly two hundred. Ellen White was for a larger building, one that would seat three hundred, but she held back. She was so happy that the brethren sensed fully the need and were willing to venture that she, as she said, "was glad to carry these brethren with us in this," feeling that in time "additional light would be given."

Then that Friday afternoon mail brought a pleasant surprise that to Ellen White was an omen of God's favor: a letter from the Harmon Lindsay family in Africa, accompanied by a draft for £100. Ellen White in her thank-you letter wrote:

> When your draft came, we felt to praise the Lord, who had put it into your hearts to give of your means to help in building a house for the Lord, that His people might worship Him decently and in order. . . . We had decided to make a beginning with the £100 [on hand], knowing that the Lord would not leave us without means to complete the house.—*Ibid.*

Sabbath, Daniells took the morning worship service and spoke to 175 people who crowded into the upstairs temporary chapel. Ellen White rejoiced that they could now see their way and would soon have a simple, neat chapel erected (MS 175, 1897). Daniells and Baker left Sunday morning, but the church project was not forgotten. On Monday morning Ellen White was requested to join others in considering where the meetinghouse should be erected. She wrote:

> There is a beautiful spot of land, forming a gentle rise, at a little distance from the main road. I remembered distinctly seeing this spot of land when we first visited this place in 1894. . . . We remarked upon this spot, and admired it. It is not thickly timbered, and there is no underbrush. . . .

THE NEW CHURCH BUILDING AT AVONDALE

We were impressed that this was the place on which to erect the church. We saw no valid reason why this building should not be on the very best location that the land afforded.—Letter 90, 1897.

On Monday evening Ellen White conversed with Metcalfe Hare concerning the proposed church, but found him less enthusiastic than was she and others. As they parted she told him, "We will not hasten the building of the meetinghouse." But this decision was short-lived. Writing to Hare the next day, she told of a change in her position:

Last night has changed my ideas materially. . . . I received instruction to speak to the people, and tell them that we are not to leave the house of the Lord until the last consideration. . . . I was instructed that our place of worship should be of easy access, and that the most precious portion of the land should be selected as a place on which to build for God.

The question was asked, "Have you shown proper respect for the Master? Have you shown the eloquence of true politeness toward God? . . . You cannot worship God in a correct manner where you are now. You cannot bow before Him in a suitable position. Build a house for God without delay. Secure the most favorable location. Prepare seats that will be proper for a house of God."—Letter 56, 1897.

THE HASTENING PACE

On Wednesday, August 18, Ellen White noted in her diary:

In the afternoon we visited Brother Hare and we came to an understanding upon some points in regard to building a church without delay. We cannot see the necessity or the least excuse for delay. When reproof comes that we have been negligent in regard to building a house for the Lord that we can dedicate to Him, we will feel clearly that we have not acted our part.—MS 175, 1897.

Things were now beginning to move. On Thursday, August 19, Ellen White told of developments:

Sara and I visited Brother Haskell and had a profitable talk

THE AUSTRALIAN YEARS

with him in regard to the meetinghouse—plans for the size of the building, and the preparing of material. Sara and I rode again to the site which we thought the best place for the meetinghouse. Certainly it is the most beautiful spot upon the whole grounds. We cannot see where there can be a spot that will have greater advantages. . . . We will honor God in preparing a place where He can meet with His people who love God and keep His commandments.—*Ibid.*

Friday morning Elder Haskell came to Sunnyside and had breakfast with the family, and there were further discussions of plans for the new church. Then he, Ellen White, and Sara rode to the school grounds to select the precise site for the church. They could see that they must have more than just one of the lots available, and talked of four or five. "Work will commence on Sunday morning, August 22," she noted in her diary.—*Ibid.*

Ellen White spoke at the worship service on Sabbath morning. She had no difficulty in selecting a text for the sermon, and read from Haggai 1:14 and 2:4, the call for God's people of old for the building of a house of worship. This had been urged upon her mind. She reported the matter in this way:

> I bore a clear and decided testimony, and appealed to all to rise up and build a house for the Lord. Elder Haskell spoke to the point, and we know the people felt indeed in earnest in the matter to do all they could.—*Ibid.*

There was need for haste, for they wanted to dedicate the building not later than the close of school. A meeting was called for on Sunday evening to consider the plans for building. Sunday morning Elder Haskell was again at the White home, coming before breakfast. After breakfast there was further discussion regarding the erection of the church *"now, without delay,"* Ellen White wrote, underlining the words in her diary. They talked of carpenters, and she proposed that they visit Brother Hardy, a skillful workman and a good manager. They could also draw in Fred Lamplough, another master workman. It was raining, but they started by carriage through the woods to the Hardy home. Ellen White reported:

> He was at home and we laid the rough sketch before him, and

THE NEW CHURCH BUILDING AT AVONDALE

he thought the dimensions proportionate. We advised with him, and he decided to stand with Fred Lamplough as directors over a large number of hands.—*Ibid.*

That Sunday evening as the church family met, it was to study the proposition that they build a church, and build it "without delay." Haskell and Lamplough reported to Ellen White on Monday morning that it was "a very stirring meeting." When a show of hands was called for, all present, except Metcalfe Hare and C. B. Hughes, voted in favor of proceeding at once. Commented Ellen White in her diary, "I was sorry in my heart that these men did not unite with those who were in favor. May the Lord help us and open ways before us and strengthen the purpose of everyone to 'arise and build.'"

Tuesday, August 24, Haskell and Lamplough went to Sydney to purchase lumber; Hare came over to Sunnyside to converse with Ellen White in reference to the building of the chapel. "We talked about one hour," Ellen White noted, and continued, "We hope that our words and ideas were not materially apart, but in harmony generally."—*Ibid*. At family worship that evening Ellen White prayed "most earnestly" for the "Lord to manifest unto us His mercy and His will." A voice spoke to her, "Tell the people, 'Arise, shine; for thy light is come, and the glory of the Lord is risen upon thee.'"—Letter 177a, 1897. A little later that night, as she slept, instruction came to her.

VISION CONCERNING SIZE OF THE BUILDING

Last night, August 23, I seemed in a vision of the night to be in Ashfield. Several of our brethren were present. I said to Elder Haskell, "This church will answer for this place, but the church at Cooranbong must be larger in width and longer than this building. It must be larger than you have estimated, and should seat four hundred people."

Then I saw papers where the length and breadth were marked out and the figures given. I had thought thirty-two by fifty was not enough, and we were saying it must be lengthened. Then the width of the Ashfield church was given, and the width of the chapel, which was wider than the Ashfield church, and after consideration the chapel was enlarged, and as the size was stated in figures, all seemed to be pleased with width and length.—MS 175, 1897.

Wednesday morning, August 25, Haskell called on Ellen White to report a very successful buying trip to Sydney; materials had been secured at lower figures than anticipated. Later in the day, sample seats were displayed at the school, and Ellen White was invited to participate in the decision of the type to be ordered. Four experienced carpenters were employed at six shillings per day, and some would make a donation of half their wages.

Ellen White's letters and diary entries through the next month provide almost a day-by-day account of the work on the church building and of God's special providences. Interestingly enough, hers were not on-site observations, for Ellen White decided it would be best to keep away as the work progressed. "I felt," she wrote, "that the building was under the especial supervision of God; and it was so, the circumstances had been arranged by the Lord, without any of our wisdom."—Letter 162, 1897. So what she wrote of the work was based on reports brought to her by Sara and the Haskells.

She wrote:

> The workmen have put heart, cheerfulness, willingness, into the work. They have expressed that they felt the angels of God were round about them. . . . We had stated seven weeks to complete the building. Ten days—lumber did not come. If we had had the lumber, it would have been done before the seven specified weeks.—Letter 162, 1897.

"We know," she wrote, "that the angels of God were with the workers. When anything came up that was perplexing to the workmen, Elder Haskell was on hand to encourage them. He would say, 'Let us have a season of prayer'; and the presence and blessing of God came upon them. Their hearts were subdued and softened with the dew of Heaven's grace. I never saw a building where we had greater evidence that the Lord managed the matter as in this."—Letter 91, 1897.

THE NEW CHURCH IS DEDICATED

Ellen White was to speak in the chapel at the school on Sabbath afternoon, the day before the dedication service. There were many

THE NEW CHURCH BUILDING AT AVONDALE

visitors at Cooranbong, for the church dedication and for the closing exercises of the school on Sunday evening. The school chapel was totally inadequate, and so her meeting was held in the new church—the very first. Sunday, October 17, was a beautiful day, and in the afternoon all gathered in the church for the service of dedication. Ellen White describes it:

> Every seat was occupied, and some were standing at the door. Between two and three hundred were present. Quite a number came from Melbourne and also from Sydney, and from the neighborhood, far and nigh.
>
> Elder Haskell gave the dedicatory discourse. Seated on the platform where the pulpit stands were Elder Daniells, Farnsworth, Haskell, Hughes, Wilson, Robinson, and your mother, whom they insisted should make the dedicatory prayer. Herbert Lacey conducted the singing, and everything passed off in the very best order. We felt indeed that the Lord Jesus was in our midst as we presented our chapel to God and supplicated that His blessing should constantly rest upon it.
>
> And we have not heard one word of criticism. All are surprised at such a house built in so short a time, and so nice and tasty and presentable.—Letter 162, 1897.

The *Bible Echo,* in reporting the dedication, described the building as situated on the school land near the Maitland Road and three quarters of a mile from the school buildings, built of wood, well constructed, neatly painted, and presenting a very nice appearance.

> The land for the church was donated by the school. The building itself cost only about £550 and is capable of accommodating 450 persons. And one of the best features connected with the whole enterprise is that it was dedicated free from debt, every penny's expense having been provided for beforehand. So there was no collection called for on this occasion to clear the church from debt.—BE, Nov. 8, 1897.

One feature of the developing enterprises at Cooranbong was the determination to avoid debt, even though the work was at times slowed, and all concerned had to sacrifice and deprive themselves of ordinary comforts and needs. Earlier in the year Ellen White had commented:

> There is no necessity for our meetinghouses to continue year after year in debt. If every member of the church will do his duty, practicing self-denial and self-sacrifice for the Lord Jesus, whose purchased possession he is, that His church may be free from debt, he will do honor to God.—Letter 52, 1897.

The last paragraph of the November 8 *Bible Echo* report of the dedication significantly declares:

> In conclusion, it should be stated that the erection of this building at this early stage of the school enterprise is mainly due to the faith and energy of Pastor S. N. Haskell and Mrs. E. G. White, and the rich blessings of God on their efforts. But for them, the building would perhaps not have been built for some time yet. With but £100 in sight, they moved out by faith and began to build, and the results are as already stated.

But of special significance to Ellen White was the fact that in this new start in Christian education, not only was it a success, but was, as she observed, "the best school in every respect that we have ever seen, outside our people, or among Seventh-day Adventists."—Letter 101, 1897. And:

> Twenty of the students have been baptized, and some came to the school who had not an experimental knowledge of what it means to be Christians; but not one student leaves the school but gives evidence of now knowing what it means to be children of God.—Letter 162, 1897.

CHAPTER 27
(1897)

Sunnyside and Beyond—1897

WHILE the physical development of the Avondale school drew heavily on Ellen White's time and strength through much of the year 1897, she was also involved in the home activities, in an outreach in coming to the aid of needy families in the community, and, of course, deeply engrossed in discharging her responsibilities as the messenger of the Lord. There was her writing for publication, and she was producing an almost constant stream of letters, many bearing messages of counsel or reproof.

As noted earlier, W. C. White was in the United States on a tour of activity that, as it worked out, kept him from home until late October. We have noted that as the year 1897 opened, his wife, May, with the four children, Ella, Mabel, and the 8-month-old twins, had just moved from the convent where they had lived for some months, to Sunnyside, and were occupying the little "house" at the rear—the two-room washhouse and woodshed where the twins were born. It was not large enough; Ellen White's proposal to build on a kitchen and veranda turned out unfeasible, and several alternatives were considered. It was hoped that W. C. White could sell his Battle Creek home and build a cottage across the road from Sunnyside.

GRANDMA AND THE TWINS

"Grandma White" doted a bit over the twins. "They both know me," she wrote to their father in mid-January, "and laugh and crow as soon as I come in sight. I take one, and the other will work his arms and make every maneuver to have me take him, too. But one, you know, is an armful. It is a treat to me to see and tend the little ones whenever I can."—Letter 169, 1897.

In mid-March she wrote to Willie, "Both are very spry at creeping, something you, their father, never did do."—Letter 189, 1897. And three months later she reported that they were "trotting around now" (Letter 138, 1897). They were delighted when grandmother would take them for a ride in her carriage. She wrote of this to Edson on July 4—midwinter for Australia:

> Willie's family are all well. The boys are healthy, rosy-cheeked, rollicking little fellows. When Sara and I go to Morisset, four miles and a half, or to Cooranbong, one mile and a half, or to Dora Creek, three miles, we manage to tuck in the children and give May a little resting spell. . . . Having to manage the two, she cannot do much else.
>
> The lads have learned when the horse comes to the piazza, they will both run to grandma, their two pairs of little arms stretched out, saying, "Gegee, Gegee." This is about all the words they speak. They are in such ecstasies over getting a chance to ride that I have not the heart to say, No. So they bundle in with their little red coats and white plush caps. We are all caught in the mistake of not distinguishing them one from the other. . . .
>
> They have been good-natured and not troublesome, but now they are so lively we will have to watch them. They have lived very much in the open air, and can scarcely be content indoors. Their great delight is in being on the ground. . . .
>
> Willie has been having a one-story cottage built. We have arranged that the piazzas shall be eight feet wide and on two sides of the house. The railing is made so that there is not a possibility of their getting out or falling over, and there is a gate that will have a spring catch which will keep them corralled, so the young White colts will not be straying out in the woods like lost sheep.—Letter 164, 1897.

THE BUILDING OF WILLIE'S HOUSE

The building of the cottage for Willie's family was, of course, being done in his absence. Ellen White and Sara McEnterfer

SUNNYSIDE AND BEYOND—1897

supervised the work. To Willie she wrote on June 10:

> We have gone ahead to build your house, and if anyone wants to grumble, you will be out of it altogether. Those who are now on the ground will take the blame. But I meant that everything should be done that could be done, in a plain, wholesome way, for your family. The house may look unnecessarily large, but I have looked it over and over, and could not bring my mind to diminish one foot in any direction. I have never been required before to do so much thinking and planning in so many lines, especially in reference to this house. I want your house to be a comfortable home, and there is not a thing I would detach from the building.—Letter 138, 1897.

Writing to Edson and Emma of some of the problems she was confronted with, she mentioned the expense of building in Australia:

> It costs just about double to build a house here, and takes three times as long as to build a house in America. Before the weather boards can be nailed on the house, every one has to be bored with a gimlet to put the nails through the wood, it is so hard. The wrought-iron nails will double up if this is not done. So you see everything takes longer and lumber is more expensive. Then here our boards for floor come from Oregon, America. All the lumber here will shrink very much. The buildings which should not cost in America over £100 cannot be built here for less than £200. This makes all meetinghouses and all dwelling houses cost much more than in America.—Letter 164, 1897.

THE MISSIONARY OUTREACH

"We have located here on missionary soil," wrote Ellen White on June 9, "and we design to teach the people all round us how to cultivate the land. They are all poor because they have left their land uncultivated. We are experimenting, and showing them what can be done in fruit-raising and gardening."—Letter 33, 1897. They tried also to set a good example in animal husbandry. Their animals were well fed and well cared for. The white cow that recently had given

THE AUSTRALIAN YEARS

birth to a heifer calf, which they were raising, was giving twenty-two quarts of milk a day, and the nearly dry red cow, four quarts. Both Ellen White's large family of workers and guests, and W. C. White's family, were supplied abundantly with milk (Letter 141, 1897).

In the economically depressed times, Ellen White continued to help needy families. Of this she wrote on February 10:

> We have a supply of poor families that must be kindly cared for and helped to help themselves. We have these poor as a legacy from God to us. Inasmuch as ye do this to one of the least of these, my brethren, ye do it unto Me. Then we will work on, doing our level best to alleviate the care of the poor, helping them when we can and strengthening them all we can in correct methods.—Letter 187, 1897.

Her home and office helpers also participated. She gave a report of this on June 9:

> Last evening we had a Dorcas Society in our home, and my workers who help in the preparation of my articles and for the papers, and do the cooking and sewing, five of them, sat up until midnight, cutting out clothing. They made three pairs of pants for the children of one family. Two sewing machines were running until midnight. I think there was never a happier set of workers than were these girls last evening.—Letter 113, 1897.

THE LITERARY WORK

The day-by-day entries in Ellen White's diary tell of the relentless demands of her literary work. As the reader has often noted, this usually began in the early hours of the day. In one entry she explains:

> The morning hours, from 3:00 A.M. until 7:00 A.M., are my best hours to write, for then I am not broken in upon and obliged to give my time to advise with my brethren and counsel with them.—MS 175, 1897.

But beyond the writing, she needed to give diligent attention to the proofreading of materials copied. "I have been awakened at half past 3:00 A.M. . . . I see I have several articles put under my door to

SUNNYSIDE AND BEYOND—1897

read this morning, to see if all is correct."—*Ibid*. In a letter to G. A. Irwin, newly elected president of the General Conference, she disclosed in her appeal for more literary help something of the way she worked:

> I have a very large amount of matter which I desire to have come before the people, but I have no one to consider these matters with me. If I could have Sister Peck and Willie, I could get off many important things much more perfectly. I ought to have someone to whom I can read every article before sending it to the mail. This always helps the writer, for the helper often discerns more clearly what is wanted, and the slight changes that should be made. It is an important matter to keep in its simplicity all that matter that I write. I am sure my two editors endeavor to preserve my words, not supplying their own in place of them.—Letter 76, 1897.

Shortly before this, the General Conference had officially released W. C. White from administrative duties in Australia so that he might give more of his time to his mother's literary work, but he was still in America performing errands for the Australasian Union Conference. A few months later, Sarah Peck was released from teaching in South Africa to join Ellen White's staff.

SARA MCENTERFER—COMMUNITY NURSE

It was not too long after Sara McEnterfer, a graduate nurse from Battle Creek, rejoined Ellen White's staff until she was involved in caring for the sick and injured in the community for some miles around. The nearest physician was twenty miles distant, and charged £5 to make a visit.

On Friday, July 23, a young man named Cloutsen came running to the house all the way from Dora Creek to report that a young man there was very sick with inflammation of the lungs and would die unless he had help.

Wrote Ellen White:

> The family is large and they are not poor, but most bitterly opposed to Seventh-day Adventists. The father of this large family will not allow one of our faith to step foot on or across his premises. We thought this might be an opportunity to break

down this prejudice. Sara and May White went as soon as they could gather up articles to take with them to help the sick man. They found him with his eyes glazed; he was unconscious. . . . The room was full of his parents and brothers and sisters. There were no windows open—not a crack of air for ventilating the room.

Sara took charge at once, told them that they were killing him, that the lungs must have food—good, pure air. All must leave the room but those required to wait on him. She examined the house and told them he must be moved into the sitting room. First, she directed that his bowels, which were burning hot, be relieved by an enema, administered by two brethren who were present. Then a cot was brought in, and Sara made it up. Then, all unconscious of everything, he was moved by four men onto the cot, and plenty of air was given him. He fell asleep for the first time since Monday. After remaining until the afternoon was nearly gone, Sara and May returned.—MS 174, 1897.

But the good work started by Sara was cut short. A physician who had been sent for before Sara was called, and who had waited on the young man earlier in the week, came belatedly on Friday evening. He was surprised to find the young man had made a change for the better and was rational. When told what treatment the patient had received, the doctor said it could not be bettered, declared the young man free from fever, and left word to give him a drop or two of liquor if he had sinking spells. When William Cloutsen came in a bit later, he found a blazing fire in the room and the windows all closed. He put the fire out, threw the wood out of doors, opened the windows, and bathed the patient's face and head.

"You are a good fellow, Billy Cloutsen," the patient said. "You know what to do for a fellow. I feel better."—*Ibid.*

The father and brothers were drinking rum when Cloutsen left, and proposed giving some to the sick man.

"Don't give him a drop. If you do, it will kill him," Cloutsen admonished.

They said they would not give him any. His brothers told Cloutsen that he was the only member of the family who would not

SUNNYSIDE AND BEYOND—1897

drink—"He would never touch it." But after Cloutsen left, they thought he was weakening and gave him liquor. When Cloutsen called in the morning, he found the young man was dead. "You gave him liquor," he charged.

The family admitted they had, and in doing so were responsible for the death of the son.

NUMEROUS OTHER CASES

But other cases had a much happier ending. Many times it was children who were involved in accidents of one kind or another. Sometimes the patient would be brought to Ellen White's or W. C. White's home and nursed back to health.

A few excerpts from her diary through the early part of September, 1897, yield a picture of this work of community ministry:

Wednesday, Sept. 1: While I was reading the mail, a woman from Dora Creek came up with her baby for instruction on what to do for the child.

Thursday, Sept. 2: We went to see the child that was brought to our house yesterday that was sick. Sara prescribed for her, and the mother followed the prescription. We learned today the child was relieved. . . .

The father of the first child that had appealed for help asked me if we did not receive pay for our trouble. We told him no, we did not do the work for pay, only to relieve suffering humanity as Christ did when He was in our world. They seemed very thankful.

As soon as this case was off our hands and we were nearly home, we learned a messenger had come for Sara to see if she could come to see a suffering boy who had stepped in a hole where there was a broken bottle, and had cut his foot fearfully. She went in the house for flannel fomentation cloths, Vaseline, and several necessary articles with which to work, turned her horse, and was away again. She found a very aggravated case. It had been hurt two weeks, was fearfully cut, and proud flesh was revealed.

Friday, Sept. 3: Sara visited the afflicted sick boy whose foot and ankle were so badly mangled. She found the poor suffering one weary and distressed.... He was crying, "Oh, she does not come; she will not come today. Oh, I want her to come. Oh, what will I do?" She opened the door, and he was pleased. She remained with him until noon, ministering to that suffering foot. The blood poisoning must not be allowed to advance. She left him quietly sleeping....

She went again in the evening. I told her to take the child and bring him to our home. We would treat him under better circumstances. In case of necessity our house shall be used as a hospital.

Sabbath, Sept. 4 (written after the Sabbath): This morning we did such kind of work as Christ would have done had He been in our world. We harnessed our team, and Sara went to visit the suffering boy with the cut foot. She took the mother and the boy to Mrs. May White's, my daughter-in-law's, close by our own house. The boy enjoyed the pure air and the ride in the easy phaeton. Then Sara had the conveniences to dress the afflicted limb.

She greatly feared at first that he would lose his limb, but by working with it twice a day for hours with hot compresses, the pain was removed, and the poor little sufferer, who had not slept day or night, fell into slumber, saying, to Sara's words "Now try to go to sleep," "I can't sleep, I can't sleep, I can't sleep, I can't sleep," until he was fast asleep.—MS 176, 1897.

Two days later Ellen White reported that he was recovering. Early Wednesday morning Sara was called to the home of Iram James, Ellen White's farmer, to attend his wife, who gave birth to a son. It was an easy delivery, and the family now consisted of two boys and four girls.

After effectively treating the badly cut foot for ten or twelve days, Sara allowed the boy to return home, with the understanding that she would go see him once a day as long as it was necessary.

A pattern was being established, and much of Sara's time was given to serve as a "community nurse." In time, a hospital was built on the grounds of the Avondale school. Were the full story of this phase of ministry fully told, it would fill several chapters. In 1958, when the author spent a few weeks teaching at Avondale College,

SUNNYSIDE AND BEYOND—1897

he was told of the long-lasting influence of such ministry.

Many years after the college was built and following World War II, it was necessary to provide some new buildings for the school, but building materials were still in very short supply, and of necessity imported. It was anticipated that the best that could be done in securing them would be to get a little here and a little there, from different suppliers. At the first firm called on in Newcastle, they found the proprietor to be an elderly gentleman who listened interestedly to their request for help in securing materials for Avondale College. In essence, he replied:

> Yes, Avondale College at Cooranbong. I grew up as a boy within a few miles of the school. And there was a Mrs. White who lived there. If there was anyone in need, or anyone sick in the community, she was there to give help. Her nurse would travel for miles to treat a sick child, or anyone suffering. I shall never forget what Mrs. White did for us in those days. Gentlemen, I will see that you get all the materials you need. You need go no further.—As told to the author.

The school representatives returned home with light hearts, and the buildings went up. The unselfish ministry of a little woman and her nurse fifty years earlier had not been forgotten, and unexpectedly yielded gratifying returns.

INVITATION TO JOHN J. WESSELS

In the autumn of 1897 Ellen White wrote to John Wessels in South Africa, inviting him to come to Australia to lead out in building and managing a sanitarium that could be provided with his own money. He had suggested to the president of the General Conference that he was "going to some place to build a sanitarium," and both Elder Olsen and Dr. Kellogg had suggested to Ellen White that she urge Wessels to help out in Australia. She reminded him of the generous contributions that had already been made by members of the Wessels family to Australia, and she told of the needs. Then in a way quite unique to one who so often wrote of the direct biddings of the Lord, she stated:

> I have not been given the message "Send for Brother John

Wessels to come to Australia." No; therefore, I do not say, "I know that this is the place for you." But it is my privilege to express my wishes, even though I say, "I speak not by commandment." But I do not want you to come because of any persuasion of mine. I want you to seek the Lord most earnestly, and then follow where He shall lead you. I want you to come when God says, "Come," not one moment before.

Nevertheless, it is my privilege to present the wants of the work of God in Australia. Australia is not my country, only as it is the Lord's province. The country is God's. The people are His. A work is to be done here, and if you are not the one to do it, I shall feel perfectly resigned to hear that you have gone to some other locality.—Letter 129, 1897.

While she had her own personal convictions and desires, Ellen White was careful not to set before people, as a message from God, that which did not have its source in the visions given her.

Wessels did not at the time choose to respond to this invitation, but in 1899 he was there, and in later years managed two sanitariums in California.

COUNSEL ON DRESS

That winter Ellen White received urgent letters from two leaders in educational institutions in the United States, Joseph Haughey, principal of South Lancaster Academy, and E. A. Sutherland, president of Battle Creek College. They were confronted with the work of a Mrs. Porter, a self-styled prophetess who, in her profession to believe the testimonies, was urging that Seventh-day Adventist women return to the "reform dress" of the 1860s. Haughey's wife was about convinced this was the course to follow, and he wrote in the hope that God would reveal to them what they should do (Joseph Haughey to EGW, May 2, 1897).

As the matter was also urged on Professor Sutherland in Battle Creek, he persuaded those interested to wait until word could come from Ellen White on the matter. He could see that if such were pressed, it could cause "quite a disturbance to the church," for, as he wrote Ellen White on May 12, "there are many good sisters here who would put the dress on cheerfully and wear it if the time has

SUNNYSIDE AND BEYOND—1897

come to put it on." While he did not believe in carrying everything to Ellen White that came up, he did feel the need of counsel in this. He urged a reply at her earliest convenience.

Ellen White responded:

> In answer to the questions that have recently come to me in regard to resuming the reform dress, I would say that those who have been agitating this subject may be assured that they have not been inspired by the Spirit of God. The Lord has not indicated that it is the duty of our sisters to go back to the reform dress. . . .
>
> The dress question is not to be our present truth. . . . I beg of our people to walk carefully and circumspectly before God. Follow the customs in dress so far as they conform to health principles. Let our sisters dress plainly, as many do, having the dress of good, durable material, appropriate for this age, and let not the dress question fill the mind. Our sisters should dress with simplicity. They should clothe themselves in modest apparel, with shamefacedness and sobriety. Give to the world a living illustration of the inward adorning of the grace of God.—MS 167, 1897.

The communication with its balanced message is found in full as the appendix to the book *The Story of Our Health Message*.

Whether by mail or to those who came to her home for counsel, she was ever ready to endeavor to present that which would give safe guidance. On Monday, October 4, after writing on the life of Christ in the early hours of the day and writing some letters, she laid aside her pen for "an interview or visit with Elder Haskell" about the church edifice that was under construction at Cooranbong. As they talked, she picked up her sewing. She wrote:

> I had an interview or visit with Elder Haskell. Read to him writings in regard to Haggai—"Arise," et cetera—and about allowing debts to remain on the church buildings. . . . While conversing with Elder Haskell, finished the babies' dresses.—MS 177, 1897.

Ellen White was a homemaker at heart.

CHAPTER 28
(1897)

The Stanmore Camp Meeting and the Health-Food Business

IN EARLY August, 1897, A. G. Daniells and W. L. H. Baker, presidents of the two principal conferences in Australia,* had gone up to Cooranbong to counsel with Ellen White and others there regarding the two camp meetings to be held in the early summer. The first was to be held in a suburb of Sydney, October 21 to November 1 (BE, Oct. 4, 1897), and the second in a suburb of Melbourne, November 18 to December 5 (*ibid.*, Dec. 13, 1897). Ellen White was requested to attend both, and she planned to do so, particularly the meeting in Sydney. On receiving a letter from Daniells suggesting that a company of workers should be put in Sydney some weeks in advance of the camp meeting to work up an interest, Baker wrote to Ellen White seeking advice. He enclosed a copy of Daniells' letter.

"That night," she wrote, "after receiving Brother Baker's letter, enclosing a copy of the letter from Brother Daniells, the Lord gave me light":

> I saw that it was not the best thing to do to make our plans known and advertise the meetings to be held, for in doing this we would prepare the ministers of the churches to arm themselves with all their implements of warfare, and by their falsehoods in their publications make the people bitter opponents to the truth.

---

*Note: When the General Conference at its 1897 session released W. C. White from administrative responsibilities to enable him to give more assistance to his mother in her literary work, A. G. Daniells was appointed in his place to the presidency of the Australasian Union Conference. Daniells continued to serve as president of the Australian Conference, with headquarters in Melbourne. Baker was president of the New South Wales Conference.

THE HEALTH-FOOD BUSINESS

I was shown that the best plan on this occasion was to come on the people as a surprise, and let them have an opportunity to hear for themselves before the ministers of all denominations should rally their forces to misinterpret our work and pour in their false reports. . . . . The light given was, When the seed of truth has been sown in the hearts of the people by the laborers at the camp meeting, then those who remain to follow up the work will, through the Spirit's power, be prepared to ripen off the work and gather in the harvest.—Letter 37, 1897.

Immediately Ellen White addressed a letter to "Dear Brethren," bearing the date of August 27, 1897. It opened, "I must place before you ideas that I cannot withhold. Is it at this time best to let everyone possible know that there is to be a camp meeting held by Seventh-day Adventists? . . . Will it not rather be best to set up the tents, and then let the people know, after the meeting has commenced doing the work of advertising? In spreading the intelligence of a Seventh-day Adventist camp meeting, are we not furnishing ammunition to our foes?" She added:

After an interest has been created by the camp meeting, then is the time that a special work should be done in following up the interest created. The greatest secrecy is needed in some cases, lest there be created an intense opposition that will prevent the people from coming to the meeting to hear for themselves. . . .

If a camp meeting can be started to break in upon the community unexpectedly, the opposing elements will not be aroused with an intensity moved by Satan's agencies to hold the people in error and darkness. The warning must be given, but let us give as little chance as possible for Satan to work, by moving cautiously and making no stir before. Let all the effort possible be put forth after the meeting closes.—Letter 13, 1897.

The suburb of Stanmore was chosen for the meeting. Ellen White described it:

Stanmore is only a few stations from Sydney. It is a thickly settled suburb, and is a very popular place. Here we found a most beautiful, grassy plot of ground, so thickly carpeted with grass that we needed no board floors.—Letter 136, 1897.

THE AUSTRALIAN YEARS

Just before the meeting opened, Ellen White sent her entire staff, except Marian Davis, who would not leave her work on *The Desire of Ages*, to the camp meeting. She followed the next day. W. C. White's entire family also went, not only for the camp meeting but to meet W. C. White, who arrived in Sydney from America the day before the meeting opened.

The village of tents, speedily erected, surprised the inhabitants of Stanmore. At the last moment small notices were distributed by diligent workers. Eagerly the workers and campers awaited the hour for the first meeting, Thursday evening. Then the people began to pour onto the grounds. The big tent was crowded, and Ellen White, in a letter to Edson, reported:

> A wall of people several feet deep stood around the tent. Elder Daniells spoke with excellent freedom. Friday morning there was an early meeting at six o'clock, and a good representation of our people was present.... The meetings have opened well.—Letter 148, 1897.

With this propitious opening, the meeting moved along well. The big tent was crowded, and people stood outside in the afternoons and evenings. Ellen White's first meeting came Sabbath afternoon. Through the ten-day meeting she spoke six times to the large assembly and five times at smaller meetings of church members and workers.

But to the Whites, a high point was the reunion of the W. C. White family after a separation of ten months. "The twins soon became acquainted with their father. May feels very well indeed over the arrival of her husband. She has behaved excellently."—*Ibid*.

As to the accelerating interest in the meetings, which continued over two Sabbaths, she wrote to a friend in America:

> I spoke Sabbath, Sunday, and Wednesday afternoons. At each meeting the large tent was crowded. To the very last of the meeting there was no falling off in numbers. On Sunday, in order that the crowd might be seated, the children were called into a forty-foot tent to a meeting of their own. Then our own people were invited to give the outside people room. I believe

THE HEALTH-FOOD BUSINESS

the angels of God were upon the ground.—Letter 136, 1897.

The light given her concerning advertising the camp meeting, she said, "has been followed to the letter" (Letter 148, 1897).

THE CRUCIAL FRIDAY-MORNING WORKERS' MEETING

There was one special meeting that was particularly trying to Ellen White. That was the October 29, Friday-morning meeting with all the ministers and leading workers in the reception tent. With her special insights into situations, which gave her glimpses of the soul experiences of individuals, she had called this meeting. She saw a repetition of some of the situations that she had dealt with at the Ashfield camp meeting in 1894, "which will, if known," she stated, "help some to take heed to be very careful in their words and in their deportment." Her diary carried the record:

> We met at half past five, and I read many pages of that which the Lord had presented to us at that camp meeting. Then I bore a very plain testimony to correct existing evils that would lead to serious consequences. Confessions were made, and all seemed to feel that the Spirit of God had appealed to them in the testimony given.
> Elder Daniells expressed himself as greatly relieved, and all who spoke seemed to feel it was a real blessing to have their mistakes and dangers laid open before them.

She noted further in her diary, "This duty was done at great cost to myself. I returned to my room and for some hours my heartache was so intense it seemed to me I could not live. But the Lord mercifully gave me rest and relief in my efforts to lay my burden upon Him. I was afflicted with physical suffering throughout the day."

She was to speak in the big tent Sabbath afternoon. But she would not speak of her feeling of helplessness lest the adversary, who cannot read man's thoughts, should take advantage of her depression. Her diary continued:

> Oh, how helpless I felt, how utterly weak, compassed with infirmities, yet not daring to express unbelief by drawing back. I

could only say over and over again, "Without Thee, My Saviour, I can do nothing. Become my Strength. I may venture only because Thou hast promised, 'Lo, I am with you alway, even unto the end of the world.'"

I dared not open my lips to say to anyone, "I am weak; will you take my place?" lest I give the enemy advantage over me. Yet, sensing my littleness, I said, "Lord, I will go not in my own strength, but in Thy strength. Thou canst strengthen me."—MS 177, 1897.

Sabbath afternoon she spoke for one hour and twenty minutes to an audience that crowded into the tent and overflowed, and held their interest to the very close.

She spoke again on Sunday afternoon. Monday morning she found herself exhausted, and she noted in her diary, "I was admonished this morning that it was wisdom for me to return home without delay."—MS 178, 1897. Accompanied by Mrs. Haskell, she did so. Tuesday morning she reported that she had had a hard night, and she could "reason from cause to effect" (ibid.). Plans for her to attend the next camp meeting to be held in Melbourne were called in question.

THE CAMP MEETING FOLLOW-UP

Interest was at its very peak when they came to the last Sunday of the camp meeting. The question was put to the audience, "Shall the meetings be continued one week longer?" "The outsiders," Ellen White wrote, "voted decidedly for it, with upraised hands."—Letter 136, 1897.

The decision was made to continue night meetings. The big tent had to go to Melbourne for the meeting that would soon open there, but a splice was put in the forty-foot tent, and with a few key ministers remaining to foster the interest, the meetings continued (Letter 91, 1897).

Ellen White gave up any expectation of going to Melbourne for the camp meeting there, but she promised to run down from Cooranbong to Sydney for some weekends. On November 22 she reported: "Forty have now commenced keeping the Sabbath in Stanmore, and still the interest is widespread. I believe we shall

THE HEALTH-FOOD BUSINESS

have a church of one hundred souls."—Letter 20, 1897. People were beginning to ask, both Sabbathkeepers and some not yet decided, "What about your meetinghouse? Are you deciding to build?"—Letter 205, 1897.

On December 20, she wrote:

> I am to look at the site for the meetinghouse here, and it is considered a good location in Newtown. . . . We must "arise and build." We cannot delay.—Letter 163, 1897.

Nothing pleased Ellen White more than to engage in an evangelistic thrust, and she seemed energized by the eager interest of those who for the first time were hearing the message. She was true to her promise to return frequently for speaking engagements. On January 1, 1898, she reported:

> Since the camp meeting I have visited Stanmore often, and have spoken eight times, on Sabbath and Sunday afternoons. The interest is wide and extended.—Letter 143, 1898.

On the occasion of one visit, Ellen White remained longer than usual and stood before the people again on Tuesday night. Describing the meeting, she wrote that no effort on her part was required to speak, for it seemed that the Spirit of the Lord spoke through her. The response was excellent, and someone proposed that she stay over and continue with night meetings. The people promised that they would come every night to hear her. But for two good reasons she could not accept the invitation. Evening meetings were too great a drain on her strength, and the book work at Cooranbong pressed hard (Letter 38, 1898). However, the movement to erect a meetinghouse to serve this new company of believers and become the "Sydney church" continued gaining impetus (Letter 6, 1898).

BEGINNING THE HEALTH-FOOD BUSINESS

The session of the Australasian Union Conference was held in connection with the Stanmore camp meeting. Ellen White attended but few of the meetings, but the groundwork was laid there for the manufacture of health foods in Australia. While in the United States, W. C. White, at the request of the union conference

THE AUSTRALIAN YEARS

committee, had made quite a thorough investigation in Battle Creek of what might be done in health-food manufacture in Australia.

On July 2, 1897, he had addressed a communication to the executive committee of the Australasian Union Conference reporting on his findings regarding the arrangements that could be made with the Kelloggs. In this letter he stated:

> Believing that the granose [wheat flakes] was a very valuable health food, that it would find a large sale in the colonies, and that it would aid us greatly in building up the market for a fine line of health foods, I had several conversations regarding its manufacture, during which I learned that the doctor [Kellogg] had expended more than £1,000 in experimenting with the manufacture of granose and developing the method of making it, and that his plan for permitting those in foreign countries to make the product was to lease them the mill and charge them a small royalty on all that they made. . . . I concluded to accept the terms and have ordered a granose mill which will be forwarded with some other machinery to Sydney to be held in bond there until we shall decide where it shall be put in operation.—11a WCW, pp. 63, 64.

Two days later he reported in a letter to the Australasian Union Conference executive committee that he had secured the services of Mr. Halsey, who was skilled in the manufacture of the Battle Creek health foods, to come to Australia and lead out in the making of the new products. White also sent samples of the foods for the members of the board to taste, so they would be better prepared to make decisions on his return *(ibid.*, p. 80). So following the union session in Sydney, W. C. White, after spending just a few days at home, was off to Melbourne, where he would give full reports to the appropriate committees, and actions could be taken in pioneering this new line of work in Australia.

W. C. White's work in Melbourne moved slowly, and his mother grew a bit impatient. She felt he was not treating his wife and children and her fairly by being away for so long a time following so closely a ten-month absence. On December 7 she wrote first of activities at Sunnyside that involved her books in preparation, and then disclosed her feelings:

THE HEALTH-FOOD BUSINESS

I think you should be with me and not spend weeks just now in Melbourne. One thing, the Lord has not appointed you to be an agent in the manufacture of home health foods. You have other work to do. I seem to be hedged about on every side. In regard to the manuscript for the life of Christ, it is done, waiting for you to look it over. There are several chapters on temperance waiting for you to look over. . . . I have no objections to your staying in Melbourne two months if you know it is the Lord's will. But there are matters on this end of the line fully as urgent as the matters on that end of the line. But I have no more to say.—Letter 206, 1897.

Three days later she wrote again. The opening paragraph contains an intimation that the Lord was tempering her thinking about what W. C. was doing:

I have been in great perplexity what to do. I cannot say anything more to you in reference to our work here. There is need enough of help, but the situation of things in Melbourne has been opened to me, and I have no more to say. . . . If you would tell us when we expect to see you, then we could know better how to act.—Letter 208, 1897.

This gave W. C. White the assurance that he should carry through his endeavors in the interests of health-food manufacture. As the church leaders worked in Melbourne, there emerged a "Report of the Committee on Health Foods" consisting of thirteen points, among them:

6. That we proceed at once to establish a health-food factory in Melbourne. . . .

10. That immediate steps be taken to make and place upon the market Granola, and Caramel Cereal, and that these be followed by Granose Biscuits, and a general line of healthful biscuits, and other foods, as quickly as possible.—11a WCW, p. 358.

The Adventist-sponsored manufacture and distribution of health foods in Australia was on its way.

CHAPTER 29
(1898)

The First Half of 1898

THROUGH early January, 1898, Ellen White passed through some days of perplexity at Sunnyside. On Tuesday, the eleventh, she attended a school board meeting where problems loomed. Later in the day in writing to Edson she opened her heart:

> In about six weeks the second term of school is to commence. I seem to shrink from the burden of being in any way connected with the school. Elder Haskell and his wife, Brother and Sister Wilson, and myself carried the load of responsibility during the last term. I wish to be counted out, and find some place where I can be away from the school, and give myself entirely to the work of getting out my books. But I will wait the opening of Providence. I will not choose for myself. I have asked this privilege of the Lord, and if He thinks best, He will make a way for me. I know not where to look or which way to turn, but I shall ask the Lord to help me.—Letter 36, 1898.

The Lord helped her, but not in separating her from the interests of the school. A few days later she wrote: "I sometimes seem to be bearing my testimony in America. This may yet be so. The Lord knows all about the future."—Letter 1, 1898.

THE VISIT TO MELBOURNE AND BALLARAT

In her next letter to Edson, written on February 2, she laid before him the plans for the coming weeks. Letters from A. T. Robinson, conference president residing in Melbourne, told of plans for a

THE FIRST HALF OF 1898

general meeting to run through several days; these had influenced her planning:

> For some time Elder Robinson has been pleading for Elder Haskell and Sister White to visit Melbourne. Sixty have taken their stand for the truth there, and he wants me to bear my testimony to the people. I shall leave for Melbourne in about ten days. W. C. White and Sara will accompany me. I shall probably visit Adelaide, and hold some public meetings, for there the apostasy of McCullagh and Hawkins occurred one year ago, and I have been daubed with all kinds of mud. For this reason I wish to visit Adelaide, and speak the truth as a witness for Christ.—Letter 38, 1898.

As she contemplated this trip to the south, she mentioned her high hopes of the fruitage of the two camp meetings held in late 1897:

> The work in Melbourne is just as promising as it is in Sydney. Since the camp meeting held there, forty-three have decided to keep the Sabbath. Brother A. T. Robinson and his wife are the main workers, and Brother Herbert Lacey and his wife are also engaged in the work. I have no doubt . . . that no less than one hundred souls will be added to the church in Melbourne, and one hundred souls in Sydney.—Letter 6, 1898.

So in company with her son and Sara McEnterfer she left Cooranbong on Wednesday, February 23, and arrived in Melbourne before the Sabbath. She found the camp meeting tent at Balaclava, near Melbourne, still standing, and night and weekend evangelistic meetings being held. Over a period of four weeks she spoke seven times. On March 20, when the tent was blown down in a sandstorm, the evangelistic meetings were moved to a hall. That weekend Ellen White and Sara McEnterfer, along with the conference president, A. T. Robinson, were in Geelong, some forty miles southwest of Melbourne. Money was scarce, and they made the four-hour trip by boat for eighteen pence each; this included the return fare. By train the cost would have been eight shillings each. Writing of it Ellen White commented, "A penny saved is as good as a penny earned."—Letter 176, 1898.

Back in Melbourne on Tuesday, March 22, Ellen White

THE AUSTRALIAN YEARS

determined that her strength should not be used in casual visiting, even with close friends. Of this she made an enlightening comment to Edson:

> It is a tax I am not called to endure. . . . When I do the things the Lord gives me to do, then I can endure the strain. When I step out of the channel He has given me, I am not sustained.—Letter 177, 1898.

She visited the publishing house in Melbourne, speaking to the workers there. She later wrote to two of the employees:

> The Echo publishing house is God's own institution, and had it not been for the Lord's care for it, it would not now be in existence. . . . The publishing institution has struggled hard to bring in, through the grace of God, a pure, sacred, holy atmosphere in every department of the work. But while a great change has been made, and there is a better class of workers, there is not yet a true appreciation of the distinction between an institution which bears the divine credentials and a common workshop. . . .
> Let everyone now at work in the Echo office, in every branch of the work, bear in mind that it is not common but sacred things you are handling. Treat this work as the work of God.—Letter 39, 1898.

DEDICATION OF THE STANMORE CHURCH

After spending six or seven weeks in Melbourne and vicinity, and speaking twenty-two times (Letter 171, 1898), she journeyed back to Sydney, expecting that the new Stanmore church might be dedicated on April 17. It was not yet ready, so the appointment was postponed to Sunday, April 24.

The weather was good on the twenty-fourth. Writing of the new house of worship, she described it as "a very nice building, and there are no debts upon it. . . . It is a neat, wholesome, commodious building."—Letter 172, 1898. She found it easy to speak in.

THE SECOND TERM OF SCHOOL

The second term of school opened on March 16. There were fifty-three students present on the opening day, but a week later

THE FIRST HALF OF 1898

there were seventy. Accommodations had been expanded through the addition of new buildings. The March issue of the newly started *Union Conference Record* carried word from W. C. White on this:

> The buildings erected during the summer have doubled the capacity and the general comfort of our school home. And it is our hope that the number of boarding students may increase to sixty, and that the day students in both departments may number fifty.

C. B. Hughes stated in the May *Record* that the faculty at Cooranbong was much the same as during the first term and the program also much the same. The students divided their time between study and work, with two and a half hours each afternoon devoted to the latter.

In describing the daily program, Hughes wrote:

> At three o'clock, students and teachers may be seen in their workclothes wending their way to work. The young men engage in the various duties of farm, garden, orchard, and carpenter work. The young ladies find employment in the kitchen, laundry, and garden. Work closes at five-thirty.

While proving a success, the school was entering upon a period of financial distress even greater than had been foreseen or expected. W. C. White, now chairman of the board, had to contend with this problem rather relentlessly, and this was to be the story for the next year or two. Ellen White attributed it somewhat to tuition set at too low a point, and to discouraging rumors and false reports that were carelessly bandied about. The May *Record* carries "An Appeal for Help" as the first article in which White reports on accomplishments and describes activities at the school and then presents its needs. It closes with the suggestion that as in the days of Israel of old, when the people came to the feasts carrying liberal offerings, so should it be in the forthcoming Week of Prayer, May 28 to June 5, which would extend over two weekends. There was a call from church leaders not only for the payment of pledges already made to the school but for liberal offerings on the Sabbaths—at both the beginning and the close of that convocation. As the story of the Avondale school will surface here and there in this account of Ellen

THE AUSTRALIAN YEARS

White's life and activities during 1898 and 1899, there will be several allusions to financial problems.

In the March, 1898, *Record*, W. C. White reported on the animal life at the school, both domestic and wild:

> Of domestic animals and other living creatures on the place, the school has three farm horses, about a dozen cows, half as many young cattle, and forty to fifty fowls. Besides this, there are twenty-two swarms of bees, from whose summer gatherings of honey eleven hundred pounds have already been extracted and stored for the winter use of the students.
>
> Of the wild animals on the place, we cannot speak so definitely. There is a small family of large kangaroos, which show themselves occasionally. The wallabies are quite numerous, although many have recently been shot. Thus far they have not done serious injury to our crops. The native bears are getting scarce. We seldom hear their cry. Opossums can be heard any night, although they have been thinned out by the hunters. Snakes are much talked about, but rarely seen. Each year we see less and less of them. Occasionally a tiger cat makes a raid on our fowls. Then we trap him, and he suffers the death penalty for his fowl murders. Flying foxes have done us no harm this year. Of magpies, there are plenty. The laughing jackasses, though not numerous, are very sociable. Groups of cockatoos and parrots are occasionally seen. The bell bird and the whip bird can be heard every day.

CORRESPONDENCE WITH MRS. S. M. I. HENRY

Early in 1898 Ellen White opened correspondence with Mrs. S. M. I. Henry, national evangelist of the Women's Christian Temperance Union and one of its early leaders. Daughter of a Methodist minister, Mrs. Henry had often accompanied her father on his itineraries in her girlhood and youth. She was now widowed, with three children. She at first supported herself and family by writing and publishing poetry and prose, but became involved with the WCTU and traveled and lectured widely in its interests.

She became a Seventh-day Adventist in 1896 while a patient at the Battle Creek Sanitarium, confined to a wheelchair. After an unusual experience in which she was healed through the prayer of faith, she again entered the lecture field and used her influence to advance the cause of temperance, and at the same time to deter the women of the United States from giving support to Sunday legislation.

W. C. White met Mrs. Henry in Battle Creek in 1897 and carried back to Australia with him some of her publications, among them an envelope-sized tract of forty-eight pages titled *How the Sabbath Came to Me*. Mrs. Henry wrote this as a means of introducing the Sabbath question to her WCTU friends. In the follow-up work in Stanmore, Ellen White saw in it a very useful tool, and wrote to Mrs. Henry on January 2, 1898, requesting permission to reprint it at the Echo office.

As Ellen White learned of Mrs. Henry's experience in accepting the Sabbath and then the Spirit of Prophecy, and also of her experience as a writer and public speaker, there quickly grew an affinity between the two.

Her first letter to Mrs. Henry, written on January 2, opened with the words:

> I would be very much pleased could I be seated by your side and converse with you in regard to the incidents of our experiences. I have an earnest desire to meet you. It is not impossible that, even in this life, we shall see each other face to face. When I learn of the gracious dealings of God with you, I feel very grateful to my heavenly Father that the light of the truth for this time is shining into the chambers of your mind and into the soul temple. Across the broad waters of the Pacific, we can clasp hands in faith and sweet fellowship.—Letter 9, 1898.

Mrs. Henry's response was wholehearted and immediate. She wrote February 18 from her Battle Creek Sanitarium base, granting permission for the reprinting of the tract. Her response began with the words:

> Your letter was a genuine and very delightful surprise to me. I have often thought of you, of course, and wished that I might know you personally. I have felt myself drawn out many times toward you during the experiences which I have had, especially as I have come to realize more concerning your own work.

She too expressed the wish that she might sit down beside Ellen White and that they might talk of their experiences, and added:

> My one wish is to know what God wants me to do, and to do it; to know the whole truth and follow it.—DF 38.

In the months that followed, letters of encouragement and counsel were written to Mrs. Henry, both concerning her work with the WCTU and the work she initiated among Seventh-day Adventists in the interest of Christian homes. She, in turn, kept Ellen White informed about her work and its reception. For a year or two she maintained a column in the *Review and Herald*.

Mrs. Henry had not found it easy to accept the proposition of a prophet in the Seventh-day Adventist Church. Then she saw this agency as a telescope focused on the Word of God. She wrote of her experience in an article titled "My Telescope," published in the January, 1898, issue of *The Gospel of Health* issued in Battle Creek. This proved helpful to many, and it has been recently reprinted in facsimile form in *Witness of the Pioneers Concerning the Spirit of Prophecy*.* Correspondence passed between the two women until Mrs. Henry's untimely death from pneumonia in early 1900.

WEEK OF PRAYER AT COORANBONG

The time for the Week of Prayer in Australia was set by the union conference committee as May 28 to June 5, and the readings prepared for the daily meetings were published in the April issue of the *Union Conference Record*. As the time neared, Elder and Mrs. Haskell visited Ellen White at Sunnyside. They counseled together as to just what should be planned in the way of meetings for both Cooranbong and the newly established Stanmore church. It was agreed that Haskell would lead out at Cooranbong and Ellen White would be at Stanmore.

It proved, however, not to be so. The Lord stepped in, as Ellen White explained in her diary:

> I have been, through the grace of Christ, able to decide the question of where I shall be during the Week of Prayer. I talked the matter over with Elder Haskell and I consented to be at

---
* Published by Review and Herald Pub. Assn.

THE FIRST HALF OF 1898

Stanmore to help there, and Elder Haskell [will] remain here.

But during the night season I was laboring in this place, and I saw much that I should do here. I have no light to leave for Stanmore. I have borne my testimony in this place but once in three months, and I have words to speak to the people here.

She wrote to Elder Haskell about it, pointing out other considerations. W. C. White and Sara McEnterfer would have to accompany her there. She continued in her diary:

That leaves Willie's family without a head during the season of prayer, and my family without our help during this period when they need us the most, that all may blend together. Then here are people to get acquainted with—our neighbors at Dora Creek and Martinsville—and our horses and wagons must bring all who cannot . . . get to the meetings.

She mentioned also the forthcoming book on the parables that called for her attention, and the upcoming American mail, and added:

My duty was laid out plainly before me in the night season, Tuesday night, and I present this to you, Elder Haskell.—MS 182, 1898.

In the interest of making this week a time of evangelistic thrust, attention was given to the village of Dora Creek. A vacant schoolhouse had been rented, and Herbert Lacey was conducting Sabbath meetings. On Wednesday, May 25, Ellen White and Sara went down and arranged for the use of the building for weeknights, as well.

As for the Cooranbong church, groundwork had already been laid for the meetings. As Ellen White spoke to the church on Sabbath, May 21, she gave a clear call for an evangelistic outreach right there in Cooranbong. She cited the gospel commission and urged a missionary thrust in the community. She called for a meeting the next evening, Sunday night, with invitations to attend to be carried to all the community. "We are not to put our light under a bed, that is, confine it to our family and forget that all who have been privileged to hear the truth must hear not only for themselves but to communicate to others that which they hear."—*Ibid.*

THE AUSTRALIAN YEARS

The next day, Monday, she wrote in her diary an enthusiastic report:

> The meeting Sunday evening was a success. The chapel was full. Quite a number walked or came with their conveyances five and six miles. We have now appointed regular Sunday-evening meetings. All seemed to be interested, even all that were not of our faith. We welcomed them and were rejoiced to have them in the meeting. This is the very object of these meetings, that we may impart to the people the knowledge we have in regard to the Word, to encourage them to cultivate their lands.
>
> There were fifteen-minute speeches by different ones—W. C. White, Professor Hughes and his wife, Herbert Lacey, and several others. I think an excellent impression was made and a better and more correct understanding was gained in regard to muscular Christianity, which should be brought into the education in all our schools.—*Ibid.*

The approach was practical and prejudice-effacing. The plans for the Week of Prayer did not call for a meeting on Friday night, for it was thought families should be in their homes, with an opportunity to study their Sabbath school lessons (UCR, April, 1898). The plans did call for morning and afternoon meetings on the two Sabbaths.

THE MEETINGS BEGIN

In the first few days the pattern of labor was established. Ellen White demonstrated her deep interest by a faithful record penned in her correspondence and from day to day in her diary. Of the meetings on the first Sabbath she wrote:

> There was a meeting in the forenoon after the Sabbath School. Quite a number of our neighbors at Dora Creek and Martinsville attended the meeting. Some brought luncheons, but we prepared food for most of them. They took their refreshments under the trees. About forty-five united in this partaking of food together, and all seemed to have an enjoyable time. At three o'clock I spoke to the people in regard to the parable Jesus gave to His disciples concerning the leaven which the woman put in the meal.—MS 182, 1898.

THE FIRST HALF OF 1898

Writing to Haskell, she related an experience that came to her during the week. She seemed to be standing before a company speaking on the subject of faith, and showing that because of deficiencies in the experience of church members, they were far behind in faith.

> Then the Word of God was opened before me in a most beautiful striking light. Page after page was turned, and I read the gracious invitations and words of entreaty to seek God's glory and God's will, and all other things would be added. These invitations, promises, and assurances stood out as in golden letters.
>
> "Why do you not grasp them?" I said. "Seek first to know God before any other thing. Search the Scriptures. Feed on the words of Christ, which are spirit and life, and your knowledge will enlarge and expand. Study your Bible. Study not the philosophy contained in many books, but study the philosophy of the Word of the living God."—Letter 47, 1898.

And so it was from day to day through the whole week. The program for the last Sabbath was much like the week before. "There are one or two from Dora Creek keeping their first Sabbath," Ellen White joyfully reported. She sent her horses and carriages to Dora Creek to bring all that they could carry. Some forty people joined in the lunch under the trees. Sunday's morning and afternoon meetings brought the fruitful Week of Prayer to a close as reported by Ellen White, with "the house of worship . . . full" on Sunday afternoon and "many not of our faith" present (MS 183, 1898).

Each day brought new opportunities, with attendance at all meetings accelerating. Ellen White seems to have struck the keynote when in writing to Elder Daniells concerning the spiritual revival:

> We are doing all we can to enlighten minds in regard to exercising faith and trust in God. Here lies our great deficiency. . . . Oh, let us know what it is to have living faith in the Word of God. We must talk faith, we must sing faith, act faith, and then we shall see the deep moving of the Spirit of God. We are weak on this point, when we should be strong.—Letter 50a, 1898.

CHAPTER 30
(1898)

Divine Guidance in Important Moves

T HE Lord is giving to His people a rich treasure of light and instruction regarding the work they are to do, and the way to do it." So wrote W. C. White to a church leader in America. He continued, "Almost daily He speaks to Mother in the night about how the work is being done, and how it ought to be done. And she is told to bear her testimony to His people."—WCW to I. H. Evans, June 6, 1898 (12 WCW, p. 48).

He had expressed much the same thought to A. G. Daniells a month earlier as he wrote:

> Day by day and night by night the situation is presented to Mother. She is prepared to give us counsel much, much needed, and I think very much appreciated. She tells us plainly that we have not too many teachers and that we cannot afford to cut down our teaching force, but that it is our duty to fit ourselves to the work, so that everyone's labor will count.
>
> She tells us that we are presented to her as separate, independent threads, standing apart, whereas we ought to unite our energies one with another, and all be woven together as a perfect web. Mother is giving us precious information regarding the importance of organization and the necessity of making every feature of our work educational.—11a WCW, p. 669.

A thoughtful reading of the above suggests the presence of problems in relationships in the working force at Avondale. They were not to be "independent threads, standing apart." Considering the diverse nature of the personalities and the experience, and the

DIVINE GUIDANCE IN IMPORTANT MOVES

age differences in the working force, these words had meaning. The matter is more clearly understood by reading Ellen White's diary and the personal messages directed to several individuals.

Matters at Avondale had reached the place where, because of jealousies, narrow-mindedness, and shortsightedness, it was difficult for the school board to function properly. W. C. White was chairman; with his broad experience and his close connection with his mother's work providing a special insight that not all others could grasp, he often sensed what needed to be done. But of the dissension he said nothing to his mother. "W. C. White tells me not a word," she wrote in her diary, "but I know." And she added, "The Lord has presented the matter before me, and as things are, there would be a better state of things without any board."—MS 184, 1898.

To Elder Prescott she also stated:

> The Lord has given to W. C. White a special work to do in this country ever since he first stepped upon its soil. God has used him in a special manner as an organizer. This is the work to which he is appointed.—Letter 57, 1898.

He saw the objectives and the goals before the school enterprise and pushed forward dauntlessly. Criticism weighed him down, but he bore it in silence.

"OUR SCHOOL MUST BE A MODEL SCHOOL"

Coming from a school board meeting on April 28, W. C. White wrote to a fellow worker, W. M. Crothers, in New Zealand:

> This morning we had a long board meeting, and Mother read us some very important instruction. From what she has said to us from time to time, we conclude that the present school term is a very important time, and that it is our duty to do everything in our power to give this school the right mold.—11a WCW, pp. 642, 643.

In September, Ellen White declared: "Our school must be a model school for others who shall establish schools in Australia; every movement we make must tell."—MS 186, 1898.

On this point Ellen White spoke again in a letter dated October 5.

THE AUSTRALIAN YEARS

Writing of the orchards and grounds surrounding the school, she stated:

> The land is to be our lesson book. After being cleared, it is to be cultivated. Orange, lemon, peach, apricot, nectarine, plum, and apple trees are to occupy the land, with vegetable gardens, flower gardens, and ornamental trees. Thus this place is to be brought as near as possible to the presentation that passed before me several times, as the symbol of what our school and premises should be.—Letter 84, 1898.

That the attendance for this term of school passed the one hundred mark, with the young people "hearing, learning, and practicing as if they desired to occupy a right position in the home and school firm," brought satisfaction to the leaders (MS 76, 1898).

THE CONFERENCE SESSION IN STANMORE

The officers of the New South Wales Conference did not see how they could hold a camp meeting in 1898, so it was planned that the annual conference session would be held in the Stanmore church, beginning Friday, July 22. Ellen White was present for the opening meeting and talked on faith, and Sabbath morning she spoke on what constituted health reform. Sunday morning her address was on education and the Avondale school (MS 184, 1898).

The conference president, W. L. H. Baker, asked to be released from his work so he could return to America to spend more time with his aging father.

S. N. Haskell, the Bible instructor at Avondale, was called to the presidency of the New South Wales Conference. He and his wife sought Ellen White's counsel on that point. Several times within the past two years Ellen White had been given light in regard to his work, particularly in his connection with the school.

Almost two weeks before, on July 11, she had written in her diary of being shown in vision workers moving from one place to another. In the representation she heard Elder Haskell say, "I know not whither I shall go or where I shall remain. I think I will go to America." One stood before Haskell. He said, "Your work is in this country for the present. When you are called to another place, you will understand His [God's] voice. . . . When He calls you to

DIVINE GUIDANCE IN IMPORTANT MOVES

America, you will know it."—*Ibid*. Haskell accepted the conference presidency.

MEDICAL MISSIONARY WORK

The first step in the line of medical missionary work in Australia was the opening of the Health Home in Sydney in late 1896. The next step was the publishing of a health journal, the *Herald of Health*, launched in Melbourne in 1898. As the Battle Creek Sanitarium Health Food Company in the mid-1890s forged ahead in making wheat flakes, a coffee substitute, "caramel cereal," and in the development of vegetable protein meat substitutes—beginning with peanut butter and soon more sophisticated products as "nuttose" and "nut cheese"—a serious interest along these lines began to emerge in Australia.

But it was in the winter of 1898 that the various lines of medical missionary work really began to blossom in Australia. One matter of concern was that of priorities in the use of available funds. Responding in June to questions asked by A. G. Daniells, president of the union conference, Ellen White enunciated two principles:

> All should be able to see eye to eye before we determine how means shall be appropriated. It is necessary that we see how we stand financially in all our lines of work.
>
> I am fully in harmony with the medical missionary work, but that mission must, to a large extent, make its own way, and be self-supporting. And it will be this if it is conducted properly.—Letter 52, 1898.

THE MEDICAL AND SURGICAL SANITARIUM, AND THE USE OF MEAT

In June she reported, "The Health Home is full. . . . We see a large number of people who are destitute of a knowledge of how to take care of themselves. We feel a great desire to advance the work."—Letter 56, 1898. In July she observed, "The Health Home is the means of reaching many souls that would not otherwise be reached."—Letter 58, 1898. Then came a report indicating progress, published in the *Union Conference Record* of July 15.

> Those of our people who read the *Herald of Health* . . . will have

noticed that the Sydney "Health Home" has changed its name. Henceforth this institution will be known as the "Medical and Surgical Sanitarium" of Summer Hill.

Nor is this a change in name alone. The entire institution has been placed upon a higher scientific plane; in fact, a sanitarium plane.

A physician has taken charge of the medical and surgical work. . . . A thoroughly competent chemist and microscopist is at the head of a new complete laboratory of investigation. Medical gymnastics and other special facilities are being added to assist in the recovery of the sick.

While at the session of the New South Wales Conference held in the Stanmore church, Ellen White attended an early-morning meeting on Monday, July 25, to discuss the dietary program of the new sanitarium. Drs. E. R. Caro and S. C. Rand, newly come to the institution, were present; also A. W. Semmens, W. C. White, and G. B. Starr. In her diary she reported what took place:

> The consideration was in regard to the meat question. Shall the Sanitarium maintain the principle of nonmeat eating for the patients who have not been instructed in a vegetarian diet? The question was, "Would it not be well to let them have meat at first, educate them away from the appetite by lectures, and then bring them where they will be instructed by the lectures on the evil of meat eating?"
>
> I replied that to condemn meat eating and show its injurious effects and then bring the injurious article and give it to the patients, and prescribe it for some of the patients as some had thought best to do, was a denial of their principles and would not be in accordance with the teachings of our people on this question of health reform. We felt there must be no drawing back on this question.—MS 184, 1898.

She pointed out that the increase of disease in the animal kingdom was a strong argument in favor of her position. The subject in various aspects came up in formal and informal discussions at the conference on both Monday and Tuesday, and Ellen White noted:

> We are to be sure that we commence the work in right lines.

DIVINE GUIDANCE IN IMPORTANT MOVES

No tea, no coffee; avoid drugs. We are to take our position firmly in regard to the light given us that the consumption of the dead flesh of animals is counterworking the restoring of the sick to health. It is not a safe and wholesome diet. . . .

However great the goodness of God and however abundant His promises to any people, continued transgression of the laws of God in our nature brings disease. Therefore we cannot present meat before the patients.—*Ibid.*

The impact of the discussions and Ellen White's firm position were reflected in the resolutions passed at the session, two of which read:

> 3. *Resolved,* That in the prosperity attending the work of the "Health Home," which has now grown into a "Medical and Surgical Sanitarium," we recognize the blessing of God upon right principles in dietetic reform, and the use of rational, or nature's remedies in the treatment of disease; . . .
>
> 4. *Resolved,* That we pledge our support of these principles by our practice and our influence, and with our means.—UCR, Aug. 15, 1898.

A few days after returning to Cooranbong, Ellen White wrote:

> We greatly hope that our physicians in the Health Home may be soundly converted to correct principles in health reform. I was glad that up to the present time flesh meat has not found its way upon the tables at the Sanitarium, and we hope it never will disgrace the health-reform tables.—Letter 180, 1898.

THE HEALTH-FOOD BUSINESS

The next day, July 31, she reported that Willie "leaves Wednesday for Melbourne to have plans laid in regard to medical missionary work, to establish it upon a good basis" (Letter 181, 1898). Medical personnel generally would be there, and of course, plans would be laid for the developing health-food business.

By this time, health foods were being imported on a regular basis. P. B. Rudge was brought from New Zealand to manage sales, which were promising. The June 15, 1898, *Record* carried an interesting advertisement:

THE AUSTRALIAN YEARS
"TRY THEM"

We invite all our readers to improve their diet by eating granola and nut butter, and by drinking caramel cereal. They are the great food correctives for indigestion and constipation. We also invite you to assist this good enterprise by selling the foods to others. Liberal discounts are offered to all agents. Address, Sanitarium Health Food Agency, 251 St. George's Road, North Fitzroy, Victoria.

Two months later the *Record* reported the arrival in Australia of G. W. Morse who was to "devote his time to the interests of the Australasian medical missionary work, giving special attention to the health-food business." He was present at the Melbourne meeting of the newly formed Australasian Medical Missionary and Benevolent Association. An early and prime concern was where the food factory should be located. Melbourne was the well-established center of the work in Australia, and workers and believers there quite naturally felt that there was little need for such a study. Others felt there were other important considerations, and a committee on the location of the manufacturing plant was appointed, made up of A. G. Daniells, Dr. E. R. Caro, G. W. Morse, W. C. White, and E. R. Palmer.

THE MOLLIFYING INFLUENCE OF A VISION

In addition to the possibility that Melbourne might not be chosen as the location of the proposed plant, consideration was being given to moving the union conference office from Melbourne to Sydney. A vision given to Ellen White in Stanmore and repeated some weeks later prevented a serious rift when these matters were under study at the council meeting in Melbourne.

Ellen White had told her son of some of the things revealed to her that, now as he was in Melbourne studying certain moves with others, took on considerable significance. W. C. White hastened off a postcard to his mother, urging her to write out the matter for their immediate use at the council meeting. But while some things stood out clearly before her, "other things," she wrote, "are not laid out as distinct as I could wish." She added, "I must wait. It will come to me, I feel quite sure."—Letter 63a, 1898.

DIVINE GUIDANCE IN IMPORTANT MOVES

Then on Tuesday night, August 9, she had a unique experience in which just that took place. The next day she wrote:

> Last night . . . I thought I must write a few lines before retiring. I began about the Sabbath meeting, when, like a flash of lightning, I had presented to me so sharply some things which had been presented to me at Stanmore, and I wrote on and on, until I had written four and a half pages.—Letter 62, 1898.

She promised to have the matter copied and sent to them, which she did in a document dated August 12. The instruction came to her in symbolic form, and now she wrote: "As these things revive in my mind, I am trying to put them with pen and ink where I cannot lose them."

> There was instruction given in an assembly. Words were addressed to men in responsible positions. . . . After the council meeting I saw quite a change being made. As I told you, there was a transferring of workers, and our Counselor was saying the same men should not continue a length of time in one place. . . .
>
> There were families with their goods being drawn away to be transported to other places. There was a necessity for this in order to leave a positive influence on the work and the cause of God, and its advancement. I would encourage the movement you suggest, and believe the Lord is in Elder Daniells' moving to Sydney at this time, and the Lord will tell him what to do next.
>
> I did have some things presented that there was now a more decided work to be done in Sydney and the vicinity. . . .
>
> The advantages now presented in doing medical missionary work need more calculation and experience brought into the management of the work. I shall be relieved if this change is made. I believe Brother Morse will be less experienced a help in Melbourne, but with Elder Daniells here in New South Wales, the working force seems more evenly balanced.—Letter 63a, 1898.

THE EARLIER INTERVIEW AT SUNNYSIDE

Just before the Melbourne council meeting, G. W. Morse, who had just arrived in Australia, and Dr. E. R. Caro spent a morning in an extended interview with Ellen White at Sunnyside. They discussed many things relating to the medical missionary work, including the lines of work getting well under way at the Summer Hill Sanitarium and the health-food business. In addition, the young and energetic Dr. Caro, having in mind Dr. Kellogg's work in Chicago, urged that as a part of the medical missionary program in Sydney there should be "an infants' orphan home" and a place "to help fallen women." As she wrote of the interview in her diary she observed that "the want of means is the great barrier to doing that work that should be done."—MS 184, 1898. She felt the Lord would give them wisdom needed at every step.

Now in her letter presenting the revived, fuller view given to her at Stanmore, she wrote:

> One thing was certain, changes must be made for the more healthful warfare before us in the health missionary work. There is needed in council and management of the work in Sydney, men of larger experience than those who are now connected with the work. Counsel with these young men who certainly need all the experience of those who have been taught of God, that the work shall not become disproportioned in any of its lines.
>
> There are many branches that will grow out of the plans now made in Sydney, and every line of work needs experienced managers, that part may unite with part, making a harmonious whole. More than two or three minds must be given to all.—Letter 63a, 1898.

The letter was mailed at Cooranbong on Friday, August 12. In Melbourne, on Monday, August 15, a meeting of the managing committee was held, considering the manufacture of health foods. W. C. White had in hand the letter from his mother in which she pictured the moving of interests and workers. It removed all question as to the wisdom of considering other places for the location of the food manufacturing establishment. The committee on location could now enter on its work with enthusiasm and confidence. Many points had to be considered, from the cost of raw materials to transportation facilities and the potential in employees. Here are excerpts from G. W. Morse's report of the committee as

DIVINE GUIDANCE IN IMPORTANT MOVES

published in the September 15 issue of the *Record:*

SEVERAL LOCATIONS FOR THE FOOD FACTORY CONSIDERED

The committee gave very careful consideration to the matter while at Melbourne, taking into its counsel several of the leading brethren of that city, and securing such items of information as would lead to a correct conclusion. Sydney was also visited, and the same investigation made as at Melbourne. Cooranbong was the next place visited, and here the whole matter was gone into very carefully, and the evidences, pro and con, as pertaining to each location under consideration, were impartially canvassed. . . .

There were a number of points concerning which it seemed to the committee that Cooranbong presented inducements that were superior to any other locality. And so it transpired that when all things were taken into account, and allowed to have their full weight, it seemed conclusive that Cooranbong was the place for the factory, and a decision was made accordingly.

The points enumerated in considerable detail can be summarized:

1. The sawmill plant at Cooranbong, a one-and-a-half-story building of sixty by sixty-two feet, with its power equipment together with two acres of land, was offered by the school for £400. The school had decided to sell the mill, as it had served its primary purpose in the erection of the school plant.

2. There was water transportation available with oceangoing boats carrying twenty to thirty tons able to dock within a few rods of the factory located on the banks of Dora Creek. The railroad station was within three miles.

3. Fuel for power was abundant and about half the cost in Sydney or Melbourne.

4. Not mentioned in this report, but noted elsewhere, was the fact that raw materials were less expensive in New South Wales than in Melbourne.

5. An important point was that student labor, male and female, was right on the premises, as it were, and the factory would offer opportunities for the students to earn. The committee saw the

THE AUSTRALIAN YEARS

advantages of the school enterprise and the food production enterprise working hand in hand in a natural manner.

The report in the *Record* pointed out that "in harmony with direct instruction that the Lord has given regarding the interests involved, the food manufacturing business will be carried forward in a way to prove a valuable auxiliary to the school enterprise."

W. C. WHITE REVIEW OF THE EXPERIENCE

On October 18, W. C. White, in a letter to W. L. H. Baker, who had been at the Stanmore conference session but was now in America, summarized in perspective the fast-moving developments. Coming to the point of the location of major interests, he described the steps taken that looked forward to moving the office of the union conference from Melbourne to Sydney, and the suggestion that possibly the health-food business should center at Cooranbong. He suggested to Baker, "I think you are well enough acquainted with our brethren in Melbourne and their feeling that most of the good things should be centered there, to believe me when I say that Brethren Faulkhead, Michaels, and some others seemed to be preparing for a strong protest against the transfer of men and business to Sydney."

> But just then we received letters from Mother, telling us more about what was presented to her that night in Stanmore. Among other things, she said that she saw drays being loaded with the household goods of families who were moving away from Melbourne to take part in the work in other places. . . . She also cautioned us repeatedly against allowing our personal ambition, our selfish interests, and our local views to interfere with such plans as were for the general interest of the cause. These letters saved us much unpleasant controversy.—12 WCW, p. 179.

In the meantime the Ellen G. White-sponsored medical missionary program right there in Cooranbong went quietly on. This was in the form of Sara McEnterfer serving as community nurse without charge, and help to families in which there was dire need of food, clothing, and bedding. In her letters, and at times in her oral presentations, Ellen White continued to call for a hospital at Cooranbong.

CHAPTER 31
(1898)

The High Point in Australian Camp Meetings

WHEN word was brought to Ellen White that the camp meeting to be held in the colony of Queensland was appointed for October 14 to 24, five hundred miles to the north at Brisbane, and she was reminded that a year ago she had promised to attend, she demurred. "It is not consistent," she reasoned, "that I go so far. My workers are here, and the work which I wish to do will be retarded for two months at least, if I go."—Letter 109, 1898. But her thinking was changed by a vision of the night. Of this she wrote:

> In the night season I seemed to be making preparation to attend a meeting, not at Cooranbong, but at a distance, where companies in the most destitute spiritual condition were stretching out their arms, and saying, "Oh, give us food; give us the bread of life. We are hungering for the knowledge of the truth."
>
> "What can we do?" I said.
>
> And the cry came back, "Feed us, feed us from the Word."
>
> Then these words were spoken, "Say not ye, There are yet four months, and yet cometh harvest? behold, I say unto you, Lift up your eyes, and look on the fields; for they are white already to harvest." . . . I saw companies eagerly searching the Scriptures and praying together.
>
> Again I saw a camp meeting gathered in regions beyond, waiting to hear the truth. I saw a representation of cattle, horses, and sheep standing round one who was holding in his hands a sheaf of oats. The hungry animals were seeking to get at the

tempting favor, but could not reach it. A voice cried out, "You place the food too high."

Cribs had been made for the sheep, but they could get but little food, for the cribs were too high. We gave a most earnest, painful study as to how we should feed these animals. Again the voice said, "Let down the crib, that the hungry animals may feed." . . . After this dream, I decided to go to Queensland.—Letter 86, 1898.

As she reported the experience to the readers of the March 21, 1899, *Review and Herald*, she declared:

I dreaded the journey to Brisbane, and would fain have believed that this meant Maitland, Newcastle, and the smaller places within thirty miles of Cooranbong. But again the scene of people calling for help was presented before me, and a voice said, "They are as sheep that have no shepherd." Then I said, "I will go to the camp meeting, for the Lord has been teaching me my duty."

Accompanied by Sara McEnterfer, her secretary Minnie Hawkins, and several of the young women from the school who were going to join Mrs. Haskell in Bible work, Ellen White took the train Wednesday evening, October 12, for Brisbane. She was favored in having a little room at the end of the car, shared by Sara. As the train sped on through the night, Ellen White slept, and in her dreams she was standing before many people. With great earnestness she was urging them to trust in God and to have increasing faith in Jesus. Then she awoke and looked out of the window, and saw two white clouds. The *Review* account continued:

THE TWO WHITE CLOUDS OF ANGELS

Then I fell asleep again, and in my dreams these words were spoken to me: "Look at these clouds. It was just such clouds as these that enshrouded the heavenly host who proclaimed to the shepherds the birth of the world's Redeemer."

I awoke and looked out of the car window again, and there were the two large white clouds, as white as snow. They were distinct, separate clouds, but one would approach and touch the

THE HIGH POINT IN AUSTRALIAN CAMP MEETINGS

other, and for a moment they would blend together; then they would separate, and remain as distinct as before. They did not disappear, but continued in sight throughout the forenoon. At twelve o'clock we changed cars, and I did not see the clouds anymore.

She was led to ponder the thought of the angels of God going before them. She rejoiced in their guardianship and the assurance of heaven's special blessings in the work to be done in Brisbane. It was thought that it would not be a large camp meeting, for there were not more than 175 Sabbathkeepers scattered throughout all of Queensland, and few of these had much to boast of in the way of this world's goods. A. G. Daniells in his report, published in the October 15 *Union Conference Record,* spoke of some of the problems they faced:

> In the first place, the difficulty the camp meeting committee experienced in securing a campground made it seem for a time that there was no place in Brisbane for such a meeting. . . . Then came the difficulty of securing an attendance of our people large enough to make the meeting appear like a camp meeting. We have had the impression that in order to have our camp meetings draw the public we must have a large showing on the ground. . . .
>
> Another difficulty was a lack of funds. The treasurer was not able to send those managing the meeting a single pound before the meeting began. They put their own personal money in where it was needed, and borrowed from their friends.
>
> At first we were perplexed to know how we would be able to get all the preliminary work done. There were but few men, and they were scattered over a vast area of country. Altogether there were as many difficulties connected with the holding of this meeting as any we have held in this country.

But the Lord wrought for them marvelously. A good lot was found three miles from the Brisbane city post office. It was set back from the street far enough to escape the noise of passing vehicles. Men from all parts of the colony came in early to help pitch the camp. Including the children, 118 Seventh-day Adventists came to the camp meeting, some traveling nearly a thousand miles. Thirty-one

THE AUSTRALIAN YEARS

family tents were pitched, and there were two large meeting tents. The counsel given the year before, to take the people of the city by surprise, was followed here. The camp was quickly pitched; then two or three days before the meeting was to open, short articles appeared in the daily papers, a few large cards were placed in shop windows, and five thousand copies of a four-page camp meeting paper were distributed from house to house. Added to this, "the tramway company placed, on all the trams passing the campground, calico signs, five feet by two feet six inches, on which were neatly painted the words 'Camp Meeting, Logan Road.' "—*Ibid*. These trams ran the full length of the main street of Brisbane every seven minutes. This advertising was provided without charge.

THE BRISBANE CAMP MEETING OPENS

By Friday night and the opening meeting, all anxiety regarding attendance quickly melted. Hundreds of men, women, and children poured onto the grounds. The tent was well filled, with an estimated eight or nine hundred present.

Sabbath morning, the Sabbath school was well attended. Stephen Haskell spoke at the worship hour, taking as his text, "We would see Jesus." Ellen White spoke in the afternoon on the call to the wedding supper and the guest who came without the wedding garment. Attendance and interest were excellent. In the evening Haskell spoke again to a large congregation.

Three of the six workers who were on the grounds and had been counted on to speak fell ill. This left Elders Daniells and Haskell and Ellen White to carry forward the work (Letter 86, 1898). She reported that the singing talent was not the best.

Saturday night, Ellen White was given a vision concerning worker relationships:

> In the night I was instructed that in this meeting we must each one look to the Lord, and not to one another, saying, "What shall this man do?" Each one must seek the Lord earnestly to know for himself what he is to do in the service of the Lord. . . . It takes all kinds of timber fitly to frame this building, and Jesus Christ Himself is to be the Chief Cornerstone, "in whom all the building fitly framed together groweth unto an holy temple in the Lord."

THE HIGH POINT IN AUSTRALIAN CAMP MEETINGS

This is the work to be done in our camp meetings. We are to build together, not separately. We are to work unitedly. Every stick of timber is to find its place, that a united framework may be made—a habitation of God through the Spirit.—RH, March 28, 1899.

Sunday Daniells spoke in the morning and Ellen White in the afternoon. She reported of this meeting:

The tent was full, and many who could not enter stood outside while I spoke . . . on the subject of Christian temperance.—*Ibid*.

I felt that an angel of God was by my side. In my weakness I was made strong. I spoke one hour and a half, and after the meeting closed the people told those who came on the ground later that they never heard anything like the talk Mrs. White had given them. One man, who wore the blue ribbon [of the temperance forces], said he never saw the temperance question more clearly presented than by a woman of 70. "What a voice she has," he said, "and she is 70 years old and uses neither tea nor coffee nor meat."—MS 187, 1898.

Those in her audience observed somewhat with astonishment that she spoke without notes (Letter 86, 1898). Ellen White was pleased to learn that in her audience were members of the legislative assembly. Every chair and seat on the campground was brought to accommodate the large crowd. Most of the church members left their seats to give room to the strangers, and still hundreds had to stand (UCR, Oct. 15, 1898; MS 187, 1898). Noted Ellen White, "The people seem more interested than even those of Stanmore, and the congregation was fully as large, both on Sabbath and Sunday."—MS 187, 1898. The notices in the Brisbane newspapers that Mrs. White, a woman of 70, would speak Saturday and Sunday afternoons, undoubtedly enhanced the interest of the general public (MS 153, 1898).

A Wesleyan minister in the city, observing the large attendance and the deep interest in the meetings at the camp, proposed to some of his members that he would pitch a tent in the yard of their church and hold meetings every day through the week. "But this," Ellen White observed, "did not seem to satisfy them entirely. We can

THE AUSTRALIAN YEARS

understand this. The minister wished to hold them, that they might not stray away to hear that which was preached at the tent."—MS 187, 1898.

THE MEETINGS EXTENDED ANOTHER WEEK

The camp meeting was scheduled to close on Monday, October 24. Ellen White was the speaker again on Sunday afternoon. She was weary and somewhat distracted, but she met her appointment, speaking to an audience of one thousand. She relates her unique experience:

> On the last Sunday of the meetings the Lord gave me a great victory. I was much exhausted. . . . I seemed to have no strength at all, but at 3:00 P.M. I went on the platform. I had a portion of Scripture to speak upon, but I could not remember what I meant to bring before the people. I stood up, and another portion of Scripture came into my mind. I had been a little hoarse, but I felt that the angel of the Lord was by my side, for my voice was clear and full and distinct.
>
> Some who had given up their seats to strangers, and had gone into their tents, said that they heard every word from the beginning to the close. I spoke for one hour and a half upon the subject of temperance. After I returned to my home [room], I had no fears that I had not done as well as I ought. I felt that it was not Ellen G. White who had spoken, but that the Lord had spoken through the frail instrument. I felt my soul softened and subdued by the power of God. My heart was full of peace and joy in the Lord.—MS 153, 1898.

Some of the crowd had attended meetings on the previous Sunday and had come again bringing friends. She gave an interesting word picture:

> Many we recognized as those who had attended the evening meetings; but there were hundreds who had come to the meeting for the first time. According to appointment, our meeting was to close the following day, but it was evident that the work of the meeting was not finished. It was too busy a time for consultation, for every worker on the grounds was busy visiting, entertaining the interested and the curious, distributing

THE HIGH POINT IN AUSTRALIAN CAMP MEETINGS

reading matter, and holding short Bible readings with those who questioned about the doctrines taught at the meeting.—RH, April 4, 1899.

As had been the case several times in connection with this camp meeting, the Lord on Sunday night gave Ellen White special light. She wrote of it in her report in the April 4, 1899, *Review*.

> It was represented to me that the cloud still rested over the tabernacle. The cloud had not yet lifted, and the tents must not be taken down. This was our time to seek the Lord earnestly for wisdom and strength, and to labor with all our powers to give the warning message to the people. The people were under conviction, and this camp meeting remained a necessity.
>
> I was not able to speak at the early meeting, but sent word that according to light given to me, there ought to be nothing done unnecessarily to give the impression to the people that the meeting had closed.

Earlier in the week as the interest was observed, the decision had been reached to leave the large tent standing for a week or two for continued meetings, but plans to take down the family tents were now dropped. Meetings were appointed for the evening and each morning, and the campers invited to stay on. Many could not, but some did. Monday night, the public congregation took a strong vote to have the meetings continued. About a dozen workers of varied experience and gifts remained to follow up the interest. Concluding her report of the Brisbane camp meeting, Ellen White could say:

> This, which we had looked forward to as a very small meeting, has proved to be one of the most interesting and profitable camp meetings held in Australia.—RH, March 28, 1899.

After the Brisbane meeting, Ellen White accompanied by Sara McEnterfer and W. C. White went on north another four hundred miles to Rockhampton, where she spoke four times.

BACK HOME AT SUNNYSIDE

Back at her Sunnyside home, quite worn from the journey to Queensland and the intensive labor there, Ellen White rested a few days and then turned to her literary work. Arrangements had been made for W. A. Colcord, who had been editing the *Bible Echo* and other journals published in Melbourne, to join her literary staff. He arrived at Cooranbong on Friday, November 25. She spoke that morning to the students in the summer school program. Sabbath, her seventy-first birthday, she spoke at the church and then early in the new week applied herself to the writing of letters.

The evening after the Sabbath, December 10, the first copies of *The Desire of Ages* reached Cooranbong and Ellen White's home (12 WCW, p. 356). On December 16 W. C. White hastened off a letter to C. H. Jones, manager of the Pacific Press, telling of receiving copies of the book and extolling it:

> We received copies of *The Desire of Ages*. I am very much pleased with its general appearance, and I think the Pacific Press has done a noble work in the illustrations, in the typographical work, in the press work, and in the binding, and as we see the book completed we are well pleased with its general plan and form. . . . I am pleased to be able to tell you that Mother is very well pleased with the book.—*Ibid.*, p. 386.

Thursday, December 15, the American mail brought letters from G. A. Irwin, Mrs. Henry, and Dr. Kellogg.

The letter from Elder Irwin, president of the General Conference, was an invitation to attend the session of the General Conference to be held at South Lancaster in February, 1899. She responded:

> You ask me to come to your conference in America. I was 71 years old the twenty-sixth of November. But this is not the reason I plead for not attending your conference. We have done what we could here. We have advanced slowly, planting the standard of truth in every place possible. But the dearth of means has been a serious hindrance. We have had to work at a great disadvantage for want of facilities; we have had to meet and breast many discouragements. We dare not show one particle of unbelief. We advance just as far as we can see, and then go far ahead of sight, moving by faith. . . .
>
> We strip ourselves of everything we can possibly spare in the line of money, for the openings are so many and the necessities

THE HIGH POINT IN AUSTRALIAN CAMP MEETINGS

so great. We have hired money until I have been compelled to say, I cannot donate more. My workers are the best, most faithful and devoted girls I ever expect to find. In order to advance the work I have donated the wages that should have been paid them. When the last call was made, my name was not on the list for the first time. The openings are abundant, but we are obliged to move very slowly. The work that ought to have been done has not been done, and I cannot feel at liberty to leave here now. . . . I have written these particulars that you may understand why I cannot attend your conference. . . . There is nothing for me to do but to remain here until the work is placed on a solid foundation.—Letter 125, 1898.

THE NEWCASTLE CAMP MEETING

While still in Brisbane, near the close of the second week of meetings, a letter was received from A. G. Daniells setting forth the opportunities and needs of such cities as Newcastle and Maitland, cities within twenty or thirty miles from Cooranbong. In eight weeks a thrust begun in Newcastle would be tapered off, and Ellen White saw it as a time to "see who can be brought to stand with us in obedience to the Sabbath" (MS 187, 1898). As she and W. C. White considered the matter, they were impressed that they should fit in a camp meeting in December just before the meeting in Melbourne appointed for January. Others concurred.

Newcastle was a seaport in a coal-mining district about twenty miles from Cooranbong. Ellen White states:

> We thought we could plant the banner of truth here, and a church be raised up, as in Stanmore. It would be a special strength to Cooranbong, for Newcastle is our nearest place of trade, and it is a matter of importance to us to see a company raised up here.—Letter 131, 1898.

The large tent used for the meetings in Brisbane was needed in Melbourne, so a new tent was hired for the Newcastle meeting. The rental was £15, with the option to purchase it if money could be raised to meet the price. Ellen White described it as "a very large tent, the largest we have ever had the privilege of speaking under. . . . It has proved to be the most substantial tent we have ever seen."—*Ibid*. In his report of the camp meeting, G. B. Starr spoke of it as "the largest pavilion yet used by our people in these colonies" (UCR, Jan. 15, 1899).

For several months Herbert Lacey had been holding evangelistic meetings in the city (Letter 128, 1898). Reading matter had been circulated freely, and the place had been well canvassed with books. The time was ripe for reaping the harvest. The working force in the conference thought of this camp meeting as "the smallest of the season held in the Australian colonies—just a little one, tucked in between the Queensland and Victorian meetings" (UCR, Jan. 15, 1899). W. C. White wrote that "when this meeting was appointed, we thought that we might gather about one hundred of our own people" and a modest attendance from the city (12 WCW, p. 402).

But to the surprise of everyone, when the meeting opened on Thursday night, December 22, there were a thousand people present (Letter 131, 1898). Ellen White drove over from Cooranbong with Sara McEnterfer on Friday, a hot and oppressive day (Letter 130, 1898). From a conference of four hundred members, two hundred were there at the camp meeting.

New South Wales had suffered a long and severe drought, but the first weekend of the camp meeting this was broken by strong winds and heavy rains, beginning Friday night. Ellen White describes the storm:

WORKING THROUGH THE STORM

We have had a terrible tempest of rain and wind. It did bad work for our small tents, but the large tent was new, and staked with poles and cross poles inside, so that it would be difficult to blow it down. . . . The wind became a howling gale, and continued over the Sabbath. Sabbath the rain just poured down, as if the windows of heaven were opened. Nevertheless our meetings went on, and there was a good attendance from the camp. Men had to leave the meeting and attend to securing the tents in the tempest of wind and rain.—Letter 129, 1898.

Ellen White was the speaker for the Sabbath-afternoon meeting, and the Lord gave her freedom as she addressed the audience that filled the tent. When the storm raged too fiercely, and the speaker could not be heard well, the congregation sang. The meeting lasted from three o'clock till nearly sundown (Letters 128, 129, 1898). Saturday night, in spite of the bad weather, the large tent was again well filled. But Sunday morning, the storm over, there were no early meetings. The whole camp was busy repairing the damage done; by eleven o'clock they were ready for the preaching service in the big tent.

On Friday night Ellen White passed through an impressive experience that molded her Sabbath-afternoon presentation. She reported it in detail in her account of the Newcastle camp meeting sent to the *Review and Herald*. She wrote:

> During the night of the first Sabbath of the Newcastle meeting, I seemed to be in a meeting, presenting the necessity and importance of our receiving the Spirit. This was the burden of my labor—the opening of our hearts to the Holy Spirit. . . .
>
> In my dream a sentinel stood at the door of an important building and asked everyone who came for entrance, "Have ye received the Holy Ghost?" A measuring line was in his hand, and only very, very few were admitted into the building. "Your size as a human being is nothing," he said. "But if you have reached the full stature of a man in Christ Jesus, according to the knowledge you have had, you will receive an appointment to sit with Christ at the marriage supper of the Lamb; and through the eternal ages, you will never cease to learn the blessings granted in the banquet prepared for you."—RH, April 11, 1899 (see 1SM, pp. 109, 110).

In this vision of the night the angel presented the elements of salvation and the key to a successful Christian life.

Elder Starr reported that the Newcastle camp meeting "grew until it was the largest in outside attendance, and one of the most important in its counsels and results" (UCR, Jan. 15, 1899). Midweek, Ellen White reported:

> We have this morning, December 28, decided that the meeting must be continued over the third Sabbath and Sunday. Those who are attentive and interested must have a chance to hear the Word of God.—Letter 129, 1898.

And hear the Word of God they did. As she described the meeting to longtime friends in the United States, she explained:

> I think we entered Newcastle at the right time. . . . The best class of people, it seems to us, attend our meetings, and they are deeply interested. We do not conceal our banner of truth at all. We let them know that we are Seventh-day Adventists because we believe the Bible. The Bible and the Bible only is the foundation of our faith. Before these meetings close, the people will know from the Scriptures why we are a peculiar people. The Word is the foundation of our faith. Our dependence is upon Christ.—Letter 131, 1898.

The speakers at this meeting, in addition to Ellen White, were Elders Tenney, Daniells, Colcord, and Robinson, and Dr. Caro (UCR, Jan. 15, 1899). On weekends the audience numbered up to 2,500. After running for seventeen days over three Sabbaths and Sundays, the camp meeting as such was brought to a close, but not the public meetings. The large new tent that had served so well was exchanged for a smaller one, which was purchased and pitched in a favorable location in nearby Hamilton for the continuation of evangelistic meetings. Elders G. B. Starr, W. A. Colcord, and H. C. Lacey and his wife were left to follow through in binding off the interest (12 WCW, p. 402). During January, Ellen White visited Hamilton each weekend and continued frequent visits while the work was developing. By the end of April, thirty-five were baptized (Letter 83, 1899), and the interest still was running high. Within a few months a house of worship was erected, and on September 2, Ellen White preached the dedicatory address. So the hastily planned Newcastle camp meeting, as "just a little one" to be held at year's end squeezed in between the well-planned meetings in Brisbane and Melbourne, surprised everyone and laid the foundation for another church.

In the Brisbane and Newcastle meetings it would seem that Australian camp meetings reached perhaps the highest point of evangelistic thrust.

CHAPTER 32
(1892-1898)

Writing on the Life of Christ— The Desire of Ages

THE arrival of copies of *The Desire of Ages* in December and the acceptance of the book in the field marked for Ellen White and her staff the climax of book preparation in Australia. This point offers an opportunity in this biography to draw together a connected account of the work that it was hoped could be accomplished in a year or two but took seven.

When Ellen G. White left San Francisco for Australia in 1891, in her accompanying baggage were two precious four hundred-page volumes on the life of Christ. They were the center volumes in the four-book set titled *The Spirit of Prophecy* and known also as *The Great Controversy Between Christ and Satan*. Volume 2, bearing the more specific title *Life, Teachings and Miracles of Our Lord Jesus Christ*, had been published in Battle Creek in 1877. The other carried the title *The Death, Resurrection and Ascension of Our Lord Jesus Christ*, and had been published a year later.

These two relatively small books were in the Australia-bound luggage because Ellen White planned that, away from the distractions of the work in North America, she would, with the assistance of Miss Marian Davis, who accompanied her, perfect and amplify the presentation they carried. It had been nearly fifteen years since they had come from the press, and Ellen White was eager to introduce into the story additional light and information that had come to her from time to time that had been set forth in her letters, periodical articles, and transcribed sermons. The projected volume, or volumes, would join the larger, more comprehensive *Patriarchs and Prophets*, just published, and *The Great Controversy*, issued in 1888. Together they traced the story of the Conflict of the Ages, and were prepared with both the church in particular and the world at large in mind as potential readers.

With Ellen White's knowledge of the situation in Australia she was not as sanguine in regard to the opportunities for literary work there as were her fellow workers, who were without the benefit of her prophetic insights. Mention has been made in the preceding chapters of her often futile attempts to work on the life of Christ. Some years provided more favorable opportunities than others. While Ellen White's work on the project was intermittent, Marian Davis kept right at the task. The latter often felt it was about finished and then would be frustrated and at the same time delighted when light was received by Ellen White in vision that, when written out, added rich sources of materials. The work on the manuscript stretched from 1892 through 1897 and into 1898. Even then, with the receiving of the finished book on December 10, 1898, there was still more to do on the life of Christ. That was presented in *Christ's Object Lessons,* published two years later. Now we will trace, rather sketchily, the story of the preparation of *The Desire of Ages.*

INITIAL WRITING ON THE LIFE OF CHRIST

In 1858 as Ellen White first wrote the account of what had been revealed to her in the great controversy visions of 1848 and 1858, she devoted fifty-two small pages to the life of Christ. Sixteen of these gave a very brief review of His ministry, and thirty-six were devoted to the few days of the last scenes of His life. These pages were expanded in volumes two and three of the Spirit of Prophecy series in 1877 and 1878; 387 larger pages were given to His general ministry and 254 pages to the Passion Week and His closing ministry. With *Patriarchs and Prophets* and *The Great Controversy* in the field, it was planned that the work, in its preparation called "The Life of Christ," would represent a further amplification, particularly of the account of the three years and more of the life and ministry of our Lord up to the Passion Week. It was to this that Ellen White and Marian Davis turned their attention in Australia.

It was early in 1873, while James and Ellen White were in California for the first time, that she began her writing on the life of Christ. Between this date and the spring of 1875, as her travels and

WRITING ON THE LIFE OF CHRIST

other work allowed, she wrote somewhat intermittently. Portions were first published in the *Review and Herald*.

In 1876 she was again on the Pacific Coast, living in their new home in Oakland. James White, president of the General Conference, was detained in Battle Creek in administrative work. She had good literary help in her niece, Mary Clough, and she pushed ahead with her writing on the life of Christ.

The first drafts of her materials were in her own handwriting. Mary would edit the pages and put them into the form of a chapter, and then copy it. Of course, the finished work was also in handwritten form, for it was six or seven years later that typewriters came into use in Mrs. White's work. Every morning she would write diligently in her upstairs room. After the noonday meal she would go to Mary Clough's room, lie on a sofa, and listen as Mary read the material prepared from her first written draft. "The precious subjects open to my mind well," she wrote in early April.—Letter 4, 1876.

Writing at this time to her close friend Lucinda Hall, she declared:

> I have a special work at this time to write out the things which the Lord has shown me. . . . I have a work to do which has been a great burden to my soul. How great, no one but the Lord knows. Again, I want to have my mind calm and composed. I want to have time to meditate and pray while engaged in this work. . . . This is a great work, and I feel like crying to God every day for His Spirit to help me to do this work all right.—Letter 59, 1876.

Bible study, visions, prayer, meditation, discussion with her literary assistant, even "hard thinking," all under the general superintendence of the Holy Spirit, were involved in the writing. "I feel great peace and calmness of mind," she noted. "There seems to be nothing to confuse and distract my mind, and with so much hard thinking my mind could not be perplexed with anything without being overtaxed."—Letter 13, 1876. "I cannot rush business. This work must be done carefully, slowly, and accurately. The subjects we have prepared are well gotten up. They please me."—Letter 14, 1876.

As the two women worked together with dedicated purpose,

they had at hand for reference several standard works by other authors, such as William Hanna's *Life of Our Lord*, Cunningham Geikie's *Life and Words of Christ*, and most likely some others. The finished product gives evidence, for instance, that they made some use of Hanna's book. While there are no paragraphs or, to our knowledge, even complete sentences taken from it, there are phrases here and there that can be easily identified, and in some cases the order in Ellen White's presentation follows Hanna rather closely. Hanna and Ellen White were both covering the same ground, leaning heavily on the gospel accounts. In Ellen White's writing there appear interesting details found in neither the Gospel writers or the writings of commentators, points in which she deals in sufficient detail to make it very evident that her basic source in writing was the visions given to her. In these visions she witnessed, sometimes in panoramic views and at other times in great detail, the events in the life of the Lord.

WHY DID SHE COPY FROM OTHERS?

Responding to this question in 1928, W. C. White wrote significantly of how this reading aided her:

> Notwithstanding all the power that God had given her to present scenes in the lives of Christ and His apostles and His prophets and His reformers in a stronger and more telling way than other historians, yet she always felt most keenly the results of her lack of school education. She admired the language in which other writers had presented to their readers the scenes which God had presented to her in vision, and she found it both a pleasure and a convenience and an economy of time to use their language fully or in part in presenting those things which she knew through revelation, and which she wished to pass on to her readers.—WCW to L. E. Froom, Jan. 8, 1928.

W. C. White mentions to Froom several other reasons as well that are worthy of thoughtful consideration:

> The great events occurring in the life of our Lord were presented to her in panoramic scenes as also were the other portions of the great controversy. In a few of these scenes,

chronology and geography were clearly presented, but in the greater part of the revelation the flashlight scenes, which were exceedingly vivid, and the conversations and the controversies, which she heard and was able to narrate, were not marked geographically or chronologically, and she was left to study the Bible and history and the writings of men who had presented the life of our Lord to get the chronological and geographical connection.

Answering still further the questions put to him by Elder Froom in 1928, W. C. White explained further:

> Regarding the reading of works of contemporary authors during the time of the preparation of these books, there is very little to be said, because when Sister White was busily engaged in writing, she had very little time to read. Previous to her work of writing on the life of Christ and during the time of her writing to some extent, she read from the works of Hanna, Fleetwood, Farrar, and Geikie. I never knew of her reading Edersheim. She occasionally referred to Andrews, particularly with reference to chronology.

The knowledge that Ellen White read from other authors, and at times employed some of their phraseology, has led some to lose sight of the fact that the many visions given to her by God through the years constituted the main source of her information and insights. Were it not for these visions, she would never have written on the life of Christ. Her reading was primarily an aid in presenting precious truths through her pen.

W. C. White mentioned Hanna, Fleetwood, Farrar, Geikie, and Andrews. He did not recall that she had read Edersheim, although recent study indicates that at some point she had. These were the books Ellen White had easy access to and was familiar with, and probably the ones she took with her to Australia. There were some others, but not a great number. It has been reported that there is evidence of some similarities in wording to expressions in twenty-five or thirty other authors. Ellen White did not carry a great library around with her, nor did she take such to Australia where she thought to stay only two years, or to New Zealand for the three months she expected to labor there. The time in New Zealand grew to ten months, as mentioned earlier, and she did considerable writing on the life of Christ while she wintered there.

The numerous authors some have referred to is most likely accounted for in the fact that it was a prevailing practice for one commentator to borrow the wording of another, considering truth common property. It could well be that some of the books Ellen White had easy access to may have contained materials traceable to a number of authors. Ingram Cobbin in his preface to his *Condensed Commentary and Family Exposition of the Holy Bible,* page iv, declared: "All the commentators have drawn largely from the fathers, especially from St. Augustine," and then points out the borrowings of one from another, naming authors so involved. See *Ellen G. White and Her Critics,* pages 404-407, for insights into the literary borrowing of commentators.

W. C. White in his letter to Froom made a further important point that should be taken into account:

> Another purpose served by the reading of history, *Life of Our Lord* [Hanna, 1863], and *Life and Epistles of St. Paul* [Conybeare and Howson, 1851, 1852] was that in so doing there was brought vividly to her mind scenes presented clearly in vision, but which were, through the lapse of years and her strenuous ministry, dimmed in her memory.

The full W. C. White letter appears in *Selected Messages,* book 3, pages 453 to 461, as a portion of appendix C.

The reader who turns to Ellen White's first writing in 1858 on the life of Christ as found in *Spiritual Gifts,* volume 1, pages 28 to 79, or *Early Writings,* pages 153 to 192, will find a vivid and clear narration, at times enhanced by details found neither in the gospels nor the writing of others.

WORK IN AUSTRALIA ON THE LIFE OF CHRIST

So the work in Australia on the life of Christ did not consist in producing creatively, chapter after chapter, but rather in Ellen White's writing more fully what had been revealed to her on Christ's life in many visions. Her time was much taken up with the developing work in Australia; Marian Davis, of whom little has been said, was busily occupied in drawing out from the various E. G.

WRITING ON THE LIFE OF CHRIST

White sources materials that would broaden and enrich the presentation of the 1870s. Writing of this a decade later, Ellen White explained:

> I feel very thankful for the help of Sister Marian Davis in getting out my books. She gathers materials from my diaries, from my letters, and from the articles published in the papers. I greatly prize her faithful service. She has been with me for twenty-five years, and has constantly been gaining increasing ability for the work of classifying and grouping my writings.—Letter 9, 1903 (see also 3SM, p. 93).

At another time, writing of Miss Davis' work, Ellen White explained:

> She does her work in this way: She takes my articles which are published in the papers, and pastes them in blank books. She also has a copy of all the letters I write. In preparing a chapter for a book, Marian remembers that I have written something on that special point, which may make the matter more forcible. She begins to search for this, and if when she finds it, she sees that it will make the chapter more clear, she adds it.
>
> The books are not Marian's productions, but my own, gathered from all my writings. Marian has a large field from which to draw, and her ability to arrange the matter is of great value to me. It saves my poring over a mass of matter, which I have no time to do. . . . Marian is a most valuable help to me in bringing out my books.—Letter 61a, 1900 (see also 3SM, pp. 91, 92).

In this letter she mentioned Marian as her "bookmaker."

ELLEN WHITE WRITES ON CHRIST'S LIFE AND MINISTRY

It was during her ten-month-long illness in 1892 that Ellen White actually began to do much writing on the ministry of Christ. In her diary for July 12, 1892, she noted: "This afternoon I wrote a number of pages on the life of Christ. I long for a large portion of the Spirit of God, that I may write the things which the people need." Thus she continued in the days that followed:

Wednesday, July 13: In the morning I wrote on the life of

Christ, and in the afternoon I rode out. . . .

Thursday, July 14: After arranging my position so as not to bring any strain on arms or shoulders, I go to work at my writing, asking the Lord to bless that which I write. I know that He helps me. . . . I am now writing on the life of Christ. . . .

Friday, July 15: I cannot manage to keep comfortably warm in these high rooms, with only a grate fire. I have had two severe chills, and this has greatly increased my lameness in my shoulders and hips. But notwithstanding this, I was able to spend most of yesterday writing on the life of Christ. I praise the Lord because I feel a nearness to my Saviour.—MS 34, 1892.

On that Friday, in a letter to O. A. Olsen, president of the General Conference, she wrote of how as she undertook this work she was almost overwhelmed with the subject:

This week I have been enabled to commence writing on the life of Christ. Oh, how inefficient, how incapable I am of expressing the things which burn in my soul in reference to the mission of Christ! I have hardly dared to enter upon the work. There is so much to it all. And what shall I say, and what shall I leave unsaid? I lie awake nights pleading with the Lord for the Holy Spirit to come upon me, to abide upon me. . . .

I walk with trembling before God. I know not how to speak or trace with pen the large subject of the atoning sacrifice. I know not how to present subjects in the living power in which they stand before me. I tremble for fear lest I shall belittle the great plan of salvation by cheap words. I bow my soul in awe and reverence before God and say, "Who is sufficient for these things?"—Letter 40, 1892.

Only occasionally at this time did she mention specific visions in which scenes pertaining to the life of Christ passed before her, but in connection with first writing on the subject in 1858, the terms "I saw," "I was shown," or other terms indicating divine revelation and inspiration, frequently occurred. As the reader has observed the frequency of the visions given to Ellen White in Australia dealing with the various features of the work and the experience of individuals, it is reasonable to assume that as she wrote, views on the life and work of Jesus were frequently given to her also. In 1889 she told of how "the betrayal, trial, and crucifixion of Jesus" had passed before her point by point (Letter 14, 1889). In 1900 she wrote:

> Heavenly scenes were presented to me in the life of Christ, pleasant to contemplate, and again painful scenes which were not always pleasant for Him to bear which pained my heart.—MS 93, 1900.

As the work of preparing the book progressed, Marian Davis would search the writings for additional material, and Ellen White would fill in the gaps. Miss Davis gives a glimpse of her task as she pleaded that relevant materials be copied out from various sources, so that they would be more readily available. Such a request is more understandable when it is known that she herself did not use the typewriter.

> Perhaps you can imagine the difficulty of trying to bring together points relating to any subject, when these must be gleaned from thirty scrapbooks, a half-dozen bound [E. G. White] volumes, and fifty manuscripts, all covering thousands of pages.—Marian Davis to WCW, March 29, 1893.

But it was Ellen White alone who performed the task of filling in to complete the text. Marian did none of the writing. Ellen White made mention of this at the death of Miss Davis in 1904, when her mind turned back to their labors together:

> We have stood side by side in the work, and in perfect harmony in that work. And when she would be gathering up the precious jots and tittles that had come in papers and books and present it to me, "Now," she would say, "there is something wanted [needed]. I cannot supply it." I would look it over, and in one moment I could trace the line right out. We worked together, just worked together in perfect harmony all the time.—MS 95, 1904.

ELLEN WHITE IN NEW ZEALAND AND MARIAN DAVIS IN MELBOURNE

Ellen White spent most of 1893 in New Zealand, and as noted in telling the story of her work there, she made some progress in writing for her book. Marian had remained in Melbourne, so Mrs.

THE AUSTRALIAN YEARS

White shipped off new material to her as she was able to write it. The correspondence between the two throws some light on how they worked together. When examining the chapters after Marian had worked on them, Ellen White would add here or there and strengthen the presentation. Further, as Ellen White would write an article on a particular incident or subject, she would place it in the hands of her office staff with the expectation that it might serve in several ways. Such articles often gave new and fresh materials for Marian to draw from.

While Ellen White was in New Zealand, Marian found that a course on the life of Christ was being offered in the newly opened Bible school in Melbourne. Eager to get all the background help she could for her task, she enrolled as a student. On October 18, 1893, she wrote to Ellen White:

> The Bible class coming in the middle of the forenoon is rather inconvenient, but while the life of Christ is studied, I can't afford to lose it, for it is the only thing I have bearing on my work, and it wakes one's mind up to hear the matter talked over.

The interchange of correspondence during this year showed the concern of each of the two women as they made progress in the preparation of the manuscript. Prompted no doubt by attending the class, Marian suggested some topics she thought she would like to see represented in the book. Ellen White did not see the real need, and significantly declared:

> These I shall not enter upon without the Lord's Spirit . . . to lead me. The building a tower, the war of kings, these things do not burden my mind, but the subjects of the life of Christ, His character representing the Father, the parables essential for us all to understand and practice the lessons contained in them, I shall dwell upon.—Letter 131, 1893.

THE SEQUENCE OF EVENTS

As the materials were assembled and arranged into chapters, careful attention had to be given to the sequence of the events in the Saviour's life. To what extent and in what detail visions provided the sequence in ministry and miracles in Christ's life and work is not

WRITING ON THE LIFE OF CHRIST

known. It is known that a decade earlier she made a significant request: "Tell Mary to find me some histories of the Bible that would give me the order of events."—Letter 38, 1885. The Gospel writers in their accounts did not help much in the point of sequence. In the absence of direct instruction from Ellen White, or clues in the materials themselves, Miss Davis consulted carefully prepared harmonies of the Gospels, and as the work progressed made considerable use of S. J. Andrews' *Life of Our Lord Upon the Earth,* which as noted on the title page took into account "Historical, Chronological, and Geographical Relations."

As the work was thought to be nearing completion in 1896, Marian, working on the three general introductory chapters, " 'God With Us,' " "The Chosen People," and " 'The Fullness of the Time,' " sought the counsel of Herbert Lacey of the Avondale school on the arrangement of paragraphs. He was a rather youthful graduate of the classical course offered at Battle Creek College. He made some helpful suggestions in the matter of the sequence of the thoughts presented, which, when it became known, gave birth in later years, when he was known as a seasoned college Bible teacher, to rumors that Lacey had a prominent role in authoring the book. In both oral and written statements he flatly denied such a role (DF 508, H. C. Lacey to S. Kaplan, July 24, 1936).

TITLES FOR THE CHAPTERS

Chapter titles came rather naturally as the material was prepared, being representative of the subject matter. The Bible narrative suggested some, but there was some paralleling with chapter titles used by others who wrote on Christ's life. Selection was based on appropriateness and reader appeal. The title for the finished book would wait.

Reference has already been made to the use Ellen White made of William Hanna's *Life of Our Lord* and Cunningham Geikie's *Life and Words of Christ* twenty years earlier when she was in California writing on Christ's life. She was acquainted with Daniel March's *Walks and Homes of Jesus,* and his *Night Scenes in the Bible.* Geikie's *Hours With the Bible* and Edersheim's works on the Temple and its services and Jewish social life were known to her as well as some others. While, as noted these books did not constitute what might be said to be her sources, they proved an aid to her in her descriptions of places, customs, and historical events.

EXTRA-SCRIPTURAL INFORMATION

In her writing in the 1870s and again in the 1890s on the life and ministry of Christ, two significant points should be noted. First, she did not fall into the pitfalls that some of the other writers fell into; second, she often introduced significant extra-Biblical points in historical narrative not mentioned by the Gospel writers—points in which she deals in sufficient detail to make it evident that her basic source in writing was the visions given to her. Limitations in space allow for but three illustrations, drawn one each from the three E. G. White published accounts of the life of Christ:

At His trial before Herod, *Spiritual Gifts,* volume 1, page 51: "They spit in His face. . . . He meekly raised His hand, and wiped it off."

In feeding the five thousand, *The Spirit of Prophecy,* volume 2, pages 260, 261: "The disciples, seeing Him pale with weariness and hunger, besought Him to rest from His toil and take some refreshment. Their entreaties being of no avail, they consulted together as to the propriety of forcibly removing Him from the eager multitude, fearing that He would die of fatigue. Peter and John each took an arm of their blessed Master and kindly endeavored to draw Him away. But He refused to be removed from the place."

The resurrection, *The Desire of Ages,* pages 779, 780: " 'The angel of the Lord descended from heaven.' . . . This messenger is he who fills the position from which Satan fell. . . . The soldiers see him removing the stone as he would a pebble, and hear him cry, 'Son of God, come forth; Thy Father calls Thee.' They see Jesus come forth from the grave."

A careful reading of chapters 79, 80, and 81 of *The Desire of Ages* will disclose many interesting details not cited by the Gospel writers. There could have been many more extra-Biblical points of interest in the book were it not for the fact that it was intended to be widely distributed among those not familiar with Ellen White's call and work. Marian Davis explained this in a letter written to J. E. White, December 22, 1895:

Since these books are sent out without explanation as to the authority by which the author speaks, it was thought best to avoid, as far as we could, statements for which the Bible seems to furnish no proof, or which to the ordinary reader appear to contradict the Bible. Better to give readers what they will accept and profit by than to excite criticism and questioning that will lead them to discredit the whole. . . .

Sister White says that Christ was twice crowned with thorns, but as the Bible mentions only the second crowning, it was thought best to omit the first, or rather to give the second instead of the first.

A passage in *The Spirit of Prophecy*, volume 2, that pictures the solicitation of Peter and John for their Lord is another example of material not included, for the reason cited by Marian Davis. The new book was intended for wide distribution beyond the ranks of those who understood Ellen White's work.

THE PROPOSAL OF TWO VOLUMES

As the work progressed and the manuscript grew, the staff working at Sunnyside proposed issuing two volumes of about six hundred pages each. W. C. White felt that if this plan met the approval of the publishers, the materials for the first volume would be ready in March or April, 1896 (9 WCW, pp. 198, 199). Assuming this would be done, Ellen White was reading the manuscript for the first volume (Letter 90, 1896), and in writing to Edson on February 16, 1896, she indicated that "we now have it about ready for the printer."—Letter 144, 1896. At Cooranbong they were in the midst of the Bible institute, and Ellen White jotted in her diary on February 18:

> In the afternoon Brother and Sister Prescott came. We had a good visit with Sister Prescott. Brother Prescott was with Marian in the interest of the book "Life of Christ." He is reading it, for it is the last reading before publication.—MS 62, 1896.

So Ellen White and her staff thought; but it did not work out that way. Three or four months later there was more material to be added. Wrote Ellen White on June 1, 1896:

> In the last discourses reported, Marian has had precious

matter to insert, and this has necessitated her obtaining a new set of copies with the addition.

In this letter to Elder Haskell she wrote of ambitious plans for book production, making reference to the decision to lift the parables out of the forthcoming "Life of Christ" and issue them in a separate volume:

> Sister Burnham . . . is now to work with me in getting out books which I am anxious to prepare. The book on temperance comes first, then *Testimony* No. 34, and then the parables which Sister Davis will get out in a small book; then close up the second volume on the "Life of Christ"; then the life of the apostles, then to finish the second book of Old Testament history. You see I have work to do.—Letter 167, 1896.

On June 19, Ellen White was still producing material that needed to be included in the early chapters of the book. She wrote: "I am writing upon subjects which stir every fiber of my being. The preexistence of Christ—how invaluable is this truth to the believer!"—MS 65, 1896.

WHO WILL PUBLISH IT?

This was a time, too, when the matter of the publisher had to be settled. Consideration had been given to offering the manuscript to Fleming H. Revell, who had handled *Steps to Christ* in a very acceptable manner. W. C. White wrote:

> [Mother] says that there are people who will be reached by the publications through outside publishers, who are not likely to get them from any of our agents; and she believes that much good has been accomplished through our placing *Steps to Christ* in the hands of Revell to publish.—8 WCW, p. 36.

W. C. White felt that there were important and far-reaching advantages of Revell doing the publishing. He mentioned one, perhaps little known to the average person: "He is brother-in-law to Moody, [who is the] leading American evangelist and [who] as far as I can see has the lead in evangelical literature."—*Ibid.*, p. 35.

Both SDA publishers, the Review and Herald and the Pacific

WRITING ON THE LIFE OF CHRIST

Press, had issued a number of the E. G. White books, but things had become complicated since the enlarged and strengthened General Conference Association was handling denominational book publishing. That organization carried the responsibility of negotiating with the printers, and sent much of the work to the nearby Review and Herald. By contract, the Pacific Press stood in a reasonable degree of independence, and Ellen White could negotiate with them directly. The experience of the General Conference Association in publishing *Thoughts From the Mount of Blessing* (a spinoff of the "Life of Christ" manuscript), particularly in the matter of illustrations, led W. C. White on May 10 to exclaim, "Never, *never*, *NEVER!*" (9 WCW, p. 436). Working through a second party in getting out books just didn't work well.

On May 6, 1896, Ellen White wrote Edson:

> I have decided to negotiate with Pacific Press to publish "Life of Christ." We are now waiting for them to obtain cuts to go in the book. The first book is completed; the second is in the process of completion.—Letter 150, 1896.

DECISION ON THE TITLE

Up to this point the project had been referred to as the "Life of Christ," and it was assumed that that would be the title. With the possible exceptions of *The Great Controversy* and the *Testimonies*, Ellen White did not select the titles for her books. As the time approached when a final decision on the title had to be made, suggestions came from various ones in Australia and America. Writing to C. H. Jones, manager of the Pacific Press, on October 22, W. C. White said, "As regards the title, I do not wish to say much till I have the criticism of others."—11 WCW, p. 20. Some, he felt, were "a hundred miles nearer being appropriate than the best of the others that have been recommended to us." He promised to send a cable after consulting "the wise men here, and have Mother's opinion, and that of Sister Davis." The suggestion of the publishers narrowed down to "The Desire of All Nations" and "The Desire of Ages," both based on Haggai 2:7, "The desire of all nations shall come."

On November 9, he wrote Jones:

THE AUSTRALIAN YEARS

We came to agreement, after much consideration and discussion, to propose that the title for the first book shall be "The Desire of Ages." Before the title page is printed, we will decide whether it is better for both books to carry this title, or if we can select another title for the second volume.—*Ibid.*, p. 51.

ILLUSTRATIONS AND FINANCE

At the time *The Desire of Ages* was published, Adventist publishing houses had limited capital to invest in large books, and the authors at times assisted in providing funds for illustrations and initial expense such as typesetting and the making of the printing plates. With the decision that the book would be published by the Pacific Press, in Oakland, California, interest at both the author's end and the publishing house turned to these arrangements. With *Thoughts From the Mount of Blessing*, handled by the General Conference Association as publishers and the Review and Herald as printers, the results as far as illustrations were concerned proved disappointing; many of the cuts had to be made over. With *The Desire of Ages* there was, over a period of months, quite a volume of correspondence, the examining of proofs, et cetera, for it was determined that the illustrations had to have the author's approval.

On July 16, 1896, Ellen White wrote of the financial side in a letter to Mrs. Wessels in South Africa:

> The manuscript for the "Life of Christ" is just about to be sent to America. This will be handled by the Pacific Press. I have employed workers to prepare this book, especially Sister Davis, and this has cost me $3,000. Another $3,000 will be needed to prepare it to be scattered broadcast through the world in two books. We hope they will have a large sale.—Letter 114, 1896.

While in the United States, W. C. White was able to give attention to the illustrations, consulting with the Pacific Press and with the artist, W. A. Reaser, in New York City (11 WCW, p. 332).

THE LAST TOUCHES

In July Ellen White was still writing on the closing scenes of the life of Jesus. Her diary for July 28 shows how deeply she felt about her subject:

WRITING ON THE LIFE OF CHRIST

In writing upon the life of Christ I am deeply wrought upon. I forget to breathe as I should. I cannot endure the intensity of feeling that comes over me as I think of what Christ has suffered in our world. He was a "man of sorrows, and acquainted with grief"; "he was wounded for our transgressions, he was bruised for our iniquities: the chastisement of our peace was upon him; and with his stripes we are healed," if we receive Him by faith as our personal Saviour!—MS 174, 1897.

A letter written to W. C. White on December 12, 1897, reflects the joy of finishing a long, protracted task:

Marian seems cheerful. The last chapters are done. "Oh," she says, "I could never, never have completed the book had you not been right here where you could supply the live links necessary. Now the life of the book is fully kept up to the close."

And I feel very much relieved and do not feel as if I am stealing if I take up other subjects before the book is closed. But nearly everything I could write has been on the matter which concerned the book, that she could select some things for the book and Maggie [Maggie Hare, who took Fannie Bolton's place] could make articles of the subjects for the papers. I shall now breathe more freely.—Letter 209, 1897.

The manuscript for the second volume went to the publishers in mid-January, 1898.

CHECKING PROOFS AND ILLUSTRATIONS

The next few months entailed the checking of proofs of the text of the two volumes as the type was being set. Ellen White, as well as Marian Davis and W. C. White, gave very careful attention to this. Close scrutiny was also given to the artwork, including many new designs. Let it not be supposed that Ellen White did not concern herself with such details. She was paying for the paintings, and she wanted them right. On December 20 she wrote to C. H. Jones:

I wish to say to you that I am sadly disappointed in the cuts prepared for such a book as the "Life of Christ." I consider that if Brother Reaser accepts such figures, his eye and taste has lost its cunning. You cannot expect me to be pleased with such productions. Look at these figures critically, and you must see that they are made from either Catholic designs or Catholic artists. The picture of Mary has a man's face; the representations of Christ with the two fingers prominent, while the others are closed, is wholly a Catholic sign, and I object to this. I see but very little beauty in any of the faces, or persons.—Letter 81a, 1897.

The reading of the proofs at times called to Ellen White's mind some things she wanted to add. In a letter written in mid-February, 1898, she stated, "Matters must be prepared on the 'Life of Christ,' and after I thought it was done. In reading the manuscript, I saw that some other things must be written."—Letter 8, 1898.

The making of changes in the manuscript after it had been sent to the publisher, and the changing of the text in pages already set in type, was frustrating to the publishers and expensive all the way around. W. C. White wrote to C. H. Jones on July 14, 1898:

> The getting out of this book is a great enterprise, and though it costs us much in money and in labor and in patient forbearance, we are confident that when issued, it will be worth, to the cause, all that it has cost and many times more. And while we may truly say that it is a trying thing to work along with author and publisher so far apart, yet it may be that the book is enough better to pay for all this.
>
> As I now have opportunity to see the volume, and the value of what Mother is now writing, I daily feel to thank the Lord that she is here in Australia, where she is comparatively *free to write what the Lord presents to her mind.*—12 WCW, p. 96. (Italics supplied.)

The Desire of Ages first came from the press in two beautiful art volumes, with continuous numbering of pages. Shortly thereafter it was published in a single volume of 865 pages. Very near the close of the year, December 10, 1898, copies arrived at Cooranbong and were eagerly examined by Ellen White, W. C. White, and her staff of workers (*ibid.*, p. 386). The monumental task was completed. Now the book would bless millions in the years to come.

The first edition of *The Desire of Ages* was distributed largely to the

WRITING ON THE LIFE OF CHRIST

public through literature evangelists. Then the Pacific Press turned to the production of what is termed a "trade edition"—the book in less elaborate form, to be sold largely to Seventh-day Adventists.

The publishers chose to issue it in a *Testimonies*-size page, using smaller type and putting it out in a cloth binding for $2. It carried an appendix and a subject index, and was a rather stubby volume of 1,042 pages. In this form it was not popular and had a limited life span. Soon the trade book printing was done from the same plates as were used for the colporteur edition, but without full-page illustrations.

A BOOK THAT SHOULD BE IN EVERY HOME

On May 21, 1900, Ellen White wrote:

> God would be pleased to see *The Desire of Ages* in every home. In this book is contained the light He has given upon His Word. To our canvassers I would say, "Go forth with your hearts softened and subdued by reading of the life of Christ. Drink deeply of the water of salvation, that it may be in your heart as a living spring, flowing forth to refresh souls ready to perish."—Letter 75, 1900.

Looking back in 1906, Ellen White freely attributed the truths set forth in the books tracing the great-controversy story to the work of the Holy Spirit. She mentioned only three of the Conflict books, for *Prophets and Kings* and *The Acts of the Apostles* were not yet published.

> How many have read carefully *Patriarchs and Prophets, The Great Controversy,* and *The Desire of Ages?* I wish all to understand that my confidence in the light that God has given stands firm, because I know that the Holy Spirit's power magnified the truth, and made it honorable, saying: "This is the way, walk ye in it." In my books, the truth is stated, barricaded by a "Thus saith the Lord."
>
> The Holy Spirit traced these truths upon my heart and mind as indelibly as the law was traced by the finger of God, upon the tables of stone, which are now in the ark.—Letter 90, 1906 (CM, p. 126).

CHAPTER 33
(1899)

The American Mails and Agonizing Situations

FOLLOWING the account of the preparation and publication of *The Desire of Ages*, we return now to the activities at Sunnyside as the year 1899 dawns. The Sabbaths and Sundays she spent at Maitland took Ellen White away for a few days each week, but the literary activities at her Sunnyside office continued. Marian Davis pressed on with the parables book, and Ellen White turned her attention to the American mails. Several matters of vital importance pressed hard upon her. Foremost among these was the distressing course being pursued in the medical missionary work in America.

Dr. John Harvey Kellogg was taking steps to divest this work of its denominational ties, in the Battle Creek Sanitarium, the medical school, and in the work for the outcasts and socially deprived classes in Chicago. This last mentioned was a fast-burgeoning work that divided his interests and overburdened his body and mind.

Calling for earnest attention were the inroads of pantheistic philosophy insidiously creeping into the teachings of Seventh-day Adventists, threatening the basic theology of the church. A three-week-long General Conference session would open at South Lancaster, Massachusetts, on February 15, and she applied herself to the preparation of messages to sound solemn warnings and to guard the cause.

The pressure of the Newcastle camp meeting, which lasted into January, 1899, deterred her writing. It was not until near the close of the General Conference session that her messages arrived and were read to the delegates by G. A. Irwin, president of the General

THE AMERICAN MAILS AND AGONIZING SITUATIONS

Conference. Some were read on Wednesday morning, March 1, and others on Sabbath afternoon, March 4. The messages that dealt with the various phases of the medical missionary work were presented first. In the main these were but an amplification of what she had been writing in letters to Dr. Kellogg over a period of a year or two. Some of the letters contained words of commendation for certain phases of his work; some just newsy reports of developments in Australia, particularly in medical missionary lines; some sounded an alarm, some solemn warnings. All were written kindly, carefully, and with understanding. On February 13, 1898, she introduced her message to the doctor, whom she had known since he was a lad and whom she loved as her own son:

> It would give me great satisfaction to have a long visit with you. I have much to say to you, and you have much to say to me. Sometimes I have a strong impression that I shall again bear my testimony upon the old field of battle, Battle Creek.—Letter 21, 1898.

Another communication written around the same time opens with the words:

> Special light has been given me that you are in danger of losing sight of the work that is to be done for this time. You are erecting barriers between your work and those you are educating, and the church. This must not be. . . .
>
> Do not, I beg of you, instill into the students ideas that will cause them to lose confidence in God's appointed ministers. But this you are certainly doing, whether you are aware of it or not. . . . Temptations will come to you that to carry forward the medical missionary work you must stand aloof from the church organization or church discipline.—Letter 123, 1898.

> You are to remember, my brother, that the Lord has a people on the earth, whom He respects. But your words and the way in which you express them create unbelief in the positions we occupy as a people at the present time. You do not believe the present truth.
>
> You will remember that I wrote you that the banner you should hold firmly was being taken from your hand, and a banner with a different inscription put into it. You remember the

warning given you that you were in danger, as was Nebuchadnezzar, of exalting yourself. Other symbols have been given me which lead me to write you now. You are in danger of not holding fast the faith once delivered to the saints, of making shipwreck of your faith. The words were spoken, "A very small leak will sink a ship."—*Ibid.*

Enamored with the work of a Dr. George D. Dowkontt, who had developed an undenominational Medical Missionary Society in New York City, through the middle 1890s, Dr. Kellogg cherished something of this kind as the ideal for the work he was leading out in, in Battle Creek and Chicago. In progressive steps he worked toward ushering the medical work of Seventh-day Adventists toward a nondenominational status. As Kellogg led out in the establishment of the American Medical Missionary College in 1895 (as explained in chapters 23 and 24 of *The Story of Our Health Message*), he rather stealthily imposed on this important phase of educational work an undenominational identity. The students who enrolled in this medical college were told by Kellogg:

> This is not a sectarian school. Sectarian doctrines are not to be taught in this medical school. It is a school for the purpose of teaching medical science, theoretically and practically, and gospel missionary work. It is not to be either a Seventh-day Adventist or a Methodist or a Baptist, or any other sectarian school, but a Christian medical college—a missionary medical college, to which all Christian men and Christian women who are ready to devote their lives to Christian work will be admitted.—*Medical Missionary,* October, 1895 (quoted in SHM, pp. 294, 295).

Kellogg's veering away from the church and what it stood for, accompanied by an attitude of increasing criticism of the ministry, placing the ministerial work as secondary to the medical missionary work, brought agony to Ellen White. "The medical missionary work," she wrote Kellogg, "is not to supersede the ministry of the Word." She continued:

> I have listened to your words in jots and tittles to demerit the ministers and their work; it was not to your credit to do this. It

THE AMERICAN MAILS AND AGONIZING SITUATIONS

was against the Lord's organized plans, and if all had been done to please your ideas, we should have strange things developed; but God has held in check some things, that they should not become a specialty.... You have become exalted; you have come to think that the message God has given for this time is not essential.—Letter 249, 1899.

WORK FOR THE OUTCASTS

Dr. Kellogg was reaching out to bring aid to the deprived, the drunkards, the prostitutes and outcasts in Chicago. This work, at its inception, brought commendation from Ellen White, but as it grew disproportionately, cautions and restraints were called for. Alarmed, she wrote to him on December 14, 1898:

> Constant work is to be done for the outcasts, but this work is not to be made all-absorbing. This class you have always with you. All the means must not be bound up in this work, for the highways have not yet received the message. There is work in the Lord's vineyard which must be done. No one should now visit our churches, and claim from them means to sustain the work of rescuing outcasts. The means to sustain that work should come . . . from those not of our faith.
>
> Let the churches take up their appointed work of presenting truth from the oracles of God in the highways. As in the days of Christ, we are to minister to all classes. But to make the work of seeking for the outcasts all and in all, while there are large vineyards open to culture and yet untouched, is beginning at the wrong end. The means now given by the churches is needed to establish the work in new fields. The glad tidings are to be proclaimed to every nation, tongue, and people.—Letter 138, 1898.

Through the year 1898 she penned seventeen letters to Dr. Kellogg, aggregating some 113 pages; many were messages of caution. On December 18, 1898, she warned:

> You are in positive danger. You are placing too many duties upon yourself and those connected with you. Unless you give yourself time for prayer and for study of the Scriptures, you will be in danger of accommodating the Scriptures to your own ideas.

THE AUSTRALIAN YEARS

Take heed that in the work you are doing, you do not misapply your powers, giving all you have to a work which is not a whole, but only a part of the work to be done. Keep the part you are doing in symmetrical proportion with the other lines of the work.—Letter 126, 1898.

Her last letter to him in 1898 was a most earnest appeal, dated December 29.

> Brother John Kellogg, my mother heart goes out toward you with weeping, for by symbols I am warned that you are in danger. Satan is making masterly efforts to cause your feet to slide; but God's eye is upon you. Fight these last battles manfully. Stand equipped with the whole armor of righteousness. By faith I lay you, in earnest prayer, at the feet of Jesus. You are safe only in that position. Never for a moment suppose that you are in no danger. You are God's property. You are to consider that you are under God's supervision. Your strength is in learning of Jesus Christ, His meekness, His lowliness of heart.—Letter 132, 1898.

One of her letters contained a strong appeal to Dr. Kellogg for financial help with which to build the much-needed Sydney Sanitarium. She urged that the Battle Creek Sanitarium, now in a prosperous time financially, should give aid to the medical work in Australia. Dr. Kellogg responded to the appeal, but not in the way Ellen White intended or expected. By the terms of the new charter for the Sanitarium designed by Dr. Kellogg in 1897, none of the profits of the institution could be used outside of the State of Michigan. Pressed by Ellen White, the doctor informed her that within a short time he would see that the work in Australia would receive $5,000. This he would raise himself. It was easier to respond to the appeal for money than to the appeals for changes in the course he was following in an unbalanced medical missionary work, in disparaging the ministry, and in steps being taken to make the medical work undenominational.

THE BURDEN OF HEART NOT LIFTED

Her messages to the General Conference penned during the early weeks of 1899 did not lift from her heart her concern for

THE AMERICAN MAILS AND AGONIZING SITUATIONS

Kellogg. Through the year 1899 she wrote another twenty-six letters to him, averaging nine pages each. Not all were sent at the time of writing, for she could see that her messages of counsel were not accomplishing what they should and she wrestled to find a way to save the doctor from shipwreck. When she could, she wrote and spoke with commendation and encouragement. It was so as she related to workers in Australia the manner in which God especially blesses the work of consecrated physicians:

> I have seen Dr. Kellogg fall on his knees in an agony of distress when an operation was to be performed which meant life or death. One false movement of the instrument would cost the patient's life. Once, in a critical operation, I saw a hand laid upon his hand. That hand moved his hand, and the patient's life was saved. . . .
>
> The medical work has been represented as the right hand of the body of truth. This hand is to be constantly active, constantly at work; and God will strengthen it. But it is to remain a hand; it is not to be made the body. I desire that this point shall be understood.—UCR, July 21, 1899.

Her message to him written April 17 was one of encouragement. In this she declared:

> On no account should you be entangled and woven up in any work that will endanger your influence with Seventh-day Adventists, for the Lord has appointed you to fill a place of His appointment, to stand before the medical profession, not to be molded, but to mold human minds. . . . He has a work for you to do, not separated from Seventh-day Adventists, but in unity and harmony with them, to be a great blessing to your brethren in giving to them that knowledge which God has given you.—Letter 73, 1899.

But at this time Kellogg was not prone to receive messages of caution and reproof. He took offense at the cautions Ellen White sounded and declared that she had turned against him. He threatened to resign from his work and all connection with Seventh-day Adventists. This almost stunned her. On August 15 she wrote in her diary:

THE AUSTRALIAN YEARS

I lose my courage and my strength and cannot call to mind the very things I ought to say and the many things I ought to write. I have a letter—two, yes, three—written for Dr. Kellogg, but I am so afraid of being misunderstood that I dare not send them. I feel intensely, and want to help his mind in many things, but how can I do it? My words are misapplied and misunderstood, and sometimes appear to be so misunderstood by humans that they do more harm than good. This has been the case with Dr. Kellogg.—MS 189, 1899.

The next day she wrote in her diary:

The mail went this morning. There are the letters to Dr. Kellogg, uncopied, unsent. Perhaps it is well. I do not think we see things alike, and he feels sure his work has been under the leading of the Lord. I see his dangers, which he does not see. The Lord has presented his case before me, and the result must, I fear, come upon him.

He is carrying the responsibilities he has been accumulating for years. If he falls under the load he has piled upon himself, he will leave the impression it is because he was left without the cooperation of those who ought to have helped him. May the Lord have compassion upon Dr. Kellogg is my prayer. May the Lord help him to see he is accumulating too many responsibilities in the medical missionary work.—*Ibid.*

Some months after this, in a letter to George Irwin, Ellen White pointed out the critical nature of Dr. Kellogg's case, and spoke of the terrible crisis that must be met:

He is writing Dr. Caro letters which declare he is going to give up and separate from Seventh-day Adventists. This is the result of his getting himself overloaded and so crowded with financial embarrassments he does not know what to say or to do to extricate himself. I am so sorry that things are as they are—but Satan has played his cards well, and the game is falling into Satan's hands unless something can be done to save Dr. Kellogg.—Letter 170, 1900.

To see the man who had been used so mightily by God and by

whose side she had stood through the years veer away from the message and lose sight of the real objectives of medical missionary work tore Ellen White's soul. Nonetheless, she continued to labor and pray and to communicate through letters. As the materials were assembled for *Testimonies,* volume 6, a section of nearly one hundred pages was devoted to medical missionary work and the balance that should be maintained in carrying forward its many features. The later compilation *Welfare Ministry* also carries a section on working for the unfortunate, appropriately titled "The Outcasts."

AT THE 1899 GENERAL CONFERENCE SESSION

The first of the E. G. White messages read before the 1899 General Conference session on March 1 carried the title "The Work for This Time," and opened with the words:

> We are standing on the threshold of great and solemn events. Prophecies are fulfilling. The last great conflict will be short, but terrible. Old controversies will be revived. New controversies will arise. The last warnings must be given to the world. There is a special power in the presentation of the truth at the present time; but how long will it continue? Only a little while. If ever there was a crisis, it is now.

The message pointed out that with the advance of the work in its many features, dangers would arise that must be guarded against, and "as new enterprises are entered upon, there is a tendency to make some one line all-absorbing; that which should have the first place becomes a secondary consideration." Then she addressed herself to the work for the social outcasts:

> Of late a great interest has been aroused for the poor and outcast classes; a great work has been entered upon for the uplifting of the fallen and degraded. This in itself is a good work. ... This will have its place in connection with the proclamation of the third angel's message and the reception of Bible truth. But there is danger of loading down everyone with this class of work, because of the intensity with which it is carried on. There is danger of leading men to center their energies in this line, when God has called them to another work.—GCB 1899, p. 128.

THE AUSTRALIAN YEARS
MEETING THE INROADS OF PANTHEISM

Only as God had revealed it to her could Ellen White have known that pantheistic teachings would be presented at the General Conference session. She was led to write and send in advance an article to be read entitled "The True Relation of God and Nature." At the Tuesday-morning meeting, February 21, as the health message was being discussed at the session, Dr. Kellogg declared that he would be glad to hear from Dr. E. J. Waggoner and W. W. Prescott "on this question of healthful living," for both had been giving interesting and helpful talks at the Sanitarium. As Waggoner spoke, he did so in the framework of pantheistic philosophy, which carried apparent support of at least a part of the audience. Some days later the mail brought Ellen White's message, which was read to the session on Sabbath afternoon, March 4.

It opened with these words:

> Since the fall of man, nature cannot reveal a perfect knowledge of God, for sin has brought a blight upon it, and has intervened between nature and nature's God.—*Ibid.*, p. 157.

Excerpts from her address reveal the straightforward way she came to grips with the issues that had been so subtly raised at the church's world headquarters:

> Christ came to the world as a personal Saviour. He represented a personal God. He ascended on high as a personal Saviour, and He will come again as He ascended to heaven—a personal Saviour. We need carefully to consider this, for in their human wisdom, the wise men of the world, knowing not God, foolishly deify nature and the laws of nature. . . .
>
> The Father in heaven has a voice and a person which Christ expressed. Those who have a true knowledge of God will not become so infatuated with the laws of matter and the operations of nature as to overlook or to refuse to acknowledge the continual working of God in nature. Deity is the author of nature. The natural world has in itself no inherent power but that which God supplies. How strange, then, that so many make a deity of nature! God furnishes the matter and the properties with which to carry out His plans: Nature is but His agency.—*Ibid.*

THE AMERICAN MAILS AND AGONIZING SITUATIONS
COUNSEL ON SEEKING COUNSEL

As mentioned in an earlier chapter, there was in the late 1890s a deterioration in conditions in the publishing house at Battle Creek. Ellen White's nephew, F. E. Belden, an employee there, reported the situation, which rolled a heavy weight on her soul. When the letter came to her, she read the opening paragraphs and then handed it to W. C. White, asking him to reply. From the visions God had given her she was familiar with the circumstances, but reading of them from the pen of another engendered distress. Because of the uniqueness of the situation we give here a part of what W. C. White wrote of this in a letter to Belden on September 25, 1899:

> After Mother had read the first of your letter, she laid it down, saying that she was weary and heartsick of thinking of matters at Battle Creek, and that she must ask me to read the letter and to write to you about it. I am sorry for your sake that she has laid this duty upon me, but for my own sake I am glad, because it gives me an opportunity to express to you some thoughts which I am anxious that both you and Edson [White] should consider.
>
> It is not necessary that you or Edson or any other person shall give particulars regarding the work at Battle Creek in order to get Mother's counsel as to the course that should be pursued, because the matters which transpire there are laid open before her clearly from time to time. Mother is carrying a very heavy burden regarding the work at Battle Creek, and especially at the Review and Herald, and she is writing frequently to the managers and to the officers of the General Conference, laying out principles and calling attention to dangers.
>
> It is not advisable at present for anyone to write to Mother particulars about the lack of harmony, the lack of tenderness, and the lack of missionary spirit in the office of publication and in the church, because it seems to bring upon her a burden which is greater than she can bear.
>
> When the Lord opens these matters to her mind, He gives her strength to bear the load, but when individuals present these things, it seems to almost kill her.
>
> Another reason why it is not best for individuals to lay before

Mother the shortcomings of others is the fact that this very action puts them in a position where they cannot so fully appreciate the counsels and reproofs sent as [they can] if they have adopted the plan of carrying their burdens, their complaints, their questions to the Lord, asking Him to send His answer through whatever agency He may choose, then waiting patiently for that answer.

It may come through a message given to Mother; it may come in another way, but I think that . . . when we wait patiently upon the Lord, we are in a better position to appreciate the answers which come to our questions, whether they be in special testimony, in the sermons of our ministering brethren, in our study of the Sacred Word, or in our seasons of counsel and prayer with our colaborers in the work.

Believe me, dear Frank, that these suggestions are offered in tenderest love and sympathy. I do appreciate to some extent your burdens of mind, your perplexity, your anxiety regarding the progress of the work, and your feeling of distress and indignation as you see a wrong course followed in the dealings between institutions, and the dealings of the institutions with enterprises and individuals.—14 WCW, p. 127.

SCHOOL DEBTS AND ELLEN WHITE'S GIFT

The American mails had brought to Ellen White a letter from Battle Creek seeking counsel as to the erection of another building there in the headquarters city. She wrote in her diary of her answer and of the outcome:

> The letter was answered. The light given me of God for them was given them distinctly that not a brick should be laid to incur additional debt, and close investigation should be made to ascertain the reason for so heavy a debt already existing.
>
> But the counselors in Battle Creek, notwithstanding, concluded that the testimony coming to them did not mean what it said. The appearance was that they must have more buildings and they did build, following the imagination of their own hearts, and now they are involved in embarrassment. . . . They went directly contrary to the light God gave them, and the counsel of men was accepted, for it looked so wise to them to make additions that they imagined they must have.

THE AMERICAN MAILS AND AGONIZING SITUATIONS

There will be every excuse made for men to follow their strong imagination, and the instruction the Lord—who knows the end from the beginning—gives is cast aside as a mistake. . . . If men will refuse light they shall have trouble. The yoke of perplexity which they have chosen for their own necks always galls when this is the case. But how much might be saved if those who claim to believe the testimonies [would accept those] the Lord has sent them rather than to cast them aside and crowd forward their own human decision which costs heavily in the end. This is the work that is now being done.—MS 89, 1900.

ELLEN WHITE RELATES TO THE MISTAKE

More than $20,000 was consumed in creating that additional building. Writing of the experience, she showed her tolerance, and the bigheartedness of a mother:

We feel very anxious to do all in our power to lift the heavy debt on our schools. I have proposed to give to the benefit of the schools my book on the parables [*Christ's Object Lessons*]. They may have the avail of this book in every place for the benefit of the schools to pay the great debt that has been created through not heeding the messages that the Lord has sent.—*Ibid.*

What she had in mind was laid before the readers of the *Review and Herald* on May 1, 1900. The General Conference appointed a seven-man committee to foster a well-organized campaign. With the cooperation of thousands of church members, this gift yielded more than $300,000 in debt-paying funds.

CORRESPONDENCE WITH G. I. BUTLER

Some of her correspondence buoyed her soul. This was the case in the exchange with G. I. Butler. At the time of the General Conference session of 1888 held in Minneapolis, Minnesota, Butler, who had long served as president of the General Conference, was ill and could not be present. Relieved of his responsibilities at that meeting, he retired in Florida, planted an orange grove, and for more than a decade faithfully cared for his wife, who, soon after moving to Florida, suffered paralysis. Being for some years on the negative side of the issues that had surfaced at Minneapolis in 1888, he felt that Ellen White had about written him off. When he received word that at her direction one of the first copies of *The Desire of Ages* to come from the press was to be sent to him, he was elated and took heart. He wrote to her expressing his gratitude for her thoughtfulness of him.

After five years in retirement he had come to see some things more correctly and had changed his attitude. He wrote a letter of confession in 1893, published in the *Review and Herald*. In this he stated:

> I freely admit that for a period I stood in doubt in regard to the agitation of these subjects ["the doctrines of justification by faith, the necessity of appropriating Christ's righteousness by faith in order to (attain) our salvation"] I have here so freely endorsed. I did not attend the General Conference in Minneapolis, where differences were agitated, being at the time sick in Battle Creek. . . . My sympathies were not with those leading out in bringing what I now regard as light, before the people.

He was glad that he could testify:

> I am well satisfied that additional light of great importance has been shining upon these subjects, and fully believe that God has greatly blessed it to the good of those who have accepted it.—June 13, 1893.

Now a letter to Ellen White in late 1898 initiated a fresh correspondence. Ellen White responded to him a few months later, on April 21:

> I received your letter a few days since, and read it with interest. Every mail I have designed writing to you, but each time something has come in to crowd me upon other things, and I could not get your letter written. But now I will write you a few lines.
>
> You misapprehend me when you suppose I have lost all hope of you. This has never been the case. I have had a great desire to see you, and to converse and pray with you. I would be pleased to see you take hold of the work again and move forward, drinking in the rich truths which God has given us. I desire to see

THE AMERICAN MAILS AND AGONIZING SITUATIONS

you stand on vantage ground and realize the blessing of God in your own heart and life.

Then, as if conversing with an old friend—which she was—she continued:

> This field is large, and has been represented to me as a new world, a second America, but very different from America in its government. But America is far from being what it once was. I feel sorry when I consider this.
>
> In regard to your situation, be assured that if I had the opportunity, I would grasp your hand with gladness, and call you brother. I think I am unchanged from the simple, humble servant of Jesus Christ you have always known me to be. You and I are getting along in years. But as far as my memory and activity are concerned, I have never in any period of my life done more earnest, hard work in speaking and writing than during the year 1898.
>
> I see so much to do. I cannot see any place where I can let go my hold. Souls are perishing, and I must help them. I speak in the church and out of the church. We drive out into the country places, and speak in the open air, because the prejudice against the truth is so great that the people will not consent to our speaking in the little rough house where they assemble for worship.

Ellen White "chatted" about her experience in Australia for six pages with one she had known for nearly fifty years. She closed with this paragraph:

> But I must stop writing. It is now 5:00 A.M., one hour before daylight. I left my bed at one o'clock. I have written this letter to you and two pages to Dr. Kellogg since then. Tell me in your next letter if you can read my writing. I cannot always get my letters copied. If you can read them, I will send some in this way. I would say to you, "Have faith in God. Trust in Him, for He knoweth all things. He is true and patient with all His erring children." God bless you is my prayer.—Letter 74, 1899.

CHAPTER 34
(1899)

Wrestling With Distressing Financial Problems

FROM term to term the attendance at the Avondale school steadily increased. The dormitories, which at first also housed classrooms, needed every bit of space for student housing, and in the summer of 1898-1899 it seemed that there was no other way to meet the need but to erect College Hall. This would provide classrooms, a chapel, and administrative offices. Before the sawmill was turned over to the health-food industry, much of the lumber for the new building was cut from local timber. The General Conference promised to match pound for pound for the project (EGW, in GCB 1899, p. 130; DF 312d, AGD, in *Australasian Record*, Aug. 27, 1928). Depending on this promise, and anticipating the receipt of funds from America in due time, carpenters were employed, supplies were purchased, and construction was begun. Funds immediately available would allow for the payment from week to week of only a fraction of the wages of the workmen, just enough for families to subsist; full wages were promised when the remittance should come from America, anticipated in early April, 1899.

As the work advanced, Ellen White made it a point to visit the families of the workmen frequently to see whether basic needs were being met. Was there sufficient food? How about the children's shoes and clothes? Were there other very special pressing needs? When she found such, she saw that they were met from her own funds. Morale must not be allowed to sink. In the meantime she addressed an appeal to the General Conference in session, which was read the morning of March 1. As she came to the point of

WRESTLING WITH DISTRESSING FINANCIAL PROBLEMS

presenting specific needs, she introduced the appeal for financial help with these words:

> When the General Conference sent me and my helpers to Australia, our people should have understood the situation, and should have provided us with means and facilities for establishing the work in this country. For seven years we have labored here; but except the publishing house in Melbourne, we have no institution that can give character to the work.
>
> In our school work something has been done; but we have not yet the means for erecting our main hall, which will contain the chapel and recitation rooms. We have not means for the necessary improvement of the land and equipment of the buildings.—GCB 1899, p. 129.

Then she turned to other pressing areas, the medical work and the need of a sanitarium in Sydney and a hospital in Cooranbong. There was a need also to establish clinics and to build churches. She added:

> It was not the design of God that our work in this country should be so hard and advance so slowly. It is His purpose that there shall be a true pattern in Australia—a sample of how other fields shall be worked. The work should be symmetrical, and a living witness for the truth. God would have us cherish a noble ambition.—*Ibid.*, p. 130.

Ellen White told of how the Lord's instruction on this point came to her:

> I seemed to be in a meeting where our necessities were being reviewed. We were considering what should be done. One stood up among us, and the word of the Lord was spoken:
>
> "Those in America can relieve the situation here, and should have shared with you their abundance years ago." . . . "When I send My servants to establish My work in a new field, and build up the interests essential to give it character, I call upon My people to sustain that work with their prayers and with their means. . . .
>
> "When My servant whom I have called to make known My will was sent to Australia, you in America should have

THE AUSTRALIAN YEARS

understood that you had a work to do in cooperation with her. Who was it that carried out My directions in laying the foundation of the institutions in America, which have grown to such large proportions?

"And when My servant was sent to establish the work in a new field, could you not see that He who owns all the gold and silver was calling for your cooperation? You had obtained a standing fully abundant and ample. And when the work was to begin in another field, I would be with My servant to indicate the work; and you should have been ready to aid in lifting up the standard of truth by precept and example in a way that would recommend it to a gainsaying world."—*Ibid.*

It was an attentive audience who listened to the messages. Ellen White made one final appeal:

I have tried to set things before you, but the attempt falls far short of the reality. Will you refuse my plea? It is not I who appeals to you; it is the Lord Jesus, who has given His life for this people. In my request I obey the will, the requirement of God. Will you improve this opportunity of showing honor to God's work here, and respect for the servants whom He has sent to do His will in guiding souls to heaven?—*Ibid.*, p. 132.

THE DELEGATES RESPOND

When the reading ended G. A. Irwin declared: "Here is an earnest appeal to us. What shall we do with it? Shall we begin right here to reform, or shall we forget what manner of men we have been, and continue doing as we have done? I, for one, want to have a part in this, and I will give $100 to go to that field." There was a silence, for $100 represented more than a month's pay. W. W. Prescott spoke, saying, "Shall we . . . go on, and do nothing, or shall we do something?"

"Do something!" the congregation responded.

Then Prescott proposed that a cablegram be sent to Ellen White promising to send $25,000 from personal donations and from the conferences. The very atmosphere seemed charged.

Elder Irwin responded, "It seems to me we ought to give opportunity to those who feel free to give $100 or more or less, now, to do so." Voices were heard, "I will give $100!" "I will give $50!" "I'll give $100!" "Another $100 here!"

The secretary could not get the names down fast enough, so the stenographers were summoned to help make the record, which started out:

George A. Irwin and wife	$100
J. N. Loughborough and wife	100
W. W. Prescott and wife	100
A. O. Burrill and wife	100

And so it went, until more than a hundred had pledged from $5 up to $100. Then a comparative stranger stood to his feet and pledged $5,000! The audience gasped. It was Henry Norman, a sea captain whom F. H. Westphal had met on his way from South America to the session. Finding him interested in Bible truth, Westphal invited him along. He came and faithfully attended the meetings. Step by step, he took his stand for the Seventh-day Adventist message. Some days later, having kept his first Sabbath, he testified:

> Here is the baby of the family. Of course you all know that I am not a minister of the gospel, but I thank the Lord that I found this people. . . . I am here to stay. . . . With the Lord's help, I intend to serve God faithfully. I have given myself and all that I have to the Lord.—*Ibid.*, p. 170.

To those who were acquainted with him, this statement was significant, for he let it be known that he was the owner of several oceangoing steamships. As the conference proceeded, he made other generous pledges, totaling $400,000. Of this, $200,000 was for the General Conference Association; $100,000 was for the Foreign Mission Board; and $100,000 was to be divided up among different countries, with an additional $10,000 specified for Australia. In addition, there was his yacht, costing $11,000, which he pledged as a gift for missionary work in New York harbor. Elder Irwin explained in a letter to Ellen White, written soon after the session, that the captain's fortunes were in the Bank of England in London, and his pledges would be paid in late May. Of the $3,400 pledged by the delegates for the work in Australia, $2,394 had been paid in by

THE AUSTRALIAN YEARS

late March and would be held until the whole amount was on hand (DF 368, G. A. Irwin to EGW, March 26, 1899). What a plum to tantalize the money-starved workers in Australia—$3,400 almost immediately and $15,000 more by the end of May! It was late April when Elder Irwin's letter was received at Cooranbong; a few days later the *General Conference Bulletin* brought further word.

FINANCIAL AGONY PERVADED THE AVONDALE COMMUNITY

In the meantime, the workers at the Avondale school writhed in agony. In March, Ellen White wrote, "Laborers working on the school building need their money, but they cannot have it, for there is no means in the treasury. But they have borne this bravely."—Letter 47, 1899. Workmen were pressing for long-overdue wages. Suppliers were pressing for the payment of accounts. School opened February 1, and the till was empty, so empty, in fact, that as the students came in A. G. Daniells, the acting principal, asked each one if he had some money that could be lent to the school—a pound or two or three? (as told to the author by AGD).

Ellen White described the situation as of April 2, 1899:

> We could not obtain money to pay the workmen on the school buildings, and a large debt has accumulated at Newcastle for provisions, and at Sydney for lumber. But all we can do is to wait and hope and believe, and keep working in faith.
>
> I have not paid my workers for a large share of last year, and nothing as yet for this year. But we hope that the next mail may relieve the situation. . . . The Lord understands every rope in the ship, and I am not at all confused or confounded. He has the means to help us, and help will certainly come. It is no use to get tired and impatient over delays.—Letter 61, 1899.

RECALL OF A LOAN OF £300

Just at this juncture, a sister in Melbourne who had loaned the school £300 asked for her money, saying that she must have it at once. The school board met to study the situation. Visiting Australia some years later, Daniells told the story. Money had not come from America. "We knew not what to do," he stated.

> Naturally we blamed ourselves for going ahead without the

WRESTLING WITH DISTRESSING FINANCIAL PROBLEMS

money. After a long, fruitless discussion we adjourned in discouragement until the next morning. I went to my room, but I could not sleep. I rolled and tossed and perspired. I was in agony of mind. I rose and went out in the bush where I could be alone. I had to have help from some source. . . . There in the dark I prayed and cried to God to send us help. I prayed on until the morning light began to appear. With all my heart I cried to the Lord to send me an answer, to give me some light. And there came to me a most positive answer. "I have delivered thee. I will meet this situation. Be of good cheer."

The presence of God was so powerful that I could not stay on my knees, I could only lie on the ground and thank and praise God for deliverance. Something was going to be done by the Almighty, and I knew it as well as I knew that I lived.—DF 312d, A. G. Daniells, in *Australasian Record,* Aug. 27, 1928.

When he met the committee early Monday morning, he told them that deliverance had come, but he could not explain just how. He asked for authorization to visit Sydney, Melbourne, and Adelaide, and assured them he would bring the needed funds back with him in several weeks' time. The board did not hesitate to authorize the trip, and he left that morning.

On Tuesday, April 4, Daniells arrived in Melbourne, and met the sister who was calling for her money by the following Thursday. He endeavored to persuade her to renew the loan for another year, but she insisted she must have it "the day after tomorrow." As he retired Tuesday night he was greatly troubled. Wednesday morning, while praying in his room, he reminded the Lord of the experience in the night at Cooranbong. He felt impressed that he would get an answer from the Bible. In his recital, years later, he told what happened:

> Then I did what I had never done before, and I do not know that I have ever done it since. I put my finger on the margin and opened the Book. The very first words I read were these: "Thy God whom thou servest continually, He will deliver thee." Daniel 6:16. I wrote in the margin of my Bible, "Salisbury's room, 7:20 A.M., 4/5/99." That evening at five o'clock, I wrote, "Fulfilled 5:00 P.M., 4/5/99."—*Ibid.*

He added, "I seldom tell the marvelous way in which it was fulfilled, but I shall do so on this occasion." He went to the publishing house to see what would happen. By Wednesday noon he was still waiting, and after lunch he called Salisbury, the manager, and Faulkhead, the treasurer, together and reminded them that the next morning he must deliver £300 to the church member calling for her money. The publishing house just did not have that much money in the treasury, but Faulkhead thought of a man who some months before offered the publishing house a loan. They went into the country to see the man, but found he had invested the money elsewhere.

THE LOCKED BANK DOOR FOUND OPEN

It was four o'clock when they returned. Faulkhead suggested they might possibly get a loan from the bank with which the Echo Publishing Company did business. Inasmuch as it was closed, Faulkhead suggested they call on the banker at his home. Daniells did not see much light in that, but what else could they do? It seemed their only hope. The two men started down the street. As they passed the bank, they saw that the door was open enough to allow a man to enter. The two men slipped in and found the banker and his assistant with the contents of the vault spread out on the counters. The bank inspector from London was expected the next day, and they were checking their cash holdings.

"Faulkhead!" the banker exclaimed in startled surprise. "How did you get into this bank?"

"We walked in," he replied.

"Yes, I know, but how did you get the door open?" queried the trembling banker. "I shut, bolted, locked, and chained that door myself. How did you get it open?"

"We did not touch it, it was open" was all they could say.

Pale, and almost in a state of shock, the banker hurriedly relocked the door. Returning, he asked, "What is it that you want?"

"We want to see you in your private office. We want £300 to meet an obligation in the morning."

"What security can you give?" the banker asked.

"Only our word tonight," they replied, "but we will give you something more later."

WRESTLING WITH DISTRESSING FINANCIAL PROBLEMS

Faulkhead and Daniells were certain that an angel had opened the bank door. The banker was profoundly impressed, and the two men left the bank carrying "three hundred shining sovereigns." The next morning Daniells met the woman who was demanding her money, and placed them in her hands. Continuing his reminiscence, Daniells declared:

> These experiences, I can assure you, made a deep impression on my mind—that assurance under the tree at Cooranbong, the assurance in Brother Salisbury's room that morning, the open door at the bank, and the money in my hands that evening—and that is why I wrote "Fulfilled" in the margin of my Bible.—*Ibid.*

Sabbath morning, in the worship service, Daniells could not refrain from telling the experience of finding the bank door open and the deliverance that came. After the service the woman who had called for her £300 asked whether the school could still use the money, and promised to add £75 as a "penalty." This was a good omen. The tide was turning.

AT THE "RED SEA"

When they had learned of Capt. Norman's promised gift, the workers at Avondale took heart (MS 185, 1899). But reports of promises could not buy food for hungry families. Conditions rapidly worsened. On April 14, Ellen White wrote:

> There are workmen here waiting to get their pay. We are hoping and praying that means will come. . . . Everything that comes to our hands is swallowed up as quickly as possible, and still we want more.—Letter 70, 1899.

Elder Daniells was at Adelaide at about this time, and felt impressed to go to the home of a certain woman church member and endeavor to secure means. The husband was not a member of the church, and while Daniells was searching for a way to bring up the subject, she asked whether he did not think it would be well if her husband would make "our cause his banker." The result was a loan of £400 (DF 312d, A. G. Daniells, in *Australasian Record*, Aug. 27, 1928). One evening, after presenting the needs of the school to the church in Adelaide, one member said he would let them have £100. The next day he raised it to £300, and a little later to £600 (*ibid.*). From

THE AUSTRALIAN YEARS

place to place Daniells went, and the Lord favored him.

But at Cooranbong people were hurting badly. On April 24 Ellen White wrote in her diary:

> We have many perplexities to meet. We see everything pressing in upon us and we have no money to handle these things. . . . We did suppose our statement of our necessities would have brought immediate relief, as the money was raised when the [*General Conference*] *Bulletin* came to us. But the matter has gone into the papers so that it is considered a sure matter that we are well supplied with funds. We are supplied with anticipation, and that is all, with the exception of the draft from Dr. Kellogg.—MS 185, 1899.

Three days later she told of how the workmen could not pay their grocery bills and of how "money must come from some source."—Letter 252, 1899.

One of the non-Adventist plasterers working on College Hall, Conley by name, was taunted by some of his acquaintances: "Why do you work for those Adventists? You will never get your money!" "Oh, yes, I will," he replied. When asked why he was so sure, he answered, "Because Mrs. White is behind it." When the men got paid in full, there was a strong feeling the God of heaven was behind it (as told by J. B. Conley to A. L. White in 1958).

When Daniells returned in late April, a little more than three weeks after he had struggled with the Lord in the Avondale woods, he brought with him sufficient money to pay the workmen and the suppliers.

COLLEGE HALL IS DEDICATED

Thursday, April 13, 1899, was a day to be remembered. College Hall was finished and ready for use. The first meeting of the day was held in the morning at six o'clock. Ellen White explains why:

> This early hour was chosen as appropriate to accommodate those who had worked with decided interest on the building. There was assembled the entire company of students and principal, preceptor and teachers. W. C. White and Brethren Palmer and Hughes spoke. I then spoke to the students and all

WRESTLING WITH DISTRESSING FINANCIAL PROBLEMS

present thirty minutes. At the close of the exercises there was the dedicatory prayer.—MS 185, 1899.

The more formal dedication took place in the afternoon. Ellen White reported in a letter to S. N. Haskell:

> The room was decorated and festooned by flowers from our gardens, and beautiful tree ferns, some of which were placed before the entrance of the building. W. C. White spoke well. Brethren Palmer and Hughes followed. Herbert Lacey then addressed the people. . . . He spoke well.—Letter 70, 1899.

Of the gifts pledged at the General Conference session in March, which were to yield some $18,000 or more for the work in Australia, the part pledged by self-sacrificing workers in the amount of $3,400 was soon available. They waited with baited breath for the $15,000 pledged by Capt. Norman, which was to come in late May.

On May 4, still in anticipation of the gift, Ellen White addressed a letter to Capt. Norman, thanking him for his generous gift and asking whether he would not help with some specific projects. Then word came from Battle Creek that the whereabouts of Capt. Norman were unknown, and the deadline for the payment of his pledges was marked with default. Ellen White commented:

> It is a strange thing that occurred in reference to Captain Norman. I understand all that business of his liberal donations is a fraud. He has not the means he so liberally donated. . . . Well, we did hope for donations to help us out of our difficulties, but if we cannot obtain means in that way, the Lord can open up some other way to help us.—Letter 243, 1899.

Mrs. White's letter to the captain lay unclaimed at the General Conference office in Battle Creek for a month or two, then, after being furtively opened and read, was returned to her. Some have been surprised at her writing to the captain. It should be remembered that as in Bible times, not every line of information was given to the prophet. She did not have total knowledge.

On July 19, writing to Mrs. Henry, Ellen White declared:

> The $3,000 raised in the General Conference assembled at South Lancaster is all that came from that wonderful donation.

THE AUSTRALIAN YEARS

The $15,000 appropriated by Mr. Norman, where is it? If he had kept out of the way, then the work begun there would have gone through the churches, and we could have had sufficient to erect a sanitarium. But the spirit of sacrifice stopped there and then.—*Letter 96a, 1899.*

CAPTAIN NORMAN DISAPPEARS

A whirlwind love affair developed between the captain and one of the General Conference secretaries. Shortly thereafter he informed his fiancée that he was unexpectedly called to New York on urgent business. Being without ready cash, he asked whether she could lend him $300, which would be paid back when he returned. The young woman withdrew the money from her savings account and happily put it into the hands of her wealthy suitor. Capt. Norman left Battle Creek on the eastbound train, expected back in a few days (DF 368). As the days slipped by and the May deadline for the captain to pay his pledges came and passed, his fiancée and the workers in Battle Creek grew increasingly uneasy and finally disillusioned. The captain and his wealth had disappeared.

G. A. Irwin was in Australia. L. A. Hoopes, secretary of the General Conference, wrote to W. C. White on June 7, 1899:

> You will remember that in my letter I made mention of the offer that Capt. Norman had made, and that I could tell you more in the next mail. . . . I had every evidence to believe, from the human standpoint, that the offer was genuine. Doubtless Elder Irwin has told you ere this something of the situation. We have heard nothing from the captain since Elder Irwin left; and as the pledge was to be paid in the month of May, everything seems to indicate that there is nothing to it. . . . I can only say that I am disappointed thus far, and await with patience the developments, and trust that God will help us to see all that is needful for us to see and understand.—*Ibid.*

Ellen White spoke of the matter a few months later:

> When I read in the *General Conference Bulletin* that $20,000 had been donated to Australia, and that large donations had been made to the General Conference to help in other places, a feeling

WRESTLING WITH DISTRESSING FINANCIAL PROBLEMS

of sadness came over me. I felt that if this donation came to our people in this way, it would deprive them of a blessing, according to the eighth and ninth chapters of 2 Corinthians, so that rich supplies of grace might flow in upon God's people, because of their self-denial and self-sacrifice.

Christ says: "If any man will come after me, let him deny himself, and take up his cross daily, and follow me."—UCR, July 28, 1899.

Hoopes later wrote to Ellen White of the experience, particularly of what took place subsequent to the Norman pledge at the General Conference session:

I have no doubt that the Lord has revealed to you the fearful state into which we all have fallen in reference to the spirit that actuated the conference after the Norman gift was proposed. It is simply horrifying as I review the history at the present time. For one, I mean to profit by the experience. I never was so convinced of the utter necessity of our being where we can discern the leadings of the Spirit of God as I am in this whole transaction.—DF 368, L. A. Hoopes to EGW, Oct. 3, 1899.

The promise of a new day in which the wealth of the Gentiles would flow into the coffers of the church resulted in a failure on the part of the church leaders to come to grips with sound financial planning at the General Conference session of 1899. The sense of release and relaxation that came to the members of the church throughout the world field as the result of promised large gifts that would make individual sacrifice no longer necessary bore an ill harvest severely felt for a number of years.

But to Australia, the cumulative adverse circumstances that greatly reduced the flow of means from America forced the field to financial self-reliance, and proved an awakening blessing. The work in Australasia was coming of age.

CHAPTER 35
(1899)

The Work in Australia Comes of Age

ON JANUARY 1, 1899, Ellen White, reviewing the accomplishments in Australia and particularly at the Avondale school, wrote: "Two school buildings are completed, and the main building is now going up. The meetinghouse is finished and paid for, but there are fences to be built and trees to set out to make the place pleasant and attractive. . . . The things that need to be done in order that the work of God in our school shall not be hindered must be done."—Letter 49, 1899. The third term of school opened a few weeks later, on February 1, to run thirty-six weeks to October 8. S. N. Haskell, who taught through the first two terms of the school and was a strong influence in the institution, was now serving as president of the New South Wales Conference. His wife, who had also taught some of the Bible classes, was, of course, with him in Sydney. This loss of staff members, and the rapid growth of the school, called for some major adjustments in both administration and faculty.

Agriculture, a very important part of the Avondale program, needed to be managed and taught by one well qualified. C. B. Hughes, who had served as principal, was assigned that responsibility. The teaching of higher mathematics was added to his duties, as well as that of business manager. A. G. Daniells, president of the Australasian Union Conference, was asked to come to Cooranbong and fill the office of principal temporarily. E. R. Palmer, the general canvassing agent, was to come also as one of the teachers and eventually serve as principal. Several teachers were brought in from Australasia and America to build a proper faculty.

THE WORK IN AUSTRALIA COMES OF AGE
THE SCHOOL GAINS UNOFFICIAL RECOGNITION

As the school became favorably known in the surrounding communities, several non-Adventist students were enrolled in the school. A minister residing in Newcastle sent his son, as did several businessmen (Letter 74, 1899), including the well-known biscuit manufacturer Mr. Arnott (MS 191, 1899).

In February, 1899, there appeared in *The Agricultural Gazette of New South Wales* an article written by W. S. Campbell, a government fruit expert, titled "The Seventh-day Adventist Settlement and Industrial College and Cooranbong." He reported very commendably on developments at Cooranbong. Mr. Campbell mentioned that in the year 1894 his counsel was sought by three men who belonged to a denomination he had never heard of, who were looking for a suitable tract of land on which to locate a school and establish a colony. While W. C. White had several times invited him to visit the school at Cooranbong, it was not until requested by the Minister of Agriculture that he did so, most likely in late 1898. Describing his visit, the article stated:

> I must say . . . that I was more than pleased with my visit, for I found the settlement to be an extremely interesting one, and the progress made . . . remarkable, considering the short time it has been established.

Mr. Campbell had with him Mr. Fegan, a member of Parliament. He wrote of going to the home of Mrs. E. G. White, and was surprised to find there "an orchard of well-grown fruit trees of different kinds. Peaches of many varieties, bearing heavily magnificent, luscious, well-flavored fruits, such as would do credit to any orchard." The report continued:

> Here we met Mr. C. B. Hughes, the business manager. . . . Mr. Hughes took us through the buildings, which are very extensive, well built, and comfortable. A large two-storied building for girls, another extensive one for meals, et cetera, with separate laundry, kitchen, et cetera, at the rear. Some distance away, a three-storied building for boys, and between the boys' and girls' residences is a place of two stories, a building for lectures and so on.

THE AUSTRALIAN YEARS

On the eastern side of the knoll, and extending to a level area, originally a ti-tree swamp, lies an orchard of ten acres. The task of clearing the heavily timbered land and draining the swamp was heavy work, a deal of which was performed by the students and staff.

About one thousand fruit trees of various kinds were planted, and within three years they began to bear most satisfactorily. Their growth has been excellent. . . . Vegetables of all sorts thrive here admirably, and maize has given remarkable results. The work altogether has proved most satisfactory.—DF 170d.

As noted earlier, College Hall was dedicated on Thursday, April 13. W. C. White, chairman of the school board, had, on April 7, invited several government officials to visit the school and participate in the dedication service. It was short notice, and the day was rainy, and none of the officials came. However, on Thursday, April 20, a week later, a group of about twenty dignitaries came up Dora Creek from Lake Macquarie by steam launch to visit the school. White's invitation to the opening of College Hall to the Honorable Mr. Cook, Minister for Mines and Agriculture, had been effective after all. This invitation read:

> Dear Sir: In behalf of the managers of the Avondale School for Christian Workers, I have the honor to invite you to visit our place next Thursday, April 13, to open our "College Hall," which is just completed and ready for use, and which we shall dedicate that day to the cause of Christian education.
>
> Believing that you have heard, through Mr. W. S. Campbell something of our efforts to establish, here in the bush, an institution where we may give young people an "all-around" education, as well as a training for Christian work, and trusting that you approve of our idea that agriculture is properly the ABC of physical and manual training, we have dared to hope that you would take time to visit us on this occasion.—13 WCW, p. 80.

The article in the *Agricultural Gazette* was doubtless also a factor.

The group of visitors who came April 20 were curious to learn why a band of dedicated people would leave the city to establish a

THE WORK IN AUSTRALIA COMES OF AGE

college in such a retired and insignificant place as Cooranbong. In the group was the brother of the premier of New South Wales. They had come unannounced, but W. C. White was at the school at the time. He hastened off a messenger to borrow his mother's carriages and horses to supplement the school's conveyances so they could take the visitors around the grounds. In the meantime they were invited to have lunch at the school (Letter 74, 1899). Writing of the experience, Ellen White stated:

> I am so glad that the main school building is up and furnished. . . . It looks nice. We treat all who come with deference and respect. We desire to make a good impression.
>
> We have had bankers and men of high repute call upon us to see what is going on here in Cooranbong. This place has been regarded as so insignificant, and the inhabitants so poor and degraded, as to be unworthy of notice. But all are surprised at that which is being done here.—Letter 75, 1899.

In June, W. C. White, writing to his old friend J. N. Loughborough, informed him that "there are over one hundred students now in the school, and we are crowded and cramped in every department. We shall soon consider turning the work of our boys to getting out material for another building."—12 WCW, p. 47.

THE UNION CONFERENCE SESSION

The third biennial session of the Australasian Union Conference was held at the Avondale school, July 6 to 25, 1899 (UCR, May 20, 1899), and really marks the maturing process in Australia. The students found temporary sleeping quarters where they could, and turned over their dormitory rooms to the forty-six delegates and visitors. Schoolwork continued, and the schedule was arranged to conform as far as possible with the work and study program of the students. The session was, in a measure, incorporated into the school program. The report was that the arrangement was satisfactory, although some of the delegates were not enamored with rising at five o'clock in the morning.

One interesting feature of the program was the two-hour period each afternoon at two o'clock when delegates joined the students in manual labor.

THE AUSTRALIAN YEARS

The published reports of the three-week-long meeting tell of an unusual group of denominational workers rarely together, taking an active part in the session and activities. Among them were G. A. Irwin, president of the General Conference, and such pioneer workers as Ellen G. White, Elder and Mrs. S. N. Haskell, Elder and Mrs. E. W. Farnsworth, and Elder and Mrs. A. T. Robinson. All participated actively.

W. C. White and E. R. Palmer gave reports relative to the school, its history, its finances, and its program. The financial report surprised everyone, especially that the school was operating in the black. When the books were closed after the end of the sixth school term [including the Bible school at Melbourne], they could report a gain of £331 *(Ibid.,* Dec. 1, 1899).

Ellen White was the speaker on the afternoon of the last Sabbath of the session. First she read from a manuscript titled "The Avondale School Farm" (reproduced in the July 31, 1899, *Union Conference Record),* based on a vision given to her some months before, and having a very practical bearing on the development of the school:

> I have words of counsel for our brethren regarding the disposition and use of the lands near our school and church. I have been learning of the great Teacher. Many particulars regarding the work at Cooranbong have not been opened before me until recently, and not until now have I felt at liberty to speak of them. . . . At the beginning of the Sabbath I fell asleep, and some things were clearly presented before me.

Among these things was the hindrance to the work of the school and the disappointment that would follow the selling of any land the school might need. The vision was specific.

> All the land near the buildings is to be considered the school farm, where the youth can be educated under well-qualified superintendents. . . . They are to plant it with ornamental trees and fruit trees, and to cultivate garden produce. The school farm is to be regarded as a lesson book in nature, from which the teachers may draw their object lessons. . . .
>
> The light given to me is that all that section of land from the school orchard to the Maitland road, and extending on both

sides of the road from the meetinghouse to the school, should become a farm and a park, beautified with fragrant flowers and ornamental trees. There should be fruit orchards and every kind of produce cultivated that is adapted to this soil, that this place may become an object lesson to those living close by and afar off.

The industrial work, she pointed out, should include "the keeping of accounts, carpenter's work, and everything that is comprehended in farming."

Preparation should also be made for the teaching of blacksmithing, painting, shoemaking, cooking, baking, washing, mending, typewriting, and printing. Every power at our command is to be brought into this training work, that students may go forth equipped for the duties of practical life.

When she finished reading, she laid her manuscript down and continued to speak to the audience on the objectives of the school:

God designs that this place shall be a center, an object lesson. Our school is not to pattern after any school that has been established in America, or after any school that has been established in this country. . . .

From this center we are to send forth missionaries. Here they are to be educated and trained, and sent to the islands of the sea and other countries. The Lord wants us to be preparing for missionary work.—UCR, July 28, 1899.

The Avondale school had come of age. It was now a strong training center and soon would be a home base for mission field activities. It was becoming a positive influence in the community; it demonstrated what, with intelligent and diligent efforts, could be accomplished in that backward region. Somehow God's special blessing attended the developments in agricultural pursuits at Cooranbong. Shortly after Ellen White had returned to America, Australia suffered a prolonged and distressing drought. G. A. Irwin, representing the work in Australia at the General Conference session of 1903, told the story of God's special providences.

For the past two years the school has had marked evidences of the protection and prospering hand of our heavenly Father.

THE AUSTRALIAN YEARS

While the drought was so severe all around that practically nothing was raised, the school estate of fifteen hundred acres was blessed with frequent rains and abundant crops, so that sufficient was raised to supply the school and leave a surplus for sale. During the three months of the last vacation . . . about $700 worth of products were sold to those outside.—GCB 1903, p. 143.

Speaking of this a few days later, he declared:

It is really remarkable; there is just as marked a difference between that school estate and the surrounding country as we have reason to believe existed between the Egyptians and the children of Israel in the time of the plagues.—*Ibid.*, p. 174.

THE PUBLISHING HOUSE

When Seventh-day Adventists began activities in Australia in the winter of 1885, publishing work was begun almost at once. With borrowed type and equipment, the type for the first numbers of *The Bible Echo* and *Signs of the Times* was set in the bedroom occupied by one of the workers. The form of set type was taken by a handcart to a nearby printer, where it was run on the press. As soon as they could purchase a press and a small engine, quarters were rented. Four years later, land was bought on Best Street and a building erected to house the emerging Echo Publishing Company and to provide a meeting hall on the second floor. Commercial work was taken in to supply work to justify the sophisticated equipment needed to produce denominational publications. After printing in a commendable manner a pamphlet for the governor of Victoria, the Echo Publishing Company was officially appointed "Publishers to His Excellency Lord Brassey, K.C.B." This gave the house standing and enhanced business. From one person employed in 1885, the work grew, until in 1899 there were eighty-three employees. This gave it the third position among Adventist publishers, following the Review and Herald which employed 275, and the Pacific Press, with 150 workers (UCR, July 19, 1899).

With an establishment standing first among the publishing houses operated outside of North America, the Echo Publishing Company was indeed "of age."

THE WORK IN AUSTRALIA COMES OF AGE
EVANGELISM IN AUSTRALIA AND NEW ZEALAND

The final objective of all efforts of the Seventh-day Adventist Church is that of preaching the gospel and preparing men and women to meet the Lord. Evangelism, which had moved rather slowly at first in Australia and New Zealand, was vitalized by the extended evangelistic camp meetings introduced in 1893 and 1894. Year by year methods were refined, and in the late 1890s evangelism was forging ahead, yielding rich harvests. Of this type of successful work Ellen White wrote in 1898 to Dr. J. H. Kellogg:

> Our camp meetings are the greatest and most efficient mode of witnessing to the truth and making it impressive. The religious exercises of the meetings are a constant confession of the truth. There are also most favorable opportunities in these meetings, which last from two to three weeks, to engage in work for the children. The smaller children are gathered into a large tent, and special instruction adapted to their years is given them.
>
> All these meetings are carried on in an orderly manner, and they have a telling influence. There are always a number of conversions made. But now we see that the effort made after our camp meeting is more effective in holding the people than that which we gain while the meeting is in session. This is gathering up the fragments, that nothing be lost. The afterwork secures from forty to fifty converts, and the experiences of these converted ones have a great influence upon their friends and relatives.
>
> But this is a very meager estimate of the work that has been done by our camp meetings in this country. In every place where a camp meeting has been held, a church has been organized. This is presented to me as one of the best methods we can use to reach all classes.—Letter 140, 1898.

These camp meetings, into which were poured careful planning, money, and the best dedicated talent available, enriched the church in Australasia in converts from all classes, but often from among the experienced and the better educated. Thus were provided some who would enter the business operations and management of the various activities and institutions in a rapidly growing work. Few of these converts were wealthy, but there was furnished a sound

THE AUSTRALIAN YEARS

backlog of resources that was much needed. Thus evangelism, together with the training of the youth of the church in the Avondale school, very largely supplied the ministerial and related needs of the cause, such as literature evangelists and Bible instructors. Evangelism in Australia had come "of age."

THE MEDICAL MISSIONARY WORK

The medical missionary thrust in Australia got under way with a humble and slow beginning. First there was the selfless and dedicated work of Miss Sara McEnterfer, Ellen White's traveling companion, nurse, and private secretary who, soon after her arrival in 1896, was pressed into work in the community surrounding the Avondale school as a missionary nurse, supported by Ellen White. In 1897 Mr. and Mrs. A. W. Semmens, nurses trained at Battle Creek, opened a little medical institution in Sydney. In the winter of 1898 Dr. Edgar Caro, of the New Zealand Caro family, having graduated as a physician at the American Medical Missionary College in Battle Creek, joined the forces in Sydney. The name of the institution was changed to the "Medical and Surgical Sanitarium" of Summer Hill (UCR, July 15, 1898). The next step was the development of a school for nurses. The *Union Conference Record* of January 15, 1899, carried the following notice:

SANITARIUM TRAINING SCHOOL FOR NURSES

The Sanitarium school for nurses is an institution for the training of young men and women to engage in various lines of medical and other philanthropic work under the direction of regularly organized missionary boards of the Australasian Medical Missionary and Benevolent Association. The school is evangelical, but highly scientific.

As to what might be expected in training and financial arrangements, the notice stated:

The Course: The course of instruction covers a period of three years, the terms commencing April 1 and October 1 each year.
. . .
Remuneration: During the first year of the course, students receive uniforms and books, besides room, board, and tuition,

THE WORK IN AUSTRALIA COMES OF AGE

and are required to work full time—ten hours each day. After the first year's examinations are passed, a small salary, as determined by the Sanitarium medical board, will be paid in addition to room and board, provided the work is done satisfactorily.

Soon Dr. S. C. Rand joined the forces, bringing the medically trained staff to four—two physicians and two graduate nurses. God blessed the work carried by the dedicated personnel laboring with limited facilities in cramped quarters. In response to Ellen White's almost heartbreaking pleas pointing out the dire need of building and equipping a sanitarium in Sydney, Dr. J. H. Kellogg, his brother, W. K. Kellogg, J. N. Loughborough, and others sent some funds with which to make a beginning in the erection of a well-planned medical institution. Just then word was received in Australia of the generous pledges of Capt. Norman at the General Conference session. This gave heart to all the workers and led to a forward-looking action of the Medical Missionary Association on April 27, 1899. Further steps in the development of the medical work can be seen in the annual report of the Sanitarium at Summer Hill, given at the July union conference session and recorded in the July 26 *Union Conference Record:*

> The matter of more suitable accommodation for the Sanitarium work was again very earnestly considered, and it was decided [on April 27] that in view of the encouraging prospect for means, we should proceed at once with preliminary steps. Accordingly, A. G. Daniells, Dr. Caro, and G. W. Morse were appointed a committee on location for a sanitarium and plans for the same.

It was reported that at the end of June there were twenty-one employees in the little Medical and Surgical Sanitarium of Summer Hill.

FIRM PLANS FOR ERECTING A SANITARIUM

In connection with the union conference session held at Cooranbong, a formal meeting was held of the Australasian Medical Missionary and Benevolent Association on Thursday morning, July 20 and recorded in the July 24 *Union Conference Record.* Fifteen resolutions were brought in for consideration. Three related to a proposed new building, the first of which read:

> 7. That we earnestly invite a hearty cooperation of our conferences and associations, and friends of our cause in general, in the erection and equipment of a medical and surgical sanitarium, to be located in the vicinity of Sydney; and that we suggest that this enterprise be undertaken according to plans for a building capable of accommodating one hundred patients.

This was followed by two lengthy resolutions relating to finance, the opening sentence reading:

> That we undertake to raise the sum of £8,000 for the purpose named in the foregoing resolution.

The resolutions appealed to the constituency for strong support and the exercise of self-denial and "strict economy, that all may have means to offer for this cause." The common sentiment was that they should "look directly to God for help, committing our cause to Him and appealing through Him to the friends of the work."

At this point Ellen White was given an opportunity to speak. Her statements filled more than six columns in the July 21 *Union Conference Record*. She opened with the words:

> My husband and I took an interest in the Sanitarium in Battle Creek from the time it was first started. It was very hard work to get right ideas fixed in the minds of the workers in regard to what the Sanitarium should be. We had to go over the ground again and again, teaching them line upon line, precept upon precept, here a little and there a little.

After reviewing the initial steps taken in Sydney, she declared: "From the light I have received, I know that if ever there was a country where a sanitarium was needed, it is New South Wales, and I may say also, Victoria." She told of how the hospitals of the world could not suffice and declared:

> We should have a sanitarium under our own regulations, that the truth of God on health reform may be given to the world. Those connected with such an institution who are being educated as nurses should be trained to go forth from the

THE WORK IN AUSTRALIA COMES OF AGE

institution as solid as a rock upon the principles of health reform and other points of truth.

She assured the delegates that it could be done. "The Lord has instructed me," she said, "that we can have a sanitarium here if everyone will do as I was reading this morning in the eighth and ninth chapters of Second Corinthians." She referred to the dire needs of the believers driven from Jerusalem, and the manner in which means were raised for their relief.

"Their deep poverty abounded unto the riches of their liberality. For to their power, I bear record, yea, that beyond their power they were willing of themselves." Some who had no money gave part of their wearing apparel. Some divided the store of food they had, living poorly, that those who were suffering in Jerusalem might be fed. "Praying us with much intreaty that we would receive the gift."

She drew lessons from this experience and recounted God's providences in the beginning already made in Australia. "We need a sanitarium," she urged. "We desire that every soul here shall be interested in this work, because God is interested in it."

> This is the work the Lord desires to have done. Then let it be hindered no longer. God help us to take hold of it. No one man is to do the whole work. Let us all help to the best of our ability. . . . Nothing that we have is our own. All is the Lord's, and we are to do His work. God will put His Spirit upon those who will do something, and do it now.

At this point a vote on the resolutions was called for, and it carried unanimously.

A SURPRISE MOVE

Then E. W. Farnsworth stood and said that he did not know whether or not what he was about to propose was in order, but it seemed to him that they could not do better than to make a practical beginning of the matter right there. To start the fund, he would pledge £50. This pledge was quickly followed by others, and a list of the pledges (which was reproduced in the July 31 *Union Conference Record*) was made. The opening lines read:

THE AUSTRALIAN YEARS

	£	s.	d.
E. W. Farnsworth	50	0	0
Mrs. E. G. White	100	0	0
C. B. Hughes	40	0	0
S. N. Haskell and wife	55	0	0
G. B. Starr and wife	10	0	0
F. Martin	10	0	0

The list grew to seventy-one entries and £905, or the equivalent of something more than $4,500.

There was no hint in any of the addresses or comments calling for money from America. Australia was reaching maturity and self-sufficiency, even though it demanded economy and sacrifice.

A few months later Ellen White wrote of the fruitage of sanitarium work in Sydney:

> Several wealthy people who have come to our Sanitarium in Sydney have embraced the truth, among them a man who has donated £500 to our Sanitarium. He is an invalid. He and his wife have taken their stand fully.—Letter 11, 1900.

The sanitarium work in Australia was coming of age! The new sanitarium building planned for Sydney opened January 1, 1903, with Dr. D. H. Kress as medical director.

THE HEALTH-FOOD WORK

It took quite a struggle to get the health-food work in Australia on its feet. While the delegates and visitors in July, 1899, were spending three weeks at Cooranbong attending the union conference session, they could observe the steps being taken to convert the sawmill structure into an efficient food factory. As Ellen White brought her Sabbath-afternoon address on "The School and Its Work" to a close, she was asked a question regarding the connection of the health-food business and the school. In her answer she indicated that there was a very close connection between the two:

> The habits and practices of men have brought the earth into such a condition that some other food than animal food must be substituted for the human family. We do not need flesh food at all. God can give us something else.

THE WORK IN AUSTRALIA COMES OF AGE

When we were talking about this land, it was said, "Nothing can be raised here." "Nevertheless," I said, "the Lord can spread a table in the wilderness." Under His direction food will go a long way. When we place ourselves in right relation to Him, He will help us, and the food we eat in obedience to Him will satisfy us. . . .

The health-food business is to be connected with our school, and we should make provision for it. We are erecting buildings for the care of the sick, and food will be required for the patients. Wherever an interest is awakened, the people are to be taught the principles of health reform. If this line of work is brought in, it will be the entering wedge for the work of presenting truth.

The health-food business should be established here. It should be one of the industries connected with the school. God has instructed me that parents can find work in this industry and send their children to school. But everything that is done should be done with the greatest simplicity. There is to be no extravagance in anything.—UCR, July 28, 1899 (CH, pp. 495, 496).

Seventh-day Adventists throughout Australasia were informed through the *Union Conference Record* of December 1, 1899, that the manufacturing of health foods at Cooranbong was under way. Readers were told that after a long and determined and persevering effort, the Sanitarium Health Food Factory was well fitted up and able to turn out health foods rapidly. The arrangements of the factory were said to be "clean, roomy, and pleasant," and as to the products:

They are now manufacturing granose biscuits, granose flakes, bromose, nuttose, antiseptic [charcoal] tablets, granola, caramel cereal, nut butter, wheatmeal biscuits, gluten biscuits, gluten meal. . . . White and brown bread, for the school and the immediate neighborhood, are also made at the factory. We are thankful to see this enterprise at last on its feet.

The health-food business in Australia was just coming of age, and the prospects were bright.

CHAPTER 36
(1899-1900)

Finishing Touches of Ellen White's Ministry in Australia

As THE union conference session closed on Sunday, July 23, and the delegates parted, none realized the changes that would take place during the year ahead or how, in the providence of God, the field was becoming well prepared to cope with these changes. They knew, of course, that they were losing Elder and Mrs. Haskell, for Elder Irwin, feeling America's need, was taking them back with him. They had been a bulwark of strength, both in the school and in evangelism. They would sail within a few weeks. The delegates did not know that A. G. Daniells, who had been in the Australasian field for more than ten years and had developed into a strong leader, would be leaving the coming April for South Africa and then the United States. Nor did they have any idea that Ellen White and her staff would be leaving in August, 1900, just a year away, and of course, W. C. White and his family would be going with her. Not even Ellen White dreamed of such changes.

For her, things would go on, following the union conference session, for some months about as they had. At her Sunnyside home she would continue with her writing, and with her staff continue article and book preparation. She would continue to go out over weekends to meet with the churches and companies of new believers. As summer came she would attend the camp meetings at Toowoomba in Queensland; at Maitland, nearby; and then Geelong, near Melbourne in Victoria. Not until March, 1900, would she make it known that she must return to America, a decision reached reluctantly, motivated by direction from heaven.

FINISHING TOUCHES IN AUSTRALIA
THE EARLY CAMP MEETINGS

It was planned that the camp meeting season would open in Toowoomba, Queensland, and the dates were set for October 12 to 23. The notice appearing in the October 1 *Union Conference Record* stated that Ellen G. White would be attending. Writing on September 11, she stated:

> The next camp meeting held in Queensland will be at Toowoomba, a beautiful city about one hundred miles west from Brisbane. It is the business center of a large, fertile, and wealthy district. There is a small band of Sabbathkeepers in this place, and much prejudice against the truth, but we trust that the camp meeting will sweep this away, and that this may become the center of an important work.—Letter 139, 1899.

The city, with a population of seven thousand, was some 1,800 feet above sea level and located in a region of great natural beauty. Twenty family tents were pitched on neatly kept grass on grounds provided by the Agricultural Society. The new canvas pavilion, eighty by fifty feet, stood near the entrance (UCR, Nov. 1, 1899). Toowoomba was a resort city, strongly Catholic, and attendance at the meetings, in spite of a wide circulation of notices, was disappointing (Letter 248, 1899). Ellen White spoke the first Sabbath afternoon to about a hundred persons and on Sunday afternoon to two hundred. Her six addresses during the meeting were on practical subjects.

Of the location and surroundings she declared:

> We have never had a tent meeting, since my acquaintance, in any place so pleasant and so beautiful, with trees and with green grass. The tents so clean and new make a nice appearance.—Letter 234, 1899.

There were four churches in Queensland, with an aggregate membership of 211, and those at the camp meeting urged the organization of a conference. Elder Daniells, the union president, was there, and joined in the steps appropriate to form the new organization (UCR, Dec. 1, 1899). G. C. Tenney was chosen president, and Herbert Lacey, assigned to Queensland for evangelistic work, was selected secretary. As evangelistic meetings were to

THE AUSTRALIAN YEARS

continue in the tent after the close of the camp meeting, Lacey and his wife were left in the town for the follow-up work.

THE MAITLAND CAMP MEETING

The next camp meeting was in Maitland, a little less than thirty miles northwest of Cooranbong, in the mountains. The meeting, opening Thursday, November 2, was to run for ten days. Ellen White and Sara McEnterfer drove from Cooranbong Thursday morning. The weather was rainy and attendance small the first day or two, but on Sunday the sky cleared, and there blossomed forth a large and gratifying attendance. The meeting was very much like the one held in Newcastle the year before, with good interest and good attendance (six hundred to one thousand), and even included a bad storm that struck the camp midweek, flattening twenty-two of the twenty-seven family tents.

> [The storm] damaged quite a quantity of literature, and thoroughly drenched a large number of the campers and their effects. Although soon over, its fury was terrific while it lasted, breaking large ropes like threads, bending one-inch iron stakes into semicircles, and tearing several of the poorer and older tents into shreds.—*Ibid.*

But the campers kept up their courage. As at Newcastle, the occupants of nearby homes invited the distraught campers into their homes; tents were repitched, and the large tent, wet and torn, was soon repaired and up again, and meetings were in progress. The principal speakers were A. G. Daniells, G. B. Starr, W. A. Colcord, Mrs. E. G. White, and Dr. Edgar Caro (*ibid.*). Ellen White spoke on all three Sabbaths and Sundays (Letter 194, 1899). The interest was such that the meetings were continued through the third weekend. When the camp meeting was over, the large tent was moved near the center of the city, and evangelistic meetings continued.

On the first Sunday after the moving of the tent, Ellen White spoke. It was her birthday, and she was entering her seventy-third year. As she recounted the experience in a letter to Dr. Kellogg, she declared:

> Before me I saw the very faces that were presented to me more than a year ago as sheep having no shepherd, men and

women who were receiving from their ministers chaff instead of wheat. Many of them I have seen bowed before God in prayer. Others with arms outstretched pleaded, "Come over and help us. We are hungering for the bread of life." Still others I saw coming from the different churches who were distressed and cast down. All were in need.

My Guide said to me, "These are as sheep having no shepherd. Speak My word faithfully to them, for unless their ministers are converted, they will sleep on until the judgments of God will come upon the world. Cry aloud, spare not; lift up thy voice like a trumpet and show My people their transgressions, and the house of Jacob their sins."

She wrote of the influence of Dr. Caro's work and told of how gratefully the medical missionary work was received in Australia, and added:

This place has been presented to me as second in importance to America, and the same work which has been carried forward there is to go forward in this country, only in more advanced lines.—Letter 198, 1899.

So keen was the interest following the camp meeting that for several weeks she insisted on being there for weekend meetings.

Ellen White and Sara made the twenty-seven-mile trip between Cooranbong and Maitland by carriage. As it was in the heat of the summer, they usually started very early in the morning, one time at three o'clock.

THE AVONDALE HEALTH RETREAT

Again and again in 1897 and 1898, Ellen White had mentioned the dire need of a small hospital in Cooranbong. Writing on April 21, 1899, she made the situation plain:

Sister McEnterfer is nurse and physician for all the region round about. She has been called upon to treat the most difficult cases, and with complete success. We have at times made our house a hospital, where we have taken in the sick and cared for them. I have not time to relate the wonderful cures wrought, not by the dosing with drugs, but by the application of water.—Letter 74, 1899.

W. C. White pointed out why the particular need existed: "With no physician living nearer than Newcastle [twenty-five miles distant], it is impossible to secure proper attention for the sick, even when the sufferers can afford to pay the usual charges." In the case of emergencies, the city hospitals were just too far away (13 WCW, p. 84). During this time, Sara, working night and day with the sick, was nearly dead with exhaustion. Ellen White earnestly declared: "We want that hospital so much."—Letter 73, 1899.

On March 26 the newly appointed board of the Cooranbong Hospital held its first meeting and organized the work. Its objectives were set forth by W. C. White:

> The purpose in view is to provide a place in which to properly treat the sick of the neighborhood; a convalescent home for the Sydney Sanitarium patients; and a health retreat for worn and weary aged workers in the cause. A place to accommodate about thirty to forty persons will be the ultimate capacity.—13 WCW, p. 70.

Earlier in the month, a self-appointed group—A. G. Daniells, Dr. Edgar Caro, Ellen G. White, W. C. White, Iram James, and Sara McEnterfer—had driven over the school grounds and had selected a likely site near the entrance to the school grounds from the Maitland road. There were nineteen acres comprising the site thought to be most suitable (MS 184, 1899). In early April, work began, and Ellen White wrote to Elder and Mrs. Haskell:

> We are now at work on the hospital ground. We are securing volunteers to clear at least two or three acres. Today the students from the school under Brother Palmer's direction will make a bee to help in this work. . . .
>
> I expect to speak today to those who shall work on the hospital ground. A dinner is to be prepared by the school, and served on the grounds for the whole school family, making the occasion a kind of picnic in the open air.
>
> We are trying to make every move possible to advance. This hospital must now be erected without delay. If the Lord favors us, we shall put up a two-story building, and several small houses around it for patients sent out from the Sydney hospital.

FINISHING TOUCHES IN AUSTRALIA

Regarding finances she wrote:

> As yet we have received not quite $1,000 for the hospital. The appeals sent to America have not yet brought returns. Dr. Kellogg states that if I say so, he will raise $5,000 from our people.—Letter 61, 1899.

The terms Kellogg proposed were unacceptable to Ellen White. A short time later she wrote to John Wessels that she had directed that everything she had in America should be sold, which would provide but little, but it would help (Letter 63, 1899). This was just the time the school was suffering so severely for want of money and Elder Daniells was in Melbourne and Adelaide seeking relief. A few months later, at the union conference session held in Cooranbong when the building was under construction, Ellen White reviewed the experience, and told of the part played by repeated visions given to her relating to the health retreat.

> In the night season I was looking at a building. "What is this?" I asked. "The building in which you shall take care of the sick and suffering." "But," I said, "I did not know that we had such a building." "No," was the answer, "but you must have it." This building presented was very nearly like the building now being erected here.
>
> The building is so placed that it will get all the sunshine possible, not only in the sleeping rooms, but in the rooms where the patients sit. The sun is God's doctor, which brings health and strength, purifying and giving color to the blood, and we must have it.
>
> It was objected that the building would be askew with the road. "Askew let it be," I said; "that building must be where it will get the sunshine, in whatever position it is." The building is just right as it now is. It will get the sunshine, and I am well pleased with it.—UCR, July 26, 1899.

In late April when the decisions were being made, Ellen White told, in a letter to Dr. Kellogg, of the committee meeting held on the site. Some sat on the trunk of a freshly cut eucalyptus tree; she and Sara sat first in her carriage and then on cushions on the ground. They all debated the way the building would face so as to get the sunshine. She presented redrawn plans that she, Sara, and Miss Peck had spent two days preparing, putting the rooms in the most favorable position. Then the committee knelt among the eucalyptus logs and sought heaven's guidance. She at first feared that the arguments for appearance would prevail. She told Dr. Kellogg, "The matter came out all right. The building will be blessed with plenty of sunshine."—Letter 252, 1899.

Again in the night season light came as the committee, so pressed financially, considered a plan that would cut the size of the building down by four feet.

> But a building was presented to me, tall and narrow and disproportionate. I asked what building that was. One came forward and said, "That is the structure that will appear if you take out four feet." I said, "This must not be. Give the full size and merely enclose the building, finishing off a few rooms, but it must not be made smaller."—*Ibid.*

Thus God guided in the planning stage. Writing of this project to his brother Edson on May 9, W. C. White stated:

> Tomorrow we shall begin to dig the foundations and hope to have it enclosed in time to form a shelter for the delegates to the union conference, which is appointed to open July 6.—13 WCW, p. 142.

The scarcity of funds delayed the work, and they were disappointed in having the building serve as they had hoped. On September 11, Ellen White wrote to an old friend, Mrs. Josephine Gotzian:

> I am much burdened regarding the dearth of means which delays the opening of our Avondale Health Retreat. The principal part of the building is up, roofed, floored, and enclosed, but it is not plastered. And we are losing precious time, which ought to be filled with effective work in behalf of those for whom this building is erected.—Letter 139, 1899.

Mrs. Gotzian responded with a gift of $1,000, which helped spur the work along (Letter 190, 1899). One gift brought from Ellen White a recognition of sacrifice. It was a dime given by a child in America,

FINISHING TOUCHES IN AUSTRALIA

and it called forth a tender thank-you note:

> My little sister Elsie Wilson,
>
> I thank you for your precious offering. It is a small sum, but it is more precious in the sight of God than a large sum given grudgingly. If all the little children would present their dimes to the Lord as you have done, little rivulets would be set flowing which would swell into a large river.
>
> The Lord looks with pleasure upon the little children who deny themselves, that they may make an offering to Him. The Lord was pleased with the poor widow who put her two mites into the treasury, because she gave all that she had, and gave it with a willing heart. . . .
>
> Sister White appreciates your words "This is all I have, but I want to help Sister White"; and the Lord is pleased. God is made glad when the little ones become laborers together with Jesus, who loved the little children and took them in His arms and blessed them. He will bless your gift to Him.
> In love,
> E. G. White
> —Letter 155, 1899.

The *Union Conference Record* dated January 1, 1900, carried an announcement of plans for the dedication of the Avondale Health Retreat on December 27, and stated that it would be open for boarders December 28 and be fully prepared to treat the sick on January 1, 1900.

RECREATION AT THE AVONDALE SCHOOL

The Avondale school opened its fourth year on Thursday, February 1, 1900, with more students than any previous year. Ellen White addressed faculty and students with appropriate remarks for the occasion, based on the character of Daniel, a man who had a well-defined purpose in his heart that he would not dishonor God by even the slightest deviation from the principles of righteousness. The noticeable change in the faculty was in the Bible teacher; A. T. Robinson had been appointed to that post. The prospects were good for a profitable school year. But there is an enemy who is constantly alert to divert that which is planned as a benefit into a drawback, and

THE AUSTRALIAN YEARS

this showed up on April 11, the day set aside as the first anniversary of the completion of College Hall.

E. R. Palmer and C. B. Hughes, principal and business manager, respectively, planned for the day what they thought to be appropriate—a morning service at which Ellen White was invited to address students and faculty, and in the afternoon various recreational games, including cricket for the boys and tennis for the girls. Faculty members and students joined in raising money with which to purchase the equipment (DF 249e, C. B. Hughes to WCW, July 22, 1912). Other games, as remembered by Ella White Robinson included three-legged races; eating apples suspended from a string, with the players' arms tied behind them; carrying eggs in a teaspoon in a knee race, et cetera (*ibid.*, E. M. Robinson to David Lee, Nov. 9, 1967). Wrote Professor Hughes in his July 22 letter to W. C. White:

> The students enjoyed the day very much, and at the close of it felt very grateful toward me, especially, for planning such a pleasant time. You know the Australians very much enjoy holidays and sports. When Mark Twain visited Australia, he found this such a characteristic of the people that he exclaimed, "Restful Australia, where every day is a holiday, and when there is not a holiday, there is a horse race."

After giving her morning address, Ellen White returned to her Sunnyside home and her work. But "during the following night," as she was to write later, "I seemed to be witnessing the performances of the afternoon."

> The scene was clearly laid out before me, and I was given a message for the manager and teachers of the school. I was shown that in the amusements carried on, on the school grounds that afternoon, the enemy gained a victory, and teachers were weighed in the balances and found wanting.—MS 73, 1912 (see also CT, p. 348).

In her diary she noted, "The whole transaction was presented to me as if I was present, which I did write out."—MS 92, 1900. She later declared:

> The Avondale school was established, not to be like the schools of the world, but, as the Lord revealed, to be a pattern

school. And since it was to be a pattern school, those in charge of it should have perfected everything after God's plan, discarding all that was not in harmony with His will. Had their eyes been anointed with the heavenly eyesalve, they would have realized that they could not permit the exhibition that took place that afternoon, without dishonoring God.—MS 73, 1912 (see also CT, p. 349).

Apparently there was much involved, in a country given to holidays and sports, in allowing any beginning toward what could easily become an infatuation.

The next morning, as Hughes was leaving his house for the school, Ellen White's carriage drove up, and he was informed that she wished to speak to him. As he wrote of this in 1912, Hughes bared his soul:

> I went out to her carriage, and she leaned out toward me and said in very earnest tones, "I have come over to talk to you and your teachers and your students about the way you spent yesterday. Get your teachers together. I want to speak to them before I go in to speak to the students."
>
> If Sister White had struck a blow full in my face, I do not think I would have felt so hurt as I did at her words. What she said sounded so unreasonable to me. I believed that what I had done the day before was for the best interests of the students. . . .
>
> I was very much troubled, knowing as I did the attitude of the Australians toward holidays and games. I felt that Sister White was acting rashly. . . . I was very much tempted to advise her not to talk to the students that morning.
>
> We went into the chapel and she delivered her talk, but it did not produce the commotion that I had expected. In fact, the students generally seemed to receive it quite well, but not so with myself.—DF 249e, C. B. Hughes to WCW, July 22, 1912.

We cannot here trace in detail the personal struggle Professor Hughes experienced. When, through Miss Peck, he inquired of Ellen White why, in the light of her counsel that teachers should play with their students, he should be reproved for what they had done, the answer came that the students at Avondale were not children but young men and young women preparing to be laborers for God. Then, with his concordance, he searched his Bible. One of the first references he turned to related to the children of Israel, when they "sat down to eat and drink, and rose up to play." Nor were other texts any more helpful. When he came to recognize that winning in games meant others must fail, he was led to conclude that the spirit of most games and sports was not the right spirit of the adult Christian. "These thoughts," he declared, "brought me out of darkness into light, and I left behind me an experience which was a very trying one."—*Ibid.*

As was usually the case when counsel was given regarding the perils of a certain course, constructive alternatives were suggested. Ellen White did so along two lines:

> In the place of providing diversions that merely amuse, arrangements should be made for exercises that will be productive of good. Satan would lead the students, who are sent to our schools to receive an education that will enable them to go forth as workers in God's cause, to believe that amusements are necessary to physical health. But the Lord has declared that the better way is for them to get physical exercise through manual training, and by letting useful employment take the place of selfish pleasure. The desire for amusement, if indulged, soon develops a dislike for useful, healthful exercise of body and mind, such as will make students efficient in helping themselves and others.—MS 73, 1912 (see also CT, p. 354).

After Hughes and Palmer sought Ellen White's help in planning activities, she wrote:

> They said they were perplexed to know what to do with the students' Sunday afternoons. They thought they could unite with them in these games and they would not be strolling around in the bush. I said, "Is there not an abundance of work to be done on this farm where all the energy and tact would be turned to the most useful account in a good work?" . . .
>
> All are to be rightly educated as in the schools of the prophets. . . . Let another teacher . . . educate how to do work in helping some of the worthy poor about us. There are houses that can be built. Get your students under a man who is a builder and see if you cannot find something that can be done in the lines of

FINISHING TOUCHES IN AUSTRALIA

education and in the lines of holiness.—MS 92, 1900.

As Ellen White addressed the sudents and faculty, she was disappointed that there was dead silence. She wrote a few days later:

> I knew after I had borne my testimony that the teachers and students might have taken a stand. . . . But not one word was said in response to the testimony; not one word spoken before that school to say, "The Lord has spoken to us through His servant and we will thank God for the light that is come to us and will receive the light and prayerfully ask God to give us clear perception of right and wrong."—*Ibid.*

It seems that teachers and students were too stunned to speak. But the message sank into hearts and was effective. Faculty and students did some prayerful studying and thinking. Hughes reported that the equipment was disposed of, and recreation was found in activities other than sports and games.

The author, when visiting Australia in 1958, talked with a physician who was one of the students at Avondale in 1900. He volunteered the experience of some of the students, the memory of which had not dimmed in his mind. He and another young man banded together, in the light of Ellen White's counsel, to study what they could accomplish in helping others in the community. They found many places where they could help those in need, and this positive type of recreation provided soul-warming experiences in Christian service. In just a short time they sensed the advantages of finding recreation in activities that bring strength to the character as well as to the body. The grueling experience bore a good harvest.

On June 11, 1900, Ellen White could joyfully record in her diary:

> I can but praise God for His goodness and mercies and blessings which are coming to the school and to the church. The Spirit of the Lord has come into the school, and the report is that every student is now a professed Christian. May the Lord bless them and sanctify them and refine them by His Holy Spirit that they may from henceforth reveal the character of the only true Model which is the character of Christ.—MS 94, 1900.

THE AUSTRALIAN YEARS

The *Union Conference Record* included the following under a note entitled "Students Building Churches":

> Many of the older students, under the direction of Brother and Sister Robinson, are working up the missionary interests in the neighborhood. Children's meetings and a Sunday school are being held at Awaba, Sabbath services and Sabbath school at Dora Creek. . . . A little church is now being erected at Morisset for the accommodation of the meetings held there. This undertaking originated with the students. They have raised the *money*, and with the exception of a little help from experienced carpenters, they have done the work. Thus the students are learning the ABCs of church building. One important feature of the lesson is to be how to dedicate a church with *no debt* upon it. When this church is finished, they intend to build another at Martinsville.—August 1, 1900.

In the April confrontation Ellen White had suggested as an alternative to engaging in sports, "There are houses that can be built."

BALANCING COUNSEL REGARDING SIMPLE BALL GAMES

The review of this experience cannot properly be left without calling attention to Ellen White's balanced counsel to a medical student in Michigan. Edgar Caro, from New Zealand, in 1893 had made inquiry of her by letter. Her reply sets forth several principles worthy of close study:

> I do not condemn the simple exercise of playing ball; but this, even in its simplicity, may be overdone.
>
> I shrink always from the almost sure result which follows in the wake of these amusements. It leads to an outlay of means that should be expended in bringing the light of truth to souls that are perishing out of Christ. The amusements and expenditures of means for self-pleasing, which lead on step by step to self-glorifying, and the education in these games for pleasure produces a love and passion for such things that are not favorable to the perfection of Christian character.
>
> The way that they have been conducted at the college does not bear the impress of heaven. It does not strengthen the

intellect. It does not refine and purify the character. There are threads leading out through the habits and customs and worldly practices, and the actors become so engrossed and infatuated that they are pronounced in heaven lovers of pleasure more than lovers of God. In the place of the intellect becoming strengthened to do better work as students, to be better qualified as Christians to perform the Christian duties, the exercise in these games is filling their brains with thoughts that distract the mind from their studies. . . .

Is the eye single to the glory of God in these games? I know that this is not so. There is a losing sight of God's way and His purpose. The employment of intelligent beings, in probationary time, is superseding God's revealed will and substituting for it the speculations and inventions of the human agent, with Satan by his side to imbue with his spirit. . . . The Lord God of heaven protests against the burning passion cultivated for supremacy in the games that are so engrossing.—Letter 17a, 1893 (AH, pp. 499, 500).

Ellen White also recognized the importance and place of the school gymnasium:

> The question of suitable recreation for their pupils is one that teachers often find perplexing. Gymnastic exercises fill a useful place in many schools; but without careful supervision they are often carried to excess. In the gymnasium many youth, by their attempted feats of strength, have done themselves lifelong injury.
>
> Exercise in a gymnasium, however well conducted, cannot supply the place of recreation in the open air, and for this our schools should afford better opportunity. Vigorous exercise the pupils must have. Few evils are more to be dreaded than indolence and aimlessness. Yet the tendency of most athletic sports is a subject of anxious thought to those who have at heart the well-being of the youth. Teachers are troubled as they consider the influence of these sports both on the student's progress in school and on his success in afterlife.—Ed., p. 210.

CHAPTER 37
(1900)

Ellen White's Last Year in Australia

As THE year 1900 opened, Ellen White was dividing her time and strength between the evangelistic interest at Maitland and her literary work. With this in mind on January 1, 1900, she wrote to Edson calling for her library to be sent to Australia:

> I have sent for four or five large volumes of Barnes' notes on the Bible. I think they are in Battle Creek in my house now sold, somewhere with my books. I hope you will see that my property, if I have any, is cared for and not scattered as common property everywhere. I may never visit America again, and my best books should come to me when it is convenient.—Letter 189, 1900.

After sending the final chapter of *The Desire of Ages* to the publishers in early 1898, Marian Davis turned her attention to the book on the parables, since it had been decided to lift these out of the manuscript on the life of Christ. She thus had in hand a sizable collection of E. G. White materials she had been laying aside for use. But as the work moved into this area, Ellen White was stirred to write rather copiously on this phase of Christ's ministry. In the year 1898 she wrote thirty-two manuscripts, averaging nearly ten pages each, dealing with the various object lessons by which Jesus taught. To these she added another seventeen during 1899. In some cases she wrote two or three times on the same topic, as she did on the wedding garment and the ten virgins. The resulting 487 pages provided bountiful resources from which Marian Davis could draw as she pulled together the chapters for the new book.

ELLEN WHITE'S LAST YEAR IN AUSTRALIA

W. C. White, on June 18, 1899, mentioned the book in a letter to the manager of the Pacific Press:

> Much valuable work is being done on the manuscript for the parables. This work has often been interrupted, but is nearing completion. The book will be larger than we had first intended, and much more valuable.—13 WCW, p. 291.

And to his brother he wrote on September 24:

> For some days I have been engaged in giving a last reading to Mother's work on the parables, and I am deeply impressed that it will be one of the most useful and most popular books she has ever brought out. It will make a book of four hundred pages, I think, and if well illustrated, I have thought it would be a great seller.—14 WCW, p. 121.

As the finishing touches were being put on this volume, which came to be known as *Christ's Object Lessons*, Ellen White was thinking of books yet to be brought out. On June 16 she wrote to Edson:

> My health is good when I do not have to stand on my feet to speak so often; but I am getting old. What I have to do I wish to do quickly and solidly.
>
> I wish now to take the Old Testament history from Solomon to the last chapter of Malachi, and the New Testament history from the ascension of Christ to Revelation. . . . My writing ability continues, but how long this will be I know not.—Letter 102b, 1899.

CHRIST OUR SAVIOUR

At about the same time she stated that "the book *Christ Our Saviour* is not yet completed."—Letter 243, 1899. Her son Edson, working in the Southern States among the blacks in the mid-1890s, saw a fruitful field for a book of modest size on the life of Christ in simple language. Being a good writer himself, he began to prepare the chapters, and then some of his mother's writings on the life of Christ came to his hands. Feeling it excelled his own work, he selected some of the materials, simplified the wording, and blended them with what he had written. In 1896 he published it as a popular book of 158 pages. The idea of blending his writing with that of his mother's was not acceptable to either Ellen White or the field. So as plans were laid for future printings, it was determined that it would all be from her pen, the wording simplified in her Sunnyside office by one of her staff. This work was accomplished, and in 1900 the 182-page book *Christ Our Saviour* was published. On the title page it carried the words: "By Ellen G. White (Adapted)." It has had a wide distribution in several languages, and now reaches the public under the title *Story of Jesus*.

Other book tasks to which attention was being given included a book on health intended for general distribution; in 1905 it emerged as *The Ministry of Healing*. Chapters from the 1890 book *Christian Temperance* formed the initial basis for this, supplemented by an abundance of other materials. Ellen White wrote several chapters particularly for the opening of this volume, presenting Christ and His ministry as the example in true medical missionary work (11a WCW, pp. 624, 625).

As Miss Sarah Peck, a teacher who had worked in South Africa, was drawn into Ellen White's literary staff, she was assigned the task of assembling the counsels on education written largely in the 1890s as the new start in Christian education was made in Australia. Ellen White had written much along this line. Wrote W. C. White in late September:

> During the past two years I think Mother has written more upon the principles of education, the importance of Bible study, and the importance of combining labor with study, and the value of agriculture as the ABC to all agricultural training, than in all the years before. I think she has written more largely upon it than any other branch of our work, and Sister Peck, who came from South Africa to assist her with her work, is preparing these writings for publication.—14 WCW, p. 145.

Miss Peck soon discovered that these writings divided themselves into two groups—those appropriate for Seventh-day Adventists, and for the world generally. The latter found their way into the volume eventually published under the title *Education* (1903). Then there were those more particularly for the church, which made up one of the sections of *Testimonies*, volume 6 (1900), and provided

ELLEN WHITE'S LAST YEAR IN AUSTRALIA

resources for *Counsels to Parents and Teachers* (1913).

Volume six of the *Testimonies,* then in preparation, would carry nearly one hundred pages on education.

ORGANIZATION OF THE E. G. WHITE MANUSCRIPT AND LETTER FILES

As Miss Peck searched the E. G. White manuscripts and letters for materials on the subject of education, she clearly sensed the need of a better organization of these files. As noted in an early chapter, copies of the letters and manuscripts were taken to Australia in oilcloth bags, and they had served in the preparation of articles and books. Marian Davis was so well acquainted with these that she could quite readily find materials she needed. Not so with the new workers, including Miss Peck. Writing to P. T. Magan on May 23, 1899, W. C. White explained:

> About four years ago the word came to her [Mother], "Gather up the fragments, let nothing be lost," and this has been repeated many times since. But not till Sister Peck came were we able to do more than keep copies of the newly written documents.
>
> For some months Sister Peck has devoted a portion of her time to sorting, filing, reading, and indexing all of Mother's manuscripts within our reach, and Mother has been looking over her old diaries and manuscripts that were never copied on the typewriter. In these she finds many precious things that are being copied, filed, and indexed with the rest.—*Ibid.,* p. 189.

First, the typewritten copies of manuscripts and letters brought from America and those produced in Australia were sorted out by years. Then the general manuscripts were separated from the letters. Manuscripts were placed in chronological order and numbered serially. Letters were sorted out alphabetically and then numbered in sequence. These were punched at the top and filed in "Shannon" file drawers. This formed the basic E. G. White manuscript file as it stands today. From that time on, as the materials were copied they were given file numbers. This put the letters in chronological order. The record books started by Miss Peck, while valuable and still used occasionally, have been superseded by more

THE AUSTRALIAN YEARS

comprehensive records that better serve the work of the White Estate. A subject index was made of the manuscripts and letters on four-by-six-inch cards, which serve today, and copies of which serve in the Berrien Springs, Michigan, branch office and the Ellen G. White SDA Research Centers.

These several lines of literary work, together with the relentless correspondence, absorbed the time and strength of the staff working at Sunnyside.

THE SYDNEY SANITARIUM

The one matter of primary concern to Ellen White through much of her last year in Australia was the choice of a site for, and the erection of, a representative sanitarium in Sydney, or close by. During the month of September, 1899, she slipped away from Cooranbong to look at three places thought to be favorable for such an institution, but priced beyond their reach. During the month of October, John Wessels, who had come from Africa, was asked to continue the search. Near the close of the month he found at Wahroonga, near Hornsby Junction, what seemed to him a very favorable proposition, seventy-five acres of land, with fifteen in orchard, and on the place a small cottage. A group consisting of W. D. Salisbury, A. G. Daniells, F. L. Sharpe, and Ellen White joined Wessels in looking over the place. Before the day was over, W. C. White and Sara McEnterfer met with them. All were favorably impressed. The property could be secured for £2,200, or about $11,000. With £900 raised at the union conference session, this seemed within reach, and on November 1, John Wessels closed the deal. The agreement called for a down payment of £100, then another payment of £200 in three months; the balance would be due within a year.

The next step was to find money for land and buildings, and Ellen White made this a prime point in her correspondence during the next few months. In the heat of early January, 1900, she and Sara McEnterfer decided to get away from Cooranbong for two or three weeks and spend the time on the "Sanitarium farm," living in the little cottage. It was crowded, for the caretaker family lived in two of the four rooms. They also found the building full of vermin, but Sara cleaned the place up, and the wide porches served as living and dining rooms. As for getting the needed rest, soon various workers, eager to see the new Sanitarium site, beat a pathway to the little cottage.

She and Sara did like the place—the broad veranda; the large front yard beautified with flowers, a feast to the eyes and fragrant to the senses; and the fruit, ripening fresh and palatable (MS 89, 1900). The *Record* reported that she "returned home much benefited in health" (February 1, 1900).

Even before finding the site, Dr. Merrit Kellogg, a builder from his younger years and the physician-carpenter who in 1878 designed and built the health retreat near St. Helena, California, had drawn up plans for the Sanitarium building. He was somewhat restricted in size, for there were other places needing such institutions. When the question of building materials came up, wood was chosen in place of masonry—for comfort, roominess, and economy. *Testimonies*, volume 7, pages 83 and 84, present the counsel that grew out of the consideration of this point in Australia.

AT THE GEELONG CAMP MEETING IN VICTORIA

Ellen White was urged to attend the camp meeting in Victoria, scheduled for March 8 to 18 in Geelong (UCR, March 1, 1900). Geelong is a beautiful, well-laid-out city about fifty miles southwest of Melbourne. A Mr. Watson, a church member, gave £25 to encourage the church leaders to have a camp meeting held there, and a tent 55 by 104 feet was pitched in the center of the city. As it was a conservative city, there was some question about attendance, especially when it was known that the local ministers warned their people not to go to the meetings. There were about two hundred church members on the grounds for the meetings, but attendance ranged from five hundred to 1,500. G. B. Starr reported that the Spirit of God stirred the place (*ibid.*, April 1, 1900). A. G. Daniells, E. W. Farnsworth, and Mrs. E. G. White were the principal speakers.

It was here that she met the reconverted Stephen McCullagh. Of this she wrote:

> Elder McCullagh and family are here. He seems to be fully in the work and expressed himself at this early-morning meeting as being in full harmony with the testimonies coming from God to

THE AUSTRALIAN YEARS

Sister White. The more he reads the Bible and the testimonies, the more deep and terribly solemn they appear to him. He talked intelligently.—Letter 198, 1900.

The *Union Conference Record* of April 1, 1900, reported one especially interesting feature of the camp meeting. Delegations from Melbourne on weekends included "the Echo office brass band, composed of sixteen of our own brethren, who had been practicing for some three months on the sacred music usually used in camp meeting. They did well, and added much to the effectiveness of the song service."

By popular vote of the audience, decision was made to continue the Geelong camp meeting for a second week. After this, follow-up meetings were moved to a good rented hall.

"I AM NEEDED IN AMERICA"

It was in connection with the trip to Melbourne to attend the Geelong camp meeting that Ellen White was suddenly overwhelmed with the conviction that she must return to America.

On March 7 she wrote to W. C. White about the struggle with her conviction and of her desire to know God's will:

> I slept not. I was in conflict all night, pro and con. Reasons would urge themselves as though a voice was speaking to me, and I bringing up objections—why it seemed to me I could not go to America. And thus I reasoned and prayed, unwilling to admit that I must go, or that it was my duty to go, but the decision was not made.
>
> Last night I had it all over again, and I am more decided that it will be my duty, as soon as I can adjust matters, to go to America without delay. . . . I cannot say all now; but I am needed in America. My testimony is needed just now, and I really believe it is my duty to go.—Letter 196, 1900.

Two weeks later, in writing to Stephen Haskell, she told of her decision:

> Well, what shall I tell you is on our minds? We are now planning to attend the next General Conference [session], taking the boat that sails in August. My mind has been wrought upon,

and I shall come. If the Lord has not wrought upon my mind, then I do not know what spirit has taken hold of me. I wrestled three nights in prayer at different times. I could not consent to go, and finally I decided.

I cannot think of being gone longer than two years, leaving here the first of August. This is as soon as I can get ready to leave. Shall leave my home just as it is, and come back to it. That, at least, is my calculation [a calculation she ultimately changed]. . . .

Now we are glad that you are in America, and we shall expect to come to your help, and we meet in September or October. We do not want to come later in the cold period of the year. . . . Things have come to a pass in America when I know the Lord would have me to go to my own country, on my old stamping ground.—*Letter 174, 1900.*

Again, two weeks later, she confided in her diary on April 7, "I try to rest in my mind and thoughts, but I cannot. My mind is *upon America*. . . . I wish to go, and I wish to remain."—*MS 92, 1900.*

The next day she wrote:

We are preparing our American mail. I have many things I desire to see accomplished before we shall leave for America. I am greatly burdened. I have been instructed decidedly that the work Dr. Kellogg has been doing in Chicago is not the charge and work God has called him to do. He has his certain work appointed him which others cannot do.—*Ibid.*

In mid-May a cable from George Irwin urged her to come to America on the August boat. She still hesitated, and declared:

I dread everything like confusion. I have stood on the battlefield at Battle Creek. I tremble at the thought of repeating the experience. We know they need help in America, but is it my duty to take this long journey? I cannot do this without further evidence.—*Letter 70½, 1900.*

As she wrote to Edson on July 1 about the proposed trip she remarked:

This is the best climate for me by far that I have ever been in, and I am so bound up with the work here it is very difficult for me to leave the work. I seem to be a part of the very work, and I tear myself away. I am not the least homesick. Nothing but duty would cause me to make the change. I am desirous to be just where the Lord would have me, and do the very work He has for me to do.—Letter 186, 1900.

In writing to longtime friends Elder and Mrs. Haskell, Ellen White discussed where she might locate on arriving back in the United States. She still owned a home in Healdsburg, a few blocks from Healdsburg College. She might locate there. "But," she wrote, "W. C. White objects. He thinks we should not be near any school. . . . We will know better what to do when we reach Oakland and have opportunity to look about."—Letter 121, 1900.

Settling in or near Battle Creek seemed to be quite out of the planning. "W. C. White has felt very strongly," she wrote, that "under no circumstances should we locate in Battle Creek or east of the Rocky Mountains. Our position must be near the Pacific Press."

> We have planned to go into the country, in or near Fruitvale, so that we might have no connection with any duties or offices that would demand our attention. Here we hope to complete the bookmaking we now contemplate.—*Ibid.*

FINAL ARRANGEMENTS

When Ellen White first let it be known that she must very soon leave Australia, one problem loomed large. That was the early disposition of her Sunnyside property and the W. C. White home across the road. It was he who spoke of how this was solved, as he made his remarks in a farewell service before they left:

> Since our decision to sail in August, many favoring providences have been seen. Mother has sold her house and land, with furniture, farming implements, and livestock, to a family wishing to be near the school.
>
> I have exchanged places with Brother Metcalf Hare, and then sold his place to the school. Many kind friends are helping us in numberless ways.—UCR, Sept. 1, 1900.

Another point of concern was the securing on short notice of suitable travel accommodations. As W. C. White took up the arrangements with the Union Steamship Company in Sydney, he found that they could take passage on the *Moana*, leaving Wednesday, August 29. The bridal stateroom, with its comfortable bed and nearby bunk, was available for Ellen White and Sara McEnterfer. Good staterooms in the second-class section would comfortably accommodate the others.

TRANSFERRING RESPONSIBILITIES

Ellen White and W. C. White had been active in so many lines of work and carried such numerous responsibilities that their rather sudden leaving seemed to pose somewhat of a problem.

It was decided that the union conference should meet a little early. A hasty call was sent out for a "union conference council," to which were invited, in addition to the members of the committee, "representatives of the different lines of work throughout the Australian field" (*ibid.* Aug. 1, 1900). This would be held at Cooranbong, August 16 to 27. E. W. Farnsworth had taken Daniells' place as union conference president.

Thirty-four delegates along with Mrs. White were present for what proved to be an outstanding meeting. They represented 1,986 baptized believers throughout Australasia. Farnsworth reported:

> That which seemed to impress all minds the most was the presence of the Holy Spirit. All came desiring harmony and peace, and under such circumstances nothing else could be expected. I have attended a large number of gatherings among our people, but I have never attended one before where such perfect union of feeling and judgment prevailed. There was free discussion on all points; but, when that was over, all saw eye to eye, and not one dissenting vote was cast on any proposition that was passed. I do not think that this can be said of any other meeting ever held by our people of equal length and importance.

With Ellen White about to leave them, her presence seemed especially precious. Wrote Farnsworth:

> We all appreciated, as never before, the counsel of Sister White. All felt that if God ever sent light to any people, He certainly did to us. We praise Him for the light.

THE AUSTRALIAN YEARS

There was also the transfer of responsibilities in which W. C. White was involved. In his farewell remarks he commented on this:

> From the day that my brethren on the union conference committee consented to begin to release me from responsibility, we have seen that the Lord had men in waiting, fitted to lift the burdens that I was laying down. Therefore we go with light hearts, feeling assured that the work will progress steadily, with increasing rapidity and power until the work is finished and the Master says, "Well done."—UCR, Sept. 1, 1900.

FAREWELL SERVICE

On Sunday afternoon, a few hours before the union conference council was to close, and three days before the *Moana* would sail, a farewell service was held in the Cooranbong church. The general community was invited to join the delegates. Several made appropriate remarks. As this was still a part of the union conference council, a resolution was introduced that read:

> That in view of Brother and Sister White departing soon for America, after a stay of nine years in Australasia, we hereby express our appreciation of their active and earnest efforts to establish the work in this country, our thankfulness for the success which has attended their labors, and wish them the rich blessing of God, and a safe and pleasant voyage homeward.—*Ibid.*, Oct. 1, 1900.

Two autograph albums had been prepared, one for Ellen White and one for the W. C. White family. Both were beautifully bound, and each contained original drawings, photographs, and messages from churches and from individuals expressing appreciation, friendship, and love. As Elder Farnsworth presented these, he remarked "that they might find in these gifts a similarity to the ones taken to Egypt by the sons of Jacob, in that they were made up, figuratively speaking, of 'a little balm, and a little honey, spices and myrrh, nuts, and almonds'" (Gen. 43:11).—*Ibid.*

Ellen White's response was eagerly awaited. She declared that she was changing work but was still under the same Leader:

> Yesterday when I spoke to the congregation, all the time I felt

my heart welling up with gratitude to God. Now we have but little time, and I want to say that I do not go to America because I feel driven to go on account of the burdens I have been carrying here. I feel that God has assisted me in the work here. I leave all the churches and the brethren and sisters with the most pleasant feelings. It means very much to me to know that our hearts are united, that we are one in the body of Jesus Christ, one in faith, one in hope. . . . I expect you will press the battle to the gate. I expect you will each act your part and close up the ranks. . . .

I have not a tear to shed. I am only changing my work under the same General, and I go to another part of the field where they are calling earnestly for our help.

I thank you for this token of your kind regard and remembrance. I shall esteem it highly. I shall bear in mind those I have met here, and our prayers will ascend that the blessing of the Holy Spirit shall be upon these believers who live in my heart, that they may advance from character to character, till in the heavenly courts, it shall be said, "Ye are complete in Him."—*Ibid.*

GETTING OFF TO AMERICA

Ellen White had been successful in selling her home and little farm with its furnishing and equipment to the Minchin family, so there was little packing to do beyond her personal effects and the precious literary materials. These included the files of letters and manuscripts and the working materials for book production, and were taken in trunks as a part of the baggage. One article of furniture did go with them—Ellen White's writing chair with its swinging, green, felt-covered writing board.

A three-hour train trip carried them to Sydney. With Ellen White were four women assistants: Sara McEnterfer, Marian Davis, Sarah Peck, and Maggie Hare. The W. C. White family numbered seven: himself; his wife, May; his two older daughters by his first marriage, 18-year-old Ella and 13-year-old Mable; the twins, 4 years old; and baby Grace, nearly 3 months old.

At the wharf they bade goodbye to friends and fellow workers, and were off to America.

Bibliography

Daniells, Arthur G. *The Abiding Gift of Prophecy.* Mountain View, Calif.: Pacific Press Pub. Assn., 1936.
Harris, John. *The Great Teacher.* Amherst, Mass.: J. S. and C. Adams, 1836.
Hook, Milton R. "The Avondale School and Adventist Educational Goals, 1894-1900." Unpublished doctoral dissertation, Andrews University, 1978.
Neufeld, Don F., ed. *Seventh-day Adventist Encyclopedia.* Washington, D.C.: Review and Herald Pub. Assn., 1976.
Nichol, Francis D. *Ellen G. White and Her Critics.* Washington, D.C.: Review and Herald Pub. Assn., 1951.
———, ed. *The Seventh-day Adventist Bible Commentary.* Washington, D.C.: Review and Herald Pub. Assn., 1953-1957. 7 vols.
Robinson, Dores E. *The Story of Our Health Message.* Nashville, Tenn.: Southern Pub. Assn., 1943, 1955.
White, A. L. *Ellen G. White: The Later Elmshaven Years.* Washington, D.C.: Review and Herald Pub. Assn., 1982.
White, Ellen G. *The Adventist Home.* Nashville, Tenn.: Southern Pub. Assn., 1952.
———. *Christian Service.* Washington, D.C.: General Conference of Seventh-day Adventists, 1947.
———. *Colporteur Ministry.* Mountain View, Calif.: Pacific Press Pub. Assn., 1953.
———. *Counsels on Diet and Foods.* Washington, D.C.: Review and Herald Pub. Assn., 1938.
———. *Counsels on Health.* Mountain View, Calif.: Pacific Press Pub. Assn., 1923.
———. *Counsels to Parents and Teachers.* Mountain View, Calif.: Pacific Press Pub. Assn., 1913.
———. *Early Writings.* Washington, D.C.: Review and Herald Pub. Assn., 1945, 1982.
———. *Education.* Mountain View, Calif.: Pacific Press Pub. Assn., 1903.
———. *Evangelism.* Washington, D.C.: Review and Herald Pub. Assn., 1946.
———. *Life Sketches of Ellen G. White.* Mountain View, Calif.: Pacific Press Pub. Assn., 1915.
———. *The Ministry of Healing.* Mountain View, Calif.: Pacific Press Pub. Assn., 1905.
———. *Prophets and Kings.* Mountain View, Calif.: Pacific Press Pub. Assn., 1917.
———. *Selected Messages.* Washington, D.C.: Review and Herald Pub. Assn., 1958, 1980. 3 books.
———. *The Southern Work.* Washington, D.C.: Review and Herald Pub. Assn., 1966 reprint.
———. *Special Testimonies to Ministers and Workers.* Nos. 3, 4.
———. *The Spirit of Prophecy.* Battle Creek, Mich.: Seventh-day Adventist Pub. Assn., 1870-1884. 4 vols.
———. *Spiritual Gifts.* Battle Creek, Mich.: Seventh-day Adventist Pub. Assn., 1858-1864. 4 vols.
———. *Testimonies for the Church.* Mountain View, Calif.: Pacific Press Pub. Assn., 1855-1909. 9 vols.
———. *Testimonies to Ministers.* Mountain View, Calif.: Pacific Press Pub. Assn., 1923.
———. *Welfare Ministry.* Washington, D.C.: Review and Herald Pub. Assn., 1952.
——— et al. *Historical Sketches of the Foreign Missions of the Seventh-day Adventists.* Basle: Imprimerie Polyglotte, 1886.
White Estate. *Notes and Papers Concerning Ellen G. White and the Spirit of Prophecy.* Washington, D.C.: General Conference of Seventh-day Adventists, 1971.

Index

(Entries in italics, except for names of books, et cetera, refer to direct quotations from Ellen G. White.)

A

Adelaide, 45-47
Affliction, EGW's, was part of God's plan, 33
Anderson, A. W. and Richard, 117
Andrews, S. J., 379, 385
Angels, God commissions, to render help, 63
Arnold, William, 12
Association of boys and girls at school, 312
Atonement, McCullagh's views on, 280
Auckland, 21, 72
Australasian Conf. session, 23, 58
Australasian Union Conf., organization of, 120-124
    session, 423
Australia, EGW's doubts re, 15, 31, 39
    why God allowed EGW to go to, 258
Australian Conf., 171
Avondale, animal life at, 346
    best school EGW had ever seen, 322
    Daniells' confession re, 314
    financial difficulties at, 267, 288, 345
    land of, to be a lesson book, 354
    literature evangelists sponsor students at, 300
    opening of, 301, 302
    staff of, 303, 420
    to be a model school, 353
    visited by government officials, 422, 423
    volunteers help in building, 296-298
Avondale Health Retreat, 437-441

B

Babylon, question of SDA churches as, 80-85
    fallen churches are, 81
Baker, W. L. H., 124, 334
Ballarat, 47
Bank, door of, opened, 414
Baptism, at a lake, 182
Battle Creek, developments at, 252-257
    no breezes from, to be held at Avondale, 304
Battle Creek College, 12
Battle Creek Sanitarium, 254, 394
Battle Creek School, 122
Belden, F. E., 403
Belden, Stephen, 29, 138

463

Bell, John, 272-275
Benson, A. H., 150
Bible School, Australasian, 42-45, 48
Bismark, 69, 191
Bolton, Fannie, 18, 138, 187, 227, 234, 237-250
   likened to Korah, Dathan, and Abiram, 244
Borrowing, literary, by EGW, 62, 63
Brown, Martha and family, 100-104, 110, 111
Butler, George I., 88, 405-407

C

Caldwell, W. F., 83, 85, 220, 237
Camp meeting, Adelaide, 270
   Armadale, 229-233
   Ashfield, 166-171
   Brighton, 113-124
   Brisbane, 364-369
   Colorado Springs, 17
   Geelong, 453, 454
   Maitland, 436, 437
   Napier, 77-80
   Newcastle, 371-374
   Stanmore, 335-339
   Tasmania, 234-236
   Toowoomba, 435
   Wellington, 108-111
Camp meetings, most efficient mode of evangelism, 427
   public press, response of, to, 170
   reasons for attending, 114, 115
Campbell, Emily, 18, 46, 76, 89, 139, 251
Canright, D. M., 92, 148, 172
Caro, Dr. (Mrs.), 77, 98
Caro, Dr. Edgar, 356, 359, 428
Children can understand lessons of Christ, 90
Christ, came as personal Saviour, 402
   lessons of, can be understood by children, 90
   life of, EGW writing on, 30, 35, 36, 93, 94, 125, 143, 148, 156-158, 187, 189, 244, 261, 262, 289, 336, 341, 375-393
   mind of, needed by workers, 99
Christ Our Saviour, 449
Christian Temperance, 261
Christ's Object Lessons, 376, 405, 449
Church, *as fortress*, 63
   building, at Avondale, 315-322
   is only object of Christ's supreme regard, 82
Church school, when to have, 301
Church's prosperity, secret of, includes organization, 60
Clough, Mary, 377
Cobbin, Ingram, 380
Colcord, W. A., 230, 369

INDEX

Cole, J. M., 167
College Hall, 408, 416, 417
Conybeare and Howson, 380
Cooking, classes in, 29
    scientific, subject at Avondale, 299
Cooranbong site for school, 147, 151, 158, 159
Copying, question of EGW, 378
Corliss, J. O., 12, 115, 124, 173, 230
Councils, God to be acknowledged in, 176
Counsel of men who do not trust in God, 176
Counsels to Parents and Teachers, 451
Courting, not to be allowed at Avondale, 312
Cross purposes, Echo workers at, 27

D

Daniells, A. G., 21, 28, 41, 43, 76, 120, 122, 171, 216, 412-415, 420
Davis, Marian, 30, 138, 271, 336, 380-387, 448
Debate on Sabbath question, 173-175
Debt at Battle Creek school, 404
Desire of Ages, The, 370, 375-393, 405
    Holy Spirit traced truths of, 393
Disease caused by transgressing laws of nature, 357
Dowkontt, Dr. Geo. D., 396
Dress, counsel on, 332
    question of, not our present truth, 333

E

Earnestness, if heaven is not sought with, God is dishonored, 259
Echo Publishing Company, 22, 26, 344, 426
Edersheim, 379, 385
Education, 450
Education, proper, combines physical, mental, moral, 218
Ekron, god of, going to inquire of, 177
Errors of God's workers, not to be exposed, 134-136
Evangelism, EGW participation in, 106-111

F

Faith, we must talk, act, live, 291
Farnsworth, E. W., 431, 453, 457
Farrar, 379
Faulkhead, N. D., 49-56, 190
Federal Hall, 22, 23, 34
Fleetwood, 379
Fleming H. Revell, 12, 36, 388
Flesh meat, banned from EGW table, 118, 119, 140
    not served at camp meetings, 140
Foreign Mission Board, 14-16, 122, 146, 152, 158, 159, 177, 181
Freemasonry, 49, 50, 52

Future, nothing to fear for, 61

G

Geike, Cunningham, 378, 385
General Conference, 13, 59, 401
Gifts from Gentiles, God motivates, 185
Government favors and grants, 183-186
Great Controversy, The, 11, 66, 92, 105, 143, 230, 264, 375, 393
Great Teacher, The, 62, 63
Gymnastic exercises, 447

H

Hanna, William, 378, 380, 385
Happiest months, for EGW, were of suffering, 32
Hare, Edward, 21, 72
Hare, Joseph, 72-76
Hare, Maggie, 229, 234, 391
Hare, Metcalfe, 218, 219, 226, 296, 317, 319
Hare, Robert, 70, 76
Harper, Walter, 163
Harris, James, 17
Harris, John, 62, 63
Haskell, Hettie, 294, 298, 303, 307, 308
Haskell, Stephen, 12, 13, 67, 104, 183, 282, 290, 294, 420
Hawkins, C. F., 275, 280, 281
Health foods, 288, 289, 339-341, 355, 357-362, 432, 433
Health Home, 289, 291, 292, 355
Heavenly Father, work of, not to be conducted as an embarrassment, 27
Henry, A. R., 253-256
Henry, Mrs. S. M. I., 346-348
Hickox, A. S., 141
Himes, Joshua V., 178-180
Honolulu, 19
Hoopes, L. A., 418, 419
"Hotel, free" 157, 158, 220
Hours With the Bible, 385
Hughes, C. B., 298, 303, 305-308, 420

I

Illustrations for *The Desire of Ages*, 390-392
Israel, M. C., 12, 89, 100, 104

J

James, Iram, 141, 330
Jones, A. T., 64, 127-129, 131
Justification by faith, 11, 49, 87, 406

INDEX

K

Kellogg, John H., M.D., 15, 56, 291, 394-401, 455
    did not believe present truth, 395
    EGW's mother heart went out to, 398
    instructed to move cautiously, 38
    needs humble heart, 38
    special light given re, 395
Kellogg, Merritt G., M.D., 109, 111, 115, 230, 453
Kneeling in prayer, 105
Kress, D. H., M.D., 432

L

Lacey, Herbert, 268, 287, 292-294, 303, 305-309, 349, 385, 435
Lacey, Lillian, 299
Lacey, May, -White, 182, 188, 193-198
Laodicean message applicable to SDAs, 84
Lawrence, L. N., 148, 149
Laws of nature, transgression of, brings disease, 357
Levity, spirit of, not to be tolerated, 309, 310
Life and Epistles of St. Paul, 380
Life and Words of Christ, 378, 385
Life of Christ, writing on, must be done carefully, 375
Life of Our Lord, 378, 380, 385
Life of Our Lord Upon the Earth, 385
Lindsay, Harmon, 17, 180, 181, 253, 254, 316
Literature ministry, 58
Littlejohn, 133
Loan, miraculous way of meeting, 412-415
Love, sympathy, courtesy, lack of, absolutely forbidden, 169
Loyalty, Christ demands, 313

M

Mail, American, 36-38, 75, 126-137, 394-407
Managers, wise, need for, 311
Manual training, 217, 262, 263, 299, 309
Maoris, 105
March, David, 385
Masonic Lodge, 49, 52, 54, 55
McEnterfer, Sara, 18, 229, 234, 298, 327-331, 362, 428, 437
McCullagh, Stephen, 78, 151, 152, 275-286, 453
Meat eating never a test of fellowship, 281
    See also Flesh meat.
Medical and Surgical Sanitarium, 356
Medical missionary work, 233, 355, 357, 394, 428-432
    not to supersede ministry of Word, 396
    right hand of truth, 399
Medical work, 289
Ministry of Healing, The, 41

Minneapolis Conference, 11, 65, 66, 85-88, 405
Miracle, every soul converted is a, 190
Missionary interests of students at Avondale, 446
Missionary work to be conducted around the world, 43
Mistake to present what God has not shown, 130
Model school, Avondale to be, 353
Moral purity, Anna Phillips' teachings on, 126
    EGW's position on, 131, 132
Morse, G. W., 358-361
Mouthpiece, Corliss was, for God, 174
Muscular Christianity should be brought into schools, 350
"My Telescope," 348

N

Natural world has no inherent power, 402
New South Wales Conference, 233
New Zealand, EGW's visit to, 69-113
Nicola, Leroy, 86
Night Scenes in the Bible, 385
Norfolk Villa, 156, 178
Norman, Henry, 411-419
Nursing, home, classes in, 29

O

Offshoot teachings, 80-85
    God is not leading, 81
Olsen, O. A., 13, 14, 85, 105, 109, 111, 121, 256
Open-air meetings, 106
Opinion, differences of, not to be put in enemies' hands, 65
Organization, church, 59
    included in church's prosperity, 60
    of EGW materials, 451, 452
Outcasts, constant work for, 397

P

Pacific Press Pub. Assn., 388, 389
Palmer, E. R., 420
Pantheism, 394, 402-404
Parramatta, 69
Patriarchs and Prophets, 11, 143, 230, 375, 393
Pattern, Australia to provide a, 409
Peck, Sarah, 327, 450, 451
Per Ardua, 138, 139, 156
Phillips, Anna, 125-132
Philosophy, of EGW re suffering, 33
    study of, in Word of God, 351
Phrenology, 78
Physical culture, need for, 308

INDEX

Pitcairn, 105, 108, 109
Porter, Mrs., 332
Prayer, kneeling during, 309
Prescott, W. W., 13, 129, 229-233, 262, 263, 387, 402
Press, Capt. and Mrs., 118, 124
Preston, EGW home in, 29, 33, 45
Promises of Bible seen as in golden letters, 351

R

Rand, S. C., M.D., 356, 429
Reaser, W. A., 390, 391
Rebellion, is it ever curable, 286
Recreation at Avondale school, 441-447
Revell, Fleming H., see Fleming H. Revell.
Review and Herald Pub. Assn., 388
    workers at, need self-examination, 57
Rice, Anna, see Phillips, Anna.
Rice, J. D., 127
Righteousness by faith, 11, 49, 87, 406
Ring, wedding, question of, 196, 197
Rockhampton, 369
Rousseau, L. J., 43-45, 122, 219, 226, 288, 299
Royalty from EGW books, 44

S

Sabbath, travel on, EGW's attitude toward, 76, 190
Samoa, 20
Sawmill, 226, 263, 268
School, establishment of, not advisable in city, 151
    Cooranbong, development of, 215-221
        to be object lesson in horticulture, 224
        with God's blessing will produce good crops, 161
    need for, in Australia, 13, 24, 25, 42
    search for site for, 113, 121, 147-156
Scott, Henry, 12
Second Coming, why world has not heard warning re, 66
Secret sign, EGW gave, 52, 53
Secret societies, incident re, 49-56
Semmens, A. W., 289, 292, 356, 428
Shannon, J. G., 221
Sick, prayer for, principles re, 40
Sisley, W. C., 181, 270
Smith, Uriah, 64
Spirit of God, EGW longed for, in writing The Desire of Ages, 381
Spirit of Prophecy, The, 11
Stanton, Mr., and SDA Church as Babylon, 80-83
Starr, George B., 16, 18, 19, 29, 76, 78, 141
Steps to Christ, 11, 36, 112, 230, 250, 338
Stockton, J. H., 34, 41, 51

Sunday laws, 144, 145, 164, 165
  relationship of black believers to, in Southern U.S., 252
Sunday question, God's plan that it be agitated, 103
Sunnyside, construction of, 236
  description of, 260-262, 270, 271, 289, 290
  disposition of, 456
Sydney Sanitarium, 452, 453

T

Tait, A. O., 128, 129
Tasmania, camp meeting in, 234-236
  convention in, 188, 191-193
Tax exemption, 184, 185
Teachers, institute for, 263, 264
Temperance, topic of EGW addresses, 93, 106
Tenney, G. C., 23, 24, 43
Testimonies, *do not misinterpret and twist*, 81
  EGW's own attitude toward giving, 256
  influence of, 67
  purpose of, 68
  response to, 80, 83, 86, 87, 169, 337
Therapy, water, 292, 293
Thoughts From the Mount of Blessing, 389, 390
Thoughts on Daniel and Revelation, 105, 117, 191
Tuition should be high enough to clear expenses, 311
Tuxford, Mrs. M. H., 91, 124, 138
Typewriters, 377

U

Union conference, plan of, for church organization, 61

V

Van Horn, Isaac, 86-88
Visions, when from God, He will show, 132
  See also White, Ellen G., visions of.

W

Waggoner, E. J., 59, 61, 402
Walks and Homes of Jesus, 385
Walling, Addie, 17
  May, 17, 18, 29, 30, 46, 138, 251
  Will, lawsuit by, 17, 146, 182, 268, 269
Warnings of God should be received as blessings, 71
Week of Prayer, 58, 348-351
Welfare Ministry, 401
Wessels, John, 331, 332, 452
Wessels, Peter, 184, 185, 291

INDEX

Wessels family, 180, 181, 256, 266, 269
White, Edson, 94-97, 107, 112, 132, 449, 450
White, Ellen G., addresses by, 20, 22, 23, 34, 43, 58, 70, 77, 90, 106, 109, 167, 168, 336, 367
    altar call by, 235
    anointing of, 39-41
    cart, ride on, pulled by White and Starr, 79
    cows of, object lesson for others, 225
    dreams of, Cooranbong land, 154
        furrow, 154-156
        two clouds, 364, 365
    feelings and emotions of, 20
    financial aid by, 44, 45, 69, 105, 142, 162, 183, 193, 235, 266, 269, 305, 326, 370, 408
    grandsons of, 264, 265, 323, 324
    health of, 21, 24, 30-41, 46, 73, 98, 105, 137, 187, 222, 228
    home of, at Adelaide, 46, 47
        Cooranbong, 219, 220, 236
        Granville, Sydney, 138, 156, 178
        Preston, 29, 33, 45
        Wellington, 91
    life in tent, 227
    personal ministry of, 101-103
    received ideas while speaking, 71
    return of, to America, 459
    royalties paid to, 269
    school property, personal pledge to buy, 161
    staff of, 261
    strength given to, to speak, 91, 228, 229
    teeth of, extracted, 98
    temptations of, 71, 72
    testimonies of, 25, 26, 31, 36, 50, 64, 70
    travel of, to Australia, 18-21
        New Zealand, 69-72
        Sydney, 69
        Tasmania, 188, 189
        Wellington, N.Z., 89, 90
    visions of, re animals being fed from crib too high, 363, 364
        Ashfield camp meeting, 168
        Australia, work in, 16, 23, 25
        Avondale, church building, 319
            conditions at, 310
            selling land at, 424, 425
        Bolton, Fannie, 240, 241, 245, 246
        Brisbane meeting, 369
        Brown family, 101, 102
        Christ, life of, 382, 383
        Edson, 95, 96
        Faulkhead, N.D., 52
        financial aid from America, 409, 410

    identification in evangelism and camp meetings, 334, 335
    Kaeo believers, 76
    man with measuring line, 373
    moving of personnel from Melbourne, 358, 359
    printing presses, 12
    promises of Bible in golden letters, 351
    publishing house, 50
    Sabbath debate, 173
    trees, how to plant, 223
    worker relationships, 168
  visitors to, 139, 156, 178
    See also "Hotel, free."
  voice of, 58, 106
  willing to forgive personal affronts, 285
White, James, 12, 377
White, William C., 14, 28, 43, 59, 79, 89, 105, 108, 121, 145, 158, 182, 188
  assigned special work as organizer, 353
  chairman of Avondale school, 353
  home of, 267, 289, 323-325
  travel of, to U.S.A., 288
White family reunion, 336
Wilson, G. T., 104, 111
Work bee, called by EGW at Avondale, 296-298
Workers' meetings, 168, 169, 337

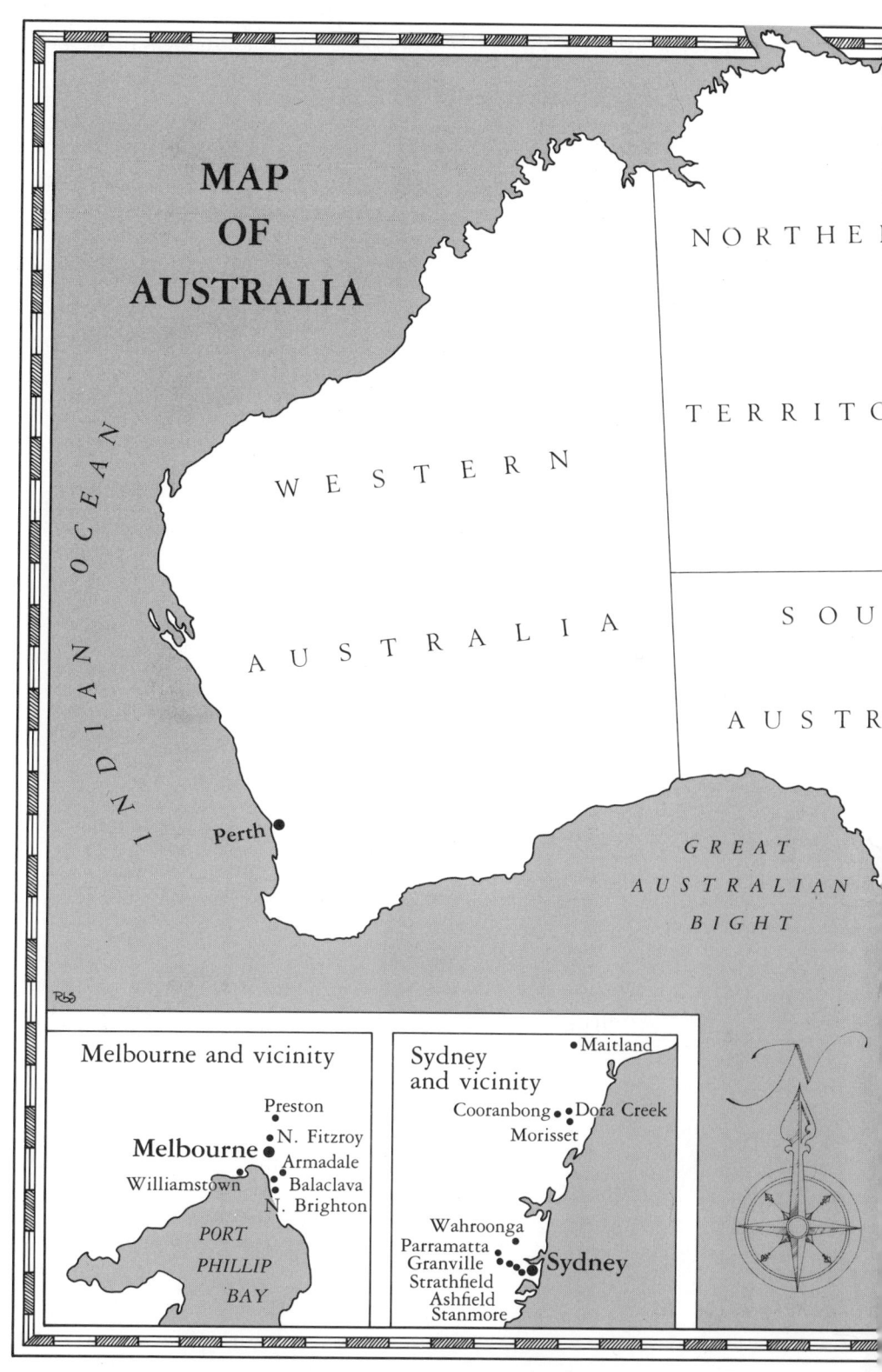